Isabel Garland in her twenties.
(Courtesy of the University of Southern California,
on behalf of USC Libraries Special Collections)

A Summer to Be

*A Memoir by the
Daughter of Hamlin Garland*

Isabel Garland Lord

Edited and with an introduction by Keith Newlin

Foreword by Victoria Doyle-Jones

UNIVERSITY OF NEBRASKA PRESS
LINCOLN AND LONDON

First Nebraska paperback printing: 2010

Library of Congress Cataloging-in-Publication Data
Garland, Isabel, 1904–1988.
A summer to be: a memoir by the daughter
of Hamlin Garland / Isabel Garland Lord;
edited and with an introduction by Keith Newlin;
foreword by Victoria Doyle-Jones.
p.   cm.
Includes bibliographical references and index.
ISBN 978-0-8032-3243-3 (pbk.: alk. paper)
1. Garland, Hamlin, 1860–1940.
2. Garland, Hamlin, 1860–1940—Family.
3. Garland, Isabel, 1904–1988.   4. Authors, American—
19th century—Biography.   5. Authors, American—
20th century—Biography.   I. Newlin, Keith.   II. Title.
PS1733.G37   2010
813'.52—dc22
[B]   2009046762

TO MY FATHER

This is Hamlin Garland as he was to me.

His full story he told himself.

Contents

List of Illustrations

Foreword

Victoria Doyle-Jones

My aunt, Mary Isabel Garland Lord, wrote the manuscript for the book that you are about to read in the 1960s and submitted it to Harold Latham, a long-standing friend of the Garland family and at that time vice-president of the Macmillan Publishing Company. Latham read my aunt's manuscript and wrote to her saying that he was willing to publish it despite the fact that it "lacked enough sex and violence to ever make it a best seller." Harold Latham died before the book ever went to press; his successor wasn't willing to take a chance on publishing a manuscript that didn't have sex and violence, the requisite earmarks of a best seller.

Rereading my aunt's manuscript decades later—and now with Keith Newlin's well-researched notations and background knowledge of the Garland family, its history, and possibly even of its psychology—I disagree with their evaluation that the book lacked "sex." Sex is most definitely in there, even if nuanced and/or repressed. In contrast, however, there is little mention of violence. Given their life and times, I find this noteworthy. My grandfather was an activist who wrote and railed against poverty and injustice, a nationally known campaigner for women's rights. Yet for all his public-spirited compassion, I sensed some great, unspoken injustices while reading through my aunt's memoir.

Keith Newlin sees in *A Summer to Be* the tale of a young woman who "rebelled against her father's loving domination" and whose "increasing interest in boys proved particularly trying to the devoted father." As much as his domination influenced the inde-

pendent path of his eldest daughter, his early disinterest in my
mother, his youngest daughter, led her to seek male attention with
an almost pathologic intensity throughout her life.

Passion, rampant and/or repressed, is the current and cur-
rency in our lives, and *A Summer to Be* has its own passions. Sex,
underlying the stories of those I can only begin to understand—my
grandparents, mother, aunt, brother, sister, myself—is but one manifestation of life's passions. However "passion" is defined, we are all
entangled in our own or someone else's pursuit and/or fear of it.
My grandfather and aunt were the writers in the family, the ones
best able to verbalize the pursuit and, to some extent, the repression
of their passions (though perhaps too often only as a between-the-
lines reading). I sense that my mother and grandmother, the artists
in the family (and the left-handed ones, as are my sister and I), were
enigmas even to themselves. Their societal roles were well defined;
they were rarely given to questioning.

Having emerged from a life of poverty and toil, Hamlin
Garland achieved for himself a place amongst the wealthiest, the
most privileged, aristocratic, and intellectual members of the
English-speaking world. Throughout their lives his two highly
privileged daughters lived exclusively on the fringes of the rich and
famous. Theirs was a male-dominated, sybaritic world; yet, as did
their lady-like mother, they seemed to accept life's inequities and
contrasts without much complaint or reflection. Suffragettes had
earned the right to vote, but distaff opinions were rarely taken into
consideration either in the Garland household or in the circles in
which the Garlands traveled. Despite my aunt's theme and original
title for her manuscript ("This Loving Daughter"), I discovered in
my rereading of it that my much-lionized grandfather was quite
capable of being hard-headed, selfish, thoughtless, and occasionally even a tyrant. Admittedly I actually never knew him; he died five
years before I was conceived.

In his defense, even my grandfather's most thoughtless
actions seem never to have been pointed out to him. (My aunt
quotes one of her father's comments, "I do not care for plain
women," and I found that comment quite revealing.) The souls of
his beautiful women were the well-earned ornaments of his life and
times. It appears his blind and unintentional wrong-doings were,
for the most part, silently and unfailingly forgiven by his wife, ador-

ing daughters, and by society in general. Yet it is clear that Hamlin Garland was given to depression and pummeled himself mentally for his discovered wrong-doings, both real and imagined. I suspect that he never really hesitated in his headlong pursuit of what he believed to be right nor sensed the hurt he had inflicted. He tried his best to do right by all—it's just that it was unquestionably and unquestioningly on *his* terms.

Hamlin Garland remained true to himself to the end—an enviable position—and it was never pointed out to him or others of his ilk that they might stop to consider the costs of the roles they were expected to assume. I'd wager that my grandfather was no different from any other high-achieving, narcissistic, alpha male of his era. He believed himself to be a very good man—as did his doting family and a myriad of friends and colleagues—and for the most part he truly appears to have been just that. If society even noticed such domineering behaviors, it tacitly forgave them in the leading males of the early 20th century. Still, much of my aunt's story seems grossly unfair.

And who am I to judge what was *fair* nearly a century after the fact? It took me until 1984 just to consider the meaning and existence of "fair." (That was during the Olympics in Los Angeles when my coach, Olympian Pat Connolly, heard me grousing about something or other not being "fair." My coach turned to me with that intense, high-energy tough love for which she was famous, and said: "Who ever told you life was supposed to be *fair*? Life *isn't fair*!" Get over it!" In that instant I discovered a new freedom: Life isn't fair, it's never been and is never going to be fair, and there is nothing *I* can do about it. Somehow, though, I've yet to master the ability to keep from feeling that it is my job to try to make things fair. I've inherited my grandfather's passion for righteousness.)

Whether their lives were fair or not, my aunt's memoir is a sequel, a chronicle of the passions, the poverty and riches of the times and of a lineage. She and her sister were, in my aunt's own words, "about as selfish as two over-indulged young women can be." (Oh what a wonderful existence!) I believed on first reading of the manuscript (and still believe today) that above all it is a pleasant read for anyone from Garland scholar to desperate housewife. It's a real-life fantasy world as described by the eldest daughter of an important figure in the American realism movement. In contrast to their father's difficult start in life, the Garland girls' young life was a whirl of exciting people, wonderful adventures, of silver tea services, black velvet evening gowns and glittering jewels, of opera and theater, of dance cards and lingering romances. Theirs is also the tale of heartbreaks and losses, of fires, floods, and of war— though my aunt's description of each calamity is only as deep as its effect on their personal lives.

Were they truly happy? Reading of their sheltered existence I find I am startled at how little my mother and aunt seem touched by the suffering load of the planet. Distaff compassion, evident only in between-the-lines reading, does not seem to have ever been nurtured in the narcissistic environment in which they were raised. Yet there was a sweet innocence to both of them that none of us can question.

During their lifetimes, both of the Garland girls' paths were more than once interrupted by fires and floods. Some of these events Isabel recounts in her memoir. Whereas others may have metaphorically drowned in tsunamis of passion, the Garland girls were far more likely to get burned by indulgences. Beyond the fires, real and metaphoric, mentioned in the confines of her book, there were other real conflagrations of great significance to Garland history. Much to his dismay, Hamlin's daughters were ever cavalier about their drinking and smoking habits. Their carelessness caused many a burn. Not long after *A Summer to Be* was written, it was Isabel's cigarette, dropped and left smoldering in an overstuffed chair, that set the top floor of her sister's house ablaze. All the occupants managed to escape, but gone were many of the Garland household treasures, the paintings, the family antiques, some of the rarest of their books, cabinets full of music and records, mother's Steinway piano. . . . But it was the Old Topanga Firestorm, started by an arsonist in 1993 (and for once not the fault of anybody we knew), that finished off the last of the Garland artifacts, the library, Connie and Isabel's wonderful life-size bisque dolls that had come to them from France at the turn of the century, the little rocking chair that Richard Garland had made for Mary Isabel, their infamous black velvet dress in its cedar chest. . . .

My aunt was four years old when my mother's arrival interrupted her starring role in the family circle. And my mother was a sickly, colicky baby whose birth was resented by more than her

Unfinished oil portrait of Isabel Garland Lord,
painted by her sister, Constance, in the late 1950s.
(Courtesy of Victoria Doyle-Jones)

older sibling. Having watched his elegant, uncomplaining wife,
Zulime, go through the waddling stages of pregnancy and agonies

of childbirth in the production of "his" Mary Isabel, my grandfather resolved that he would never be responsible for putting his beloved wife through *that* again. Somehow my mother's conception slipped past his resolve, and he transferred some of his guilt to her mere existence.

The healthy, bright, adoring, and much-adored Mary Isabel (who dropped her first name when she launched a stage career) continued to fill her doting father's days with joy, while Constance fought for her life through a series of childhood illnesses, starting with an infant's milk allergy that left her weakened and her dentition ruined. (They saved her life by feeding her goat's milk.) By the time Constance was able to toddle out of the nursery, her father's attention to her was just about nil. It was only when he discovered her artistic talents many years later that he assumed a fatherly role and interest in Constance and her career. The father called his two daughters "Tempest [Isabel] and Sunshine [Connie]," but by the time he took any real notice of Connie, the psychological damage had been done.

Connie, my mother, was the wild child, the flapper, the adventuress. Subconsciously she must have decided that if she wasn't going to get the male attention she needed by being good, then she'd durn well get it by being "bad." She was invariably sweet tempered (which probably saved her life more than once), but she smoked and she drank and she drove fast cars and she flew airplanes. Mother was very blonde and smashingly attractive and vivacious; she claimed she could make eye contact with any man and have him at her side within five minutes. My aunt claimed the same skill set: "I had been known to summon a man across a room with a speaking look." While in her sixties and seventies, Mother still retained that skill and put it to good use; my aunt no longer felt the need to keep her flirting honed. Isabel had found her grand passion (we are left to read between the lines for her other conquests), while my mother tripped through a series of husbands and lovers worthy of any Hollywood celebrity (many of whom, like the Barrymores and Amelia Earhart's spouse, she included in her personal stable of admirers). Connie spent her life searching for the "real love" that her sister had known.

Mother's third and last husband was my handsome, reserved, aristocratic, then-forty-five-year-old and never-married

Constance Garland Harper and her airplane
at Burbank Airport in the 1930s.
(Courtesy of Victoria Doyle-Jones)

father whom she called "The Poor Man's Cary Grant." He hailed from a long-line of Celtic Catholics with a propensity for alcoholism. He adored mother, forgave her most of her fascinating foibles (though the Church never forgave him for marrying a divorcee), and they drank their way through nearly fifty years of marital bliss. My half brother, John, and half sister, Constance, then in their teens, left home shortly after I arrived on the scene to take my own center-stage position with a doting father. And, like my mother and aunt before me, I was spoiled rotten (it's not my fault). My half siblings soon left baby sister and the stuffy, aristocratic, and academically oriented lifestyle of their mother and stepfather behind and opted to join the wealthy and exciting Hollywood ranks of the Cecil B. DeMille clan into which their own father had married. It was a very wise choice for Connie, my half sister, sixteen years my senior, who even then was a budding starlet.

By contrast, our mother and aunt, Constance Hamlin Garland and Mary Isabel Garland, were inseparable sisters, bitter rivals, and best friends to the day of their death, days apart in the same hospital room. Aunt Isabel was quite beautiful in her own way (and loving and generous to a fault—we all basked in her spoilings), though unlike her bolder, flashier, blonde sister, she was dark and of a far more reserved nature. Unlike my outwardly easy-going mother, my aunt was highly opinionated, strong-willed, and yet at the same time probably just a bit timid. Mother was the adventurous one (and possibly the more creative of the two), but Isabel was mother's intellectual superior, and she never let my poor mother forget it.

In retrospect it amazes me that my wild-child mother ever survived long enough to bring me into the world. She put on a happy-go-lucky front and insinuated her way into a lot of predicaments in her lifetime. My favorite tale of their sibling rivalry is one that I heard from both mother and aunt (my aunt describes her version of it in *A Summer to Be*), and it typifies both of them and their relationship: my aunt was twenty; my mother, sixteen at the time. Isabel's best beau was an Annapolis midshipman whose name, as I recall them telling me, was Sherry Berry. Midshipman Berry telephoned the Garlands' New York flat one afternoon, hoping to invite my aunt to a dinner dance at the Plaza Hotel that evening. Little sister Connie picked up the call (my aunt and a second-cut beau were elsewhere at a tea dance at the time). "She's not home," said my mother to my aunt's best beau, "But *I* am, and *I'd* love to go to that dinner dance." What was the poor fellow to do? So, he settled for escorting Isabel's little sister, a wildly attractive teenage blonde flapper worthy of the Great Gatsby himself.

Having secured the prize for the evening, my fiendish mother went to her sister's closet and donned my aunt's brand-new, black velvet evening gown, lined with pink satin and trimmed with little ermine tails. (My aunt describes them as sable, but I saw that dress in the cedar chest, and I remember those tails were black and white.) Mother slipped her slightly larger feet into my aunt's brand new, black peau de soie dancing slippers, stuffed her own lipstick, a lace-edged handkerchief, and some mad money into my aunt's lovely little beaded handbag, and off they went to the Plaza, my adorable mother and her sister's best beau.

These crimes might have gone unnoticed had my aunt and her second-cut escort not concluded that the function they were attending was not up to their standards. They decided, on the spur of the moment, to go on to the more glamorous dinner dance at the Plaza. There, when my aunt and her date arrived, was my aunt's best beau with my aunt's wretched baby sister in his arms as they swirled about the dance floor, my mother wearing my aunt's best gown and new shoes, and carrying my aunt's fanciest beaded handbag. I have no idea what transpired or what words were exchanged then and/or later, but somehow my mother survived into her eighties. I said the book lacked violence, didn't I?

The two Garland girls lived separately as little as possible throughout their eighty years together. As married ladies they had domiciles as close to each other—and to their parents—as they could manage. Even when living on opposite coasts, they spent as much time together as they could. Their father hovered around and over them as much as possible. (Their enigmatic mother, the beautiful Zulime Taft, seems to have remained, as always, warmly and gently and quietly in the background. Oh, how I wish I had known her.)

To his last days, Hamlin's daughters accompanied him on his exploits—including some outlandish expeditions under the guidance of a medium and spirit voices searching for buried crosses. Their reasoned influence and lukewarm support of this project did little to keep Hamlin Garland from delving into the world of the occult (he was ever an agnostic, though becoming hopefully mystic in his later years). My aunt and mother kept the elderly gentleman entertained, and they humored him in his psychic research, though they obviously believed that he was more often possessed by the medium than the spirits. They both described Hamlin Garland in his seventies sliding down a steep hillside on his derriere at some desert location the medium had pinpointed for a cross dig. "Well," he proclaimed at them as he slid past them in an avalanche of rocks and dirt, "Some old gentleman play *golf.*" He knew they didn't approve; he chose to ignore it. The last words my aunt ever heard him say in this life were: "Well, Children, it's full steam ahead!"

As a small child I was taken to New York to attend the same Finch School that my mother and aunt had both attended (I hated it) while they worked together on the opening night for a musical entitled *Under the Rose* that my aunt had written with the English composer Cyril Horrocks. Similar in theme and a couple years prior to the musical *Camelot*, cast recordings of *Under the Rose* were cut and ready to distribute. The musical was through dress rehearsals and set to open on Broadway when its financial backer, one exceedingly wealthy Dr. Jones (whom I suspect was "keeping" my aunt in her glamorous New York penthouse) died a week before opening night. Backing was withdrawn and tied up in probate; *Under the Rose* never opened on Broadway. My aunt left New York forever and moved back to California.

The non-launch of *Under the Rose* was just one of a series of emotional blows and creative disappointments that plagued Isabel in her later life. The manuscript for her memoir, "This Loving Daughter" (which we renamed "A Summer to Be"), was first accepted and then tabled by the publisher; it was never to appear in print during her lifetime, though I made a deathbed promise to her that I would see to it that it was published. Hardest of all for Isabel to bear was her divorce from Mindret Lord, the love of her life, followed by his suicide a few years later. His loss shattered her psyche beyond recovery. She took up fantasizing about Sir Lawrence Olivier (whom I believe she had never met, though she seemed to have met just about every other celebrity of merit). She slowly slipped into poverty, due in no small measure to a life of social excesses, and was eventually forced to sell all her belongings (though never the fabulous jewelry her father and Mindret had given her). Her health failing following a series of strokes, she moved into my mother and father's house, and lived there from that time forward until her death more than a decade later.

Isabel produced the manuscript for "This Loving Daughter" on an old manual typewriter at the desk in my childhood bedroom. She had moved in when I moved out. I had vacated my parent's house and gone on to college and my own married life, though years later I ended up sharing that same bedroom again with my aunt. First I, then she, slept in that room in the mahogany sleigh bed that had belonged to my grandmother, Zulime. (Like my aunt before me, I had felt it necessary to leave my husband to temporarily fend for himself while I moved back into the family fold to help as my aging family began to require 24/7 nursing care.) I can still hear my aunt's beautiful stage-trained voice reciting poetry as we attempted to fall asleep, she in the sleigh bed and I on a daybed, in our dark, shared bedroom. Poetry made the long, black nights of care-giver captivity almost bearable for both of us. . . .

> In a coign of the cliff between lowland and highland,
>   At the sea-down's edge between windward and lee,
> Walled round with rocks as an inland island,
>   The ghost of a garden fronts the sea. . . .

After my father passed away, the Garland girls lived out the remainder of their lives entirely together, sharing and arguing and bickering in an affable sibling way. Their last year was spent living comfortably together in a house that my husband and I had purchased for them. My less-athletic aunt was frail and wheelchair bound by that time, but her mind was ever sharp, and she was still able to recite the metered, musical words of her favorite poem, Swinburne's "A Forsaken Garden." The sisters played cards and listened to music, reminisced, read to each other, and recited poetry together. They were both excellent cooks, though mother got more and more forgetful and auntie wasn't able to get around well after her strokes. Still, they went on visits and welcomed visitors until their last days.

Living as they did, so closely together, my aunt contracted and soon shared her final illness with my mother. Isabel had gone into a local hospital for some tests and, unbeknownst to any of us, came home with a virulent staph pneumonia brewing in her lungs. Coughs developed quickly, and the two sisters slipped into ever-deepening comas as CO_2 built up in their systems. My mother went into the hospital first, and when it became clear to all concerned (my mother included) that her chances of surviving this pneumonia were nonexistent, at her wish and with her two daughters at her side, she was taken off the respirator, transferred out of intensive care, and moved into a regular hospital room. She was soon joined in that room by her sister, Isabel. Side by side, their angelic white hair tenderly beribboned by one of the day-shift nurses, they looked as peaceful and innocent as sleeping children.

Never proponents of "good clean living," their eighty-odd years of cheerful indulgences did not seem to have left them with even their fair share of wrinkles. Isabel, who never spent a full hour in the sun in her eighty-four years, still boasted the fairest and most delicate of Celtic skin; her sister, Constance, who prided herself on an adventurous and athletic life, was almost equally smooth and fair against the clean and squarely folded white hospital sheets. Nurses came in and out of their hospital room; some stayed to talk and ask questions.

"These two were famous ladies," the shift nurse explained to a newcomer on duty. "They're sisters; were together all their lives; couldn't bear to be separated even for a day."

"Who were they?" the new nurse queried.

"Isabel was a writer and an actress—published about a half-dozen books; her niece said she wrote a musical, too. Constance was a well-known artist. Their father was a famous author—won a Pulitzer Prize. Lots of famous people in their circle. They knew everybody. Ran around with the old Hollywood set, too—friends of all that old movie crowd. Constance even had her own airplane in the 30s; knew Amelia Earhart."

"Who's Amelia Earhart?" the younger nurse demanded.

"Good God, child, don't they teach you kids anything these days?"

Constance Hamlin Garland Harper Williams Doyle died peacefully in her hospital room in Sherman Oaks, California, on Wednesday, November 16, 1988. Mary Isabel Garland Johnson Lord followed her sister for the last time on Saturday, November 19th.

They made their final journey together, joining Hamlin Garland and his wife, Zulime Taft Garland, plus previous generations of the Garland family in the family burial plot under huge maple trees on the breezy slope of a coulee in Neshonoc Cemetery above the little town of West Salem, Wisconsin.

These two sisters represented the end of a magical, romantic era to many who knew them. They themselves seemed to realize that they were bringing their father's Middle Border saga to a close, and they ended their own chapters with peace and dignity. Hamlin Garland should have been proud of both of his daughters. I can hear my aunt's voice even now as finally I am able to fulfill my deathbed promise to her: "the air now soft with a summer to be," her offering to a new and far less innocent era.

A Forsaken Garden

In a coign of the cliff between lowland and highland,
　　At the sea-down's edge between windward and lee,
Walled round with rocks as an inland island,
　　The ghost of a garden fronts the sea.
A girdle of brushwood and thorn encloses
　　The steep square slope of the blossomless bed
Where the weeds that grew green from the graves of its roses
　　　　Now lie dead.

The fields fall southward, abrupt and broken,
　　To the low last edge of the long lone land,
If a step should sound or a word be spoken,
　　Would a ghost not rise at the strange guest's hand?
So long have the grey bare walks lain guestless,
　　Through branches and briers if a man make way,
He shall find no life but the sea-wind's, restless
　　　　Night and day.

The dense hard passage is blind and stifled
　　That crawls by a track none turn to climb
To the strait waste place that the years have rifled
　　Of all but the thorns that are touched not of time.
The thorns he spares when the rose is taken;
　　The rocks are left when he wastes the plain.
The wind that wanders, the weeds wind-shaken,
　　　　These remain.

Not a flower to be pressed of the foot that falls not;
    As the heart of a dead man the seed-plots are dry;
From the thicket of thorns whence the nightingale calls not,
    Could she call, there were never a rose to reply.
Over the meadows that blossom and wither
    Rings but the note of a sea-bird's song;
Only the sun and the rain come hither
            All year long.

The sun burns sere and the rain dishevels
    One gaunt bleak blossom of scentless breath.
Only the wind here hovers and revels
    In a round where life seems barren as death.
Here there was laughing of old, there was weeping.
    Haply of lovers none ever will know,
Whose eyes went seaward a hundred sleeping
            Years ago.

Heart handfast in heart as they stood, "Look thither,"
    Did he whisper? "look forth from the flowers to the sea;
For the foam-flowers endure when the rose-blossoms wither,
    And men that love lightly may die—but we?"
And the same wind sang and the same waves whitened,
    And or ever the garden's last petals were shed,
In the lips that had whispered, the eyes that had lightened,
            Love was dead.

Or they loved their life through, and then went whither?
    And were one to the end; but what end who knows?
Love deep as the sea as a rose must wither,
    As the rose-red seaweed that mocks the rose.
Shall the dead take thought for the dead to love them?
    What love was ever as deep as a grave?
They are loveless now as the grass above them
            Or the wave.

All are at one now, roses and lovers,
    Not known of the cliffs and the fields and the sea.
Not a breath of the time that has been hovers
    In the air now soft with a summer to be.
Not a breath shall there sweeten the seasons hereafter
    Of the flowers or the lovers that laugh now or weep,
When as they that are free now of weeping and laughter
            We shall sleep.

Here death may deal not again for ever;
　　Here change may come not till all change end,
From the graves they have made they shall rise up never,
　　Who have left nought living to ravage and rend.
Earth, stones, and thorns of the wild ground growing,
　　While the sun and the rain live, these shall be;
Till a last wind's breath upon all these blowing
　　　　Roll the sea.

Till the slow sea rise and the sheer cliff crumble,
　　Till terrace and meadow the deep gulfs drink,
Till the strength of the waves of the high tides humble
　　The fields that lessen, the rocks that shrink,
Here now is his triumph where all things falter,
　　Stretched out on the spoils that his own hand spread,
As a god self-slain on his own strange altar,
　　　　Death lies dead.

ᴂ ᴂ ᴂ

The real hero of this book is not its author, my aunt, Mary Isabel Garland Lord, nor any of the people she describes in this chronicle of generations. Isabel never met her real hero, and he remains quietly and mysteriously in the background, appearing here and there on the pages of her life to make scholarly note of some interesting historical fact or detail. These fascinating notes might otherwise never have been known to me, to my aunt, or to any member of the generations mentioned in *A Summer to Be* had Professor Keith Newlin not taken Isabel's project and the history of the Garland family under his wing.

My deathbed promise to my aunt slipped to a back burner after a few feeble attempts early on to secure a publisher for her memoir. Years slipped by, and the publishing project languished. Then in 1999 Keith Newlin contacted me about his plans to write a new biography of my grandfather and to republish *The Book of the American Indian* that Hamlin Garland had produced in 1923. Professor Newlin accomplished both of his projects in record time (along with teaching a full load of English courses at the University of North Carolina Wilmington), and came back to me with a publisher for *A Summer to Be*. He kept up a true professorly prodding and made several trips to California to work on this project. What emerged for me in getting to know Professor Newlin and his research is a fabulous wealth of familial history and knowledge. Not too many souls can claim the luxury of a Ph.D. scholar dedicated to their family history!

For all my aunt's love of rare jewels, the only disappointment to me in working on this project is that Isabel never knew Keith Newlin, the crown jewel in the Garland tiara. It's details like the ones Keith sent to me in an email in the fall of 2005 that made the book and the project so much fun:

> The best photo of Zulime I've ever seen is the one on the easel in your house, which was taken shortly after her wedding. It was even used in the marketing campaign for *The Captain of the Gray Horse Troop*, where it appeared as a full-page photo in *Harper's Weekly* on April 5, 1902. Things haven't changed much: photos of beautiful women sell books, just as today they sell cars. Anyway, the two I've put up [on the website] will interest you: one was taken in 1893 when she was sculpting at the World's Fair; it too appeared in a magazine feature on "girl sculptors." The other was taken in 1898 at Eagle's Nest Camp shortly before HG and Z began courting. . . .

And this was just the beginning. For example, I discovered from Keith Newlin that my pilot mother and Amelia Earhart's husband were more than friends. Each encounter with Keith brought some fascinating new tidbit of information, and his contributions have quite literally made this book happen. Keith Newlin has made the publishing, reading, and rereading of *A Summer to Be* a deeply enjoyable and rewarding project for all concerned.

Dr. Takeo Susuki and Hal Feeney kindly provided me with photographic assistance and electronic reproductions of some of the Garland family images and paintings. I would also like to express gratitude for the advice, encouragement, and support of Keith Burns, Joan Perkal Burns, Ph.D., and of my two toughest critics: my ever-patient and logical scientist husband, Robert; and forever coach and friend, Billee Pat Connolly.

Introduction

Keith Newlin

Readers who come to *A Summer to Be* because of an interest in Hamlin Garland will discover a fascinating side of the writer that he never revealed in his eight volumes of autobiography—the intensely-loving, domineering father whose deep love for his eldest daughter led him to change the trajectory of his career even as that love impeded his daughter's independence. Garland was ill-equipped by temperament for marriage and fatherhood, to which he came late, marrying in 1899 at age thirty-nine. He had spent his adulthood in almost incessant travel as he fulfilled lecture engagements and indulged his own wanderlust by exploring the West, by visiting the goldfields in the Yukon, and by journeying to England to meet the authors with whom he had been corresponding. As he entered his fourth decade, he found it difficult to break his solitary habits and enter the inevitable compromises of marriage and family life. Though he was a devoted father who spared no effort to ease the passage into adulthood of his two daughters, Mary Isabel, born in 1903, and Constance, born in 1907, his fatherly guidance was as often overbearing as it was loving—as Isabel (who dropped her first name in her late teens) amply illustrates in her memoir.

But *A Summer to Be*, which Isabel had originally titled "This Loving Daughter," is valuable in its own right as a story of a girl brought up in the shadow of her father's famous friends, enjoying all the advantages of celebrity even as she rebelled against her father's loving domination. Garland had a talent for forming friendships, and in their childhood his daughters played with the children of Solomon Guggenheim, the founder of the famed art museum; Ira Nelson Morris, Chicago financier and later U.S. envoy to Sweden; and Ernest Thompson Seton, naturalist and co-founder of the Boy Scouts of America. As teenagers, the Garland girls met Arthur Conan Doyle, George Bernard Shaw, J. M. Barrie, Joseph Conrad, Rudyard Kipling, and A. A. Milne; and as adults they formed friendships with the actors Walter Hampden, John Barrymore, and Walter Pidgeon. While Constance inherited an artistic ability from her mother, Isabel inherited her father's talent for writing. In her memoir, which begins with her earliest memories, Isabel charmingly describes her encounters with these and many other writers and actors as she honestly and movingly weaves a story of her own coming of age that is also a snapshot of American literary culture of the first decades of the twentieth century. Part memoir and part autobiography, *A Summer to Be* records a daughter's gradual emergence from her devoted and possessive father; it is a story full of moments of revelation and intrigue, betrayal and guilt, and ultimately the joy of self-discovery.

🙚 🙚 🙚

Hamlin Garland was born in a squatters' shack on the outskirts of the village of West Salem, Wisconsin, in 1860, just twelve years after that state had joined the Union. When he was three, his father, Richard Hayes Garland, enlisted in the Wisconsin Volunteer Infantry and saw action in Georgia during the Civil War. When Richard Garland returned to his farm in 1865 (an event celebrated in his son's much-anthologized story, "The Return of the Private"), he promptly transferred the rigor of military service to child-raising. "His scheme of discipline impressed itself almost at once upon his children," Garland later remembered. When Hamlin and his younger brother, Franklin, misbehaved, "we soon learned . . . that the soldier's promise of punishment was swift and precise in its fulfillment. We seldom presumed a second time on his forgetfulness or tolerance."[1] His mother, the former Isabelle McClintock, was not demonstrative. Garland remembered that "she never expressed her deeper feelings. She seldom kissed her children," and once he reached his teenage years, Hamlin recalled that "she never embraced us."[2] The combination of a stern father and an undemonstrative mother forever colored Garland's own attitude toward the outward expression of love. As an adult, he was painfully shy about interacting with women directly; as a father, he determined not to repeat his parents' practice and never missed an opportunity to remind his children of his love—with the result that his few occasions of discipline deeply wounded his daughters.

Richard Garland was an ambitious farmer who uprooted his family five times before Hamlin was sixteen.   When the Garlands moved to a patch of land near Osage, Iowa, in 1870, young Hamlin was set to work to plow the tough prairie sod. "I plowed seventy acres of land when I was 10 years old and more each year after that," he told an interviewer in 1897. "I was so small that I had to reach up to catch the handles of the plow."[3] His arms aching, at times tormented by flies or blasted by a bitter north wind, his small legs slowed by the accumulation of mud, Garland plowed two acres a day, ten hours at a stretch. It is little wonder that he later commented, "my heart was sometimes bitter and rebellious," even though he well understood that child labor was a necessity on a frontier farm.[4] Garland's early years of hard labor would forever affect him, determine the subjects for his earliest fiction, foster his belief that nothing worthwhile comes without hard work, and engender a life-long fear of poverty.

When Garland was sixteen, he entered the Cedar Valley Seminary in Osage, a combination high school and junior college, returning to the farm each spring and fall for planting and harvesting. By the time he graduated in 1881 at age twenty-one, he was determined to leave farm life forever, and in 1884, after a brief stint at homesteading in Dakota Territory, he made his way to Boston. Like many young men of twenty-four, he didn't know what he wanted to do with his life. For a time, he dreamed of becoming a great orator and, later, a playwright and actor. He drifted into what was effectively an adjunct position as a lecturer at the Boston School of Oratory, tried his hand at fiction-writing, and discovered his calling.

He soon began to flood the nation's magazines with a blizzard of short stories, poems, book reviews, and essays on various topics, all the while campaigning for agrarian reform as a lecturer for Henry George's Single Tax movement, a proposal for more equitable taxation that would, adherents hoped, end land speculation and the consequent escalation of land prices that magnified the difficulties of Midwestern farm life. He gained a reputation as a radical and began writing stories that combined George's economic theories with realistic depictions of farm life. In 1891 the best of these stories appeared as *Main-Travelled Roads*; reviewers praised his method but were disturbed by the bleak subject. Other books followed rapidly (four novels in 1892 alone), and they were often greeted with hostile criticism that focused on Garland's persona as much as the books themselves.

Garland was a naturally gregarious man who made the acquaintance of many of Boston's writers and intellectuals, a circle of friends that enlarged when he moved to Chicago in 1893. By then he had become known as one of the nation's most vehement advocates of literary realism, a campaign that he brought to the leading magazines. When he issued his literary manifesto, *Crumbling Idols*, in 1894, and his novel celebrating the independence of women, *Rose of Dutcher's Coolly*, in 1895, critics greeted them with hostility in reviews that often attacked Garland personally—and Garland thereafter determined to write no more controversial books. But controversy had also increased the demand for his lectures, and Garland traveled widely throughout the country and became involved in a number of organizations that enlarged his acquaintance with the leaders of American literary and art culture. In his travels he also discovered a new enthusiasm in the grandeur of the mountain West and decided to devote his energies to celebrating the West in his fiction, a decision cemented after a trip to the Klondike Gold Rush in 1898 in search of new literary material.

Garland married Zulime Mauna Taft in 1899. The daughter of a former University of Chicago professor of geology turned Kansas banker, Zulime (pronounced Zoo-lah-mee) had recently returned from Paris, where she had studied sculpture, a talent encouraged by her brother, the sculptor Lorado Taft, who was Garland's good friend. With the responsibilities of marriage, Garland began to write a series of western romances, beginning with *The Eagle's Heart* in 1900, which launched his pattern of issuing a book each year until 1911, when he began to tire of his subject. Two of these books—*The Captain of the Gray Horse Troop* (1902) and *Hesper* (1903)—achieved respectable sales, enabling Garland to attain, for the first time in his career, a sense of financial prosperity. Poised to capitalize on literary and financial success, his world changed with the birth of Mary Isabel. Garland delighted in the joys of fatherhood and became a devoted and affectionate parent. As Isabel remembers, "We had glorious times, my father and I. We walked, we talked, we read, we drew, we romped. Daddy would lie on the floor, holding my hands, while I, stomach down across his feet, was lifted to thrilling heights. When I was little, I used to ride on his foot, clinging to his leg as he moved slowly around the room." Amid such distractions, Garland found himself unable to focus the drive that had hitherto made him so prolific, and as sales of his books slumped, he cast about for new literary direction. After much disappointment, in 1917 he published his autobiography, *A Son of the Middle Border*, to critical acclaim. Its sequel, *A Daughter of the Middle Border*, published in October 1921, was awarded the Pulitzer Prize for biography for 1922, which Garland celebrated by taking his family to England, where he renewed acquaintance with the British authors he had met on his previous trips, alone, in 1899 and 1906.

Isabel's description of her visits with England's famous authors has a certain charm. Hers is a teenager's view, impressed with the pomp and circumstance attending the famous, worried about the impression she makes in her adolescent self-consciousness, and commenting on the incongruous, such as the omnipresence of custard at dinner or the cheating at croquet by the son of the Maharajah of Jhalawar. By the time she returned to the United States after this memorable summer in 1922, Isabel had matured into a lovely young woman of nineteen with considerable self-confidence and poise.

While Garland was practicing his craft as a writer, he also kept up a very active life as a professional lecturer. Returning from England with new material for lectures on British authors, he set out on a fresh round of speaking engagements. He developed a new program entitled "Memories of the Middle Border" that included Isabel and capitalized on the success of his autobiography. Garland and his eldest daughter would read excerpts from his autobiographies, fiction, and poetry, with Isabel costumed as her mother and grandmother. Encouraged by the success of the program, he added two more volumes to the family saga, *Trail-Makers of the Middle*

Border (1926) and *Back-Trailers from the Middle Border* (1928).

The 1920s saw much change for the Garlands. Now in his sixties and often in ill-health, Garland was prone to the carping that often comes with the infirmities of age. His work on his autobiographies had led him to dwell in the past, a time in which, in his nostalgic myopia, the country was unified in its goals and values. In the Wisconsin and Iowa of his remembrance, his neighbors had hailed from New England or Scandinavia or Germany and had made it a matter of pride to assimilate into the nation. But the eastern Europeans he saw on the streets of New York struck him, in his now-conservative outlook, as alien to the traditions he was daily describing in his writing.

Then, too, cultural changes in entertainment, brought about by movies and the rise of magazines with circulations in the millions, served to increase his disdain for the immigrant. He perceived contemporary writers not as artists but as tradesmen who were writing for a magazine industry whose primary goal was not to publish works of literary merit, but to sell advertising. The story was only an incidental hook, full of sensation and violence, provided to lure readers into buying soap and underwear. Garland attributed the changes in literature to these magazines and their lowbrow readers. His long preoccupation with his own past, with reliving his former triumphs, and especially with retracing his own battle for realism in his autobiography, served to cement more firmly the value of that movement in his eyes. One effect was to leave him utterly incapable of recognizing the significance of the burgeoning modernist movement, with its linguistic inventiveness, chronological disruptions, sense of alienation, and invention of new narrative structures that marked a perception of reality that was markedly at odds with his own practice. Garland was especially galled by the modernist assault upon decorum, the frank depiction of sex, of adultery, of violence seemingly for its own sake, all of which he dismissed as "pornography." Everywhere he turned he heard jazz—though to his ear, accustomed to the soothing melodies of folk songs or the stately rhythms of classical symphonies, the music was raucous and jarring, inflaming desires better kept under wraps.

The effect of this cultural conservatism on his relationship with his daughters—now in their teenage years—was predictably confrontational. Always his favorite daughter, Isabel's increasing interest in boys proved particularly trying to the devoted father. More disturbing was Isabel's ambition to become an actress. She and Constance were students at the Finch School, a private preparatory school for girls founded by Jessica Cosgrave, the wife of Garland's friend, John O'Hara Cosgrave, the editor of *Everybody's Magazine*. Isabel had discovered her dramatic talent in the school's theatrical productions, and it was only natural that she wanted to pursue her ambition on the professional stage. Garland's early interest in theater and his long friendships with a number of actors, actresses, and playwrights meant that he was well acquainted with the more casual intimacies of theater folk. When he couldn't dissuade Isabel from acting, he arranged for her to take parts in the theater companies of friends, believing that their watchful eyes would protect his daughter. This first experience on the professional stage was, Isabel remarks, "a liberal and raw education," for away from the protective gaze of her parents, she "learned more of the seamy side of life than I had learned before or since"—for the first time hearing profanity and smut from the lips of leading actors and encountering "the modern connotation of the word 'fairy.'" As an attractive and poised young woman with all the passions of youth, Isabel soon fell in love with a fellow actor, an affair that Garland did his best to end, which only served to increase his daughter's growing secretiveness.

Eventually, Isabel met a man who met with her father's approval. (James) Hardesty Johnson was a tenor with the Jean de Reszke Singers, a quartet that had trained in Europe (where Isabel first met him) and that had come to New York on an American tour. Always fond of musicians, Garland soon welcomed Hardesty as the son he never had. He was pleased when Hardesty and Isabel were married on May 12, 1926, mindful that Hardesty's singing career would be centered in New York, and he would have little separation from his beloved daughter. One year later, on September 12, 1927, Constance married Joseph Wesley Harper, a grandson of one of the founders of Harper and Brothers, Garland's long-time publishers. He was greatly troubled by the new couple's plan to relocate to Hollywood, but he took solace in Isabel's proximity. His world was turned upside down when Hardesty also decided to go to Hollywood to explore career possibilities in the movies.

Isabel touchingly reveals the emotional effect of this relocation on the Garland family. Now approaching his seventieth year, feeling increasingly out of touch with the literary world that had sustained him for forty years, Garland had centered his life around his daughters. Their absence was unbearable. In 1929, when he arrived in Hollywood to visit Constance and Joe Harper, he easily fell in love with California's temperate climate, so alien from the New England winters he had always known. He promptly decided to build a house for Isabel and Hardesty, conveniently located next door to Constance and Joe, who themselves had built a house next door to Joe's mother—all on DeMille Drive, named for the famed film director whose mansion graced the hilltop. He didn't foresee the difficulties this family ménage would present.

Garland had intended to visit during the winters, for Constance soon presented him with two grandchildren—John, born in 1929; Constance, born in 1930—returning to the East for the rest of the year. But in 1931 when Zulime became ill with what was eventually diagnosed as Parkinson's disease, he realized that she needed more care than he could provide. By 1932, the seasonal visit became permanent.

Garland has amply recorded the effect of this self-imposed "exile" on his career in his letters and memoirs: now separated by a continent from the clubs and writers that sustained him, he grew even more dependent upon the company of his daughters. Before long Isabel came to resent her father, for still in the process of becoming independent herself, she begrudged Garland's imperious demands upon her time. But her resentment was complicated by the continual reminder that she was living in a house her father had built for her, as well as being dependent upon his monthly allowance of $100; her guilt at not feeling more appreciative only exacerbated the resentment.

While Hardesty was busy making contacts in the film industry, Isabel was determined to follow in her father's footsteps and become a writer, chiefly of mystery stories, which were enjoying a vogue in the magazines. In the evenings Isabel and Hardesty would socialize with film folk, all the while taking care to hide their drinking from Garland, who disapproved of all but an occasional drink. Then one day Hardesty met an old flame, the singer Marguerite Namara who, like him, had trained with Jean de Reszke in Nice. Marguerite, who was married to a struggling writer fifteen years her junior named Mindret Lord, was in Hollywood to film *Thirty Day Princess* (1934). The two couples began to have regular dinners together, and while the two singers flirted over the piano, the two writers found they had much in common. Mindret had enjoyed some success with placing stories in the pulps, and he began to mentor Isabel with her writing. Not surprisingly, the two soon fell in love.

Still dependent upon her father financially, and fearful of displeasing and disappointing him, Isabel concealed her affair. Then one day, Marguerite surprised the two lovers in an embrace. For a cuckolded husband, Hardesty seems to have been unusually understanding, and he agreed to say nothing to the Garlands. Indeed, hoping that the love affair would play itself out, he even agreed to travel with Isabel to New York, where Mindret would join her. When it became clear that the affair was more than an infatuation, Hardesty agreed to take a separate apartment—and also to conceal their separation from Garland.

In November 1934, Garland learned that Isabel and Hardesty had separated. He was devastated. "This was an appalling revelation to me for I had no suspicion of it," he confided to his diary. "I could not believe it for it involved a long period of duplicity on Mary Isabels part."[5] Four weeks later he learned of her involvement with Mindret and promptly fired off an angry letter to his wayward daughter: "Your sister tells me you have left your husband and are involved with another man. I need not tell you what this means to me but I want to say I will never see this man or take him by the hand. Your monthly allowance will continue but do not expect anything else from me."[6] Isabel responded immediately, pouring out her heart to her father, trying to make him understand. His reply was a curt note: "I understand you are contemplating divorce. You will have no help from me in this matter. I have always stood for honesty and decency and I wish no part in this dangerous venture you embarked on. From now on, the subject is closed between us."[7] Thereafter, his letters, usually effusive in expression of his love and interest in his favorite daughter, were curt and impersonal. For consolation, Isabel turned to her mother, who was far more supportive and acted as an intermediary to temper the disappointed father's wrath. As soon as she and Mindret could save enough money for a lawyer, Isabel arranged for an

absentee Mexican divorce. Isabel and Mindret Lord were married
on December 21, 1936.

While Garland was fretting over his disappointment in his
eldest daughter, Constance was dealing with her own marital difficulties. In 1930 Joe Harper had been an usher at the marriage of
Cecil B. DeMille's daughter, Cecilia, to Francis Calvin. The newly-
wed couple moved into the famed director's mansion atop DeMille
Drive. The Calvin and Harper children often played together, and
soon their parents developed a warm friendship as well. One day
in 1936 Joe announced to Constance that he wanted a divorce so he
could marry Cecilia. Again Garland was devastated at this crumbling of his world and mourned to his diary, "Constance informed
us today that she and Joe—after eight years of wedded life, had
agreed to separate and so—I who have stood for decency and loyalty in social life find myself with two daughters seeking divorces!"
Adding to his pain were fears that the sensation-loving press would
learn that Cecil B. DeMille's daughter was now involved with his
son-in-law. Two days later, he added, "If ever I have a biographer
he can take this as one of my darkest weeks. Both my daughters
separated from their husbands, my wife an invalid, myself threatened with pneumonia and unable to see even the few friends I have
left."[8] By January 18, 1937, Garland had rallied and accompanied
Constance to her lawyer's office to sign the divorce decree. Joe
Harper and Cecilia DeMille Calvin were married one year later, on
January 21, 1938, and, remaining blissfully in the neighborhood,
promptly settled in to live in the Cecil B. DeMille house, directly
across the street. Little wonder that the ménage on DeMille Drive
led Constance to sell that home, and she moved out of the neighborhood and into the then sparsely settled San Fernando Valley.
As her father reflected, "These are the complications of divorce,
deeper yet are the complications in the minds of the children. They
can not understand why their father and mother do not live together as they used to do."[9]

Garland eventually got over his disappointment with
Isabel, and when she and Mindret returned to Hollywood in
November 1937, he welcomed the new husband into the family, taking great pleasure in their discussions of the writing game. Garland
expected Isabel to return to the DeMille Drive house he had built for
her, but in the intervening years she had learned how to say "no"—

indeed, she had made independence a condition of her return to Hollywood. To her surprise, Garland did not resist.

≈ ≈ ≈

A Summer to Be concludes with Garland's death, on March 4, 1940. For the next nine years, Isabel and Mindret lived contentedly in Los Angeles, with Mindret achieving modest success writing scripts for the radio and the movies (most notably, for *The Virgin Queen* [1955], starring Bette Davis). Isabel published her first novel, *Abandon Hope* (Mystery House, 1941, also published as *Death Comes Courting*, Arcadia House, 1941), followed by four others, under the name "Garland Lord," in collaboration with Mindret: *Murder's Little Helper* (1941), *She Never Grew Old* (1942), *Murder with Love* (1943), and *Murder, Plain and Fancy* (1943). Unfortunately for Isabel, Mindret's growing involvement with the film industry led to jealousies on her part. She had found fulfillment in their writing partnership and she regarded Mindret's decision to work for the movies as a betrayal. As she later explained to her attorney, "We had had such fun working together, writing together, that I was hurt and jealous that he would prefer another career without me. He says that that was the moment that opened his eyes to my complete selfishness, my possessiveness. I was selfish, I admit. I so loved our life together and what I thought was our happiness, that I hated to let it slip away from me."[10] Mindret began drinking heavily. He entered into an affair, and in 1947 the marriage collapsed. Eight years later, in 1955, Mindret was dead, a suicide.

In the 1960s, Isabel read her father's diaries in preparation to depositing them in the Huntington Library. Garland had begun keeping a daily diary in 1898 and had continued the habit until a week before his death. In them he had recorded the minutia of a busy author and also a great deal about his family, especially about Isabel, the daughter he adored. He filled the pages with her every advance, noting her first steps, her first words, recording every achievement, no matter how small. Reading the diaries gave her a renewed appreciation for the meaning and scope of Garland's life— as well as her own part in it. Before the diaries left her hands, Isabel made a selective transcript, some 146 single-spaced pages. At some point in the process she decided to use them as the basis for a memoir, and that was the genesis for *A Summer to Be*, which Isabel had originally titled "This Loving Daughter." Despite her occasional conflicts with her father, Isabel wished the book to stand as a testament to her deep and lasting love for the father who had cherished her, perhaps not fully realizing how revelatory it would prove of her own complex attitude toward him.

As a writer, Isabel well knew that every story needs a conflict, and she decided to place her own struggle for independence at the center of her memoir. *A Summer to Be* contains two stories. In it can be found a sequel to Garland's own biographical series, the story of a famous man who intensely and possessively adored his daughters to whom he represented the extremes of social privilege. The other story is Isabel's own, the tale of her rebellion against her father and her growing independence, brought about by the discovery of her one true love. But lurking behind the narrative is the knowledge that her own insecurity drove love away from her, and though she nowhere mentions the later outcome, she foreshadows it by infusing the memoir with her own tendency toward possessiveness, as at the close of chapter 20 where she implores Mindret, "Promise me that no matter what happens you'll go on loving me! Promise me that you will love me forever!" In fact, Isabel carried her undying love for Mindret to her own last day, decades after their divorce and his suicide. Just as *A Summer to Be* is an ode to her father, the second half of the memoir becomes her ode to Mindret. Isabel also casts Hardesty as a saint in his tolerance of her affair, out of his own love for her, perhaps in part as penance for her betrayal of him. Writing *A Summer to Be* thus became an act of catharsis.

⁊ ⁊ ⁊

I am grateful to the Huntington Library, San Marino, California, for permission to quote from Garland's unpublished diaries (GD 1-43) in this introduction and in the notes. For permission to quote from Garland's unpublished letters and to publish photographs in its collection, I wish to thank the Hamlin Garland Papers, University of Southern California Libraries Special Collections, hereafter abbreviated as (USC). I also thank John

Ahouse and Claude Zachary for help in acquiring materials at USC, and Stephen C. Brennan and Gary Culbert for helpful comments on a draft of this introduction.

Notes

[1] Garland, *A Son of the Middle Border* (New York: Macmillan, 1917), 7-8.

[2] Garland, "The Wife of a Pioneer," *Ladies' Home Journal* 20 (September 1903): 8, 42.

[3] "Gossip about Hamlin Garland." *Los Angeles Times*, August 8, 1897, 21.

[4] *A Son of the Middle Border*, 88.

[5] Diary, November 2, 1934 (Huntington Library, GD 1-43).

[6] Quoted in chapter 17 of *A Summer to Be*.

[7] Quoted in chapter 17 of *A Summer to Be*.

[8] Diary, November 9, 11, 1936 (Huntington Library, GD 1-43).

[9] Diary, April 12, 1938 (Huntington Library, GD 1-43).

[10] Isabel Garland Lord to Mr. O'Connon, March 2, 1949 (USC).

1. The Beginning

ᢲᢲ ᢲᢲ ᢲᢲ

The first arms I remember are those of my father, the man I loved so dearly and was to hurt so cruelly.

Two of my sister's three children knew "Grandfather" in his last years, ruddy, white-maned, alive with sympathy and enthusiasm. As a young man, his photographs show, he was clean-shaven and dangerously attractive, but when I came on the scene he was in his forties and bearded. Strangely, I cannot recreate him like that, but I do remember with great vividness the day he had the beard shaved off and came home smooth-faced except for a flowing mustache. He was anxious, a bit sheepish, and enormously relieved when I clapped my hands and announced, "I like it, Daddy!" I must have been about three at the time.

Those who have read Hamlin Garland's *A Daughter of the Middle Border* will know that no child ever was more loved than I. I adored my beautiful mother, but in my father's arms I was safe and imperious. I can see myself now on his lap, peering into his face, into the round, wide-set eyes, the irises of which were yellow-green with brown flecks like tiny islands set in mysterious seas. I would trace with my small forefinger the lines of the sensitive, smiling mouth under the gray mustache, the big, strong nose and, wonderingly, the small mound between bushy, erratic eyebrows.

"What's that, Daddy—that little bump?"

"That, daughtie, is a 'think knot.' I have to think very hard, you know, so that you and your mother can have good food and pretty dresses."

I flung my arms around his neck.

"Daddy, I love you!"

"Daughtie, I love you, too," he assured me gravely.

Anya Seton[1] maintains that she and I have a "father fixation," and if the phrase means that I doted upon him, I am proud to accept it. Yet with all the love and understanding between us, Hamlin Garland is still a mystery. In his *A Son of the Middle Border* and the three volumes that followed, Father wrote a memorable autobiography, setting down a lifetime of events and reflections with heartwarming honesty. For forty years he kept daily diaries, and when I reread them all before they went to the Huntington Library in San Marino, it was a disturbing emotional experience. When I turned the last page, I felt I had been actually living inside the brain of that brave, passionate, moody gentleman, that I knew him as no one else in the world could know him. Without question, he told his story well and frankly—but what of the things he left out?

It is not my purpose to retell Father's life history, but in the course of my reading and meditating, questions have arisen, questions to which I have yet to find an answer.

Why, for example, is there no mention of the baby boy, born in the first year of his marriage, three years before I came? Mother told me about the baby and that it had lived only a few days. Father, in his diaries and in his books, makes no reference to it.[2] Why? Was the hurt too deep?

Among Father's papers after his death, I came on a short poem titled "To My Dead Child." Was this merely a literary flight, or a lament for the first born he had lost? The poem itself was undated, conventional, and offered no explanation.

At the same time, among Father's papers, shoved way back in the files, I found the first page of a Boston newspaper. Under the flamboyant headline, "GARLAND IN APPEAL FOR UNWED MOTHERS," was an impassioned, well-written article decrying the injustice meted out to girls who had been victimized by men and calling on the State and Society to do something to ease their lot. He was a crusader in those days, I know, but I find no mention of this particular cause in either his diaries or *A Son of the Middle Border*. This was the period when his novel, *Rose of Dutcher's Coolly*, was banned from the bookstalls of Boston on the charge of sexual frankness. It was also a time when Father was deeply involved with James A. Herne and the world of the theater. At one point in his diary he says briefly, "I am tired of actresses." Hamlin Garland was a dogged, determined fighter, but I cannot help but wonder at the circumstances that led him to espouse this particular, sensational campaign.[3]

To me, one of the greatest mysteries is his relationship to his wife, my mother. Her grandchildren remember her as a wistful, silent semi-invalid, but for the major part of her life Zulime Taft was a beautiful, intelligent, and vital woman. In his books Father paid her tender and deserved tribute, but I have heard people say that as a personality "she doesn't come through." I know why, partly. Deeply emotional, Mother hid behind a facade of almost British reserve. Unfailingly kind and concerned with others, she kept her own counsel. *She* could never have written an autobiography. Was she always so remote, I wonder? It is only in her last years that she and I were able to talk together as women, not as mother and daughter. I wish I had known her sooner.

As a child I worshiped my mother for her beauty, her patience, her tenderness. I would insinuate myself into her bed and command her to "tell-me-about-when-you-were-a-little-girl." What she said comes back to me now only in fragments because, like most children, I listened avidly to the parts I wanted to hear and ignored most of the rest. I knew what the Taft homestead was like because a large photograph of it always hung in Mother's bedroom: a big, comfortable, old mansion on a shaded, small-town, Illinois street. I knew the wonders of the back yard and about the kittens and the dolls and what the family had to eat and how long the walk was to school. These details I had to have repeated over and over, but the basic facts of the family background I have forgotten, if I ever knew.

So, I can say very little about Don Carlos Taft and his wife, Mary Foster. In an old locket, they are a plain, grim, Welsh-English pair. The Professor, a formidable mentality, was a classics scholar and teacher of geology at the University of Illinois. His wife was frail and tiny and called "Little Mother" by all her handsome brood. They raised four children on Professor Taft's salary of twelve hundred dollars a year, and Don Carlos left a mark on his offspring when he named them, in order, Lorado Zadock, Florizel Adino, Zulime Mauna, and Turbulance Doctoria. Mother said she always burst into tears when she had to give her name in school. That was why, when I was born, Mother wanted me named Mary, after her

Don Carlos Taft   Mary Foster Taft
(Courtesy of Victoria Doyle-Jones)

mother. (No one has trouble with Mary.) Father, on the other hand, wanted me named Isabel, after his mother, with the result that I was saddled with both names, for a time.

When Zulime was in her early teens, the Taft family moved to Kansas, why I do not know. The poor "Little Mother" was slowly and agonizingly dying, and her elder daughter nursed her night and day and hung wet sheets around the bedroom of the dreadful little house in an attempt to keep out some of the appalling Midwest heat and dust.

Lorado Taft, the eldest, was resolved on becoming a sculptor. Where did it come from, I wonder, the artistic strain that ruled my uncle and my mother and is now passed on to my sister and her children? Supporting himself by taxidermy and the taking of death masks, Lorado moved on to Chicago and success. When his mother died, he went out to Kansas and brought Zulime, his favorite sister, back with him. There was a deep devotion between those two, and Lorado was determined Zulime was going to have more out of life than serving as housekeeper for a bitter, old man on the bleak Kansas plain. She was talented; he taught her to model and sometime later took her with him to Paris, where she stayed and studied painting and sculpture for the next five years.

As I think back on it, I am amazed at my early indifference, my stupidity. Why didn't I try to draw Mother out about those years? It was the time of Monet, Manet, Renoir, Gauguin, Degas, Sisley, Van Gogh, men whose fame is worldwide, and Mother was in the thick of it. She was a beauty. Her brother used her exquisite body in many of his figures, and her classic face was painted by the leading artists in Paris. Later, when I might have had the sense to ask questions, I was too involved in my own love affairs to go into the matter of hers. Mother always maintained that she came back from Paris heart-whole, but with a girl as warm and ravishing as that there were bound to be romantic encounters under the candles in the ateliers and cafes of Montmartre. Had her dazzling brother blinded her to other men? Was there, perhaps, an unhappy love affair that she was reluctant to recall? Strange that she was able to keep all that exotic adventure bottled up inside her. Whatever the reason, to my shame and remorse, Zulime Taft's five years in the art center of the world are a closed book to me.

Back in her brother's studio on the Midway in Chicago, Zulime was commissioned to model an heroic-size group for the World's Fair of 1893. As I remember, Education was the subject, and from the photographs it turned out to be a handsome, professional job.[4] It was not long before she met the rising Western novelist, Hamlin Garland, whose realistic literary approach was causing shocked comment in intellectual circles. Henry Blake Fuller wrote the story of their courtship in his sly, charming *Under the Skylights*,[5] and Father's own account appears in his Pulitzer Prize-winning *A Daughter of the Middle Border*, a book, by the way, that my mother steadfastly refused to read.

When I asked her why, her face shadowed and she looked away from me with her lips tightening.

"Because it isn't true," she said, and nothing could persuade her to say more.

Many years later, Mother and I came together in a way we never had before. Though I had always loved her, depended on her, used her, there was a shyness between us that prevented full confidence. Then the day came when I found a deep, rewarding, romantic love, and she seemed to want to share it with me, to prove to me that she really understood. It was an extraordinary story that she told me, and not a suggestion of it appears in either Hamlin Garland's books or his diaries.

Lorado Taft in his Chicago studio.
*(Courtesy of the University of Southern California,
on behalf of USC Libraries Special Collections)*

Zulime Taft just before her marriage, 1899. The photograph later
appeared as the frontispiece to *A Daughter of the Middle Border*.
(Courtesy of Victoria Doyle-Jones)

Zulime Taft was not in love with Hamlin Garland when she married him. She had numerous admirers, and Father was frank in explaining the difficulty he had in persuading the lovely young artist to accept him. Mother said she had admired Hamlin, and liked him, but love as a physical passion had no part in it.

"I don't quite know why I did it," she said with a half-smile, lying back on her pillows in the darkened room where I sat by her bedside. "Except he was handsome, distinguished, much talked about. And Lorado like him."

There was no question about it: Father was a strong character, and I imagine his wooing was pretty hard to withstand. They went out to Kansas for the wedding, where the bride wore a blue serge suit she had made herself, and the bridegroom was confined to a wheelchair, temporarily, with rheumatism.

"Zulime looks after me as if I were a baby," Father confided in his diary. "She is a wonderful girl."

To the Colorado Springs friends they were to visit, Father had written in his atrocious handwriting, "I am eager to have you meet my wife who is a panther."

The Ehrichs were enormously intrigued but somewhat relieved when the lady turned out to be a "painter" and not a "panther."[6]

Their marriage, at first, sounds ideal. Father was a literary lion, and money and honors flowed in upon the Garlands. Proudly he took his dazzling young bride (he was ten years older) to New York where they were feted and courted and wined and dined to the point of exhaustion. In his diary Daddy tells of returning to their hotel suite in the early evening with a bottle of champagne and two roast beef sandwiches in his overcoat pocket, to spend an evening of peace, alone.

When he took his wife back to the little town of West Salem, where his mother and father were living in the old house he had bought for them, life for Zulime became far from idyllic. Isabelle McClintock Garland was a semi-invalid and a furiously jealous and possessive mother. While she came eventually to love her daughter-in-law, it was a difficult, discouraging time.

"I tried my best," Mother said, "but she couldn't bear to have us alone together. She was always coming to the foot of the stairs and calling, 'Hamlin, aren't you coming down?' and usually Hamlin went."

I understand my mother's exasperation, but Father gives no hint of this side of the picture.[7] Never was there a more loyal and devoted son. To him these were merely signs of motherly affection. His father, on the other hand, frankly doted on his new daughter, and when she presented him with a granddaughter (me), he professed himself completely content.

It was five or six years after their marriage that it happened. Mother told me that it was months before she would even admit it to herself. The man was from out of town, dynamic, handsome, vastly rich, with just one idea in the world: to take Zulime away with him.[8]

Mother's voice faltered. "I was tempted, horribly. . . . I had never felt anything like that before. It was as if I were . . . another person. I couldn't think what to do. Hamlin was away a great deal, lecturing, attending to business in the East. Larry would take a taxi from the station and keep it waiting out there in the street hour after hour, while he tried to persuade me. . . ."

Oh, as a child I remember those stolen visits: the low murmur of voices downstairs in the fire-lit drawing room, the throb of the taxi motor in the silent, snow-filled street. I would wonder sleepily in my cozy bed who it was who came so late and stayed so long. If I had known it was Uncle Larry, I would have been down the stairs in a minute. I adored the big, striking man who, on official visits, showered me with preposterously expensive presents and swung me high in the air before he kissed me. He smelled wonderfully of tweeds and tobacco and fine masculine cologne.

I remember remarking once, artlessly, "It's too bad Daddy's never here when you come. He would like to see you so much."

I was on the floor, absorbed in a great new doll, but I remember the silence and can imagine the long look that passed between them.

Mother told me the man had a wife but they were estranged and planning a divorce. Surely, he argued, if she told Hamlin the truth, he would agree to a divorce. But there was the baby, Mary Isabel. Without question, Mother loved me as passionately as Father did and would not for an instant consider giving me up.

Yet the thought of robbing Hamlin of the light of his life was intolerable.

Mother and I were both weeping now. "I couldn't see a chance for happiness anywhere . . . so, at last, I sent him away. . . . It was worse than . . . dying. The long, empty years seemed to stretch on forever."

I was holding her small, trembling hands. "Did Daddy know?"

She drew a long breath. "Yes. . . . But we have never spoken of it since. After little Constance came, there was so much demanded of me that life became . . . easier."

Nowhere in the writings of Hamlin Garland is there a hint of this bitter, foredoomed episode, but once I had heard Mother's confession, many things about my father became clearer to me. He was a proud, self-centered man. It must have turned his world to dust and ashes.

🐦 🐦 🐦

The birth of my sister is my first sharply detailed memory. In the mornings, I had been in the habit of creeping in between my mother and father in the big brass bed in the sunny front room on the third floor. "Here we are," I would exclaim blissfully, "the whole pammy!" Little did I know what was shortly to threaten my reign.

My own birth, they told me later, had been an unspeakable ordeal for my poor mother. She was three days in labor, with only a young, inexperienced village practitioner in charge. When I was finally dragged out with forceps, I was disfigured by a blazing purple scar that covered half my face. (Another thing never spoken of by my father.) Mother was so horrified that she frantically set to work making wide-ruffled baby bonnets that would hide my mutilated little face. The scar gradually faded out, but Father's memory of that time of horror did not.

"No man has the right to put a woman through such torture!" he wrote passionately. "The whole idea of birth is animal, obscene. It must not happen to my wife again." He covered pages in the diaries with self-reproach, his agony clear in every line. Yet when I reread the diaries, before turning them over to the

Zulime and Mary Isabel, 1903. The photograph appeared in *A Daughter of the Middle Border* with the caption, "At last the time came when I was permitted to take my wife—lovely as a Madonna—out into the sunshine, and, as she sat holding Mary Isabel in her arms, she gathered to herself an ecstasy of relief. A joy of life which atoned in part, for the inescapable suffering of maternity." *(Courtesy of Victoria Doyle-Jones)*

Huntington Library, I found the pages relating to my birth had been torn out and presumably destroyed. Here again is mystery. Did Father himself do it before he died, thinking they were too revealing? Or was it Mother, after his death, shrinking, as always, from emotional display? My knowledge of the excerpts stems from the time when I was working with Daddy on his literary reminiscences. The pages had been heavily blue-penciled but they were still completely legible. I was shocked and grieved to find them gone.[9]

"It must not happen to my wife again," Father had written, but it *did* happen and there was Constance. No cuddling with my parents from then on. My nurse took me out early that day to play among the June flowers in Jackson Park. When we returned, I was taken up to Mother's bedroom. The curtains were drawn and the room was in half light, but Mother, very pale, her nut-brown hair in thick braids over her shoulder, smiled at me from propped-up pillows.

Daddy drew out the small rocking chair Grandfather Garland had made for me and set it beside the bed. "Sit down, Mizabel, we have a surprise for you." A strange nurse placed a white bundle in my arms, and I sat rocking gently and staring bemused into the face of a tiny, live doll.

"It's your sister, darling—your new baby sister," Mother was saying. "You must help us take care of her."

Daddy looked at us both fondly. "What shall we call her?"

That was easy. For some time I had been promised a baby sister and the name was ready. "I shall call her Marjorie Christmas," I said firmly.

My parent's eyes met in amusement. "Why, dear?" Mother asked.

I could be very important. "Because Christmas is the best time of the year and Marjorie is the nicest name."

They were tempted to let it stand, but Mother had a devoted friend who took a proprietary interest and suggested her own name, Constance, which everyone liked.[10]

Poor little mite. Her coming into the world was comparatively simple, but the question was how could she stay in it? Unable to assimilate the usual formula, Connie was finally raised on buttermilk, with the result that her teeth came in uncoated with enamel and were always cruelly sensitive. While Mother and Anna, the baby's temperamental Irish nurse, hung over the ailing, whimpering little creature, I was thrown more and more into my father's company.

"This is *my* child," he would say to my mother. "The other is *your* child."

We had glorious times, my father and I. We walked, we talked, we read, we drew, we romped. Daddy would lie on the floor, holding my hands, while I, stomach down across his feet, was lifted to thrilling heights. When I was little, I used to ride on his foot, clinging to his leg as he moved slowly around the room. One of my first pangs of jealousy was when the baby, in her turn, was old enough to do that.

To be honest (I was Isabelle McClintock's granddaughter, after all), I was wildly jealous of Constance, of the attention she demanded, of the fatuous adoration of our parents as she turned into a precocious, cherubic, little fiend. The joys of having a baby sister, I soon discovered, were vastly overrated, and the sooner she was put in her place the better.

I was attempting to administer a little discipline one day— as I remember I bit her—when Daddy happened on the scene and rose in his wrath. "Mary Isabel, come upstairs with me!"

He swung me off the floor and onto the bottom tread of the stairs. With his big, hard hand in one rousing spank after another he assisted me bodily to the top of the stairs and into his study. I wept and shrieked and struggled, and as he left me, after a severe lecture, closing and locking the door behind him, I shouted after him in outrage, "You hurted me and I hate you! *I hate you!*"

Eventually, the nurse released me and I headed, sobbing and snuffling in self-pity, for my mother. She was ill in bed and I had been told not to bother her, but my injury could only be soothed by her kisses. The door to her room was slightly ajar and, peeking cautiously in, I saw a curious scene: my father was down on the floor beside the bed, his face hidden, and Mother's hand was moving back and forth over his shock of hair, as he repeated brokenly over and over, "I struck her! . . . She said she hated me. She'll never love me again!"

Here was one who recognized advantage when she saw it. Conscious of unlimited power, I tiptoed back to the nursery. This is another incident that does not appear in either the diaries or the book. I imagine that Father was too shaken by the episode to wish to record it.

ᐁ ᐁ ᐁ

Our most joyous times were reading. I have heard many of the great dramatic voices of our day, Olivier, Burton, Gielgud, but Hamlin Garland would not have been far behind. He had a fine natural voice and he had been trained at the Boston School of Oratory, attended every possible performance by Edwin Booth, and was an off-and-on member of James A. Herne's theatrical company. He might have become an actor, as his brother Franklin did, but he chose literature and public speaking instead. At this time in his life he was all mine.

We had a huge *Household Book of English Verse*, 1052 pages. I know because I have it still, crumbling and smoke-stained but still cherished, and Daddy would read aloud from it by the hour. I especially loved the Scotch and English ballads and shivered with excitement over "Lord Ullin's Daughter," "The Three Ravens," and "Randall, My Son." Shakespeare, Keats, Shelley, Byron, Tennyson, Swinburne, and Lanier became as familiar to me as my own name.

"Weed some more, Daddy," I would order, wriggling with joy.

I can hear that voice now, rich, resonant, crisp of diction, in the opening lines of Swinburne's "A Forsaken Garden," one of our favorites:

> In a coign of the cliff between lowland and highland,
> At the sea-down's edge between windward and lee,
> Walled round with rocks as an inland island,
> The ghost of a garden fronts the sea.

I learned to read from Albert Bigelow Paine's inimitable *Hollow Tree Books*, Daddy reading the long words, I the little ones, and it did not take long. Soon, I was ready to start reading Hamlin Garland and delighted Father by telling him gravely that I considered his *Boy Life on the Prairie* even better than *Robin Hood*.

Our home was full of music as well. No radio, no records, but we had the piano, which Mother played with grace and skill, and many of our friends were professional musicians. One of Daddy's most intimate friends was Edward MacDowell, but his tragic illness took him out of our lives, though his dauntless, little wife, Auntie Marian, was often in our home, her small, steely hands drawing out the soul of her husband's music.[11] Another who took over the piano was Henry B. Fuller, a small, elfin, literary man who became my father's alter ego. Night after night, Connie and I went off to sleep on tides of Grieg, Chopin, and Mozart.

Father himself loved to sing and, though not professionally trained, he had a rich voice and an extensive repertoire. Out of his own youth he would bring back the songs his mother and father and aunts and uncles used to sing, but sometimes the pain of memory would become too strong and his voice would break. Many of the old songs were too sad for me, and I would creep under the piano and wail like a puppy.

"Don't sing that one, Daddy!" I would implore of "My Darling Nellie Gray." I was blessed and cursed with an excess of imagination, and the agony expressed in the songs was so real to me that sometimes I thought my heart would break. "I will never see my darling anymore" I still think is one of the most poignant lines in the world, and "I hear the children calling, I see their sad tears falling" laid all of childhood's burdens on me.

There were cheerful songs, too. Daddy sang "Bonnie Dundee" and "My Heart's in the Highlands" and all the old Irish ballads. I loved "Jock O Hazeldine," "The Pirate's Serenade," and "The Raggle Taggle Gypsies." Now and then on the lecture platform Daddy would break into "O'er the Hills in Legions, Boys" or "The Rolling Stone," a quaint tale of a pioneer husband frustrated by a quick-thinking wife.

Our house was a narrow, four-story brick building on the unfashionable South Side, but it was within walking distance of Jackson Park, the University, and the Midway studio of my mother's brother, Lorado Taft. Our house had been built by an architect for himself and, though small, had charm. On the ground floor was a small apartment we rented out, and a long, steep flight of stairs led to our main floor, which began with two small bay-windowed drawing rooms. The front one had a book-walled fireplace; the back one was almost filled by the grand piano. There were window seats in the front room, deliciously warmed by radiators underneath, and there Connie and I spent most of our waking hours, with books and crayons and paper dolls. The dining room was minute and Dutch in effect, with high-set leaded windows and dark wood paneling. Beyond was the kitchen, a maid's room, and a bath.

On the third floor in front was Mother's large sunny bedroom. A guest room was next, then the bathroom (there were pink roses in the bowl, I remember), the nursery, and at the back, over-looking the alley and the ugly service stairs of the neighborhood, was Father's study. On our house, the top landing of the service stairs was enclosed in glass, making a sort of sun porch where we loved to play. There were trunks piled in one corner, and with a down quilt and some cookies, we would climb to the top and snuggle down and pretend we were on a mountain high in the Alps.

In the early days, Connie and I and Anna, the Irish nurse, all slept in the nursery, and it was there I met with the first unfairness I had ever known. Anna was fiercely devoted to the baby, could hardly bear to share her with my parents, and was furiously resentful of me. On certain nights, when the little one was fretful, Anna would take her into her bed and sing to her and tell her stories. If I sat up in my bed and tried to listen, Anna would swoop over, deliver a stinging slap, and order me to sleep immediately. Only four, I could not understand why I should be left out and often wept myself bitterly to sleep.

It was Anna who first introduced me to horror and left a mark that exists today.

An elderly gentleman in a neighboring house died suddenly and, being Irish, a wake was held. Mother and Daddy were away from home that night, but Anna, superstitious primitive, determined to go and to take the baby and me with her. To me, at first, it was just bewildering: the close-packed people, the wailing, the long black box in the middle of the room; but when Anna commanded me to go and look into the box, I refused and backed away. She ordered again and I still refused and began to cry. Handing the baby to someone nearby, Anna seized me roughly and, despite my kicks and frantic screams, held me over the coffin so that my eyes were only an inch or two from the rigid old face with its sparse white beard.

"Look!" Anna screamed, shaking me. "Look—and don't ever forget! He's dead—and you're going to be someday. He's *DEAD!*"

It was not that occasion that saw the last of Anna, though it should have. With the secretiveness of childhood, I never told my parents what had happened, but from then on I was subject to blood-chilling, hideous nightmares. Mother and Father were thoroughly tired of Anna and her dramatics, but her love and care of the baby was unbounded, and as long as Connie ailed, Anna was sure of her place.

Connie must have been three or so when our parents went out one night to dinner and the opera. We had been permitted to watch them dress, and I was impressed with the deft way in which Mother anchored her train up under her pony coat with safety pins and swathed her lovely crown of braids in veiling. She wore quilted carriage boots and carried rhinestone-buckled satin slippers in a black velvet evening bag. She was perfectly beautiful and so was Daddy in full evening dress.

From our usual post, the warm window seat, we watched them going down the street to take the elevated at 64th and Woodlawn, waiting till they turned the corner under the streetlamp and, with a last wave, vanished from view. It was a bitter winter night and we could see how they struggled against the force of the vicious lake wind.

We were still there when they returned, long after midnight, Connie and I huddled together on the window seat, cold, supperless, and in the dark. Upstairs, Anna and the Swedish cook, having worked up a feud, were locked in their separate rooms.

Father's wrath was monumental. By morning the house was swept clean of domestics, and Mother was wearily phoning the employment agencies for another of the ignorant immigrant girls who were the only source of supply.

Notes

[1] Anya Seton (1904-1990) was the daughter of Garland's good friend, Ernest Thompson Seton (1860-1940), naturalist, wild-animal illustrator, author, and co-founder of the Boy Scouts of America. Anya would later become a successful author of a number of historical novels, including *Theodosia* (1941), *Dragonwyck* (1944), and *Foxfire* (1950).

[2] While Garland, always reserved about personal matters, does not mention this calamitous event in his autobiographies, he does include a cryptic note in his diary for June 26, 1901: "This morning at about 4 am Zulime called me. She was in great pain and Father went for the Doctor. Before he came the worst was over. She must be in bed for a week and our plans are all awry again" (GD 1-43, Huntington Library). The baby was stillborn.

3 Isabel is likely referring to a three-part series of articles in which Garland lobbied for inheritance rights for illegitimate children, which were widely syndicated in 1913. Since the Boston clipping is undated, Isabel concluded that it dated from Garland's Boston years, 1884-1893. For a reprinting of the text, see Keith Newlin, "Hamlin Garland and the 'Illegitimacy Bill' of 1913," *American Literary Realism* 29.1 (1996): 78-88. The actor and playwright James A. Herne (1839-1901), with his wife, the actress Katharine Corcoran Herne (1856-1943), were among Garland's closest friends after they met in May 1889. On July 4, 1890, Herne's *Margaret Fleming*, the first Ibsen-inspired drama to appear in America, opened in Lynn, Massachusetts. In 1891 Garland and Herne founded the Boston Independent Theater Association, modeled after the independent theaters of Europe, to produce experimental realistic drama on a subscription basis without the worry of turning a profit, after they failed to interest commercial managers in their plays.

4 For the Columbian Exposition, Zulime sculpted *Learning* for display in the Art Building, as well as a statue of *Victory* for display in the interior of the Manufacturers' Building. Her colossal figure of *Freedom Breaking Her Chains* caused one reviewer to marvel, "One can scarcely believe that the slender girlish figure has the physical endurance, or the small white hand the strength to model those great forceful figures, but all unaided she has accomplished that which will crown her with honor, for she has embodied in plaster much of the grace and dignity of her own soul." As a result, she was featured, with a striking engraving of her, in an issue of the *Illustrated American* as part of a story on Exposition sculpture by women artists. (Clippings in Zulime Garland's scrapbook, item 712c,4 [USC]; "Sculpture at the World's Fair," *Illustrated American*, March 25, 1893, 373-374).

5 Henry Blake Fuller (1857-1929) was Garland's closest friend. Garland met him soon after Fuller published his most important novel, *The Cliff-Dwellers* (1893). In "The Downfall of Abner Joyce," one of the stories in *Under the Skylights* (1901), Fuller wickedly satirizes Garland's climb into social preeminence.

6 Louis Ehrich (1849-1911) was a Colorado Springs businessman and art dealer. Garland and Zulime were married on November 18, 1899, at the home of Zulime's father in Hanover, Kansas. Garland describes his honeymoon visit with Louis and Henriette Ehrich in *A Daughter of the Middle Border* (New York: Macmillan, 1921), 140-142.

7 While Garland's autobiographies consistently portray his devotion to his mother, Zulime's recollection is borne out by Garland's diary, where he describes their contentment in isolating themselves in their room, only to be interrupted by Mother Garland, who "is jealous of our companionship and often comes to the door if she thinks we are staying up stairs too long. She likes to have us sit where she can see us" (February 11, 1900, GD 1-43, Huntington Library).

8 Zulime's lover remains unidentified. "Larry" is likely not his

name, given Isabel's concealment of other names in the memoir.

[9] When he went through his diaries as he prepared to compose his memoirs, Garland removed pages for July 14, 15, 16, 17, 1903, from the diary, redated July 13 to July 15, and described his reaction to first holding his new daughter while omitting details of the delivery. In *Daughter*, 286-287, Garland glosses over the event's trauma.

[10] Constance was born on June 18, 1907. Zulime's friend is Constance Lily Rothschild Morris, wife of Ira Nelson Morris (1875-1942), a financier and later the U.S. envoy to Sweden (1914-1923). Their daughter, Constance Irene, was one of Isabel's close friends. A 1927 letter from Henry B. Fuller to Constance explains that the new parents had so dithered in naming their new daughter that he urged them to get off the fence: "when you were quite new I looked you over and told your undecided parent that they were at liberty—a mighty narrow liberty—to choose between 'Lucy' and 'Constance.' They wisely chose the latter" (Fuller to Constance Garland, August 23, 1927, USC).

[11] Edward Alexander MacDowell (1861-1908), New York-born composer of many piano works. He was the head of Columbia University's department of music (1896-1904), but he resigned his position and suffered a nervous collapse in 1905. After his death in 1908 his widow, the pianist Marian Nevins MacDowell, established the MacDowell Colony for composers, artists, and writers at the MacDowell farm in Peterborough, New Hampshire.

2. Chicago

ॐ ॐ ॐ

On the whole, life in Chicago was exciting and rewarding. Outside of home and our neighborhood, which was full of nice children and interesting things to do, there was Uncle Lorado's studio. Our kind, witty uncle always made us welcome, put piles of modeling clay at our disposal, and paused now and then in his own monumental work, *The Fountain of Time*, to speak words of advice and encouragement. At night the studio became a mysterious and thrilling playground. With our charming Taft cousins, Emily and Jessie Louise, we played hide-and-seek through the cold, lofty rooms filled with huge, half-carved marbles, stark-white, dead-eyed casts, and mountainous shapes covered with wet cloths to keep the clay from drying out. In one room, as you opened the door you came face to face with a life-size plaster group of blind people clinging together behind a young, blind mother who held aloft a little boy, the only one with eyes to see the way. I never saw it without a thrill of terror.

At Christmas, with red capes and lanterns, we sang carols with our cousins beside the indoor pool that reflected the glow of tall candles in six-foot sconces and the sculptured beauty of my uncle's group, *The Great Lakes*: five graceful women, one of whom was our mother. Today, it stands beside the Art Institute in Chicago. *The Fountain of Time*, now at the end of the Midway, was a great, surging wave of humanity passing in review before a towering, hooded figure. The concept came from the lines,

Time goes, you say. Ah, no.
Time stays. We go.[1]

Hamlin Garland and Mary Isabel. The photograph appeared in *A Daughter of the Middle Border* with caption, "Entirely subject to my daughter, who regarded me as a wonder-working giant, I paid tribute to her in song, in story, and in frankincense and myrrh. Led by her trusting little hand I re-discovered the haunts of fairies and explored once more the land beneath the rainbow."
(Courtesy of the University of Southern California, on behalf of USC Libraries Special Collections)

Pen and ink drawing of her father and sister, by Constance Garland.
(Courtesy of Victoria Doyle-Jones)

&a &a &a

Christmases, because of Daddy's planning and enthusiasm, were always perfection. Everything had to follow tradition, which was purely our own. In Father's youth there had been no lighted trees, no carols, only an orange or a stick of candy or perhaps a pair of home-knitted mittens for a present. Constance and I were never allowed to see the tree before Christmas morning, but from the moment it was delivered and stored in the basement, the heavenly scent of pine began creeping through the house, filling our noses and imagination with delight. Smells are one of the best parts of Christmas.

Mother and Father were usually partying somewhere on Christmas Eve and came home to the task of building up a fairyland to greet our eyes in the morning—now so dangerously near at hand. They had hardly gone to bed when Connie and I awoke and piled in upon them, shouting "Merry Christmas! Get up! Get up!"

Daddy, bright-eyed as a boy, was up in an instant and down the stairs to set the stage properly. Mother moaned and dragged herself into a robe and slippers and combed our hair. We were allowed to go down in our nightgowns, and we waited, panting with excitement, at the head of the stairs, till Daddy's "Merry Christmas! Come down, everyone!" told us that the hour had come. Holding hands, awed and fearful that it might not be *quite* as wonderful as we had dreamed, we crept halfway down the stairs to the point where the full view of the drawing room opened before us, and there it was—more glorious than ever! Daddy was a fool about trees, and each year our tree was a little taller, thicker, more opulent. Of course, we had it all over the present day, for our tree was lighted by real candles that twinkled like stars among the dark foliage. It was all hideously dangerous, but Father had buckets of water behind the tree and, like a hawk, watched the angles of the candles in their pretty weighted sconces. Colored electric lights cannot begin to give the same romantic effect. I can't help feeling today that my nieces and nephew—and their children—have been cheated of something pretty important.

The first thing was to sit down and go through your stocking. They were usually Mother's long, black lisle ones, and they were crammed with wonders interspersed with candy and nuts and fruit and always, at the tip of the toe, some really lovely, valuable pin or chain or ring from Daddy. One Christmas we discovered with horror that Mother's and Daddy's stockings were filled with bits of coal tied in tissue paper to give the proper, lumpy effect, and Connie and I both wept so bitterly at our riches and their deprivation that our poor parents realized that they must never try that again. After the stockings, we had breakfast—and we had to eat it and wash and dress before we were permitted in with the tree again.

There were always too many presents piled under the tree, and Daddy would groan guiltily, "It's criminal! All that for two spoiled little girls!" The loveliest of all were the dolls Mother dressed for us—queens and brides and fairies—but our wealthy friends sent things like fur scarf-and-muff sets and doll houses and velvet dresses and party purses. One Christmas there was a small-size candy shop, complete with shelves on which stood countless jars of real miniature candies. There was a counter and tiny striped paper bags and scales and a scoop to weigh out the proper amount. We were incontestably the most popular household on the block.

Daddy always gave us books—beautiful, expensive editions of the world's best literature—but he also knew our love of dress-up and finery, and there would be rhinestone tiaras, aigrettes with pearls in the handles, feather fans, and oriental scarves embroidered in gold and silver thread. Mother's gift to us was always party-dresses, and by a miracle, they always fitted perfectly.

After we had opened all the presents, we put on our new frocks and went to Christmas dinner at the Tafts, where there was another tree that couldn't begin to equal ours, and we sat around fidgeting while they opened their presents. Aunt Ada, sweet-faced little darling, and her daughters served up a vast turkey for the assembled horde, eighteen or so, including some of Uncle Lorado's impecunious pupils. We were frantic to get back to our home and our Christmas, but I hope we were reasonably civil. Daddy and Connie and I usually went early, leaving Mother in the bosom of her family, and walked home along the snowy streets, looking at the lighted trees in the windows and singing carols softly to ourselves. When we reached home, Daddy would light the tree for one more time, we would eat corn flakes and milk and some of the candy, and, taking dolls, animals, and a selection of our gorgeous new books, we would wander off to bed, weary and replete.

&a &a &a

Despite the harshness of the winters, the Garlands had a gay social life. Daddy may have resented Chicago for its noise and crassness and dirt, but he did his best by her. A born promoter, he was into everything that had to do with the arts: founding the Cliff Dweller's Club, promoting theatrical companies, starting magazines, arranging lecture series, and encouraging talented young writers. With very little money themselves, Mother and Father were as at home in the palaces of the McCormicks, Potter Palmers, Lowdens, Cranes, Hutchinsons, and Morrises as they were in the rabbit-warren studio atop Orchestra Hall.[2] Big, black limousines or silent, gleaming "electrics" came to take us to the opera or the Thomas Concerts, Connie and I smug in our wine and blue velveteen gowns with wide, real lace collars and vast taffeta bows confining our long, regrettably straight hair. One glorious fall weekend we spent with the Charles Hutchinsons on their yacht on Lake Geneva, where they gave us a present of a yard-long box of chocolates. I have a picture of me holding it in an almost religious awe and another picture of my sister and me in the stern of the yacht, buttoned into blue serge reefers that boasted double rows of Grandfather's Civil War uniform buttons. I must say we look every inch to the manor born.

One of our close family friends was the manager of the Chicago Opera, and free boxes were always available. The first three operas I heard were *Carmen, Salome,* and *Thais.* "A fine collection to feed a child," Father said curtly. Though Mother and I reveled in it, Father had his reservations about opera. The artificiality of it bothered him, and the fat, little Italian tenors "gargling and yowling" affronted his masculinity. As a Western authority, he was asked to sit in on the rehearsals of *A Girl of the Golden West* and could scarcely contain himself in indignation and amusement. The lead actress, Blanche Bates, however, had his whole-souled admiration.

Of course, there was the theater, Father's long-time love. We were taken to everything suitable and some things that were not. Many of the actors, managers, dramatists, and producers were Daddy's friends, and free passes were showered on us. Daddy took us to see our first motion picture, *Neptune's Daughter*, with Annette Kellerman in long black tights and streaming hair. It was followed shortly after by *Spartacus* and the *Last Days of Pompeii*, which were almost too thrilling. Connie and I were both quite sick on the elevated platform going home; it was later discovered that we had chicken pox.

One day Daddy took me to see Chrystal Herne play in a vaudeville adaptation of his Rocky Mountain story "The Outlaw," and my fate was sealed from then on.[3] The footlights, the snow-capped mountains on the backdrop, the realism of the log cabin, the flowing golden hair of the Girl, the hard youth of the handsome Outlaw, the tense unfolding of the plot—I could hardly wait to get home and recreate it for myself. From that moment on, my sister and the neighborhood young people were never to know a moment's peace. It was plays, plays, plays from morning to night. I wrote them, adapted them, staged them, costumed them, directed them, and played all the parts no one else wanted. Connie, with her pretty face and long blond hair, was always the heroine, the princess, the bride, the fairy, the Little Match Girl, and whatever boy I could corral—and it took corralling—had to marry her. Admission was at first pins, then pennies, and eventually we made three dollars and twenty cents from one performance and had our names in the paper as the Greenwood Avenue Players.

In all this, Daddy aided and abetted me and loyally came to every performance. Mother patiently put her artistic genius to work in the creation of coronation robes, ball gowns, and fairy wings. In fact, designing and sewing were to be Mother's only creative outlets; she had abandoned painting and sculpture completely. Father was greatly in favor of women having careers of their own and urged, even pleaded with Mother to go back to work in her brother's studio, but Mother was caught up in a busy social life and the joys and trials of child-raising; she stubbornly refused.

I asked her once why she had given up art, and after a little pause she said slowly, "Because I'm not good enough. I'm a copyist, not a creator. In Paris I saw so much real genius that I became discouraged."

Here was one essential difference in my parents: when Mother was discouraged, she gave up. Father, swept at intervals by black Celtic depression—no one could go as low as Daddy, nor fly so high—had a native doggedness that brought him back into the fight and on to victory. Challenged, his determination grew twice as strong. Over and over he would shake his head sadly and say of Mother, "I *wish* Zulime had kept on with her career. She is enormously gifted. She could have made a real name for herself."

Mother would smile her enigmatic little smile and that was the end of that.

ঌ ঌ ঌ

The first days of spring in Chicago were lovely. All the children were out on roller skates, there were kites and little girls playing jacks on the front steps, and on May Day we made baskets of wallpaper and filled them with paper flowers to hang on people's doorknobs. As soon as it was warm enough, we would go as a family for picnics to Jackson Park and sit on the grass among the blossoms, and after the hard-boiled eggs and chicken sandwiches, we'd explore the fairy-tale Japanese houses that had been left from the World's Fair. The supreme treat, of course, was the White City Amusement Park. There was the Merry-Go-Round, of course, and the Shoot-the-Chutes and rides in little individual autos that swept you off into the darkness all by your happily-terrified self and brought you back safely to the lights and your patient, smiling parents again. There was also a plaything I have never seen before or since. It was a long flight of carpet-covered rollers, about ten feet wide, set one above the other with a slight variance, so that when you got on at the top and began to slide, the roller revolved, deposited you gently on the one just below, and so on till you reached the bottom and slid down to the gate. The slide was about twenty feet high, and it was so splendid I never wanted to get off.

ঌ ঌ ঌ

I think I was about nine or ten when our peaceful domestic existence was rocked by a family shakeup and scandal. It was my first conscious observation of the power of sex, and its impact on me was considerable.

Mother's younger sister, Turbulance, was known as Aunt Turbie and was much adored. She was dashing and brilliant and I first remember her married to a gentle, Van Dyke-bearded landscape painter, Charles Francis Browne. The Brownes and my handsome boy cousin, Charlie, were part of the summer colony of artists at Eagle's Nest Camp, a rustic settlement high on the bank of the river at Oregon, Illinois. Uncle Lorado's twenty-foot statue, *Blackhawk*, for which Father had posed in an Indian blanket, dominated the countryside, and it was at "Camp" that Hamlin Garland courted Zulime Taft. We were frequent visitors, but Connie and I were daunted by the primitive living conditions and preferred to be house guests in the luxurious Wallace Heckman home, a mile or so away.[4]

At any rate, we were deeply fond of both Aunt Turbie and Uncle Charles, and then, suddenly, by some mysterious alchemy, we were being presented to Aunt Turbie's husband, "Uncle Angus." Heaven knows what torrents of passionate drama lay between.

Turbulance was a gay girl with a roving eye. Her new husband's name for her was "Vivid," and beginning with a runaway marriage at seventeen, she was destined to make any man miserable. Despite her doting artist husband and the son she adored and spoiled, she was fretting with boredom and self-pity when she happened in the way of a spectacular, virile, Scotch-Irish lawyer, and the fat was in the fire. He had a wife and children and it meant breaking Uncle Charles's heart as well, but there was no stopping them. Mother did her best, and Daddy, loyal to Charles and furiously disapproving, raged. There were frantic conferences and rushings back and forth, most of which passed over the heads of Connie and me, and in the end, despite Father's bitter condemnation, the two were divorced and legally re-wed.

Mother told me later of frantically trying to run up a lace wedding blouse for Turbie and asking her sister to make the sleeves. My aunt went at it in her usual slapdash way, only to discover she had made both sleeves for the same arm. There was nothing to do but pick one apart again, and lace is fiendish to work with. When she had finished it the second time and discovered she had repeated the same mistake, she picked the thing up and in a cold rage tore it to shreds. That was Turbulance.

Uncle Charles, broken, retreated to a shabby little bachelor studio beside the Illinois Central tracks and, except for Daddy, who never gave up his fierce loyalty, disappeared out of our lives. The newlyweds rented a smart high-priced apartment in one of the tall new buildings and proceeded to enjoy life.

We were invited to a one o'clock Sunday dinner at their new flat, and though Father went reluctantly, at Mother's insistence he did. Connie and I were thrilled. We had always adored our aunt and we had fallen immediate victims of our dashing new uncle's sex appeal.

Because of Father, who was fanatically prompt—he was always at the door, hat in hand, ten minutes before it was time to start for anywhere—on our first visit we were early and the honeymooners were still in bed. I remember the scufflings and whispers behind the closed bedroom door and a glimpse of the tumbled bed as the lovers emerged, flushed and breathless, stammering apologies. I had a stirring sensation of being in on something exciting, even wicked. There was bold amusement in my new uncle's eyes as he contemplated Father's stoney face and the scotch he poured with a lavish hand did not improve the situation. Father removed us as soon as it could be decently managed.

Now, after all these years, I wonder—where did it come from, my father's outspoken antipathy to sex and all it represented? As he grew older, he became more and more violent on the subject, and when he launched on one of his tirades, his family would cringe with embarrassment. Did it all start back there in his Boston youth, when he was young and restless and intimately involved with a casual, attractive group of stage people? My guess is that there was some kind of early and embittering love affair that turned him against the whole idea until, at almost forty, he met Zulime Taft. In his diaries he admits to admiring several beautiful actresses but, he would have us believe, only from a platonic distance; yet his novel *The Light of the Star* is an account of a torrid love affair between a famous actress and an intense and serious young writer. The diaries that he left do not begin until 1898. Were there, perhaps, earlier, injudicious ones that he felt it was wiser to destroy? The people who knew him in the Boston days are all gone. How I would like to sit down now and ask questions of James A. Herne's wife, Katherine.

One thing I did discover: at the time Hamlin Garland was frankly pursuing Zulime Taft, he was being himself pursued by a determined young woman who told me later, with some truth, "You know, I might have been your mother." Or at least, the mother of a Hamlin Garland daughter.

Aunt Juliet, as we called her, was a brilliant and successful fiction writer and editor in New York in the late Nineties, and when Hamlin Garland was in that city, he was constantly thrown with her.[5] On his returns to Chicago a flood of letters followed him, full of rapturous admiration and girlish yearning. From the diaries, there was a time there when it sounded very much like touch-and-go, but it may have been Zulime's very indifference that finally won him. Later on, Juliet became my mother's closest friend and an important figure in our family social life.

I see it as a combination of circumstances that warped Father's sense of values. I would guess that there had been an early stage romance in Boston that possibly ended in tragedy. There was the birth and death of his first born son and the hideous ordeal of my birth, when he nearly lost both of us. Then Mother's love for another man and eventually the passionate need that led to the creation of a third child, though Father had vowed, "My wife must never go through that thing again."

Romantic, poetic love Father understood and approved, but the physical relations between male and female became anathema to him. As my sister and I left childhood, Father became increasingly bitter and savage, afraid, subconsciously, of the dangers we were about to face. It is ironic that with all his protective concern, the very thing he had hated and dreaded most was to overtake us.

Notes

[1] From the poem "A Paradox of Time," by Henry Arthur Dobson.

[2] Edith R. McCormick (1872-1932), the daughter of John D. Rockefeller, was a Chicago philanthropist who was married to Harold

Fowler McCormick (1872-1941), the son of Cyrus McCormick, founder of International Harvester. Potter Palmer (1826-1902) was a prominent Chicago real estate developer and businessman; his wife Bertha (1949-1918) was a socialite and art collector. Frank Orren Lowden (1861-1943) was a prominent lawyer and governor of Illinois (1917-1921); his wife, Florence, was the daughter of George Pullman. Charles R. Crane (1858-1939) was the president of Crane Co., one of the world's largest manufacturers of plumbing fixtures, and later a diplomat to Russia, Turkey, and China. Charles L. Hutchinson (1854-1924), Chicago banker and philanthropist, was one of the founders of the Art Institute of Chicago.

[3] Chrystal Herne (1883-1950), the daughter of Garland's friends of his Boston days, James A. and Katherine Herne. Isabel refers to "The Outlaw of Blizzard Basin," a one-act dramatic adaptation of the story "The Outlaw and the Girl" (*Ladies' Home Journal* 25 [May-July 1908]), reprinted as "The Outlaw" in *They of the High Trails* (1916).

[4] Charles Francis Browne (1859-1920), an artist and lecturer at the Art Institute of Chicago, married Turbulance in 1909; after their divorce, she married Angus Roy Shannon, a Chicago attorney. Eagle's Nest Camp was an art colony founded by Lorado Taft on the banks of Rock River, near Oregon, Illinois, about 100 miles west of Chicago. Wallace Heckman (1851-1957) was an art patron and the counsel and business manager of the University of Illinois.

[5] Juliet Wilbor Tompkins (1871-1956) was a novelist and the editor of *Munsey's Magazine* from 1897-1901. She later married Emory Pottle, editor of *Criterion*.

3. West Salem

৵ ৵ ৵

I am about five, on a train alone with Daddy in a Pullman berth, pressing my face to the window to watch the lighted villages and the crossing bells fly by in the darkness. Donald, my Scotch-kilted boy doll, and Violet, the bewitching baby, are safely asleep in the clothes hammock, but I am too excited to give up. We are on an overnight journey and at six in the morning the train will slow down for an instant and Father and I will descend into West Salem, Wisconsin. This is my kingdom, and my grandfather's, for while we only come to the sleepy little country town for the summer months, Grandfather lives here the year around. This time I am old enough to go on ahead with my Father, "to get the house ready for Mother and Constance," and my importance and exaltation are beyond words. "I kick for joy!" I announce breathlessly, and I wonder now how Father and I managed to sleep at all that night.

Despite the early hour, Grandfather was on the station platform to meet us and the dolls and I flew into his arms. He was a handsome, neat, snowy-bearded old gentleman and I was proud of him and loved him. He laid his gnarled brown hand on his son's shoulder and a smiling glance of respect and admiration passed between the two. Father's mother, Isabelle, for whom I was named, was dead, and after a period of loneliness, Grandfather had married again, not very successfully, and had now returned to end his honorable, hardworking days with us at Mapleshade.[1]

Grandfather had the buggy and the old horse and I led the way, dancing with impatience.

"May I drive, Grandfather? May I drive?"

"I don't see why not," he said promptly. "A young lady who's old enough to spend the night on a Pullman train is surely old enough to hold the reins on an old mare."

Grandfather was in his seventies, but he swung me up into the buggy with the ease of a man used to long, athletic hours in the barn and hayfield.

"Get in, Hamlin. I'll fetch the rest of the stuff."

I installed Donald and Violet in the middle of the seat, and Daddy set me between his knees and wound the reins around my hands.

"Giddap!" I slapped the reins authoritatively.

Bess looked back over her shoulder with patient curiosity. Gravel scrunched under the wheels, and we made a slow turn and set off down Main Street. My heart soared. This was home!

Most of us have one particular place deep in our inner selves. Across the years the thought of West Salem still brings a tightness to my throat. Like Byron's lady, it "walks in beauty," and yet, to be honest, it was only a graceless, little settlement of some nine hundred inhabitants, set out under huge arching maple and butternut trees in the rich, rolling Wisconsin coulee land.

As we jogged up Main Street in the clear, early morning sunlight, I pressed back against my father.

"Daddy, I'm so happy!"

His hands came down on my shoulders. "Good, daughtie— good. So am I."

Grandfather gave a satisfied sigh. "It's nice to have you folks home again. I missed you a lot this winter."

Our house, Mapleshade, was on the edge of town, on a wide, dusty street where the trees made a long, cool tunnel leading into the golden farmland beyond. Bess picked her deliberate way and there was time for me to see and excitedly identify everything.

"There's the Post Office. . . . There's the Congregational Church. . . . There's the Otterson's. . . ." Reverend Otterson was the Lutheran minister and his exquisite daughters became our closest friends.

We rounded a corner into our street and through the trees, over the tops of the lilacs, the syringas, the blooming fruit trees, I had my first glimpse of the roofline.

"Daddy, there it is! I see it!" Then, suddenly troubled by a stab of fear, I looked around into his face. "It will be just the same, won't it?" I asked. "There won't be anything—different?"

Grandfather, who was an old tease, hooted. "Well, now, I wouldn't say that. I just might have done one or two things you won't object to—like a new swing from the twin maples—and fixing the shutters on the playhouse the way they'll be able to—"

"Oh! . . . Oh!—"

Mapleshade, the Garland home in West Salem, Wisconsin, 1893.
*(Courtesy of the University of Southern California,
on behalf of USC Libraries Special Collections)*

There it was serene under its magnificent trees, exactly as I remembered it: a generous, sloping-roofed, many-windowed frame house, painted dark green, surrounded by wide screen porches, on one of which I would sleep that night. To the north stretched the smooth green of the tennis court, to the south were the vineyards, the apple and cherry trees, the vegetable garden, and straight down at the end of the driveway the big red barn stood silhouetted against the fresh green of waving corn.

Bess turned in at the gate of her own volition and made for the cool dusk of the barn. Father, gay as a boy, leaped down and held up his arms.

"Welcome, princess. Everything you see is yours to command."

How can I begin to tell the wonders of that blessed place? Outside, thanks to my grandfather's skill and care, garden and grounds were perfect. From a three thousand acre wheat farm in Dakota, Daddy had brought his father back to a half acre in his native Wisconsin, but that half acre was the pride of the village. Our corn was the first and best, our peonies the largest and spiciest, our strawberries the most luscious. Our grapes—Concords, Delawares, Muscats, Seedless—took first prizes at the County Fair. All summer long we feasted on every conceivable fruit and vegetable from currents to asparagus—which the villagers had never made the slightest attempt to eat, considering it a shade plant merely. When Connie was old enough to join me in play, we would pick large grape leaves and arrange on them a miniature banquet: infinitesimal carrots, fresh peas, baby onions, grapes, berries, ground cherries—those mysterious and delicious little Oriental husked tomatoes—anything, everything, and then we would retire with our dolls to the shade of the asparagus fern or the corn rows for a high tea beyond compare.

It was, incontestably, an Eden, yet there was menace in the countryside, too. Once, when Connie was still a crawling baby, I came out on the back porch one afternoon to see her sitting up and happily confronting a large coiled rattlesnake only a few feet away. I had been instructed by Daddy about rattlesnakes in some of our rambles over the bluffs—"Just watch where you put your feet. They'll slip away. They don't want to hurt you unless you try to hurt them first"—but I knew this was imminent tragedy. I ran screaming out to the tennis court where Mother and Daddy were playing tennis, and a few seconds later, Father had killed the snake with a hoe. Twice, I remind her, I have saved my sister's life. This was one time; the other was when she lost her footing at the head of the stairs in Chicago and came rolling down toward the landing where stood our large grandfather clock. I was playing with my dolls on the landing and had sufficient presence of mind to catch the baby just as she was about to crash into the glass front of the clock.

There were times, thereafter, when I wondered whether I had made the right decision.

There was so much to do in West Salem that the days were never long enough. There was a hay mow—and drying nuts—in the upper storey of the barn, with a deliciously dangerous chute that slid you into a manger below. There were smooth warm eggs to gather and baby chickens to hold, kittens skittering everywhere, and a charming playhouse made of louvered shutters where our family of dolls held court. There was a thrilling swing that went high, high, surely higher than any swing had ever gone before, up into the branches of the trees, smack into the face of the blue summer sky. There were hammocks for lazy hours, croquet and tennis courts for active ones. On the Johnson farm next door were two tall pine trees to climb and what if you did get covered with resin? About halfway up, you could look down on the whole village and the surrounding farmlands almost as far as Bangor. There were wild, heart-pounding games of "Run, my good sheep, run" and "Anti-I-over," with the young Dudleys and Ottersons in the long summer dusk, when everything became twice as intoxicating and Father's bedtime call had to be repeated.

Over and beyond all these enchantments was the tree house. With it we became the sensation of the village. Daddy built it for us high in the branches of the biggest maple in the back yard. It was reached by a rope ladder, and I remember being taught to climb and Daddy's admonition, "The thing to remember is—never to let go with both hands at the same time. See you've got a good grip on the next rung up or down before you start moving off the one you're on."

I don't know how far from the ground the tree house was, but once you were up there you were all but invisible from the ground below. When I became bored with my tagging little sister, which was fairly frequently, I would stuff a store of food and books in a knapsack, sneak away up the ladder and, safe in my treetop bower, pull the rope ladder up after me. No top of the Empire State Building or Eiffel Tower ever gave me the thrill that tree house did. Far from the world and its troubles, lying full length on the bench, with the flicker of sunlight through the stirring leaves and my book open, I could have stayed there hour after hour except that Constance would shortly have trailed me and be screaming and dancing with rage on the ground below.

"Let me up! I want to come up there with you!"

I would ignore her and pretend I wasn't there, but the vanished ladder was a giveaway, and before long one parent or the other would be down with my sister, saying in a voice I had learned to respect, "Mary Isabel, let that ladder down immediately and invite Constance up with you."

If the grounds of Mapleshade were fairyland, the inside of the house was equally satisfying. You entered through a wide, screened front porch that overlooked the tennis court and the Sanders' dairy farm on the other side of the unpaved, tree-arched street. Again, as in Chicago, there were two living rooms, the first one containing the huge, native stone fireplace and chimney that Father wrote the story of building in "Mary Isabel's Chimney."[2] The room beyond was called the music room, for it held the piano around which so many of our evenings were centered. Beyond the music room was a large, red-rose wallpapered guest room and bath, a south side screened porch draped in vines, and my grandfather's sunny room and bath. Off the main living room was a bay-windowed dining room overlooking the tennis court and the flower gardens, and beyond that a big, cheerful kitchen with window on three sides.

Daddy, who had spent a good deal of time in the Southwest, had a fine collection of Navajo rugs that brought warmth and color to the living room. As a young man, he had often earned his living by carpentry, and the built-in settles and bookcases were his work. Above them were set cherished oil paintings of the various landscapes that Father loved best, painted by some of the leading American artists.

A steep, enclosed flight of stairs led to an upper hall and the master bedroom, which was Mother's. On one side of the bedroom, under the sloping roof, was a long, mysterious attic full of old costume trunks and discarded furniture. On the opposite side, a double door opened onto the screened-in sleeping porch that belonged to Connie and me.

It was a heavenly place to sleep and we were out there in all weather. Mother had a morbid fear of thunder storms and Daddy was determined his children should not share it. In the fiercest of Wisconsin electrical storms he would lie out on the porch with us, a

Mary Isabel (left) and Constance, in the early 1910s.
*(Courtesy of the University of Southern California,
on behalf of USC Libraries Special Collections)*

small, trusting head on each arm, and while the heavens were riven with fire and the thunder rolled, he would talk to us calmly about the beauty and drama of it all, so that instead of feeling afraid, we came to look upon it as some sort of spectacular production arranged for our benefit.

On clear nights, when the stars were near and bright, Daddy would lie with us and pick them out for us by name and answer as best he could our eager questions. Sometimes he would talk of mythology or English history or pioneer America. At other times he would recite poetry and give us lessons in the marvelous expressiveness of words. In the late fall, before we went back to Chicago, snow would often mask the roofs of the barn and wood-shed and sift through the screening onto the porch, where Connie and I lay snug under down quilts and a mound of blankets.

We always slept together, my sister and I, huddling up to each other, talking, giggling, reliving the day's adventures. We had a song we used to sing just before going to sleep each night:

> Golden sunsets fade away, paling with the dying day,
> Father, hear our evening prayer. All Thy children crave Thy care.

If one of us was angry with the other, she might refuse to sing and we would go off to sleep in hurt silence, lying stiffly, as far as possible from each other in the big bed, but somehow during the night we came back together again and morning found us in each other's arms as usual. Neither of us could manage to carry a grudge.

Father's study, along with several guest rooms, the bath, and maid's room, was also upstairs, and it was by far the most inter-esting room in the house. It was a big, square room with a fireplace, completely walled with books, Navajo blankets, Hopi jars, and woven baskets. On the tops of the bookshelves, Lorado Taft sculp-tures, landscape sketches in water color and oil, and framed photo-graphs of literary and political friends vied with geologic speci-mens, snapshots of the mountain West, and daguerreotypes of long-gone Garlands and McClintocks. A huge, hand-hewn desk stood between two sunny windows, the big basket beneath it filled to overflowing with discarded manuscript and answered correspon-dence. On the desk was a confusion of objects: an iron model of a buffalo, a silver-topped glass inkwell, toppling piles of letters and manuscripts, and a lumbering old typewriter on which Father pecked doggedly. Saddles and bridles and stirrups and a battered old Stetson that had gone with him to the Klondike hung on pegs, and tennis rackets, fishing rods, and guns disputed the corners. It was an outdoor man's room, as well as a literary man's, and I loved to be in it.

I can recreate every inch of that beloved old house now, but my sister has maddened me for years by refusing to remember the things I remember. To her, she says, it only comes in bits and pieces.

"But *surely* you remember the cellar where the potatoes and cabbages and apples and jams and jellies and pickles were stored!"

"No, I don't."

"You must remember the night it snowed and Daddy was away and you and Mother and I had dinner in front of the fire and it was the most wonderful dinner in the world! Fresh bread hot out of the oven and Minnie Johnson's milk and sweet butter and a huge hunk of heavenly Wisconsin cheddar cheese!"

"I . . . think I remember," she says, twisting her face in earnest but unconvincing effort.

I know one thing my sister doesn't remember because she wasn't there, and I, myself, am not sure I did not dream it, yet it stands out sharp and ugly in my mind. As a tiny girl I was forced to become part of a shivaree, and the memory of the occasion makes me shudder today.[3]

Daddy and Mother had gone to dinner in La Crosse—our "big town" ten miles or so away—and I had been left in the care of a local woman who didn't "want to miss the fun," so late at night I was awakened and dressed and hustled out and down the dark streets toward a goal some blocks away. I could hear a terrible noise in the distance—the jangle of cowbells, the clash of tin pans together, the sound of rattles, shrill whistles, loud, hoarse shouts—and as we turned a corner—I, frightened, dragging back—a house came into view, theatrically highlighted by torches held in a dozen hands and surrounded by a large gathering of the town rowdies. There were women there, too, giggling, shrieking, shoving, and in the background some of the so-called respectable citizens hung about, grinning sheepishly and making no effort to interfere.

I hadn't the slightest idea what was happening, but I knew

instinctively that it was wrong—dirty. The sniggers, the drunken, derisive shouts, the catcalls were all directed at the poor little house that with closely drawn window shades stood there in silence. Except for smoke rising slowly from the chimney there was no sign of life.

"Come on out!" the crowd was yelling. "What you *doing* in there? Don't you know we're thirsty?"

"Come . . . on . . . out!" a chant began. "Come . . . on . . . out— or we'll *bring* you out!"

I shrank against the woman's side, whimpering, "I want to go home—"

She shook me fiercely. "Keep quiet. I gotta see what happens."

It wasn't till later I found out that inside that besieged bungalow were a pair of newlyweds hiding from the sadistic world that surrounded them. The crowd wanted free drinks and horseplay and they were going to get it. The mood grew more and more ugly. There were muttered conferences and at last appeared a man with a long ladder and some others with planks. With shouts and cheers from the onlookers, a red-faced young tough swarmed up the ladder that was laid against the house and crawled to a spot beside the chimney. His friends passed up the planks and he fitted them closely together over the top of the chimney. The column of smoke ceased.

"That does it!" A cheer went up and the chant began again, "Come . . . on . . . out! Come on out—or we'll *smoke* you out!"

I don't know how long it was we waited—I sick with a hideous distaste I can feel to this day. Suddenly, the back door of the house was flung open, and a pale-faced, half-dressed youth, accompanied by a billow of smoke, staggered out onto the porch.

"Damn you!" he yelled, coughing and sobbing and clinging to the porch railing. "What the hell you trying to do—kill us?"

Someone yelled, "Take it easy, fella—we're friends, don't you know?" and someone else called, "Where's the bride? We want to see the bride. Bring out the bride!"

The crowd took it up with loud guffaws. "Bring out the bride!"

The young husband, his face distorted, turned on them. "You leave her alone. She—don't feel so well—"

A chorus of jeers, interspersed with comments, answered him. He was like an animal at bay.

"Go—home!" he stammered. "You got no right to do this! Why don't you—" Another strangling burst of coughing doubled him up.

Two young bullies moved up to the porch steps. "What say we go in after her?"

The groom flung himself against the door and his voice shrilled. "You come up those steps—" his eyes were maniacal, "I'll kill you! I mean it—one more step and I'll—"

Terrified, I covered my face with my hands and sobbed hysterically. The woman gave me a sharp slap. "Shut up—"

There was complete silence for an instant, and then someone in the back of the crowd called out placatingly, "Keep your shirt on, boy. Can't you see we're just—thirsty? Shell out for the drinks and we'll go away peaceable."

Some of the frenzy went out of the boy's face. He fumbled in his trouser pockets and pulled out a handful of crumpled bills. "Here! It's all I got. Take those damn boards off my chimney and go drink till you bust."

He flung the money on the ground and, as the front spectators dove for it, stumbled back into the house again, slamming and bolting the door after him.

"Well, boys—" one of the men grinned, waving a couple of bills triumphantly, "Guess the fun's over—around here. Let's go open up a barrel!"

In groups of three or four, the crowd began to move off in the direction of Main Street and the saloons. Crying miserably, I was dragged home by Della in the dark.

If this reads like blatant melodrama, that is exactly what it was. Everything I have described seared itself on my unhappy little brain. Seeing photographs of today's mob leaders, I recognize the same kind of half humans that sickened me that night. One curious thing: I never said anything about this to either my mother or my father. The woman must have forbidden me to tell my parents and probably threatened me viciously. Being so very young, the memory of it faded into a sort of nightmare dream, yet today, when I try to recreate it, it is as vivid as the night it happened. . . .

Connie does remember the picnics.

It was a lovely countryside we inhabited, almost as lush and sweet as England's. Our house being at the edge of the village, we were surrounded by prosperous, beautifully kept farms. One of our favorites of these was "The Dudley Place" some miles away.

The George Dudleys, our neighbors across the corn field, were rare and good friends, and every week or so the two families would hire a rig and a team of horses and jog out to the Dudley family farm which, at that time, was under the management of George's younger brother, Sherman, a stunningly handsome university graduate who had lost an arm in the mowing machine but was carrying on gamely with the help of his bright, charming, city-bred wife. The farm stood on the banks of a clear, slow-moving stream, and after the excitement of inspecting the barns, the silos, the corncribs, the haystacks, the new calves and kittens, and the baby ducks, we all adjourned to the riverside where the mothers and fathers settled themselves in the shade of the weeping willows and the children paddled blissfully in the safe, sparkling water.

Toward sunset, Daddy would build an expert fire and broil steaks or chops, the mothers buttered fresh bread and sliced tomatoes, and Sherman came down from the farm with huge pitchers of milk. After the meat, we roasted corn over the embers—nothing is so good as a black-roasted ear of fresh corn—and the feast wound up with fruit pies bursting with juice, a four-layer lemon cream cake, and Father's famous camp coffee.

After dinner, in the dusk, we sang to the background of running water, while the littlest ones fell asleep with their heads in their mothers' laps and the stars thickened and brightened. Uncle George had a true tenor voice and his beloved Molly a sweet soprano which combined with Daddy's resonant baritone to make a musical trio. Our own mother, despite her musicianship, could not carry a tune or stay in pitch and was unanimously chosen to stay out. Connie and I and Wilbur chimed in and most of us were still singing softly as we rattled home in the dark. I remember lying in Daddy's arms and sleepily watching the fringe on the rig top as it moved rhythmically with the turning of the wheels.

Sometimes on our picnics we went further afield—to the banks of the great Mississippi itself or into the back country where the small hillside farms were. Once Daddy took us to Green's Coulee and showed us where the Richard Garland house once

Hamlin Garland in 1909.
*(Courtesy of the University of Southern California,
on behalf of USC Libraries Special Collections)*

stood. His old schoolhouse was still there, windowless and door-less, overgrown with vines. It was a poignant day and though Father talked cheerily, what thoughts must have swept through his mind as he stood looking out over that gentle, familiar countryside. It was a long, uphill road he had come—that little Wisconsin farm boy of the sixties. I have never gone back to Father's birthplace.[4] I have no wish to.

That was the day that on our way home we swung around past Clint's place. He was my father's last uncle, Isabelle's son, who had been a mighty athlete in his youth. Now he was a crippled old man with misted blue eyes, sitting under a ragged blanket in the sun. Around him on the ground and as far as the eye could see lay a glowing, heartbreaking carpet of fallen apples, red, white, gold, and green.

"Take all you like, Hamlin," Uncle Clint said bitterly. "Can't sell 'em, can't pick 'em up, can't give 'em away. There's just too dan-ged many apples in this world."

If the countryside was rewarding to my father's soul, the social life of the village was not. With the exception of the Dudleys, the Congregational minister, Samuel McKee and his family, and one or two ancient relatives, Father was totally without intellectual com-panionship.

Constance and I had our play world and bright neighbor children to share it, and Mother, who was quite happy with anyone, was in great demand for church socials and whist parties, but Father soon grew frantic with boredom. The old retired German and Scandinavian farmers and the gossipy village shopkeepers and loafers did not interest him. Now and then he would persuade Ernest Thompson Seton or Irving Bacheller or Henry B. Fuller to come up for a week,[5] though Uncle Henry B. detested the country and could hardly wait to get back to the soot and smells of Chicago again. Now and then Aunt Turbie and Uncle Angus drove up in their dashing new car, and one memorable time, through the gen-erosity of one of Uncle Angus's clients, the back seat of their car was piled almost to the roof with great flats of caramels of every con-ceivable variety: vanilla, chocolate, chocolate nut, chocolate marsh-mallow, caramel, caramel pistachio, caramel marshmallow, and so on. Inevitably, we were a social magnet for the next week or so.

In La Crosse were a few charming, cultivated people, chief

among them the Eastons, but until the coming of motor cars it was an awkward trip on the train and one not taken easily. While Mother went serenely from one village function to another—"She's not stuck-up like Hamlin," an old aunt commented acidly—Daddy took it out in writing, carpentry, tennis, and his children.

He was a splendid father, indulgent but firm. Mother had an artless way of saying, "Daughties, would one of you like to get Mother her sewing basket?" There would follow a pregnant silence in which neither Connie nor I made the slightest move.

Suddenly Daddy would bring his hands together. "Of course they wouldn't *like* to do it but they will. Daughties!" with another handclap, "*JUMP!*" We jumped.

Mapleshade. . . . West Salem. . . . I left it forever when I was twelve, but I still dream of it and wake up knowing I have had a good dream. When he sold it, Daddy and I wept together; so much was bound up in it, my "Fairy World of Childhood."

It was in the upper loft of the barn that I saw a fairy. I had been lying in the hay, warm and drowsy—I must have been four or five—and suddenly in through the wide, sun-filled cracks between the old boards she came: silver-white, an inch or two in height, with glistening butterfly wings, a frock of some floating stuff, and a smiling face of incredible beauty. I stared at her for a long, heart-stopping moment while she hung in the air, upright, a foot or two away, and looked back at me calmly, then fluttered her wings and flew out through the crack again.

I rushed, breathless, to Daddy who listened gravely, then nodded. "Yes, it must have been a fairy."

Doubters might say that in my half-sleep, half-waking state I had mistaken a butterfly, but my father was not one of those. He and I were one in conviction.

Notes

1 Richard Garland married Mary M. Bolles (1841-1922) in November 1901, one year after Isabelle Garland's death.

2 "Mary Isabel's Chimney" is chapter 20 of *A Daughter of the Middle Border*.

[3] A "shivaree" is a mock serenade of newlyweds, a custom along the upper Mississippi valley, in which revelers tease the couple by banging pots, pans, and other noisemakers.

[4] Isabel repeats a common misconception. Garland was born in a squatters' shack on the outskirts of West Salem and later moved to Green's Coulee, where Richard built the family's first house.

[5] Irving Bacheller (1859-1950) founded the Bacheller Newspaper Syndicate in 1884 and later published the best-selling novel *Eben Holden* (1900).

4. Fire

ৰ৶ ৰ৶ ৰ৶

Everything in West Salem was touched with magic. Our birthdays, for instance, mine in July, Connie's in June, were glorious beyond compare, with everything—guests, menus, costumes, games—to our order. This was long before the day of the coke, the hamburger, the hot dog, and from early morning the kitchen would be a whirl of thrilling activity. The birthday queen wore a wreath of roses at breakfast and later was allowed to lick the frosting bowls and crack the nuts for the sea foam candy. We ate from trestle and board tables set out under the maples and covered with pink crepe paper, and it was sliced ham and chicken salad and baked beans and hot biscuits, winding up with pure-cream ice cream and a towering birthday cake with an inch-thick frosting. There were snappers and everyone wore paper hats and drank pink lemonade and there were prizes for everyone.

There was one unfortunate occasion when Mother rebelled at the tide of hand-painted tea cups and saucers, pin cushions, and souvenir spoons that rolled in upon us and made us print "No presents" at the bottom of the flower-decorated invitation paper.

The party was an utter failure. Coming empty-handed, no child seemed to know what to do or say. Whereas heretofore the merry crackle of tissue paper and the admiring oh's and ah's had bridged over the trying first few moments, now there was nothing. I was disappointed, the guests were bewildered and uneasy, and Mother surrendered.

We invited both boys and girls to our parties, and it was not long before I became pleasantly conscious of the male sex. I can remember annoying one of the German boys next door when I was quite small. He was stretched out in a hammock reading. I buzzed around him like a gadfly, plucking at his hair, his shirt, his book, until suddenly he lost patience, threw down his book, reached out his arms and snatched me up. He released me at once but not before I had found out something: I discovered that I liked to be caught and held. From then on the poor boy had no peace and finally had to take refuge in the house with his mother.

At nine, ten, eleven it was thrilling to play "Pom-Pom-Pull-Away" on the tennis court in the half dark, to be the fastest runner of the girls and the one survivor and have all the boys thudding after me across the grass. Whoever caught you could kiss you and I found I liked that, too, though I thought Post Office was silly and embarrassing. There was a game I liked called Wink, where a boy stood behind each girl's chair and one boy with an empty chair tried by winks to get a girl into it. As she started up, the boy behind her could hold her down, but if she was off the chair, she was free to go to the winker. It was fast and furious, with more than a dash of sex in it, and we played it by the hour.

Somewhere at this point I acquired a beau, a bright, attractive lad who had a bicycle and rode me now and then on the handle bars. We usually stayed in West Salem until after Thanksgiving—at least, Mother and Connie and I did—while Father went back and forth to Chicago and New York on lecture and business trips. This meant we had two months in the local school, which was on the other side of town, past the pea factory and the creamery and across the railroad tracks. I loved the West Salem school as much as I hated the grim old pile I was forced to attend in Chicago. The walk to school on crisp October mornings, scuffling the scarlet and gold leaves, with Donald carrying my books and stealing admiring, sidelong glances, was pure delight. At recess, racing and shrieking across the play yard, I always hoped it was Donald who would catch me, and it usually was.

Gradually, however, I became aware of another admirer. Adolph was several years older than I, a long, pasty-faced Swede, with lank tow hair and pale, vacant eyes. There was something creepy about him, and his unshifting stare made me uneasy and a little frightened, not that he did anything but stare. He was slightly retarded and shy as well and hardly ever opened his mouth, but as Donald and I walked home together, I knew that Adolph was always just a little way behind.

In a village like West Salem there was no mail delivery, and one of my chores was to go every day to the post office for the mail. Behind the post office was a vacant store that Grandfather and his cronies had made their Rummy Club, and I would see them there, hard at it, as I passed the door. My grandfather was by far the handsomest of the old gentlemen, and when I blew him a kiss, I would get a loving "There's my girl!" in return. Richard Garland had been a Union soldier in the Civil War, and on Decoration Day he wore his uniform and marched in the parade to the cemetery where he and my father now lie.[1] I walked beside him proudly, carrying a small flag and wearing a white ruffled frock and big, white taffeta hair bows.

On this particular afternoon when I opened our box I found, along with Daddy's usual big batch of correspondence, a pink, slightly grubby envelope addressed to "Mary I. Garland" in large, uneven capitals. I was wildly curious but waited till I reached the privacy of the Otterson hedge before I opened it.

It was a proposition. "I want to kiss you. Meet me behind your barn tonight at 7:30," and it was signed, "Don."

I wonder now just why I was so outraged. No medieval virgin ever rose in more affronted wrath. How *dare* he! I felt as though I had been besmirched. In a white heat of passion, I marched home and straight to my desk. In a pigeonhole I had several colored post cards of villages and scenes, and I selected one at random and addressed it firmly to "Donald—Box 306." In the message space I wrote fiercely, "I hate you and never want to see you again."

Omitting to sign my name, I marched right back to the post office and mailed the card. Naturally, I did not leave the house that night, though I would have given a good deal to know how long that lecherous creature hung around in the shadows behind the barn before he realized that I was not coming. Any male who thought he could summon me to his side in that peremptory way had another think coming.

Donald was not visible when I left for school the next morning, and when the school bell rang and his desk was unoccupied, I began to have very odd feelings. Perhaps I had been a bit too cruel.

Certainly I did want to see Donald again, but I also wanted him to know his place. When he reached the point of apologizing, I would inform him. . . .

At which point, the classroom door opened, and Donald, red-faced, eyes averted, came in accompanied by his mother. There was a low-toned exchange with the teacher, then something—a colored post card—was deposited upon the desk. Miss Smith picked it up and examined it carefully, then she rose, holding up the card so that it was in direct view of us all.

"Did any of you send this post card?"

In the silence you could feel curiosity mounting in waves, though nobody moved. The teacher repeated her question in a sharpened tone.

"I asked—did any of you write this post card?"

There were scufflings and neck cranings and here and there a head shaken in denial. I sat turned to stone. Sheer horror possessed me, and I felt the color creeping up my neck and into my face. Donald stood with his back to us, staring down at the floor.

His mother was furiously angry. "I want to know who wrote this insulting post card to my son!" she shouted. "Speak up—one of you! . . . Miss Smith, ask each one in turn. I'm going to get to the bottom of this. No one is going to write something like this to my son and get away with it."

The questioning began. Along with the rest, by a superhuman effort, I managed to shake my head, but Miss Smith eyed me sharply.

"Mary Isabel—stand up."

Every eye in the room, except Donald's, was on me. I got to my feet, thinking I would collapse at any moment. Miss Smith came down the aisle and held the card under my nose.

"Have you ever seen that writing before?"

Mutely, I shook my head. The faces in front of me rippled like eddies in a pond.

Donald's mother drew a hissing breath. Donald was the only son of a widow, and though up until now she had been pleasant enough to me, the light seemed to break.

"You're lying, aren't you?" she demanded. "You're the one who wrote the card, I know it!"

I shook my head stubbornly, and now Miss Smith grew

angry. "It looks like your writing," she said coldly. "Go to the board and write out the words that are on that card."

In absolute silence I did it. The chalk squeaked as the uneven tell-tale letters sprawled across the board. I was too proud, too furious to attempt to disguise my handwriting. My schoolmates gawked and shifted in their seats. Donald turned suddenly and bolted from the room.

Miss Smith turned to his mother. "Will you come with me to the principal, please? And Mary Isabel, you come, too."

There is a family legend about my Grandfather Taft, whose stubbornness was spectacular. One day, when he was a small boy, there came from the direction of the pantry a tremendous crash. The first arrival on the scene found an upturned pan of milk on the floor and around the mouth of young Don Carlos a wide ring of cream.

No, he had not touched the cream. . . . No, he had not. . . . They pleaded with him to tell the truth, his mother wept, finally they beat him. Still he said he had not done it.

"Merely circumstantial evidence," he said airily in his last years. "What's more, if they come to me on my deathbed and threaten all the fires of hell—I will still say I did not touch that cream."

Professor Taft's granddaughter also denied. The principal questioned and threatened, Don's mother ranted, the teacher grew sorrowful, and at last they phoned my father. I can see his grim face now as he came into the office. He wasted no time on greetings.

"Now, then, Mary Isabel, what's this?" He sat down and drew me toward him. "Don't cry, daughtie. Just tell the truth and things will come out all right."

The dam burst and I flung my arms around his neck. "Oh, Daddy—Daddy—yes, I wrote it! It was because he asked me to— Oh, take me home! Please take me home!"

Curious that I remember so little of the sequel; how Adolph was finally persuaded to confess that he had written the original note and signed Don's name. In any event, Donald was guiltless— was I, perhaps, the least bit disappointed? His mother was mollified, but a subtle change had come into our relationship. We were never quite at ease with each other again.

Richard Hayes Garland and granddaughter.
(Courtesy of Victoria Doyle-Jones)

❧ ❧ ❧

Between my grandfather and me there was always a special understanding. He was so good-looking, so clean, so merry of tongue. I loved to sit on his lap and draw him out into stories of his youthful pioneering days. One day I confided to him that the dream of my life was a bicycle.

"It is, is it?" he said, looking over the tops of his spectacles. "A young squirt like you. Do you think you could ever learn to ride it?"

"Of course," I said loftily. "I've ridden Donald's and it's easy." I was stretching a point here. I had sat on the seat and been held up and pushed, but there was nothing easy about it. "I'd have to have a lady's bicycle, you know," I added hurriedly. "On account of my skirts, you see."

Grandfather nodded. "A lady's bicycle, naturally."

Grandfather died several days later.   One moment Grandfather was standing with his hands in his pockets in the sunlight before the barn door, waiting for a load of wood to be delivered. The next, he was lying full length on the grass, his hands still in his pockets, his lips curved in a half smile. The night before we had all played Rummy, his favorite game, and to his vast delight, little Constance had beaten him thoroughly. We kissed him goodnight as usual and never saw him again.[2]

A neighbor coming in on the afternoon of his death found Connie and me playing the piano in a sun-filled room and, with an exclamation of horror, jerked us off the piano bench and started pulling down the shades.

"What's the matter with you? Don't you know your grandfather's *dead*?"

Dead. . . . That terrible word again. I could see the white-bearded old man in the coffin in Chicago. My grandfather wasn't like that! I burst into hysterical sobbing and Connie joined me. Father, coming to see what was the matter, flung up the shades and turned savagely on the well-meaning neighbor.

"My children are going to remember their grandfather as he was last night—happy, loving, content. No one is going to make a horror of this. Please go."

We did not see Grandfather in death and we did not go to his funeral, but it was days before I could bear to look into his silent room. About a week later, a large wooden box addressed to Miss M. I. Garland arrived on the back porch, and when it was pried open was found to contain a new, beautiful, gleaming "lady's bicycle." The note tied to the handlebars read, "To my granddaughter, Mary Isabel, from her loving old Grandpop."

The note was in Grandfather's crabbed little handwriting, and it brought my loss home to me as never before. Grandfather was gone. One of his last thoughts had been of me. He would never see me ride my bicycle. He would never know how I loved him. I sobbed my heart out in Daddy's arms.

It was some time before I began the ordeal of learning to ride. Despite my blatant boasting, I was a timid child, easily discouraged, as my mother was, and it took all Daddy's persuasion and authority to get me on the thing. I wept and tried to beg off, but Daddy was patient and dogged and before long I could skim along the sidewalks with the best of them. No more trudging to school, now it was only a whisk away. In fact, I became *too* daring.

A mile or so out from the village on the La Crosse road was a long, long hill. I was permitted to ride anywhere in West Salem, even around "the square," where the circus and Chautauqua held forth in season, but I had been expressly forbidden to go down the long hill. More and more cars were appearing on the road and children on bicycles were a dangerous nuisance.

Donald had coasted down the long hill and one day he dared me to do so, too. Bursting with bravado, I took him up, and we started out jauntily, but it was a longer hill than I had expected, and steeper, and as the wheels turned faster and faster, the brakes didn't hold. I was frightened and wanted to stop but I couldn't. Don was way ahead of me and didn't know the trouble I was in, when all at once a big rock loomed up on the side of the road where I was riding and with a sickening crash I hit it.

I didn't know anything for several minutes. When I came to, I was lying with the bicycle on top of me in a ditch by the road. The handlebar had gone through my dress, my face and hands were badly cut, and the top of my knee had been sliced off and was streaming with blood. Far down, at the bottom of the hill, Don had turned around, saw what had happened and, leaping off his bicycle, started pushing it up the hill toward me as fast as he could come.

That was an interesting trip home. I couldn't walk, so Don put me on his bicycle and pushed me all the weary way. I was a solid child and romance must have been sorely tested.

When I reached home, aside from being bloody and in great pain, I knew my disobedience meant trouble. I sneaked in the side door and dragged myself upstairs. Mother was giving a ladies' luncheon, and I could hear the high-pitched babble of conversation from the dining room and now and then Connie's merry little crow. Ordinarily, I would have joined the party for the almond cream and mints, at least, but now my one thought was to get upstairs unobserved.

I made it to the bathroom, locked the door, filled the tub and, sloughing off my filthy, bloody clothing, climbed into the water and lay there, half fainting, while the water reddened around me and my wounds stung like fire.

All at once, there was Connie rattling the doorknob.

"Sister, are you there? Let me come in."

I didn't answer her though she called and called and at last she went away and returned with Mother.

"Mary Isabel—" Mother called sharply. "Let Connie in. Daughtie, open the bathroom door at once!"

Mother told me she nearly fainted at the grisly sight. Charlotte Corday had nothing on me.[3] Fortunately, in the drama of the occasion my parents forbore to punish me. I was in bed for the next few weeks and I remember the long nights of pain, when Mother lay beside me and recited "Gray's Elegy" over and over again, until I finally dropped off to sleep. When I returned to school it was interestingly on crutches and I played the situation to the hilt.

ta ta ta

The top holiday of the summer was undoubtedly the Fourth of July and Daddy was its leading spirit. He was always up before dawn to set off the first firecracker, while Mother groaned and covered her head with a pillow and Connie, who hated noise of any kind, crept in beside her. Father and I kept the Fourth conscientiously on the front walk, lighting one after another of the festive, popping things. Grandfather's big flag hung proudly over the front door and the acrid smell of gunpowder filled the air. Sometimes Daddy would put one of the bigger firecrackers in a tin can and set it safely out of harm's way, and when it went off, I squealed and danced in gratification.

The big anticipation, however, was nightfall. For days, Father, Grandfather, and George Dudley had been assembling the finest collection of fireworks the county afforded, and each Fourth of July our friends and neighbors were invited to a party. Mother and Minnie—our "hired girl" and neighbor on the other side of the tennis court—made gallons of celestial ice cream and yards of cakes and cookies, and as dusk fell the party gathered on the side lawn and Daddy brought out boxes of sparklers. One in each hand, we children ran rapturously about in the dark, tracing whirling patterns of tiny golden stars. Once little Connie, enchanted with the fairy things, seized a glowing end in her tiny fist and was grievously burned.

When the sparklers were exhausted, the big show began— a thing of great beauty. Dazzling rockets shot skyward, "golden rain" fell softly, silently, red fire mesmerized us. There were whirling circles of rainbow fire fastened to the trees, and strange, gilded snakelike forms writhed on the grass. We were all drunk on light and movement.

There was one unhappy Fourth when a big carton of fireworks standing on someone's porch, not ours, was ignited by a spark from a firecracker. With a whoosh and a roar, the whole thing went up—and with it the main part of the village.[4]

That was a day of wild excitement. We were far enough out of town so that the flames were no menace to us, but the McKees were in the direct path, and Mother and I went down through the pall of smoke to help Aunt Jessie pack up her treasures and move out of the parsonage. Though all able-bodied men and boys were on the fire line and firefighting equipment was brought in from neighboring towns, the entire main street and a good proportion of village homes burned to the ground. That night, around midnight, when the fire had been controlled and the menace was over, homeless, smoke-blackened villagers laid out tents and blankets on our lawns, Mother brought out gallons of peach ice cream and the cakes and cookies, and we had our belated party, this time without fire-works.

Daddy told me an amusing aftermath of that holocaust. Our little town, despite its trees and flowers, was, frankly, without charm. Main Street was the typical Midwestern eyesore of raw, yellow brick fronts, plate glass, and crude, boxlike structures behind. It curdled my father's artistic soul, but here, now, with the slate all but wiped clean, he saw a chance to remedy things.

Two of his good friends in Chicago were the Pond brothers, distinguished architects, and he asked them to draw up plans for an attractive, distinctive, economical-in-construction village Main Street.[5] Proudly, hopefully, Daddy laid the plans before the town council.

The answer was a flat no. West Salem was to be rebuilt exactly as it was before. All, that is, except for the five saloons, whose enterprising owners fell upon the new plans joyously. Before long, five delightful Swiss chalets, with steep roofs, leaded windows, and blooming window boxes appeared among the crass yellow brick and plate glass. There was a moral there somewhere but I do not think Father ever figured it out.

ès   ès   ès

A year or so later, our own home burned.

It was after one of our musical evenings. Connie and I, in rose-trimmed costumes, had danced and we all sang, and when it was time for the children to go to bed, we begged Mother to let us sleep downstairs in the guest room so that we could listen to the music that came after. If we had slept on our sleeping porch, as usual, there might have been no more little Garlands, for the sleeping porch was directly over the kitchen. A sleepy "hired girl" turned on the gasoline stove in the early morning, forgot to light it, and when she did remember and struck a match, gasoline had flooded the floor and the whole room went up in flames.[6]

Mother had slept downstairs with us in the guest rooms, and the three of us were awakened by a screaming girl, wrapped in flames, bursting into the room. Mother threw her on the floor and rolled her in the rug until she had extinguished the flames. Then she ran back through the house calling, "Hamlin!—Hamlin—"

I sat up in the darkness and saw Fern, glowing coals still on her shoulders, huddled sobbing and moaning on the floor. I remember going to the bathroom for a glass of water and pouring it on her till the glow went out. Then I followed Mother through the quiet, dark house and was just behind her when she pushed open the swinging door to the pantry. The kitchen beyond was a solid wall of flame.

Mother closed the dining room door behind her and ran back to the foot of the stairs. "Hamlin—the house is on fire! Get the children out—I'll phone for help—" I saw her wildly crank the handle on the wall phone and heard the urgency in her voice as she said, "Operator—this is Mrs. Garland. Our house is on fire! Oh, please help us!"

Daddy was downstairs by then, trousers on but barefooted and tasseled of hair. He took us back to the guest room where we gathered up robes and shoes and, snatching up some bedding, he hurried us out to the barn. The old buggy stood there and he put us into it, wrapping the quilts around us.

"Stay here. Don't move till I come back."

From where we sat, we could see the leaping flames that enveloped the kitchen wing of the house and, silhouetted against the glare, the figure of our father, holding a garden hose from which a feeble stream of water trickled. With an exclamation, he flung the hose down and started on a run around the house. Connie and I clung together, sobbing, while in the distance the village fire alarm bell began to clang. All around us, sleeping houses awoke, lights flashed, people shouted and came running.

Mother, pale, tense, her long dark hair in braids over the shoulders of her dressing gown, joined us in the barn. Under her arm she carried the family photograph albums and her bag of modest jewelry. It had been arranged between my parents that in case something like this happened, once the children were safe, she was to save the photographs and her jewels and Daddy was to look after his manuscripts and papers. Now he appeared upstairs at his study window and, wrenching out the screen, tossed it to the ground.

"George!" he shouted above the crackle and the road. "George—can you hear me? I'm going to throw down my manuscripts. Try to pick them up."

George was there and he heard. He and two or three others collected the books and papers Daddy threw down and wrapped them safely in blankets. The fire department arrived. I saw Uncle George ask one of them a question, and the man shook his head.

"Mr. Garland!" George Dudley shouted up at the study window. "You'd better get out of there. Don't try the stairs—you can't make it that way. They say the whole place is going to go!"

Daddy hesitated, gathered up one more load of his cherished papers, and tossed them down. Then he sat down on the sill and swung his legs over. We watched in terror as he dropped safely to the ground, and the next moment he joined us in the buggy. We clung to him, wailing.

"Don't let the house burn, Daddy!" I begged in anguish. "Don't let it burn!"

His face was set and gray. For the first time, he failed us. "I can't do anything, baby. There's nothing to do." He picked up little Connie. "Let's get out of here. I don't want to see any more."

We went to the Saunders house across the street, where we sat in the dining room with the shades down. We could hear the shouts, the crackle, the roar, but at least we were spared the sight.

George Dudley came in to report. "I think we'll save part of it—"

Daddy lifted his head. "Did it get the trees?"

"Not badly. I think we'll save most of those, too."

Daddy's face was alight. He hit his knee with his clenched fist. "Then I'll rebuild! If the trees are still there, I'll put it back again just as good as new. Daughties, I promise it!"

We both hugged him ecstatically. Everything was going to be all right now. Daddy had promised.

For the next week or so, Connie and I played, absorbed, in the fallen leaves on the tennis court. We had a game laid out that was called Dog and Deer and was a series of touching loops across which the agile deer might jump, while the poor panting dog had to run the length of the loops. The point was that there was only one deer and a pack of pursuing dogs, and it took all the deer's finesse to choose the right moment to cross from one loop to another and so leave his dogged pursuers behind. We also made elaborate house plans of leaves, laying out drawing rooms and bedrooms and hallways and scrupulously respecting the indicated entrances and exits. But we didn't look up at Mapleshade. From the Saunders house across the street, where we were still staying, the front of our own house seemed untouched, but we knew that once you went around to the back, the full horror of what had happened to us would be apparent. By not looking at the house or talking about it, Connie and I lived in a sort of dream world of waiting for the time when, Daddy had promised, it would be itself again. In the meantime, Mother and Daddy were sorting, planning.

Eventually, in remarkable clothing borrowed from our neighbors—we had lost all our personal possessions—Mother and Connie and I went down to Chicago to stay while Father and whatever workmen he could corral began the ugly, back-breaking task of tearing down the charred shell of our home.

All that autumn Daddy worked like a fiend, forgetting career, lecture dates, everything but the task at hand. He had promised we would have Thanksgiving dinner in Mapleshade, and the Wednesday before we came back up to West Salem.

Daddy met us at the train and his eyes were shining. A dray was to bring up our bags and we walked home, along the sweet, quiet streets where dusk had just fallen. At the corner where we had so often turned, Connie and I hung back, afraid to go on.

"Come on," Daddy urged. "It's all there, just as I promised. And tomorrow we'll have the best Thanksgiving dinner anyone ever had."

I was still afraid. The nightmare of three months before was too vivid to be dismissed. I dreaded what I would see, what I wouldn't see. Father took my hand and drew me after him, talking quietly, reassuringly.

"In a few minutes you will see the lights. . . . The trees are all right, only a few branches scorched. I haven't had time to replace the playhouse yet, but I'll get at it right away. The swing is waiting for you. You'll sleep tonight on your own sleeping porch."

There it was! Connie and I cried out in joy. Just as we remembered it. The trees, bare of leaves now but still tall, sheltering, and from every window lights glowed, while from the chimney rose up a column of violet smoke into the sharp, November air. We began to run toward it, then, suddenly afraid again, stopped short at the gateposts. Father went ahead of us up the walk and opened the front door. Golden light streamed out across the newly-screened porch. In the living room the Navajo rugs were there, paintings were there, firelight flickered over the walls, and from the direction of the kitchen came enticing smells.

Connie and I were delirious with pride and satisfaction. The Garlands were at home again. Our father could do anything.

Notes

[1] Neshonoc Cemetery, about one mile north of West Salem.

[2] Richard Hayes Garland died on October 21, 1914. Isabel disrupts the chronology of the narrative, for the events of this chapter close in 1912.

[3] In 1793 Charlotte Corday assassinated Jean-Paul Marat, one of the leaders of the French Revolution, by plunging a knife into Marat's chest while he was in his bathtub.

[4] On July 1, 1911, most of the business district of the village of West Salem burned, leveling more than forty businesses and damaging many others.

[5] Irving K. Pond and Allen B. Pond formed the Chicago firm Pond & Pond, noted for its designs of public buildings.

[6] Garland has described the burning of his home, which forms the basis of Isabel's account, in chapter 24 of *A Daughter of the Middle Border*, "The Old Homestead Suffers Disaster." News of the fire, which occurred on October 7, 1912, made the front pages of the *New York Times* and the *Chicago Tribune*. See "Hamlin Garland in Fire," *New York Times*, October 8, 1912, 1; "Hamlin Garland in Peril When His Residence Burns," *Chicago Tribune*, October 8, 1912, 1. The maid, who was badly burned, was Fern Fox.

5. West and East

ટ્ર ટ્ર ટ્ર

The next West Salem summer was broken by a trip with Ira Nelson Morris and his family to the Big Horn Mountains in Wyoming.[1] To make it perfect, Daddy was going with us. Father's love for the Mountain West was one of the deep passions of his life. Brought up on the plains, his string of Western novels were not "pot boilers," as some critics have suggested, but an expression of his own deep longing for the high peaks. He had taken his bride to this country on their wedding trip, and a harrowing experience it had proved for a non-athletic, city-bred girl. Mother confessed to me that she was in tears a good part of the time: "Hamlin wanted me to see everything and he thought nothing of a thirty or forty mile ride. He was always assuring me that there was an even better view around the next corner, and all I wanted to do was get off that stupid horse and sit down beside the trail and cry. One time I did just that and Hamlin disgustedly rode on alone and looked at his view before he came back to me. It was not my idea of a honeymoon."

Ever since Connie and I were old enough to sit on a horse, Daddy had dreamed and talked of showing the Rockies to us, but money was an ever-present problem and the cost of such a trip unthinkable. Now, however, in a private railcar, accompanied by maids, valets, and secretaries, the Garland family rolled across the country, acquiring a taste for high living that it has been hard to overcome.

Our party consisted of Uncle Ira, who had recently been appointed ambassador to Sweden—a stocky, handsome, white-haired, dynamic man with remarkable eyes—his wife, Lily, Mother's close friend, who had been a Miss Rothschild and a great beauty; their daughter, Constance, some years older than I, who was herself a beauty; their son, Ira, who was my age and my particular friend; Ira's chum, nice John Davis; and the four Garlands. The Morris home—a great stone castle on the North Shore Drive— was the scene of many lavish parties during our youth, and the trunks full of beautiful, slightly-worn clothes that were delivered periodically were a thrilling godsend to Mother, Connie, and me. Naturally, the Morrises would have a private railcar, and I must say that the Garlands settled into it quite easily.

Our base in Wyoming was Teepee Lodge, a semi-rustic, high-priced dude ranch, five thousand or so feet up, twenty miles by car and horse stage from Sheridan. Outfitted in breeches, riding boots, and Stetsons, Connie and I became Hamlin Garland heroines overnight.

The day after we arrived at the Lodge, we were all mounted and set off on a thirty-mile ride to Glacier lake, where we were to make camp at ten thousand feet. It was a magnificent ride. I will never forget the smell of hot pine needles, the whiff of sage, the rushing, ice-cold streams, the gallops across sun-flooded mesas. The Morrises did everything "regardless," and the guides told us that our pack train was the longest that had ever left the Lodge.

The pack train had gone on ahead, and by the time we reached camp everything was in order. Our tents were up and equipped with heating, electric lights, mattressed beds, every conceivable luxury. Father, who had ridden his big, faithful gray, Ladrone, into the heart of the Klondike with only saddle bags and a roll of blankets, was amused and troubled. From our earliest days Connie and I had seen and had too much, Daddy claimed, and he was bothered by the thought of our discontent when we were forced to return to earth again.

"This isn't the West I knew," he said ruefully, accepting champagne from Uncle Ira's valet, while we lounged in deck chairs around the fire after a dinner that had begun with caviar and ended with ice cream. Earlier, Mother and I had strolled over to watch the cook and his helper at work, and Mother had gasped as Slim had opened a whole pound of butter and nonchalantly slipped it into the chicken fricassee.

The cook grinned and winked, "They're so rich they won't know the difference."

Our camp was at the base of a huge glacier that glowed white in the moonlight. From sheer cliffs, a long waterfall slid down the rocks in a cloud of spray and fell, roaring but tamed, into a deep, diamond-clear pool. In every direction the mountains lifted their snow peaks against the sky and the mighty pines seemed to march away into infinity.

This was what Daddy had wanted to show us. "Look at that, daughtie!" he exulted, gripping my shoulder, turning me to face some incomparable vista. "Like it?" he would ask over and over. "Like it?" He really had no need to ask. One look at my face and he could see. I was in heaven. Daddy taught us to ride, to fish, to follow a trail, to jump a fallen log and ford a stream. The first fish I ever caught was on this trip. Daddy and I were out alone in a canoe on the lake and I was idly trailing a line when something live and strong took the hook and almost pulled me overboard.

"Daddy!" My shriek and his shout of laughter rang out across the lake. "There's something wiggling on the end of my line!"

Back at the Lodge, we came out of the cabin one morning to see what looked like a thick bank of fog moving down the mountain side toward us. Father lifted his head and sniffed and his face became grave. "That isn't fog—that's smoke. There's a fire somewhere."

The very word "fire" struck a chill into my heart and I seized his arm. "Daddy, will it get here?"

"I don't think so. Let's go down to the corral and ask some questions."

Reassured, we got out on our horses and rode to a safe viewpoint where I had my first sight of a crown fire. Those of us who live in California have been through brush fires and know the helplessness, the devastation, but a crown fire is something straight out of the Inferno. Far away down the canyon we saw the flames leap from one magnificent treetop to another, and the roar was that of a herd of savage, penned beasts. Father, who loved trees, groaned aloud. We had seen what the aftermath was on our trip up from Sheridan: mile after mile of stripped, blackened skeletons. I have my father's love of trees to the extent that the whine of a power saw in the neighborhood goes straight to my heart. I bought the little house I occupy because it is surrounded with trees, because I can lie in bed and look up into the branches and return, for the moment, to that young, sweet Wisconsin world.

But this was 1914 and not only the forest but the world ignited. Ira Morris left hurriedly for Washington. Daddy was booked for a lecture tour and departed also, and the rest of us sadly packed and prepared to return home. The last day I sat with Mother in Aunt Lily's log cabin while they chatted and the French maid stowed things in trunks. I had permission to play with the contents of a large suede jewel case, and as one who had dreamed since childhood of queens and princesses, I was especially charmed with the three tiaras. One diamond and emerald one was so ingeniously made that it could be taken apart by unscrewing and made into a variety of bracelets, brooches, earrings, and dog collars.

If Daddy could only see me now! I exulted, standing before the mirror in all my priceless trappings. Daddy and I were alike in our love of jewels. On every legitimate occasion, he would take me with him to Vantine's, the Oriental store on Fifth Avenue, to select a gift for Mother, who cared very little for such things. In fact, it was her ungracious habit to return at once whatever she had just been given to the store it came from. Her excuse was the extravagance, but to do Daddy justice, he bought only the least expensive of the topazes and rose diamonds, the jades and aqua-marines that called him so strongly. He would have gloried in me in my mass of liquid fire.

Later in my life I acquired some lovely pieces of my own, but the one I cherish most is a hammered silver Navajo bracelet I have worn on my right arm since Daddy put it there when I was fifteen. The Indian tradition is that if you have been faithful the silver will never tarnish. Mine is as bright as the day I put it on. . . .

So, down out of the high, pure air we came to spend a few days in the reek and roar of Chicago. There was tragedy there. My cousin, Charlie, diving in an unfamiliar lake, struck his head on a rock and died shortly thereafter, and with him died the soul of Turbulance Doctoria. My mother's pain and pity were beyond words. It was bliss to get back to the sleepy peace of West Salem where, despite our father's fears, we settled into our modest home again in supreme content.

Then came the morning when Father came into Mother's

room with the front page of the *Chicago Tribune* in his hand. In the biggest, blackest headlines we had ever seen, it proclaimed, "ENG-LAND DECLARES WAR!"

Father held the paper up before us and his voice was harsh. "Look at this, Zulime—daughters—and never forget it. This is the end of the world we have known. Nothing will ever be the same again. Before long, the whole world will be at war."

It didn't seem possible, there under the great, sheltering maples, where the only sound was the wind in the leaves, the cluck-ing of chickens, or a far-off moo from an impatient milk cow. Though our parents' faces became ever more grave as the days passed, Connie and I managed to put the shadow behind us. This was our home. We would live here in comfort and safety forever.

Father, however, had other plans. With Richard Garland's death his son's last tie with West Salem had snapped and he was determined to get away. For years his publishers, his lecture agents, and his literary friends were in the East, and each time he left it with reluctance. In West Salem, too, was the heartbreak of memory. He had bought the old house for his mother, and she had died here. Now, with his father gone, hating the stagnation of village life and out of sorts with Chicago, where an antagonistic faction had arisen to destroy his satisfaction in the Cliff Dwellers, Father set his face doggedly toward New York.[2] When he was away from us his let-ters were paeans of praise for the cleanliness, the stimulation, the opportunities of the East, and any friends who passed through our Chicago house were charged to make similar reports.

Invitations to visit were showered on us by Daddy's Eastern friends. Edward K. Bok, editor of the *Ladies Home Journal*, dining with us in Chicago, insisted we come and make a long stay with them in Philadelphia, adding craftily, "Tell me what you like best in the world to eat and I'll see that you get all you can manage." With one accord, Connie and I said, "Cream puffs!"

Before long there was an urgent telegram addressed to "The Misses Garland." "One thousand cream puffs ready and spoiling. Come at once. E.K.B."

First, Father had to convince his wife and daughters of the desirability of the move, and it was not an easy matter. Eventually, Connie and I were won over by the sheer adventure, by the thrilling prospect of visiting historical sights—the Louisa May Alcott house, the "House of the Seven Gables" with its hidden stairway, the Old North Church, the White House—and of meeting famous people and going to the theater and the opera. But Zulime Taft loved the West. Her beloved brother, her only sister, and their families were in Chicago; lifelong friends were close at hand. She liked the cheerful little Greenwood Avenue house and the unexacting social life in which she was involved, and like her daughters, she was happy in West Salem. Already, she had begun to suffer from nervous tension, and the long, uneventful days at Mapleshade were medicine for her. Mother knew the hectic pace of New York, the public life that would be required of her as the wife of a well-known literary figure. Hamlin Garland was in constant demand at important social functions, and Mother, who made all her own clothes and ours from the boxes that came now and then from the Morrises or the Guggenheims,[3] would be expected to be suitably attired and at his side.

There was something else, too—one of the things she dreaded most: she could not bear to hear her husband speak from a platform. It was ironic, for Father was an effective speaker, brief, easy, humorous. "Hamlin speaks very well, I know," Mother said to me once apologetically. "He's never awkward or tasteless. It's just that it—makes me so nervous."

Why, I wonder? Was it a fear of possible failure, of something going wrong? Or was it because she had heard most of it before? Wives of banquet chairman become pretty familiar with what their husbands are about to say. Mother, to be honest, was a curious contradiction of poise and shyness. She loved people of all kinds, but she hated public appearances and eventually refused to attend formal functions of any kind, and so Connie and I were conscripted in her place. Yet she was beautiful, gracious, apparently at ease and extravagantly admired.

Now, with the big decision to be made, Mother objected, vacillated, and was bombarded with telegrams from wherever Daddy was at the moment.

"What are you doing about the Chicago house? Take any reasonable offer."

"Ernest and Grace Seton say come at once. They will put us up till we find a place to live."

"George says he has a tenant for Mapleshade. Talk to him."

Finally a wire more peremptory than the rest: "Sell Chicago house at once or leave it in agent's hands. You must be here by the 15th, Hamlin."

This one brought her face down, weeping on her bed. "I can't! I can't!" As Mother's head rolled despairingly back and forth on her pillow, Connie and I grew bewildered and frightened. It was the first time we had seen an adult break down. I know I had never seen my mother cry before. I remember many times coming in and seeing her lying on her bed with her arm across her eyes, knowing vaguely that she was not well or was unhappy about something, but I had never heard her voice raised in either anger or distress. Whatever disagreements Mother and Daddy had—I think they were few, for Mother was gentle and tactful and in most cases it was easier to let Hamlin have his own way—were settled out of sight and sound of the children. To have our mother now prostrated, sobbing like a heartbroken child, was appalling.

Knowing our distress, she forced herself to dry her eyes, to sit up and speak calmly and reassuringly, and face the fact that she was going to have to surrender. A buyer appeared for the Greenwood Avenue house, Mother accepted the offer, and wired Daddy we were coming.

I have beside me now a letter of mine written to Daddy on this occasion:

> . . . Now Father dear I don't want you to think we don't want to go to N.Y. because we do and I should be broken hearted if we don't. WE HAVE SOLD THE HOUSE so do not worry any more daddy dear. I love you oh so much and in some of your letters where you are so discouraged you made me cry. Come and take us all back to N.Y. with you.

I vividly recall the day we left Chicago. Daddy was in Washington waiting to welcome us, but all the others who meant most to Mother were there on the station platform: her sister and brother and their families, her dearest friends, fellow artists she had known since Paris days, a contingent from Eagle's Nest Camp, some faithful masculine admirers. They stood in a half circle, silent in the main except for tearful sniffs from some of the women. Mother was gallant and did her best to make conversation, but finally in desperation she herded Connie and me onto the train. When we reached our Pullman section and looked out the window, they were all still standing there, their faces blank with loss. Mother gave of her warmth and sympathy as few do, and her tribute was outside there on the platform.

Suddenly her own tears gushed. She pounded on the window with her small, gloved fist and called wildly, "Go away! Oh, please—all of you—go away!"

Whether they heard her or not, they made no move to leave, and Mother flung herself back in the corner of the seat and covered her face with her hands. Mercifully, the train began to move. Connie and I, sobbing bitterly, watched all that was dear and familiar fade out of sight.

In *Back-Trailers from the Middle Border*, Father described our trip and the joy he took in showing his daughters the historical and literary shrines that had meant so much to him in his own youth. Constance and I soon forgot to look backward and had a splendid time. Mother was unfailingly brave and cheerful, but I can imagine how her heart ached. Today, when we fly across the entire continent in a few hours, it is hard to realize what that parting meant. We might have been taking a ship to a far-off land.

After doing the rounds of Washington, we descended on the Mark Sullivans in their beautiful, historic home in Fredericksburg, Virginia.[4] Since Daddy and Uncle Mark had arranged the visit without consulting Mrs. Sullivan, our welcome was cool and we remained only two days. The second night, Connie and I saw a ghost.

It was very warm, and the night was full of moonlight and jasmine. The house, where Robert E. Lee met his wife and courted her, was a Southern plantation stage set: mellow brick, tall white pillars, and two long wings extending out from a wide central hall. We were sitting out on the steps after dinner when Uncle Mark, lowering his voice dramatically, pointed at the rose garden.

"We have a lady who walks there—The Lady in White. The story is that she killed herself for love."

Connie and I were entranced, and Daddy, who had always had a lively interest in psychic research, said, "Call her up, Mark. Let's find out about it."

"We've tried but she wouldn't come. She's a whimsical lass—doesn't seem to have regular hours. Anyhow, keep your eyes open. You may have a glimpse of her."

Connie and I had twin beds in a room at one end of the house, and Mother and Daddy were in the State Bedroom at the other. We went to sleep promptly, and it must have been three or four hours later that I was awakened as sharply as though someone had laid a hand on my shoulder. I opened my eyes and lifted my head and there, standing before the closed door, was a shape, a woman's, white and transparent, for the paneling of the door showed clearly through her. I drew a sharp breath. At the same instant, Connie, in the other bed a few feet away, whispered in awestruck tones, "Do you see her, too?"

We both lay rigid for a moment or two, staring at the door, then the apparition appeared to glide toward the center of the room, and as one Connie and I leapt from our beds and charged out the door and down the endless hall to the bedroom occupied by our parents. Shivering and sobbing, we piled into bed with them and nothing could shake our story that we had seen The White Lady. I suppose it could have been a trick of moonlight, but as both my sister and I awakened at the same instant, I prefer to believe in a visitation.

From the Sullivans, we went to Boston, Concord, Cambridge, and then on to Philadelphia for our stay with the Boks. The great editor was true to his promise. On the lace-covered dinner table that night were spaced four gigantic silver epergnes, each one piled to overflowing with cream puffs. We had them for dinner, breakfast, lunch, and tea. It was a thoroughly satisfactory visit.

At last, New York City. . . . Connie and I loathed it at sight. We tried to be civil and not load Daddy with reproaches, but I know we looked them. Coming up Broadway in a taxi from the Pennsylvania Station, we were appalled by the ugly, sooty buildings, the street littered with filthy, blowing paper, the drab, hustling pedestrians. This was Daddy's "shining city"?

We spent our first night in New York in the decaying grandeur of the Park Avenue Hotel, all four of us in a huge, drab room, slightly illuminated by one unshaded light bulb hanging on a long cord from the ceiling. That night I menstruated painfully for the first time, and the world looked grim indeed. Fortunately, the

Park Avenue Hotel, for all its down-at-the-heel condition, was too expensive for the Garlands, and after a depressing hunt, Mother and Daddy rented a cheap little flat on the upper West Side, between West End and Riverside Drive, and we became New York apartment dwellers.

Connie and I must have been pretty difficult. We did not like anything: tenement life five stories up, food—for the first time I tasted store-bottled mayonnaise and it sickened me—the noise, the dirt, the crowds, the smell. Our one refuge was the park along Riverside Drive where we would sit and watch the Hudson moving sluggishly by and talk of the day when we would return to West Salem and contentment. Neither of us had any idea that our life in the West was over.

In the meantime, our parents were trying to locate a permanent place to live, somewhere on the East Side, within walking distance of the Finch School, which was to take over our education in the fall. Mrs. John O'Hara Cosgrave, the founder of Finch, was an admirer and good friend of Daddy's, and for the sake of his distinguished name agreed to take his two daughters for the price of one.[5] Rents on the East Side were prohibitively high, and poor Mother and Daddy had another long hunt before they finally found a "railroad flat" on the north-east corner of Park Avenue and Ninety-Second Street. Mother and Daddy reported it was on the top floor of a seven-story building and overlooked the whole city, but Connie and I were too disgusted with the whole prospect even to wish to go and inspect it.

There was another reason why we were not taken to see our new home and school: an epidemic of infantile paralysis had broken out and our parents were panic-stricken. For ten days we were not allowed out of our hot, smelly little flat, and as we fussed and fumed, Daddy decided the only thing to do was flee the city.

Irving Bacheller, his wife, and son, Paul, were spending the summer in a small, upstate town called Canton and wrote that they had found rooms for us in a nearby boarding house. With antiseptic masks over our faces, we took a taxi and then a train and went north for the rest of the summer.

Canton was almost like being back in West Salem: the same tree-shaded streets and screened-porch houses, the same slow, uneventful tempo. Mother, Connie, and I settled in happily, but

Daddy, aside from the pleasure he took in Uncle Irving's company, soon became restless. He felt he had exchanged one rural prison for another and before long left for the city, where he stayed at the Players Club and wrote daily letters that alternated in tone from deep depression to spectacular high spirits. As I said before, no one could go quite so high or so low, for no apparent reason, as Father. I am afraid I have inherited some of that. I remember, during my early teens, going into the bedroom to fling myself down and weep my heart out over some mysterious wave of feeling that had taken possession of me. Usually, Mother would follow and put her arms around me, coaxing me back to reasonableness, but with the two of us to contend with the wonder is that Mother survived. In the light of her nervous collapse in later years I am afraid that the answer is that it all took its toll.

The summer ended, the leaves turned to flame and gold, and the wind blew chill. Connie and I had learned to swim in the Canton River and left with reluctance for New York.

The new flat was a pleasant surprise, for it was airy and sunny at the front and back. The rooms in between, along a dark, narrow hall, had windows on a sunless areaway, and Daddy's so-called study was a minute chamber squeezed between Connie's and my bedroom and the bathroom. The view from the living room, however, was dramatic, and there was room for the piano and walls of books. Though the fire under the fake mantel was a gas log, in a few days the place began to take on the aspect of home.

In the end, the thing that persuaded us to accept Daddy's New York was our visit to the Lenox School, which housed the lower grades of Finch, from which I later graduated. The building was still under construction when Daddy took us down one afternoon and Mrs. Cosgrave showed us about. It was charming, hardly like a school at all, we told ourselves, remembering the grim, old pile of Chicago's Wadsworth. The classrooms were small and attractive with wicker armchairs drawn up around tables of silvery blond wood. Flower arrangements and handsome art reproductions were everywhere, and on the 13th floor a two-story, professionally equipped art studio was plainly going to absorb my sister, Constance. On the first floor—and here my eyes shone—was a small, perfect theater: orchestra pit, modern lighting, dressing rooms, everything one could ask for. I stood entranced in the middle of the stage and made a silent vow that I would be the leading lady on that stage before I was through.

"You have to decide," Father had put it to us, "whether you'd rather be a big frog in a small puddle, or a small frog in a big puddle." In other words, queen it in an everyday school or take a humble position in an exclusive one. One look and Connie and I made up our minds. We knew that our classmates came from rich families and that we couldn't begin to compete with them on a social level, but to Mother's relief, we were to wear uniforms: dark green wool suits and white cotton blouses. Thus turned out, you could hardly distinguish the Storrs, Guinness, Uppercu, and Rachmaninoff offspring from the Garlands. Our mentalities we would have to apply.

The school was all we had hoped it would be and more. We were completely happy there with the dozen or so brilliant, hand-picked women who had the job of opening our minds to the cultural world. Being only a few blocks from the Metropolitan Museum, it became a second home for Constance and me, and I remember Miss Dickinson, Miss Ufford, Miss Carter, Miss Grant, and Mrs. Cosgrave herself, with her classes in philosophy, civics, and comparative religion, with deepest gratitude.

My particular pet was Vida Ravenscroft Sutton, my dramatic teacher, a lovely blond ex-actress with a dedication to the theater and Greek dramatic literature that she did her best to hand on to me.[6] We tangled when we first met. I had the typical strident, nasal Western voice that was Father's frank despair. I had also his stubbornness. "I don't want to talk like an Easterner," I proclaimed. "I come from the West and I want to talk like the West." Vida, however, with exquisite tact, gradually won me over.

My first big part was the leader of the Chorus in Gilbert Murray's superb translation of Euripides' *Trojan Women*, and that glorious poetry had a tremendous impact. I quote it to this day.

Each time the curtains parted on the Lenox Theater stage, I could look out into the audience and see among the fond mothers, doting aunts, classmates, and young men admirers the handsome gray head of my father. Except when he was out of town on a lecture tour I don't think he missed a single production in which Connie and I appeared. After the final curtain, it was always Daddy I sought out first. What he had to say meant more than anything.

At the close of *Iphigenia*, in which, true to my vow, I had the leading role, overwrought and exalted, I ran into his arms.

"You did it, daughtie!" he said, his voice rough with feeling. "You made it live. You did it!"

On the other hand, he was an unsparing critic. We worked on my various roles together, he cueing me patiently, suggesting new nuances, better business. One of his frequent admonitions: "Beware of the falling inflection. The audience may fall with you."

One of our productions was Lady Gregory's fantasy *The Dragon*, in which I played the princess. I looked the part in a long, lovely gown of pleated shell-pink chiffon and a high gold crown that Mother had made out of wide, coarse lace, stiffened and gilded, but when I rushed to Daddy as usual after the final curtain, he shook his head. "I don't know, daughtie. You didn't get your teeth into it. It was too superficially pretty. Think it over, you'll get it right."

That was Father, always encouraging, tearing down only to build up. He was equally interested in Connie's drawing and set about getting her illustrating commissions and standing over her while she executed them.

"That's it, Conniekins! You're on the right track. Keep going!"

One of Father's most admirable traits was his enthusiasm for and appreciation of creative talent. Stephen Crane was one of his early discoveries, and all through his life he was generously promoting young literary talent. There was no professional jealously in Father. The thing that counted was craftsmanship. The plays and fiction of the later years of his life filled him with distaste, with actual physical pain. What he would think of this era's ugly output I would rather not imagine.

It was about here that the Garland household was increased to five with the arrival at Christmas of a small, woolly-white Maltese terrier. She had a card tied to her collar with the inscription, "My name is Blinkie and I belong to Mary Isabel and Constance." She was the gift of our friends, Dr. and Mrs. Fenton B. Turck.[7]

Connie and I detested her on sight. We didn't want a dog. We didn't want the chore of taking her down six flights of stairs four or five times a day. She would obviously yap and misbehave and fall sick, and intent as we were on our school and our planned careers, we felt we had no time for that sort of thing. But you couldn't hurt the kind Turcks, so we dragged her home, quite literally, and dumped her on Mother's bed, and there she stayed for eleven years.

Inevitably, we all came to adore her. She was the daily pest we had anticipated, but, on the other hand, she was so bright, so high-spirited, so full of overflowing love that we succumbed. In fact, she became the center of our daily life, and her tricks and ways were endlessly endearing. Nothing escaped her. A box of candy brought by a beau and opened with infinite care in the drawing room would bring Blinkie charging the length of the apartment, curls streaming, red tongue quivering with anticipation. Blinkie loved everybody and in the end even Father gave in.

I came home late one night and opened the front door quietly on a scene that twists my heart to this day. Daddy was sitting in half light before the gas log, a small, curly white mat stretched out ecstatically across his knees. His big, broad hand was fondling the long silky ears, and in a sort of tender, masculine croon he was saying over and over,

"Was a little dorgie-dorgie. . . . Was a little dorgie-dorgie."

Interesting to think that while my father had a myriad pet names for his children—*baby, daughtie, Mizabel, Mebsie, Conniekin, childababe, kidlets*—terms of affection exasperated him.

"Don't call me *dear!*" he would charge fiercely. The same applied to *darling, dearest, sweet, love*—any of the fond words that flow so easily from us all in these days. I never heard him call my mother anything except Zulime, yet he was a warm, demonstrative man.

Probably his dislike stemmed from the old stage days with their easy assumption of familiarity. Father was a formal man.

Happy as Connie and I were in our school life, Mother was under more and more of a strain. The thing she had anticipated, dreaded, was ever present. New York was worse than Chicago, for it was the center of the American creative world. Everyone came through New York to be wined and dined, and night after night, there in the center of the Speaker's Table, handsome and distinguished and competent in white tie and tails, was Father; and there, on the right of the guest of honor, Joffre or Tagore, Galsworthy or Stanley Baldwin, would be Mother, radiant in one of Aunt Lily's or

Aunt Irene's cast-off evening gowns, looking as though she hadn't a care in the world. If she hadn't hated it so, she could have had a wonderful time.

Father was pretty outspoken about it. "Your mother sits by the guest of honor and gets interesting talk. I get the dull wives."

Mother, herself, was not one of the dull wives. Gracious, sympathetic, and witty, she tried to pass on her technique to Connie and me. "Find out what they are interested in and ask questions." Her own first formal dinner party when she was sixteen proved her point, for she sat next to a middle-aged gentleman who addressed himself solely to his plate. Mother artfully discovered that his wealth and position stemmed from the manufacture of pearl buttons and professed such an intelligent interest that he scarcely left her side thereafter.

Despite the colorful social life, things with the Garlands were tough. In Chicago, we had lived in comparative affluence. In those days, on his trips to New York, Father could—according to his diaries, did—set out in the morning with seven manuscripts in his pocket and place them all before nightfall. Now, with the war raging, nothing was selling, lecture dates were few and far between, and our finances grew tighter and tighter. We walked everywhere, or took the five cent street car or subway to save the ten cents the Fifth Avenue bus would have cost, and anxious planning was necessary in all things. I asked Daddy for a dollar one day, and his face was stony as he opened his checkbook to me.

"Nine dollars—" he said harshly. "That's all we have in the bank now, daughtie—nine dollars."

It was not as bad as it sounded—there were some bonds—but it was a cruel thing to do to an emotional child of thirteen. I had always suffered from an excess of imagination, and now I was terrified, defenseless. At any moment, I expected we would be put out on the street. I shivered and wept all night and in the morning went to Daddy with my resolve. I would leave school, falsify my age, and get a job in a ten cent store. At least, my family should not go hungry. Daddy soothed me, explained that money would be coming in shortly and that his credit was good, but I imagine he felt somewhat conscience-stricken.

There was no minimizing, however, the fact that things were grim. To add to the financial worry, Father had developed a deep, painful arthritis in his shoulder and back. He wasn't able to lift his right arm high enough to dip his pen in the ink, so he would slowly and agonizingly dip it in with the left hand and transfer the pen to his crippled right. Some nights the torture was so overwhelming that he would walk the floor, tears streaming down his cheeks, while Mother or I walked behind him, pounding on his back with all our strength to counteract the pain. The despair he must have known, lying there on his narrow, sagging cot through the sleepless hours.

Yet we entertained constantly. Daddy was the most gregarious of men and rarely came home from the club without some distinguished man in tow. Carl Akeley, the African lion hunter; Stefansson, the Arctic explorer; Edward Wheeler, editor of *Poetry Magazine*; were the regulars. William Dean Howells, William Allen White, Charles Breasted, Robert Frost, Mark Sullivan, and a procession of actors, artists, and musicians—our little dining room received them all.[8]

It meant usually that the meal, never lavish to begin with, would have to be stretched to include another healthy appetite. Mother worked miracles. We were too poor for roasts and steaks and chops, so dinner would consist of a big wooden bowl of mixed green salad at Mother's end of the table and a casserole or a chafing dish of some creamed thing at the other. Milk would extend the creamed thing and so would toast underneath. There were always mashed potatoes and plenty of hot biscuits and honey, and we wound up with one of my pies or cakes or the steamed puddings that Daddy so loved. I do not think anyone ever went away hungry, but there were no second helpings. The climax, of course, was the coffee, which Daddy painstakingly brewed himself, and superb stuff it was, dark, winey, fortifying the soul.

Daddy made the coffee in the mornings, too—it was his admitted vice—and Connie and I would be awakened at seven by the entrance of Father, holding a large, saucerless cup in each hand, a slice of haphazardly buttered bread balanced across the top of the cup.

"I will not spread hard butter on crumbly bread for any child," he would announce as we sat up in bed to receive the cups. Nothing ever tasted better than that wonderful coffee in the cold, gray, New York dawn. As the heat from the coffee rose up through the bread, the butter melted and it became a very memorable breakfast.

Connie and I became good cooks and waitresses and tackled cheerfully the washing up afterwards. Some of our male guests were inclined, in a fatherly way, to become amorous, but Connie and I would escape to the kitchen, where we gossiped and giggled and broke dishes in peace. It was valuable training and we really giggled when, as part of the course in Domestic Science that Finch insisted on (Mrs. Cosgrave announced that one of her goals was to make rich girls into competent, poor men's wives), I was solemnly instructed in the scientific approach to dishwashing.

What a contradiction our lives were. Culturally, we were having the best the city offered: opera, theaters, concerts, lectures, art exhibits. Chauffeured limousines called for us and brought us home. The Plaza, where the Guggenheims occupied thirty-two rooms on the third floor, the Waldorf, the Ambassador, and the Ritz, depending on which of our rich friends were in residence, were familiar stamping grounds. We wore hand-me-down, remodeled clothing and velvet and fur coats, and thanks to Mother's skill with a needle, we always felt ourselves adequately turned out wherever we went.

Mother was so clever that she could take an original model of a Worth or Vionnet, rip it apart, spread the pieces out on new fabric, and cut from them, then reassemble the whole garment in its pristine smartness. From Mother I inherited an interest in dressmaking but not, alas, her dash.

On Sundays, after a late breakfast, Connie and I would wash our hair, then we three females would don aprons and do the week's washing—sheets, pillow cases, towels, Daddy's long winter underwear, table linen, blankets, everything—and hang it out on the roof, one flight up. Often it was so cold that everything froze stiff, and to remove a rigid sheet from a line in a strong north wind on a New York rooftop is something of an experience. Connie and I did the hanging out—assisted by Blinkie—while Mother mopped floors and cleaned the bathroom. Afterward, we would turn to and polish silver and run the vacuum. Father hated these domestic chores and would escape to the club as soon as his morning's literary stint was finished.

Mother used to see him go with frank relief. "Children,

whatever you do, don't marry a man who works at home. Marry one who goes to work at eight every morning and doesn't come home till five." In spite of that sensible advice, I married a singer-musician and a writer. As for my sister, who eventually married the desirable office-goer, she complains because he isn't home enough.

Beaux had begun to appear on the scene. Connie was too young, of course, but she did not think so and was more and more omnipresent. When callers came for me and she determinedly took over the scene, I could have wrung her neck.

My first New York escort was the son of one of Mother's friends, and the event, as I recall, was a trip to the movies and a Luxuro ice cream cake at Schrafts afterward, all arranged by our two mothers. He was a tall, burly youth with a thatch of dark hair and he was "a college man." I was thrilled, remembered my mother's advice, hung on his every word, and was promptly invited out again.

This young man was, by the way, the one who, chatting with my mother about a possible career, said he rather thought he would like to be a writer. "I can write all right," he said gloomily. "The trouble is I can't think of anything to write about."

It was, thank heaven, before the time of that social abomination known as "going steady," and before long I had, through various channels, collected an assortment of young men who could be counted upon to make my free time pass pleasantly. There was always an undergraduate or two to share our Sunday roast chicken and ice cream. Apropos of the chicken, it was always a small one, and in the division I wound up with a tiny sliver of white meat and a wing. I used to beg Mother to buy *two* chickens, just once, so that I could have anything but the cheapest of everything. I remember her saying wistfully one day as I helped her make the bed, "If I could only afford to buy the long sheets that tuck in at the bottom and don't pull out."

Poor Mother. It was certainly a school of hard knocks she inherited, but I never heard her complain. It was Father who did the complaining. He hated to have Mother forced to scrimp and save and labor and blamed his lack of moneymaking ability.

"Look at Irving—look at Ernest—their wives don't have to get down on their hands and knees and scrub the kitchen floor. What's lacking in me? What have I done wrong?"

He had done nothing wrong. A good craftsman and in his way a good salesman, he was no financial plunger. His successful friends would now and then put him in the way of some promising stock or real estate deal, but when it came right up to it, Father would buy Government bonds instead.

Father did not take kindly to the invasion of young men, and looking back on it now, I cannot blame him. Our flat was small and already crowded. Add two long-legged youths with big feet and loud laughs, roughhousing with two silly, flirtatious young females, and there was no peace for anyone. Daddy usually went to bed at ten in order to rise at five—his invariable hour for starting work—but on into the night would go the ceaseless grind of the phonograph, the pound of dancing feet, and along about midnight we would all troop down the hall—past Father's door—to the kitchen for nourishment. It was usually cocoa and sandwiches, and that meant pots and pans, crashing and banging, shrieks and muffled guffaws, and then the long noisy trek back to the front of the flat again. Mother's room was separated from the drawing room only by a sliding door. When she got to sleep I cannot imagine, but at least she did not have to get up at five.

Daddy had craftily worked out a scheme of coming to the door of the drawing room about ten with a stamped letter or two in his hand.

"Will one of you young men," he would say pleasantly, "drop these in the mailbox on your way out?"

"Surely, Mr. Garland, be glad to."

The letters would exchange hands, but Daddy would continue to stand there, waiting for the young man to be "on his way out."

One night Evan and I got into real trouble. He had asked me to go with him to Palisades Amusement Park, across the Hudson, and though Daddy was against it, Mother—who was usually on the young side—persuaded him that it would be all right.

We went across on the ferry and spent three delirious hours on roller coasters, merry-go-rounds, shoot-the-chutes and the like, and finally just made the last ferry, which should have brought us home by midnight—the absolute deadline. Unfortunately, the ferry developed engine trouble, and we were several hours in midstream before we could get underway again.

It was half past two when we got off the street car and start-ed running up the street toward the apartment entrance. I had expected unpleasantness but I was not prepared for what I found. Father, fully dressed in hat and overcoat, was standing on the out-side steps, his eyes blazing, his voice harsh with outrage.

"Mary Isabel, where have you been?"

We both started a breathless explanation, but Father seized my arm and thrust me roughly through the vestibule door.

"You go upstairs. You can tell me about it later."

"As for you—" he dismissed the unfortunate youth, "never come to this house again." With which he strode into the vestibule and slammed and locked the door after him.

The elevator did not function after twelve o'clock and here was I, once again, marching in disgrace up the stairs ahead of my father. There was no spanking this time but something even worse—absolute silence. When we reached the apartment, Mother was at the door in her nightgown.

"Darling, what happened? We've been worried."

I stammered out of my story, and she, as always, was quick to understand and forgive, but my father's face was set. Mother told me later that he had been watching out the window from eleven-thirty. "Anything might happen to her in a place like that! Why in God's name did you let her go?" By one he wanted to call the police but Mother persuaded him to wait. She could not stop him, however, from getting dressed and walking the six flights downstairs to wait on the apartment house steps in the lonely dark.

Now he looked at me in a way to chill my soul. "I thought I could trust you," he said, and went heavily down the hall to his room and shut the door.

I went to bed in tears. No coffee in bed the next morning, and when I left for school his door was still closed against me. It was the first time I had left without a parting kiss, and the whole day seemed leaden. At dinner that night he and I were both silent, not looking at each other, while Connie and Mother chatted valiant-ly, but after dinner, when Father had again gone to his room and closed the door, Mother called me out into the kitchen.

"Darling—go in and apologize to your father."

"What for?" I said fiercely. "I told the truth. It was in the paper tonight about the ferry breaking down—"

"I know—"

"He's unfair! He should apologize to me!"

She looked so tired, that darling peacemaker who had to contend with the two of us. She shook her head. "He never will."

"Why not? He's wrong! He's acting like a pig—"

"Yes and he knows it. I can see he is suffering. But it is constitutionally impossible for Hamlin to apologize. Oh, he'll make it up to you in many ways, but he just can't say the words."

"I can't either!"

She brushed my cheek with her lips. "Oh, yes, you can. Women can. You don't want to go on this way, do you? You know how much he loves you, how worried he has been. Go in now and put you arms around his neck and say, 'Daddy, I'm sorry—'"

In the end, still hot with resentment, I did. Father was at his desk and did not look up as I entered. I went behind him and folded my arms under his chin and felt him stiffen.

"Daddy . . . forgive me. I'm—so sorry."

He swung the desk chair around and drew me down into his lap. Nothing more was said, but his arms around me were strong and reassuring, and I could feel the ugliness, like a bad dream, slipping away.

He cleared his throat. I stood up and he turned back to his desk.

"William Gillette offered me a box for *Sherlock Holmes* tonight," he said offhandedly. "Do you think you can make it?"

"Oh, Daddy! Of course."

That was *that* time.[9]

Notes

[1] Garland briefly describes the trip, which occupied the month of July 1914, in *A Daughter of the Middle Border*, 389-391.

[2] In 1907 Garland founded Chicago's Cliff Dwellers, a men's club modeled after the Players Club of New York City, and served as its president. In 1915, tiring of Garland's edict that no alcohol be served in the club, the members passed a resolution barring the president from serving more than two consecutive terms, effectively staging a coup. His ouster from the club to which he had devoted so much time was in large measure responsible for

his decision to move to New York.

³ Isabel refers to Solomon R. Guggenheim (1861-1949) and Irene Rothschild Guggenheim (1868-1954). Their daughter Eleanor was Isabel's friend. In a June 11, 1917, diary entry, Garland mused upon the effect of his children's friendship with one of Chicago's wealthiest families: "The children are having a heavenly time at the Guggenheims. It may be sadly corruptive to them but they are having a taste of the luxury of kings. The Guggenheim place would have scared me to dumbness at their age. They take it all sweetly, joyously and without a trace of awkwardness. I am not sure whether to rejoice or weep over this" (Typed transcript, item 707.1, USC).

⁴ Mark Sullivan (1874-1952) was the editor at *Collier's Magazine* who published the serial version of *A Son of the Middle Border* and later became a columnist for a number of New York newspapers. Sullivan and his wife, Marie, were close family friends.

⁵ Jessica Finch Cosgrave (1871-1949) was the founder and president of Finch School, a preparatory school for women. She was married to John O'Hara Cosgrave (1864-1947), the editor of *Everybody's Magazine*, which published the serial of Garland's novel *The Shadow World* in 1908

⁶ In addition to teaching drama and speech at Finch, Vida Ravenscroft Sutton (1880-1956) was a consultant to NBC in the training of radio announcers.

⁷ Fenton B. Turck (1857-1932), biologist and physician, won acclaim for his research in cell biology. Garland, who had been suffering increasingly from arthritis beginning in 1915, found Turck's treatment to be miraculous and championed Turck frequently among his friends

⁸ Those not previously identified are Carl Akeley (1864-1926), a noted taxidermist who specialized in African mammals; Vilhjalmur Stefansson (1879-1962), an arctic explorer noted for his travels among the Inuit; Edward J. Wheeler (1859-1922), the editor of *Current Opinion*, not *Poetry Magazine*, who was the founding president of the Poetry Society of America. William Dean Howells (1837-1920), preeminent novelist and editor; William Allen White (1868-1944), the owner and editor of the *Emporia Gazette* (Kansas) and author of many books on political and social events; Charles Breasted (1898-1980), the son of noted Egyptologist James H. Breasted and the author of a memoir of his father, *Pioneer to the Past* (1943); Robert Frost (1874-1963), the poet.

⁹ Garland was similarly pained by this episode and described it in his diary for May 27, 1919: "Mary Isabel, against my advice but sustained by her mother, went away to Palisades Amusement Park and did not get home till two o'clock. It all seemed a criminally careless thing to do and I thought how easy it would be for her to go out this way and never come back—as thousands of young girls do every year. I was about to go to the home of the boy's father when I met the children on their way back. They had been held up by the ferry. We have been very happy together, Mary Isabel and I, but I

see she is about to take her divergent path. Her own life with some other man is sure to begin in a year or two more. This was a very painful night for me" (Typed transcript, item 707.1, USC).

6. Onteora

ᨠ ᨠ ᨠ

From a mass of photographs, both studio and snap shots, I see all too vividly how my sister and I looked as we moved through our teens. Neither of us had inherited our mother's perfect features, but in general we were a passable blending of Garland and Taft, Constance blonde, I a brunette. Mother said that when we were born she was in terror that we might inherit Father's big strong hands and feet, but nature was merciful and there was nothing remarkably out of proportion in either of us. We both had a great deal of very straight long hair, which Connie wore spread over her shoulders in a Burne Jones way, while I alternated between a crown of braids and a part straight down the middle of my head, with great, flat, braided rolls wound over my ears. Neither of us had good figures—I was too plump and Connie too thin—but we had small waists and good legs and feet and were more than a little vain of them. Connie's eyes were gray, like Mother's, and mine were Irish blue. Both of our mouths were too small, but lipstick remedied that.

Sartorially, it was an incredibly ugly period. I have a great many pictures of myself turned out in what I considered was exquisite chic, and I truly wonder. Cloche hats down to the eyes, flattened chests, knee-length and very tight skirts, high engulfing coat collars, and pouting, cupid's bow mouths above them. How could our young men face being seen with us? On the other hand, I look around today and shudder even more violently. What about the knobby knees under the mini-skirt, the dirty bare feet in gilded thongs, the flesh-colored, skin-tight capri pants, the bulging bosoms

Isabel (left) and Constance Garland, around 1920.
(*Courtesy of Victoria Doyle-Jones*)

in inadequate brassieres, the forests of plastic curlers above green, orange, and lavender makeup? Someone loves these creatures, one assumes, as one day brave souls loved us.

I remember one particularly humiliating episode. I had been invited to a dance at the Plaza and nothing would do but that I must have a lamé gown—the *in thing* of the season. Mother tried to talk me out of it, but I was stubborn, and eventually the sweet, patient soul abstracted the money from Daddy and went with me to purchase three yards of turquoise and silver lamé and she cut and sewed it to my specification. It was very tight and short and boasted a vast tulle bow low on one hip. With it I wore a silver bandeau, long dangling earrings, ropes of imitation pearls, and baby doll shoes with bows. I felt very chic and sure of myself, and my escort was quite overcome by all the glamour.

Unfortunately, the ballroom was overheated, and as the evening wore on and I went from "cut-in" to "cut-in," a disconcerting odor began to surround me, a metallic scent as of a tea kettle burning dry on the top of the stove. I tried to ignore it, but it became more and more pronounced, and the nostrils of my partners quivered visibly. In desperation, I began making trips to the powder room to pat myself dry and apply powder and perfume—all to no avail. I was just plain hot and the metallic threads of my evening gown proclaimed it inescapably. Eventually, I pleaded a headache and went home in the middle of the evening, and I never wore the dress—or lamé—again.

I remember something else I never wore again. One day on a bargain counter at Macy's I saw a bewitching pair of evening sandals. They were powder blue suede, studded with gold nail heads, and they looked like something worn by Gertrude Lawrence. They were also a size too small, but I could not resist them. I wore them to another dance, and by the end of the evening, feeling like the Little Mermaid dancing on red hot coals, I arrived home in agony and had, literally, to *cut* the wicked things off my feet.

One more story about clothes. I was seventeen, I think, and had been invited to a tea dance—a charming, social custom, by the way. For two or three dollars a young man could take his favorite girl to one of the nicest hotels, sit at a pretty, cozy table over plates of thin sandwiches and cakes and unlimited pots of tea, and, in the intervals of conversation, dance to the strains of some well-known

orchestra. It was all very romantic—and economical—and I wonder if today's bar habitués have half the fun.

Anyway, this time my current beau had sent me an orchid—
representing a flat outlay of about ten dollars in those days. He was
tied up at some broker's office, and I was to meet him and the rest
of the party at our favorite hotel. My coat—a lavish, lynx-trimmed
beige cashmere that had been Mrs. Guggenheim's—lay on my bed,
and in a flurry of haste and excitement, I pinned the orchid to the
collar and swept out of the apartment.

I knew I looked extremely well, and I climbed onto the
Madison Avenue street car with all the aplomb in the world. The
seats were in long rows facing each other, and I sat down smugly in
the middle of one row and looked across in the certainty of finding
admiring eyes raking me from head to foot. They were raking all
right, but to my amazement it was not admiration but out and out
laughter. Well-bred ladies tittered behind their gloves, men
grinned, boys and children stared and guffawed, and I grew hot
with incredulous embarrassment. What could be wrong?

Involuntarily, I glanced down. There, spread across my lap,
dangling tastefully from the pin that held the orchid, was a suit of
my mother's cotton underwear!

I arrived at the party almost hysterical with laughter and
launched into my tale. The other guests didn't believe me.

"It wasn't! . . . Then what did you do?"

"What could I do? I unpinned the thing, rolled it up, and
stuck it inside my coat sleeve and glared around, daring anyone to
laugh at me again."

"You're spoofing—"

"Am I? Then what do you say to this?" I pulled one of my
mother's most private garments from my wide coat sleeve and
waved it triumphantly. Since a young lady did not ordinarily go
out to a tea dance with a suit of her mother's underwear up her
sleeve, it was a gratifying moment.

The explanation was simple. My coat had been thrown
over piles of clean, folded laundry lying on the bed, waiting to be
put away, and I had inadvertently pinned the orchid not only
through the coat collar but one of the top garments as well.

ॐ ॐ ॐ

The summer I was fifteen and Constance eleven, we became involved in another big family adventure. New York in the summer—no one had even heard of air conditioning—was unspeakable. Ninety degree heat and matching humidity day and night wore us down to nubbins. Connie and I slept on the living room floor, wringing cold water out of bath towels and spreading them over the pillows on which we lay gasping. Mother roamed the apartment like a distracted ghost, with a big paper fan which she waved over us now and then. It was brutal, and suddenly Father decided to do something about it. He packed a bag and, with only the sketchiest of explanations, took off.

Three days later, one of those preemptory telegrams of his arrived: "Have taken house for summer. Come at once."

Mother collapsed, as she had in Chicago, and Connie and I were again badly frightened. Mother wept and wept, rolling back and forth on her bed and moaning, "I can't! . . . I won't!" Through frantic questions, my sister and I learned that Onteora Park in the Catskill Mountains was a rich, exclusive community far beyond anything the Garlands could afford, with a frenzied social life that demanded extensive wardrobes and all manner of pretensions.[1]

A second telegram arrived from our adamant father, and once again Mother surrendered and began listlessly to pack. We were a forlorn little group as we waited on the 125th Street pier for the Hudson River Day Boat which would take us to Catskill, where Father would be waiting. The night before had been so hellish that Mother had taken us down to the Battery, where we rode back and forth on the Staten Island Ferry until dawn. Now, all three of us were weak with exhaustion and apprehension.

Astonishingly, the trip up the Hudson was a joy. We sat in the prow of the boat, and the breeze engendered by our movement was warm but tolerable. At Catskill Daddy was waiting, brown as a berry and beaming mysteriously. He loaded our unappealing luggage into a quaint little train that was standing on a siding.

"Just wait," he kept repeating to our excited questions. "Just wait."

He was so obviously bursting with satisfaction that we all

began to take heart. By the time the train had deposited us at the foot of an incline railway that climbed three thousand feet into the heart of the Catskills, we were enchanted, for as we climbed it cooled, cooled! Soon, a light, gentle rain began to fall and the smell of wet foliage filled the air. At the top of the flight, another comic little train, with iron benches in place of seats, awaited us. It was called the "Huckleberry Train," for it transported pickers to the huckleberry fields that covered the mountainsides. Mother revived like a wilted flower, and as we put on sweaters and sniffed the fresh, chill air, we were ecstatic.

And then—the cabin! All Mother's fears of pretentious living were swept away at first glimpse. Such a dear, rustic, tumble-down place, under old apple trees on a hillside of wild flowers. Out of sight or sound of any neighbors, it crouched there happily, looking out over barley fields at the velvet-green Catskill ranges beyond. It was perfect.

Camp Neshonoc, the Garland cabin in the Catskills.
(*Courtesy of Victoria Doyle-Jones*)

Grey Ledge, the Garland home in Onteora, New York.
(*Courtesy of the University of Southern California,
on behalf of USC Libraries Special Collections*)

That night we sat around a roaring fire and sang and gloated and felt ourselves to be the most fortunate on earth. Our bedrooms had wide sideboarding shutters that pushed out and made an overhang, and we slept that night up among the treetops and could almost have imagined ourselves back in West Salem again.

When Daddy asked the next day, as we were all breakfasting out on the porch in the clear, fresh mountain air and sun, "Shall we buy it?" Connie and I screamed with excitement and Mother forgot to look worried. The whole house, adequately furnished, was ours for less than a thousand dollars, and we never had to fear New York heat again.

Everything about Onteora was satisfying. It was a colony of pleasant people, artists, writers, and professors, along with some rich, simple-living people who welcomed us with apparent enthu-

siasm. It was a long, two-mile walk uphill from the cabin to the
Club, the Inn, and the church, but we did it day after day, to play
tennis, to swim, to sing in the choir, to act in the little theater, to go
to the dances and the picnics. We could hardly wait each year to get
up there again, and the minute school closed, we were off. The
thing that made it right was that Daddy was happy there, too.
Climate and working conditions were ideal, and in place of being
buried alive in a sleepy country town, he was surrounded by intelligent, sophisticated people who gave him the intellectual companionship he needed. West Salem faded farther and farther into the
background.

The cabin became the outlet for Daddy's excess energy. The
simplest of wooden structures, nothing could really hurt it; everything was an improvement. Carpentry, by which he had often
earned his living as a young man, was Father's hobby. He was
proud of his skill, and here was an ever-present challenge. With gay
abandon, he built on porches, cut new windows—sometimes it
would be weeks before he got around to setting in the frames—
hung doors, sanded, scraped, and painted. He sent back to West
Salem for his Navajo rugs, and when they were installed and the
place colorful and familiar, he painted a sign, "Camp Neshonoc," in
honor of his native valley in Wisconsin, and nailed it over the front
door.

Miraculously, about this time, our friend and medical scientist, Dr. Turck, invented a serum which he called cytost and which,
through injection, completely eradicated the arthritis from Father's
system. Before long, he was playing tennis with us again, able to
write normally and to share without pain in anything. If we had a
patron saint, it was Fenton B. Turck.

Things were looking up for the Garlands. In fact, in a modest way, they looked so far up that Daddy decided to buy a car.

It was a combination of John Burroughs and the George
Dudleys that did it. Since we no longer visited West Salem, the
Dudleys came to us, proudly, in their brand new car—a formidable
trip in those days. For a few days there were nine of us in Camp
Neshonoc, and the little house palpitated like a Disney cartoon.
It was wonderful fun. Talking constantly of old times, we took
them to paddle in *our* brook, and we had our traditional picnics and
song feasts.

One of Daddy's close literary friends and an object of fervent admiration by the Dudleys was the old naturalist, John Burroughs, whose "Woodchuck Lodge" was forty miles or so from Onteora. One day we all drove over to call. Cars were new and still exciting then, and Daddy and I, sitting in front with Uncle George, were impressed and envious. "Listen to it purr!" Daddy said. "All that machinery going round and round and hardly a sound. And the speed—the convenience!" It was only an hour's trip by car. By train, it would have taken six. I could see the percolation begin in Daddy's brain.

John Burroughs clinched it. He not only had a car, but at seventy-eight, he drove it. In fact, only a few days later he drove it over to see us, sitting up like Santa Claus at the wheel, a nervous secretary huddled beside him.

"All right," said Father, "that does it. If Oom John can own a car and drive it, so can I."

The fact that Uncle John drove it into the barn a few days later and right on out through the back wall, getting only slightly "shook up" in the process, disturbed Father not at all. He had made up his mind.

It was a Ford, naturally, a black, incredible thing, as incongruous among the tall grasses and wild flowers of our hillside as a black beetle on a dining table. Daddy spent hours each day polishing it and "tinkering," as he called it, "with the mixture"—which was possibly why it was always so reluctant to start.

Daddy and I both took lessons from Fred, the chauffeur of our generous friend, Dr. Jones, and I am frank to admit they did not go well. If I loathed learning to ride a bicycle, I hated even more learning to drive a car. It could have sat there under its tarpaulin till Kingdom Come for all I cared, but again Daddy won out. Neither he nor I was in the least mechanically minded and had only the vaguest idea of why the thing went—or stopped. I was in the back seat one day when Fred was giving Daddy a lesson in the Joneses' driveway. In his nervous excitement, Daddy mistook the gas for the brake and clung to it, while the car went cavorting back and forth from one hedge to another. Fred was not a patient man and he was notoriously profane. Now, as we leapt and crashed and jerked, he shouted at the top of his lungs,

"Damn you, Garland! Get your foot off that gas!"

No "mister," no "please," no respect, just naked self-preservation, and my fiery father took it as meekly as a mouse.

Anyhow, every single afternoon Daddy insisted I get out and drive that car. The steering came easily enough, and when we putt-putted along I quite enjoyed it, but the thing was always breaking down. I never went down the long hill at East Jewett without burning out the brake band and usually low and reverse gear as well. Then it would suddenly cough and die by the side of the road, and Daddy would get out and "tinker," and sometimes it would cough again and start, but more often I had to phone the local garage for help.

It was in the midst of this trying period that I met my first true love. Joe drove a red Stutz roadster and wore white linen suits and a dashing panama hat.[2] He had brown curly hair, dimples, and mischievous brown eyes, and he was very, very beautiful and charming.

We were both sixteen, but he was a wealthy, worldly young man, and we both considered him vastly sophisticated. It began as another mother-to-mother arrangement, but it wasn't long before we were romantically involved, and then there were two people who were not happy. One was my small sister, who was as much in love with Joe as I was. The other was my father. In fact, Father put his foot down. I was not to go driving with Joe at night unless Constance went with us. Connie was overjoyed, but Joe and I were not. We had been in the habit of finding a romantic parking place, and it was on a mountain top overlooking the Hudson River Valley that I received my first kiss. I mean, there had been dozens of fleeting smacks, but this one was a revelation and I was quite ready for more. But there was Connie. To be sure, we put her on the outside, so that I was, at least, squeezed close to Joe, but it was a poor substitute. The night drives tapered off, and though we still swam and played tennis and held hands in the movies, other opportunities were few and far between.

I took it hard. I used to sit in my bedroom in the dark, weeping, listening for the sound of his car passing on the road, torturing myself with the thought of the girl who was undoubtedly sitting in my place. Joe, for all the attraction I had for him, was not one to repine. I remember a costume birthday party his mother gave him at which a wretched blonde dressed as a baby doll wound my happy-go-lucky friend around her little finger. That night Connie was as indignant for my sake as I was.

Fortunately, as I said before, this was not a time of "going steady," and though my heart was more or less broken, I had other beaux and many gay times. One of my favorites was Ira Morris, and our mothers hoped for a time that something might come of it, but it didn't. Another was Arthur, a strange, handsome, six-foot-four lad I had known since childhood in Chicago and who now was going to Princeton. Arthur had a great deal of money and used to take me to the opera night after night and try to instill a little musical education. To dance with him was an experience I am glad I do not have to repeat. He was so very tall that my face came to about the middle of his chest, and that was the period when the men held you bent backward while they curled over you from above. I used to wonder if I would ever be able to straighten myself up after Arthur released me. I loved Arthur but not passionately, and he was half in love with me and half in love with my beautiful cousin, Emily Taft, who was older than I and preparing to be what I wanted to be—an actress.[3]

She stayed with us all one winter in New York in the bleak, dreadful maid's room off the kitchen, studying at the Sargent School of Dramatic Art in the daytime and cheerfully doing her practicing and exercises in her cold little cell at night. She had one outfit, as I recall—the Tafts as well as the Garlands were having a financial struggle—a dark blue serge dress, with which she wore a long string of huge, red wooden beads that reached to her knees. I thought it was fearfully chic and inspired and had a yearning for one exactly like it.

When Emily finished her course—which I took vicariously by hanging around and absorbing everything she said and did—she tightened her belt and gamely started on the rounds of the theatrical agencies. She was a very pretty girl with a lovely voice and grace and breeding and had been the leading lady in the Chicago University dramatic productions and, by jove, she landed herself a job: as second woman in the Ehlich Gardens stock company!

What excitement—and what anxiety, for, as she confided to my mother, she was supposed to supply her own wardrobe, with the required number of street outfits, sport clothes, evening gowns, negligees, and the like—but she had no money. Once she was

collecting a salary she could afford to buy clothes but in the meantime. . . . Mother begged and borrowed from her rich friends,
bought materials, and cut and sewed, and at last we sent the gallant
girl off with a cheer. When I next saw Emily she was on Broadway,
replacing Florence Eldridge in *The Cat and the Canary*, and was a real
professional by then. It was all to serve her in good stead when she
left the stage and became interested in politics. Now, as the wife of
Paul Douglas, she is a splendid public speaker and a wise and witty
woman.

After Emily left, Uncle Henry B. Fuller came from Chicago
to stay with us in the same mouse hole behind the stove. The
friendship between the shy, ghostlike, little intellectual and my
ruddy, virile father had deepened through the years, and Daddy
was frankly dependent on Henry B. in everything he wrote. Henry
B.'s literary taste and knowledge were impeccable, and he was as
much interested in Daddy's career as his own. The letters that
passed back and forth between New York and Chicago—now in the
Hamlin Garland Papers at the University of Southern California—
are absorbing lessons in literary craftsmanship and would lend
themselves, I would think, to publication. Henry B. was a stern critic, nothing escaped him, and Daddy was a dogged perfectionist,
more than willing to write and rewrite to reach the most effective
presentation.

Ostensibly, Uncle Henry B. was with us to help Father in a
literary way and enjoy some of the stimulus of New York, but there
was also his long-time devotion to Mother and his insatiable interest and curiosity in what was happening to "the girls"—Connie and
me.

We always served afternoon tea on Sundays, and our young
men would come about five to eat puffy cheese toast and oatmeal
cookies and make conversation until it was time to take us out to
dinner. Uncle Henry B. joined us only briefly, but I soon realized
that when he had ostensibly departed to the back of the flat, he had
actually slipped into an adjoining room and was sitting there in the
dark, listening to every word we said. I don't think the boys ever
knew it, and Connie and I were so devoted to Uncle Henry B. that
it only amused us. We weren't saying anything we shouldn't; the
conversation with the four of us was general, if juvenile, but it
seemed to fascinate our literary friend. Now and then I'd hear his

breathy little laugh echo something amusing that one of us had said.

The next day he would catechize us gently. Which boy did we like best? What was Paul going to do when he left college? Did we think Robin was handsomer than Toby? What were our favorite dance tunes? He had all our admirers catalogued in his mind and an almost feverish interest in all of them. Where Father looked daggers at each arrival and sped him on his way as soon as possible, Uncle Henry B. would inquire eagerly who was coming this night— and where had we gone with John and Charles the night before? His questions, though prying, were so delicate that we gave him full reports on everything—something we never could have done with Father.[4]

My little sister was growing up, and a predatory kitten she turned out to be. While I was going off to college football games and proms at Princeton, Harvard, and West Point, she was answering the telephone in my name and inviting any disappointed young man to come up and have tea with *her*. Not content with her own "minnow fleet," she wanted everyone I had as well, and as time passed she grew more and more successful and relations between us more and more strained. Leave the room for five minutes and when you came back you would find her cuddled up beside the newest conquest on the couch, tossing her long, golden locks and playing flirtatiously with his necktie. We had some sharp words now and then, though our basic devotion still held.

But one night she went too far. I had a midshipman beau at Annapolis, a stunner in all his handsome trappings. He was at the time my "great occasion" beau, and I remember Army and Navy games and the balls afterward and the ride home in his arms in an ice-cold taxi, round and round the park. The lower vestibule was a semi-dark place to linger for another kiss or so, till Blinkie, on the seventh floor, would sense that I had arrived downstairs and start up a furious, tell-tale yapping. I wore John's class ring and we were almost—but not quite. Father, of course, was nervous as a cat and as rude to the young man as he dared to be. (He was also hatching in his mind something that would put an end, at least temporarily, to all this.)

Anyhow, I had my glamorous beau. I also had one of the most dramatic dance gowns in the world, thanks to Aunt Irene.[5] It was vastly full black velvet, cut devastatingly low and square, the neck and hem faced with pink satin, the cap sleeves banded in sable. In it, I knew I could not fail—at least, I never had. The frock, my treasure, hung in a garment bag at the far side of my closet and I would look in now and then to be sure it was there.

This night Connie and I were going out separately, I to dinner and the theater, she to go supper dancing later on. As I was dressing and she was lying on the bed watching me, she asked, idly, "Are you going dancing anywhere afterward?"

"Yes, I know we are, because we're going with Bob's sister and her husband to the Roosevelt after the theater. Why?"

"Oh, I just thought Toby and I might join you."

"Why not? We'll look for you in the Roosevelt Grill around eleven."

Bob's sister didn't wish to go to the Roosevelt Grill and said so, and as she was from out of town, the choice was hers. I was sorry to leave Connie high and dry, but after all, she and Toby had planned to be alone anyhow, and so we decided to go to the Plaza Grill instead.

And there, as we came down the steps, in the middle of the floor, waltzing for dear life—like Anna and the King of Siam—was my sister . . . in my black velvet dress . . . with my midshipman!

It took her days to explain and she never did, quite. She *said* John had phoned after I left for dinner and had sounded so disappointed that she had taken pity on him, cancelled out on the faithful Toby, and suggested John take her out instead. The dress she could not explain—except that it was there and so beautiful and smart and she had wanted to make a dazzling impression. Which was why she had carefully discovered that I and my party would be safely bestowed in the Roosevelt Grill before she took it out of the bag! I don't say that I never trusted her again, but it was hard and it grew harder.

Aside from my sister's companionship and despite all our troubles, we were really very close. I had several admired and adored friends. One, Edith Shearn, several years older than I, was a raving beauty.[6] Except for Madeline Carroll, I have never seen such harmony in a girl before or since, and all of it completely natural. Her face was a perfect madonna oval, her eyes were huge, wide-set, gray-blue under long, improbable lashes. She had gleaming, curling, silver-gilt hair that had never seen a rinse, flawless classic features, and a slim, graceful body to match. She was brilliant, a Phi Beta Kappa; she was modest and an utter darling. And her favorite hobby was mountain climbing.

Her father was a distinguished judge, her mother a merry Southern belle, and they both liked young people. Some of my most memorable dinner parties were at the Shearns' where I met Edith's brother, Clarence, and a succession of interesting and attractive young men. Edith, thus far heart-whole, was as generous as she was exquisite and cheerfully shared her admirers with the rest of us. Through her I embarked on my next romantic adventure.

He was lithe, he was handsome, he wrote poetry and plays, and he was the captain of the fencing team at Harvard, of which Clarence was also a member. Edith and I went up to Cambridge for one of the matches, and it couldn't have been better. Strictly speaking, Burke was Edith's escort and Clarence mine, but brother and sister were deeply fond of each other, and there were times when Burke and I seemed to be suspended somewhere together in glittering timelessness.

Cambridge was snowbound, and for all my country living I had never seen a village buried in white before. We all wore boots and heavy coats and tramped along under the snow-covered branches between huge walls of ice, talking, laughing, quoting poetry, flirting with life and each other, confident that because the moment was so desirable, the future must be too. Sitting, watching the boys at swordplay, it was easy for me to dream myself back to *The Idylls of the King* or the days of D'Artagnan. Very heady brew. Happily, I came out of that one unscathed.

My other particular friend, my lifelong friend, was Anya Seton, Ernest Thompson Seton's daughter, a black-haired beauty with a talent for trouble. We had met first at about three months of age or thereabouts, and for years a good-humored feud went on between Daddy and Uncle Ernest as to which child was the more precocious, the better behaved. Up until ten or twelve, I was jealous and heartily disliked the whole idea of Anya Seton and put up a graceless howl when my parents informed me she was coming to spend a week with us in West Salem.

"You are going to be nice to her," my mother said firmly, just before the train arrived. "You are going to share everything and make her happy. It is important to Hamlin. He and Uncle Ernest are very close, you know."

They were indeed as close as brothers for many years. What happened between them that ended their long companionship? There were years, after we moved to New York, that we never saw Uncle Ernest, never heard his name mentioned. Anya and I have since puzzled over it, and the diaries give no hint. In their later years, as elderly gentlemen, they had a brief meeting in our home in Hollywood, but there were other people there and the talk was impersonal. I know that Father felt that Uncle Ernest had gone a bit too far in his enthusiasm for Red Indian culture and philosophy, but what was the initial cause of their estrangement I have no way of knowing.

The time, however, he brought his daughter to West Salem, and he and Daddy promptly disappeared upstairs into the study. Mother was occupied with Connie, and Anya and I stood and scowled at each other in the middle of the drawing room. She was pretty, I had to admit, with Uncle Ernest's coal-black hair and her mother's lovely skin and features, but her mouth was as sullen as mine and she looked around her as if she was trapped in some unspeakable hole.

Then I had an inspiration. "Do you ever read?"

Her eyes flashed. "Do I ever read!" she repeated scathingly. "Why, that's just about all I ever do. I *hate* sports and things!"

"So do I." My spirits rose. I waved a hand at the bookcases lining the room. "Do you think you could find something you want to read there?"

"I know I could." She was on her knees in front of the shelves, selecting, discarding, and in a minute or two she was up, her arms full of books. "Now—show me where to go so I can be absolutely alone."

Better and better—but I hesitated. "Mother said I was supposed to—"

"Play with me, I suppose." She made a face. "I don't want to play with you and you don't want to play with me—so let's get on with our reading."

Mother, coming to look for us an hour or so later, found us stretched out on our beds in our separate rooms, with the doors shut and locked, and there we stayed for the major part of Anya's visit. When Anya left, she told mother she had had a "splendid time" and I could echo her. She was the ideal guest.

Years later, after a visit of mine to Anya's home, she paid me, on leaving, a supreme compliment.

"I hate to have you go," she said fondly. "You're almost as good as being alone."

After we moved to New York, we spent many happy weekends at the Seton place in Greenwich. By this time, Anya and I had begun to trust each other. Not only were our bedroom doors left open, but we took to reading books together up in the haymow on long, hot summer afternoons. The first book we read together was Rider Haggard's *She*, and if mine was an overcharged imagination, hers was more so. The perception and skill that produced *Dragonwyck* and *Katherine* was already evident, and I listened goggle-eyed. Anya was also, from my point of view, amazingly knowing and sophisticated and would let fall provocative, incomprehensible remarks that left me with an uneasy wish to know more.

When we were about seventeen, we had a never-to-be-forgotten weekend in the new house that Uncle Ernest had just finished building on his private lake. To the Garlands it was unbelievably luxurious, and Daddy was green with jealousy. He had never been able to match his two closest friends, Ernest Thompson Seton and Irving Bacheller, in income, and as he watched their magnificent stone houses rise, his own self-respect dwindled. He even came to look down on our beloved Camp Neshonoc, and frank financial gloom possessed him.

On this particular weekend, except for the housekeeper, our elders were all away, and Anya and I and three dashing young men held high carnival. From Friday afternoon to Sunday night we did not bother to go to bed at all, and I remember it as a time of breathless excitement and discovery. All, I might add, without the benefit of alcohol or even coca-cola. Anya was falling in love with one of the young men—who later became her husband—and that left me with the two discarded suitors. We sailed and swam and canoed and danced and someone taught me to drive a jeep. We lay on the floor in front of the fire and ate wonderful food that was put before us at intervals and talked and planned and dreamed. It was as perfect in its way as the Harvard weekend, without a sour note, till

Anya confessed later that at the end she had been consumed with jealousy because *her* young man elected to escort me back to New York.

I think this was the year *A Daughter of the Middle Border*—after seven complete revisions—came out.[7] Its reception by the critics was flattering, but even more so was the news that reached us in Onteora announcing that Father had been elected to the American Academy of Arts and Letters. He was also to win the Roosevelt Medal,[8] but I know that nothing could equal his satisfaction in the Academy membership. Among the gray-headed "Immortals" he told us he felt almost boyish, but with his customary zest and drive, he at once plunged headlong into Academy affairs and proved himself invaluable. It was his idea to give an award for the best voice and diction on the radio, and it was largely through him that Archer Huntington undertook to house the Academy suitably and put up the money to build the handsome stone building it occupies high up on the banks of the Hudson.[9]

Notes

[1] In July 1917 Garland arranged to buy a dilapidated cabin on the outskirts of Onteora, New York, an exclusive residence community. He paid $1,000 for it and named it "Camp Neshonoc," after the Wisconsin valley of his youth.

[2] Joseph Wesley Harper (1903-1963), great-grandson of one of the founders of Garland's publishers, Harper and Brothers, whom Constance would marry on September 12, 1927.

[3] After studying at the American Academy of Dramatic Arts, founded by Franklin Sargent, Emily Taft (1899-1994) performed in a road production of *The Cat and the Canary* (1922-1924), later married Paul H. Douglas, and was elected to the U.S. Congress, representing Illinois, in 1944.

[4] Part of Fuller's unusual interest in the girls' beaux may be explained by his homosexuality, though Isabel likely never knew of his sexual orientation.

[5] That is, Irene Guggenheim.

[6] Edith Shearn was the daughter of Clarence Shearn, a former justice of the New York Appellate Court who resigned to become William Randolph Hearst's lawyer.

[7] Isabel is confusing the events surrounding *A Son of the Middle*

Border with *Daughter*. In 1917, after multiple revisions, Garland published *Son*, which was a critical triumph. He was thereafter elected to the American Academy of Arts and Letters in 1918. *Daughter* was published in October 1921.

[8] In 1931 Garland received a gold Medal of Honor from the Roosevelt Memorial Association for "distinguished service in the field of American historical literature."

[9] Archer Milton Huntington (1870-1955), adopted son of the millionaire railroad tycoon Collis P. Huntington, was a noted philanthropist and scholar of Spanish culture. Elected to the American Academy of Arts and Letters in 1919, Huntington was largely responsible for its financial solvency in its early years, donating some three million dollars in operating funds and land between 1913 and 1936.

7. England

※　※　※

The year I was eighteen I graduated from Finch. I had thought of us as a rather attractive group of girls, but our class picture still survives, unfortunately, and I would not show it to a soul. We are wearing the white crepe dresses with long, floating panels that each graduate was required to make for herself, and we are bowered in flowers and looking pretty smug. As my last dramatic appearance, I played the lead in Maeterlinck's *Sister Beatrice* in the romantic setting of George Gray Barnard's 14th Century Cloisters. I may say, modestly, that I received a handsome volume for the best scholarship and the proud honor of a private recital of dramatic readings and piano excerpts with one of my classmates. Father, of course, attended and beamed. I had eleven boxes of flowers, many fond well wishers, and a general feeling that LIFE as one hoped it would be was about to commence.

It did. Fortune smiled and Father's dearest dream came true. Not only did he sell a number of his novels to the motion pictures, but his *A Daughter of the Middle Border* won the Pulitzer Prize.[1] Now he could see his financial way clear to take us all to England. Aside from the artistic and historical value of the trip, it would remove Connie and me from the circle of young men who were occupying most of our time. As it happened, we were both "out of love" temporarily and accepted the idea with enthusiasm. Mother, who had to provide all our clothes and look forward to another of the social rounds she dreaded, was less radiant but as always was a good sport.

Finch School Graduation, 1921. Isabel is seated, far left.
(*Courtesy of Victoria Doyle-Jones*)

Daddy, with a constitutional objection to sea voyages, sailed first by the short Canadian route to locate a flat in London and get in touch with the various literary and artistic friends he wanted us to meet. Half of Father's heart was in the British Isles, and from earliest childhood we had been familiar with the great names in contemporary English literature. The thought that we were actually to see and speak with Shaw, Barrie, Hewlett, Kipling, Conrad, and others almost equally well known was wildly exciting. Any misgivings we might have had were swept away in the cordial warmth of the letters that traveled back to us across the Atlantic in response to Daddy's announcement of our coming.

Mother worked like a beaver and, our three wardrobes assembled, she and Connie and I sailed on a small British liner.

It was a ten-day passage; there were only eighty passengers on board, and twenty of them were dashing young Englishmen, the members of a visiting cricket team!

It was our first sea voyage. To save money, the three of us shared a tiny, inside cabin with a very fat, sick, old woman who lay all day groaning in her bunk, but as we rarely came down for anything but a bit of exhausted sleep, it didn't matter. Connie and I had the time of our lives. We didn't have to go to England; England was presented to us on a platter. I have never had so much attention before or since, and I think of today's "going steady" young people with bewildering pity. Connie, as I kept reminding her, was actually still a child, but she flirted as madly as I did and worked up a secret passion for the ship's sexy young violinist, while I went from one gay kiss to another. It was on this voyage that I lost my midshipman's class ring and told myself that I would have to marry John to make up for it, except that one of the ship's officers told me it was possible to have class rings made up by the gross.

Thanks to Father, I was prepared to love England the moment I set foot there, but the railroad hotel in Liverpool took care of that idea. Sleeping three in a single bed to keep warm, amid the clamor, the smoke, and the grit, we would have taken the ship back home that very night. Mother and Connie and I all wept, and an almost inedible breakfast did its bit. The train trip down to London, through cold, gray rain, in an icy, third-class railway compartment, contributed its share of disillusion, and it was a drab trio that greeted Daddy at Paddington Station.

Father had worked out an act. "Yes," he said soberly, regretfully. "I've found a flat. It isn't much, I am afraid. You know we have to pinch pennies. . . . The district isn't the best. . . . The furniture . . . well, wait and see. I imagine it will do us if we are not too particular."

His three women, the hotel in Liverpool clear in their minds, exchanged unhappy glances. We hardly bothered to look out at Old London in its pall of smoke and mist. Father and Mother chatted of practicalities, but Connie and I sat in wretched silence. We wanted to go home.

Daddy enjoyed his joke, and before long, we did, too. The flat was in a handsome building across from Albert Hall, with Kensington Gardens only a block or so away. The elevator man, in frock coat and white gloves, took us up to the third floor in a gilded wire cage elevator, and the apartment door was opened by a smiling, pleasant lady in a big, white apron, who bobbed a curtsey.

"I'm Curzon, mum. Did you have a good trip?"

We stared about us with our mouths open. The rooms were large, high-ceilinged, and beautifully furnished. Ancestral portraits hung on the walls, red brocade draperies were half drawn against the gray London sky, and a fire blazed behind burnished brass andirons. A tea table with a lace cloth was drawn up before a big, comfortable, chintz-covered couch, and a white kitten slept delicately on a velvet cushion on the hearth.

Daddy could hardly contain his triumph. "Like it, daughties? Like it, Zulime? You don't mind my little joke, do you?"

Mother was laughing and crying. "It's heaven! Hamlin, you are a wretch!"

"Daddy, you're wonderful!" the daughters cried, hurling themselves on him. The Garlands were at home in London.

That first night, at dusk, a little before closing time, we walked through the gates of Kensington Gardens and entered upon "The Baby Walk" that led to the banks of "The Round Pond." Connie and I were breathless with anticipation. It was all here, as Barrie had described it, as Arthur Rackham had illustrated it. No need to say that we knew *Peter Pan* by heart, and it was like walking on hallowed ground.

We stood in awed silence, looking up at the sprightly little figure of Peter—not my idea of that magnificent elf at all—while around us in the dark sounded the clanging bells of the caretakers announcing the closing of the gates. As we moved, reluctantly, with the other shadowy figures toward the exits, we accepted the fact that no one could intrude on them except Sir James Barrie himself, who was the only private person in the world with a key to the Gardens. Any night, at any hour, Father told us, Barrie was privileged to turn his gold key in the lock and reenter the enchanting world his genius had evoked.

The next morning, hardly waiting to catch our breaths, we embarked on an intensive round of sightseeing. I have said it before but I must say it again, Father's energy and enthusiasm were phenomenal. Even in his old age, after a long day's motoring or social engagements, he would come down to dinner, fresh and rosy, demanding, "Well, what shall we do this evening?"

In London he was in his element, and there never was a more stimulating guide. He knew that I was deeply moved by historical association, and when he found me in tears beside the tomb of Mary Stuart, his arm went around me in complete understanding. What he said was, "Daughtie, there was a note from Maurice Hewlett in the mail this morning. I'm going to take you down to call on him next Friday." He was well aware that my two favorite books in the world were *The Queen's Quair*, by Maurice Hewlett, and his magnificent study of Richard the Lion Heart, *Richard Yea and Nay*.[2]

Two nights later we sat under the great oaks in Hyde Park and watched a performance by the Stratford Players of *A Midsummer Night's Dream*. Midway, a gentle rain began to fall, but we were all so caught up in the play's magic, in the perfection of its setting, that not a member of the audience made a move to leave.

Our first weekend in England we spent with Sir Arthur and Lady Conan Doyle. Sir Arthur and Daddy had been friends for years, though they parted ways on the spiritualistic line, and we were all devoted to Sherlock Holmes.[3] It was a memorable moment to descend from the train at Crowborough.

The weather was perfect, the countryside was perfect, and Sir Arthur, big, burly, ruddy, and good-humored, was perfect, too. The house was a rambling, many-windowed place that looked out on the rolling hills of Southern England, and so quickly did we feel at home that we might have been staying with any of our well-to-do American friends. Lady Doyle was gracious, intelligent, and two of the boys were there and promptly took Connie and me in charge.

The Doyles had recently returned from America, where the boys had been presented with a pair of large black snakes, which they wore casually draped about their necks. We were finally persuaded into touching the snakes and were surprised to find them warm and firm, not slithery, nor slimy at all. We would not agree to trying them on, however, and during the night I kept an apprehensive eye fixed on the ventilating slit under the door.

Morning brought our first experience with English tea and thin-sliced bread and butter in bed; the pretty, pink-frocked and mob-capped maid was straight out of Dickens. After a lavish English breakfast, Sir Arthur drove us to Battle Abbey and the field of the battle of Hastings. Sir Arthur knew the owner, and we were free to wander where we liked through the wonderful historic old fortress. It was our first castle and a thundering success. On later trips, I became somewhat of an authority on castles, but the six-foot-thick walls and steep, narrow winding stairways of Battle Abbey had a tremendous impact.

I think here is the time to try to describe in some detail this company of Americans descending on the literary lights of England in the summer of 1922. I cringe at the memory but also remember with gratitude that not once were we made to feel anything but admirable and welcome.

In the van would be Daddy, a striking figure, unquestionably, with his thatch of gray hair, his round, bright eyes, the sweeping mustache under a wide-brimmed black hat. He carried a cane, for the fun of it, and used it to point at striking vistas.

Close beside him was Constance, still too young to have the emotional response that was mine with four more years of history and poetry though she was intent and impressed nevertheless. She usually wore a simple homemade cotton dress, over which she buckled a too-wide black patent leather belt, cinched so tightly that she could scarcely breathe in order to show off her small waist. Over that was a shapeless gray coat, and atop her long, streaming hair was a shiny, gray pudding-bowl hat that came down to her eyebrows and was overweighed on one side with a huge cluster of grosgrain ribbon almost as large as the hat itself.

Immediately after came Mother, beautiful but ridiculous in a great straw cartwheel hat with too many iridescent bird's feathers on it, wearing a blue silk polka-dotted dress and a dangling lace jabot. Mother always seemed to have a navy and white polka-dotted dress, and it was probably the same one.

In the rear of the procession, mooning along in a semi-daze, came a singular apparition. Mother had happened into Harrods when a gigantic sale of Black Watch tartan was on at approximately twenty-five cents a yard. It was strong, handsome stuff and she bought a lavish seven yards of it and made me an outfit. It was exactly what I wanted. The skirt was tight and came almost to my ankles. There was a plain, dark blue jersey overblouse and on top of that the most dashing and enormous cape you ever saw. The collar was stiffened with buckram and stood up high and ended in two scarves that fell down to the hem of the skirt in front. There were four long points behind that waved effectively as I walked, and with gauntlet gloves, all I needed was a sword on my hip to be the very embodiment of romantic swagger. Lacking a sword, I had a hat that did it. It was black, down to my nose, of course—all hats had to be in those days—and from one side hung a wide knotted silk veil that could either swing free, adding to the Winged Horse effect of my progress, or—shades of Fatima and Mata Hari—be artfully looped across to the other side and anchored either under the chin or under the eyes. Well!

Imagine you are a quiet, well-bred English literary man, in your quiet, well-bred English country house, and you see the local taxi stop at your rose-bowered gate and spew out this group. Wouldn't you be tempted to scream and run? Or barricade yourself in your library? Not at all. You are prepared. There is your old friend, Garland, in the lead of what is obviously his family. Open the door and make them all welcome. But whoever in the world designed that preposterous tartan outfit?

I did. I loved it. In it I felt secure—siren and D'Artagnan at the same time. I made my best conquests in that outfit. What a woman is supposed to feel in a sable coat, I felt in about two and a half dollars' worth of hard-textured, blue and black and green Highland wool. I wish I had it today.

I wore it, inevitably, when Daddy and I went down to see Maurice Hewlett. He lived not far from Salisbury Cathedral, which we visited first, and as that, except for Westminster Abbey, was my first cathedral, I was speechless. My soul soared with the spire. On later trips, I became choosey about cathedrals, but on that day Daddy and I were completely satisfied. We lunched in a dim English pub, where I struggled manfully with a mug of ale and a pork pie, and about the middle of the afternoon we took a taxi out over the moors to the cottage where Maurice Hewlett was living alone. I remember Father held my hand encouragingly.

Hewlett had seen the taxi and came to open the door of a small, low-roofed farmer's cottage. He was tall and excessively thin—a sick man, I learned later—but his face was the face of an artist, lean, sensitive, gray mustached. His voice was beautiful and his choice of words a delight. He seemed genuinely pleased to see us.

He told us that a woman from the neighborhood came in three days a week to clean up and cook for him, and she had left a simple tea under a clean cloth on the table. Hewlett himself heated the water, brewed the tea, and served us. His eyes were astonishing, large and very brilliant, and his neat goatee gave him a cavalier look. I have his photograph beside me as I write, one he autographed for me that day, and my copy of *The Forest Lovers*, in which he inscribed, "Record of a charming visit." He posed for me patiently while I directed my little camera at him, the cottage, the hills beyond, and all the time he talked, wonderful talk, full of medieval music. If I could only bring it back!

I think Hewlett quite enjoyed being worshipped. I may have been inarticulate but certainly my eyes spoke, and Daddy had warned him of my fervent admiration. There is no minimizing the influence Maurice Hewlett had on my life. I shall be a romantic till the day I die.

(It was a bitter disappointment to find that the shutter of my camera had stuck open that day, and not one of the pictures came out. It was doubly bitter when I heard of Maurice Hewlett's death a few months later. To my mind there has never been anyone with the imagination, the quality, to take his place.)

Father has written in detail of our many meetings that eventful summer, but there are some I personally wish to relive. If Hewlett to me was supreme, both Connie and I agreed that Sir James Barrie came next. Aside from *Peter Pan*, we knew a great deal of what he had written. We had seen every Barrie play produced in New York, and at Finch I had acted in many of them. Barrie and Father had been friends for years, and one of the first invitations that came to us in London was one asking the whole Garland family to come down and spend a few days with Barrie in Stanway Castle.[4]

We were going to live in a castle! Connie and I were enraptured. Mother was worried because Barrie's hostess and chatelaine was Lady Cynthia Ashley, an aristocratic beauty who had been born in that very castle. It meant that we would be expected to dress for dinner, and we consulted anxiously on the subject. Fortunately, I had my white crepe graduation dress, and Constance and Mother both had suitable hand-me-downs from the Guggenheims. Daddy was always happy to don a dinner jacket, and so, in a measure of poise, we departed by train.

A limousine and uniformed chauffeur met us at the station, and a ten-minute drive brought us alongside a high stone wall set with formidable gates, now open wide, giving a vista of bright green lawns stretching away as far as the eye could see. We swept in under a beautiful old archway and around a drive to the front of a low, mellow-stoned castle as romantic as a dream.

A butler received us and escorted us through long, stone-walled and -floored hallways, up innumerable winding steps to two luxurious suites that opened on a succession of exquisite formal gardens.

"When you are ready, if you will ring, I will show you the way downstairs," the butler said with a faint smile. "It is rather difficult to find the first time. Lady Ashley and Sir James are waiting for you in the Garden Room."

Difficult! It was almost impossible. Connie and I were always getting lost and turning up in extraordinary places. The bathroom alone was a safari; up and down tiny winding stone staircases and along portrait-hung corridors, and when you reached it, the room was as large as our own bedroom. Indeed, it had been a bedroom in the days when comfort had another meaning.

That first day, washed and brushed and excited, we followed the amiable butler great distances and down a long flight of steps to a heavily barred door. The butler swung it open.

"Your guests, m'lady."

Barrie jumped from a chair and came toward us, both hands out. "Well, Garland!" he said, with just the right amount of Scotch burr. "Welcome—welcome to you all."

The beautiful, golden-haired lady behind the towering silver tea service smiled and beckoned Mother to a seat beside her. "I'm Cynthia Ashley. Do come and have some tea. I hope you're famished. The scones were made especially for you."

Extraordinary, looking back on it. Here was Father, a farm boy from Midwest America, and James Barrie, a lad from the coal fields of Scotland, having tea in a fourteenth-century castle with a genuine "daughter of a thousand earls."

Barrie was as exactly right in his way as Hewlett had been. He might have walked out of his own Thrums. Short and square, broad shouldered, silent and twinkling by turns, he left no doubt of his liking for us and his deep affection for Father. Smoking, pointing, commenting, he led us over the magnificent estate he had leased from Lady Cynthia, who followed after with Mother, chatting charmingly, quite serene about the whole transaction. Years later, I met her sister, Lady Plymouth, another exquisite English beauty who had fallen on lean days. Yet here at Stanway nothing seemed to have changed since the beginning of time.

The pride of the Castle was the sixteenth-century leaded-glass window that illuminated the Great Hall with a soft golden light. It had been installed in preparation for a visit from Queen Elizabeth, and even in the middle of winter, Barrie told us with delight, "the hall always seems full of sunlight." It was five hundred years since this hall and the great Tithing Barn had been built. Connie and I climbed up to the high musician's gallery and looked down on stone flagging that had echoed to the tread of men in armor. Here in California where our homes are made of lath, black paper, chicken wire, and stucco, what can we know of the long, precious mellowing of centuries?

Our visit went so famously that Barrie insisted we stay on several more days. Mother was doubtful about the imposition, but Lady Cynthia cheered her. "I haven't seen Sir James so happy in months. Do stay. It is doing us all good."

Barrie was a croquet enthusiast, and his croquet ground was a swath of pure velvet, smooth, flawless, that had been cultivated for generations. Connie and I rather fancied ourselves as players, and Mother and Daddy were very skillful, but we all had to give way when Barrie took over. His pipe clenched in his teeth, a plaid cap down over one eye, his face absorbed, he played with complete concentration. At one particularly dramatic moment when my ball, on which he was "dead," blocked his way through a wicket, with great deliberation he removed his jacket, his cap, and his pipe and laid them carefully to one side. Then, with a look round and a brief, "Watch this," he lifted his mallet and brought it down with a sharp crack a little behind the center of his ball. The ball lifted just enough to clear mine and sailed through the wicket without touching either. We all applauded and Barrie blushed like a boy. "That is my best shot," he said smugly.

Whenever Barrie came up to London, he and Daddy would lunch, he came to tea, and one night he came to dine. If we were entertaining the Queen we could not have been more concerned with the menu. Our "Treasure," as Daddy called Mrs. Curzon, looked after us well, but there were certain habits she had that Mother found both amusing and irritating. One was that no matter what we had for dessert, invariably beside the serving dish would appear a large white china pitcher of custard. It was meant to "go on everything" we were told. It might not have been so bad if it had been real custard, but it was, in fact, custard powder and water, a sort of jaundiced-green slop with a slightly nauseating taste. Every night Mother would inspect the table and remove the ugly custard pitcher. The next night it would be back again. As no one took any of it—except presumably Mrs. Curzon—we sometimes wondered whether it was the same custard that had appeared for weeks, or a new and loathsome batch just stirred up.

The night of Barrie's coming, everything was at its prettiest: flowers and candles, embroidered cloth on the table, the best silver and dishes. The Garlands were also in fine fig. We had asked no one else, for we wanted Sir James to ourselves, and he came in full dress, bearing a large box of chocolates and settling down among us as though he had been there always. When dinner was announced, Mother hurried ahead for a last minute look and was relieved to find everything perfection.

Barrie enjoyed his dinner, refused nothing, congratulated Daddy on the wine—Father was becoming a wine connoisseur—and looked with interest at the nut torte Mother was in the process of serving. As she handed him his plate, Mrs. Curzon appeared in the doorway of the kitchen with the familiar white jug on a tray.

Mother glanced up in horror and gave a sharp, dismissive shake of the head, but Mrs. Curzon paid no attention. She went to Barrie's side and set the pitcher down firmly beside his plate.

He looked at it. "What is this?"

"It's custard, sir," she said, tight-lipped.

His face cleared. "Custard? Ah, yes."

Despite our united gasp, he lifted the jug and poured a stream of green glue onto Mother's celebrated dessert. Mrs. Curzon turned with a look of triumph on us all as she stalked back to her kitchen.

That night as he left, Barrie produced a beautifully bound copy of his Balliol College address, *Courage*, and autographed it for Mother, with whom he was much taken.

"For Mrs. Hamlin Garland—a good wife for Hamlin," he wrote in his small, strange hand.

On shipboard, as we sailed for home, a huge, beribboned

box of candy bore a card, "Come back soon. J. M. Barrie." Connie and I dissolved into happy tears.

~ ~ ~

One day Daddy and I went down alone to call on his old friend, Joseph Conrad.[5] I do not remember the station, but beside the platform, in a funny little English car, was a very distinguished foreign gentleman with a trim goatee and round pince-nez glasses hung with a black ribbon who greeted Daddy with warmth and, when I presented my hand, kissed it gallantly. This was Joseph Conrad. Who would have imagined he would be so foreign?

Conrad drove the car himself, with me sitting beside him. He drove furiously, talking all the time, turning around now and then to say something to Father, gesturing constantly with one or both hands. It was a hair-raising trip along country lanes to an attractive house set deep in shrubbery. Mrs. Conrad was in the drawing room, a large, inert woman, a semi-invalid in a big rocking chair. She smiled amiably but seemed to have no particular interest in us, which was just as well, for Conrad never stopped talking. It was good talk, too, for all the Polish accent, and I wish I had had the opportunity to take some of it down. Father always wrote in his diary immediately after he came home, while experiences were still fresh in his mind, but eighteen is a willful, wasteful age, and though he gave me a journal and was constantly after me to keep it, I am afraid I was just too bone-lazy.

Conrad was an expansive host, answering all our questions with wit and good humor. He was excessively gallant to me, Father thought, drawing out my chair, paying compliments, kissing my hand again when we left. Strange that this sea-faring man—who had to *learn* the English language to write it—should turn out to be the picture of an effete European dandy. It was hard to believe that such a man could have written *Lord Jim*.

~ ~ ~

Sometime during the middle of the summer, we had a dramatic experience. One of Father's ardent admirers was the

Maharajah of Jhalawar, a gentleman of great wealth and an enthusiasm for learning.[6] Having met Mother and Father at an Embassy
reception, he promptly purchased every book Father had ever written and had them all bound in handsome red leather crested with
gold. He also invited the entire Garland family to spend a weekend
with him in Oxford, where he and his son, the Crown Prince, were
taking courses in agriculture and farm management. He was an
advanced and far-seeing man who knew that the old ways in India
were going to have to be replaced by new ones.

We had not thus far encountered Oxford and, arriving late
in the afternoon, we were eager to explore but had little time, for we
all met for tea in the lounge of the Mitre Hotel where we were to
stay. The Maharajah turned out to be a small, stocky, pleasant
Indian in the traditional turban and long jacket. His son was also
there, a large, rather beefy and uncommunicative young man, with
his wife, the Princess, a sixteen-year-old Indian beauty who, in her
gauzy sari, might have been straight out of *A Thousand and One
Nights*. There was also a bouncy six-months-old baby in the arms of
a doting amah and a gray-haired Indian gentleman who acted as the
Maharajah's prime minister, with his English wife, also in sari. We
were a colorful group around the tea table.

The Princess spoke hesitant English, and from her we
learned that his highness was giving a dinner party for us that night
in the Mitre but that she herself would not be present. "Women in
India do not go out to dinner in public places," she told us, "but I
and my companion would like to come over to the hotel to watch
you dress." Connie and I were enchanted with her and, though
somewhat surprised at the suggestion, gladly agreed to it.

She arrived about half an hour before dinner and sat in our
room while we put on makeup and arranged our hair. She and her
maid-companion sat side-by-side on one of the beds and watched
us with dark, unwinking eyes as we got into our dinner dresses.
Connie's, I believe, was a pale blue crepe, and mine was bouffant
black taffeta with a big, artificial red rose pinned at the waist.

The Princess gave along, wistful sigh. "Oh, I would *so* like
to have a frock like that!"

Connie and I stared at her and almost laughed aloud. Here
she sat, Eastern allure incarnate, in a rainbow-tinted sari threaded
with gold, a fabulous emerald hung from a glittering chain around

her throat, her slim brown arms weighted down with gold filigree bracelets. She was Scheherazade at the very least, and yet she was envying us our plain, modest garments of blue and black.

It was true, she was not permitted to attend the dinner. We were twelve in the private dining room on the ground floor of the Mitre—nine men and the three Garland women. The Maharajah, his son, and the prime minister were Indian, but the other men were Oxford dons of various ages and interests, all intelligent and charming. Father was given the center of the stage and had a superb time. Mother sat on the Maharajah's right and a handsome pair they made—he in impeccable white, with an intricately wound white turban in the front of which was fixed a mammoth ruby set in an aigrette, and Mother in a blue lace off-the-shoulder gown, holding herself beautifully, as she always did, her gray eyes warm with interest. We were not in the least surprised later on when she told us that the Maharajah had invited us all to visit him in Jhalawar and offered to meet us at the border with a caravan of elephants.

It was a warm summer night and the dining room windows stood open to the night breeze. I was conscious of a steady stream of passersby peering in at us curiously. We must have made a dramatic international picture. I sat on the right of the Crown Prince and found it tough going until I started asking the usual questions and discovered that the young man's enthusiasm was croquet.

"We must have a game tomorrow," he said eagerly. "You are lunching with us at home and we shall play afterward." It was a command, in effect, but liking croquet, I was more amused than otherwise. I was a bit miffed, however, because I had an attractive young don on the other side and would gladly have turned to him, except that the Prince insisted on my attention.

After dinner, the Maharajah proposed a moonlight stroll through Oxford, and though it was almost midnight, six or seven of us set out with him. It was overwhelmingly romantic: the wonderful old city, silent and sleeping, the towers against the moonlit sky, the Maharajah in his turban and jewels leading the way, pointing out memorable vistas. In fact, it was all so overstimulating that it was almost morning before Connie and I could get to sleep.

The next morning the Maharajah sent a car and chauffeur to take us wherever we wished to go, and after the usual sightseeing, we made a call on John Masefield, one of my favorite modern poets and a delightful person, who lived a little way out of Oxford. At one we were driven to the house the Maharajah had rented for his stay in Oxford. It was a conventional middle-class villa, but our Indian friends, while not attempting to change the regulation British decor, had managed to impart an exotic quality of their own. A thing that fascinated my sister and me was the fact that no one was ever permitted to open a door for oneself. As soon as you approached it, it would swing back silently and swiftly, and behind it, flattened against the wall, would be a salaaming native servant. There were ten of us at luncheon at a long table weighted down with embroidered silk, gold service, and towering epergnes of fruit and flowers. A large gaudy macaw roamed at will up and down the table, helping itself to a nut here, a bit of roll there. Behind each chair stood a native servant, and the meal itself was long and represented the very height of Indian culinary art.

The Princess and the prime minister's English wife joined us at luncheon—the Princess this time in a lemon yellow sari worked in silver—and after coffee and liqueurs in the drawing room, the baby was brought in to be admired and passed from hand to hand. It was a large, fine brown baby with what was obviously one day going to be a terrible temper. The Prince seemed to take no interest in his offspring, but the Maharajah beamed and patted the small future rajah on the head.

"Time for croquet now," said the Prince, rising abruptly to his feet. He pointed at me. "You will be my partner and you—" to the prime minister, "will be the partner of the other young lady."

Out we went to the croquet ground, the two exalted Indian gentlemen, my sister and me. The Princess, baby, and amah disappeared. The others preferred to stay and talk with the Maharajah, so there were no other witnesses to what turned out to be one of the more remarkable games.

"You go first," the Prince told me.

"You have to go by the colors on the stake," Connie pointed out. "My sister's green. I'm red, so I go first."

The Prince scowled. "Your sister goes first," he said, and as I sent Connie a swift, warning glance, she subsided sulkily.

I got off to a good start, landing up with my ball directly in front of the first side wicket. Connie moved up confidently and put her ball in place, but the Prince stepped in front of her.

"I play now," he said, knocking Connie's ball out of position and putting his own there.

Connie's jaw dropped. "But—but you *can't!*" she stuttered. "You're *partners!*"

"We're partners, yes," said the Prince, "so now I play." He took careful aim, went through the two wickets, and headed straight for my ball at the side one. "Now, I'll put us both through this wicket and then we go on to the middle—"

My sister was all but dancing with rage. "But that's not right! You have to take turns. Partners *never* play after each other! It's my turn—and then yours—and then his—" She waved at the prime minister who was standing, wooden-faced, at the side of the court. Now he moved forward swiftly and said something in my sister's ear. The Prince was not paying the slightest attention to her. Having got us both through the side wicket, he skillfully set us both in position for the middle one, then he turned to Connie and said with condescension, "You may take your turn now."

Connie swung her mallet. I thought for one heart-stopping moment that she was going to bring it down on the royal head, but with an effort she controlled herself and stalked across to retrieve her ball from the court's edge where it had been sent a few moments before. She was so angry that she muffed the first two wickets and had to go back and get in position for the second one again.

The Prince jeered. "Bad luck." He turned to me. "Now *you* play again. See what a good position we are in?"

I really thought Connie would have a fit. She was only fourteen and she had been brought up in the tradition of fair play and sportsmanship. This high-handed arrogance was simply unbelievable. While she stood there, hunting for words, the prime minister moved closer to her and said something again. She glared at him, at me, and sent a look of death-dealing contempt in the direction of the Crown Prince who, completely oblivious, was smugly studying the advantageous position of our two balls.

Under my sister's withering gaze, I hesitated and the prime minister cleared his throat delicately. "Ah—there are various sets of rules for the game of croquet and his highness, I believe, plays the—ah—other."

It seems hard to credit, but the entire game was played that way. At any moment, when either the Prince's ball or mine was in a favorable position, it was either, "I play now," or to me, "You play now." Connie, baffled and beaten, said not another word. The prime minister was all soft clucks of concern for his own stupidity or outspoken cries of admiration for the royal skill. With no difficulty whatever, we swept round the course, leaving our opponents thoroughly whitewashed.

"Out!" called the Prince triumphantly, sending his ball smartly at the stake. "Let's have another."

My sister and I exchanged speaking looks. "I'm afraid I am developing a headache," she said coldly. "Thank you very much, though. It was—interesting."

When I got her alone, I had to ask, "What in the world did the P.M. say to you when you got so mad?"

Her eyes narrowed. "He said 'no one ever contradicts the Prince. You must play the game his way.'" She drew a deep breath. "And I used to think it would be fun to be a princess."

Notes

[1] In April 1922 Garland learned that *A Daughter of the Middle Border* had been awarded the Pulitzer Prize for biography. Four of Garland's novels were filmed by the Vitagraph Company. *Hesper* was released as *Hesper of the Mountains* on July 31, 1916, directed by Wilfred North. The other three films were directed by William Wolbert: *Money Magic* (February 5, 1917), *The Captain of the Gray Horse Troop* (May 7, 1917), and *Cavanaugh of the Forest Rangers* (1918), remade in 1925 as *Ranger of the Big Pines*, directed by W. S. Van Dyke.

[2] Garland describes the family's meeting with novelist Maurice Hewlett (1861-1923) in *Back-Trailers from the Middle Border* (New York: Macmillan, 1928), 243-246; and, more extensively, in *My Friendly Contemporaries* (New York: Macmillan 1932), 464-469. The full titles of the novels are *The Life and Death of Richard Yea-and-Nay* (1900) and *The Queen's Quair or the Six Years' Tragedy* (1904).

[3] Garland first met Sir Arthur Conan Doyle (1859-1930) in 1893 when Conan Doyle lectured in Chicago. "Lady Doyle" is Conan Doyle's second wife, the former Jean Leckie. After the deaths of his son Kingsley, his brother, and other family members during World War I, Conan Doyle became a devotee of Spiritualism. At the time of their 1922 meeting, Garland was skeptical of the validity of the Spritualists' claims to communicate with

the dead. For Garland's recollection of this meeting, see *Back-Trailers from the Middle Border*, 246-249; *My Friendly Contemporaries*, 476-481.

[4] Garland met James M. Barrie (1860-1937) in 1896 in New York, after Barrie had written to praise *Rose of Dutcher's Coolly*. The Garland family visited Barrie in both 1922 and 1923; while Isabel describes the visit to Barrie's castle as occurring in 1922, Garland places it during the second visit, in 1923. For Garland's account of both meetings, see *Back-Trailers from the Middle Border*, 266-271 (1922), 322-328 (1923); and and *My Friendly Contemporaries*, 419-424 (1922), 522-527 (1923).

[5] Garland had long wished to meet the novelist Joseph Conrad (1857-1924) after Stephen Crane had introduced him to the Polish writer's novels. While in England he wrote to Conrad, who invited Garland and Isabel to visit on July 29, 1922. See Owen Knowles and J. H. Stape, "Conrad and Hamlin Garland: A Correspondence Recovered," *Conradian* 31.2 (2006): 62-78. For Garland's recollections of the visit, see *Back-Trailers from the Middle Border*, 244-246; *My Friendly Contemporaries*, 489-495, 498-502.

[6] Bhawani Singh (1874-1929) became the Maharajah of Jhalawar in 1899. The author of *Travel Pictures* (1918) and other books, Singh was a member of a number of British scholarly societies and had come to England to accompany his son, Rajendra Singh, who was attending New College, Oxford, when the Garlands met him. Other members of his entourage, referred to below, were his son's wife, Brijraj Kunverba; and his legal advisor (whom Isabel refers to as "prime minister"), Shyam Shankar, the father of the musician Ravi Shankar. Garland has described the meeting in *Back-Trailers from the Middle Border*, 234-239; and *My Friendly Contemporaries*, 460-461, 482-486, 536-540.

8. A Singer

ε❧ ε❧ ε❧

Toward the end of the summer, a gracious friend of Mother's, Mrs. Meredith, who lived in St. John's Wood, asked us to an evening musicale. She was herself a musician and music patron, and tonight she told Mother over the phone that the performing guests were to be four young Americans, all pupils of the famous opera tenor, Jean de Reszke, who had formed a quartet and were making a great hit in England and on the Continent.[1]

Mother, who had worshipped the de Reszke brothers during their triumphant years at the Metropolitan and Chicago Opera, was much interested, but I, for some reason, did not wish to attend a musicale. I much preferred to stay home and read, but Mother was firm. To demonstrate my reluctance, I elected to wear what I considered was my most unbecoming frock, the faithful graduation dress, and somewhat sulkily I climbed into the taxi with my family.

Mrs. Meredith's long music room was crowded with laughing, chattering music lovers. I had never known enough to "talk music" and everything I heard was far over my head. Besides, I hated crowds and managed to find a chair in a far corner where I sat alone and glowered. At intervals, I would catch a glimpse of a tall, broad-shouldered young man with a boyishly attractive, intelligent face which seemed to be turned pretty steadily in my direction. There were always girls around him, however, and I scorned the competition. I had been known to summon a man across a room with a speaking look, but this time I didn't bother. I wanted to go home and read.

Mrs. Meredith finally clapped her hands for silence and

everyone found a seat. The tall young man, who wore his white tie and tails with a worldly air, moved to the piano and sat down at it. Three other young men, similarly turned out, gathered behind him, and the concert was on. I was hearing the de Reszke Quartet for the first but not the last time.

The concert was completely delightful. All the boys had superb natural voices and were well trained, their arrangements original and musicianly. The top tenor, Hardesty Johnson, was also the accompanist, and I was attracted, almost unwillingly, by his half-closed eyes, the little smile that lifted the corners of his mouth as he sang, and the beauty of his shapely, competent hands on the keys.

After all the encores they could be persuaded to give, Mrs. Meredith brought the Quartet over to present to the Garlands. The next thing I knew Hardesty Johnson was sitting on the floor at my feet, and we were sipping punch and talking as easily as if we had been lifelong friends. He told me later that it was my gown that had attracted him first. "You looked like an angel with all those floating white panels. I couldn't keep my eyes off you." So much for foresight.

We saw a good bit of the Quartet from then on, and it was fun to have bright young American men at our beck and call. They were singing at the Palladium and we went to hear them, sitting in a stage box and thrilling with pride at their triumph. The British liked them immensely—their freshness, their skill, their American quality. They were riding high, with big plans for an American tour the next year.

We had acquired English beaux, too, and with them went to the theater, dancing at the Savoy, punting on the Thames, and taking long, cross-country walks, climbing stiles, passing through "Kissing Gates," and winding up at small, ancient pubs where picturesque, old painted signs swung above the doors.

Speaking of the theater, Connie and I had one absorbing week of it. The Stratford Players were in town, at the Hammersmith Theater, and with Daddy's approval, we saw every single performance. I have never before or since seen a company as flexible, as gifted as that one. There were no stars, for everyone was a star. If you played *Hamlet* one night, you would be cast as Lancelot Gobbo the next. Desdemona was equally at home in the small, comic

part of Audrey. Richard II was superbly funny as the Second
Gravedigger. It was a Shakespearean orgy and we were punch-
drunk but regretful when it ended.

We were also continuing to call on England's top literary
figures. We had been brought up on *The Jungle Book*, and one day
we visited Rudyard Kipling.[2] He lived in an ancient stone house
with an authentic smuggler's cellar, set far back from the road in a
setting of formal gardens. Oh, the gardens of England! Kipling was
stocky, swarthy, with a dark bristly mustache and bright myopic
eyes behind thick glasses. He and Daddy had known each other
intimately for years and had innumerable things to discuss, while I
talked with Elsie Kipling, whom I remember to this day as one of
the brightest, most attractive young women I have ever met.

We had dinner with Arnold Bennett in his elaborate flat furnished completely in Victorian antiques—in which Father looked as
out of place as a bull in a china shop. We went to a garden party at
the John Galsworthys, and we met the Irish playwright St. John
Ervine—the only person in England Connie and I immediately disliked. He had an unfortunate leering manner that made you feel he
was making fun of you, but I fancy he merely thought he was being
flirtatious. Daddy went to see his ailing old friend, Thomas Hardy,
but he went alone and came home saddened. For some reason, I
didn't go with Mother and Daddy and Connie to the studio of John
Sargent, but I remember with complete satisfaction our meeting
with Arthur Rackham, a strange, smiling, little gnome of a man,
who might have stepped out of one of his fantastic illustrations. We
had tea on the Embankment of the House of Commons with T. P.
O'Connor and lunched with Stanley Baldwin and at the Admiralty
House with Lord and Lady Lee of Fareham.[3]

Through the good offices of our friends, the Post
Wheelers—he was chargé d'affaires in London at that time during
the absence of the Ambassador—we were invited to a garden party
at Buckingham palace. We were as awed as the farmer's daughters,
for we were to see the King and Queen moving among their bow-
ing, curtseying guests; he small slim, frail; she a magnificent ship of
a woman, every inch a queen. The Prince of Wales, still a fairy-tale
hero, and the Princess Mary followed behind the King and Queen,
and Connie and I felt that we were part of a truly historic occasion.

The following day, I was again walking through Hyde Park

Corners when I became aware of a happy stir of excitement. People were running to take up positions on the corners and along the curbs as they had the day before, but this time all the faces were alight; there was laughter and the craning of necks as out through the Park gates, preceded by a single motorcycle policeman, came an open motor car in which sat two pretty girls in flower hats, light dresses, and white gloves. There were two men on the box, and a small, unobtrusive car trailed behind and that was all.

"The Queen! . . . Princess Margaret!" A thrill of pride and pleasure ran through the crowd. Off came hats, out came handkerchiefs, and a shout of affection filled the air. The two royal ladies had been deep in conversation, but now they turned to their people with lovely smiles of such spontaneous appreciation that it warmed your heart. No greater contrast could be imagined than the grim, guarded cavalcade of the day before and this lighthearted jaunt through the streets of London.

"They're going to lunch at the Ritz, dearie," a woman told me helpfully. "There's some kind of charity fashion show, I read in the papers. Nice looking hats they had on, wouldn't you say?"

I would say and did and went on my way refreshed and, somehow comforted.

🐛 🐛 🐛

Back to the literary scene. A. A. Milne became one of our particular favorites.[4] He and his utterly charming wife and "Christopher Robin" were living in a bright little house in Chelsea, and we had Sunday luncheon there the first time. Christopher Robin was about three and a raving beauty. Surely, English children are the loveliest in the world. This one spent most of his time with his arms clasped around a big, black satin pillow, with which he would roll over and over in a miniature tumbling act. He had recently learned the names of the colors, and his mother was showing him off by pointing at a rainbow-shaded bed cover in the guest room.

"What color is this? . . . What is this?"

He answered promptly, "Wed . . . Blue . . . Gween," but when her fingers indicated a band of chartreuse, he frowned. "It's too dif-

ficult that," he said with a crisp Oxford accent and marched out of
the room.

Milne used to drop in frequently at Albert Hall Mansions
and stretch his long, graceful body almost full length in one of our
easy chairs. He was blond and handsome, with a lovely slow voice
and a quick wit. I shall always think of him as young and on the
crest of the wave, with a wife he adored, a young son who was the
cream of English youth, and royalties from plays, books, and poetry rolling in. He promised to come to America. I wonder why he
never did.

Way up at the head of the list, of course, was George
Bernard Shaw.[5] He and Father were not only long-time friends,
they were constant correspondents, and Shaw's merry postcards
had been our delight for years. Just before I graduated from Finch,
through Vida Sutton and Dr. Norman Guthrie of Trinity Church, I
had been privileged to appear in the first American reading of
Shaw's *Back to Methuselah*, an exciting experience. It was called a
"reading," but we were costumed and appeared on a stage in the little upstairs theater that was part of the rectory. I played Eve in a
brief leafy shift, and Adam was similarly discreet. We had a beautiful Serpent in a long sinuous tail, and the whole project brought
out such a crowd that the hall had to be emptied and refilled for a
second performance.

Certain lines keep repeating themselves to me. "What is
Hope?" asks Adam, and the Serpent replies, "As long as you do not
know the future you do not know that it will not be happier than
the past. That is hope."

Again, we had been brought up on Shaw. When Father was
not reading him aloud to us, we were seeing him on the stage or acting his plays in various little theater companies, so our excitement
over an invitation to lunch at Ayot St. Lawrence was obvious. I prefer to think I did not wear the Black Watch tartan, lace-veil effect
because I remember it was a rather warm summer day as we came
puffing along from the station in a battered old taxi and nearly ran
down tall, spare, white-harried gentleman marching briskly along
with his hands rammed in his pockets.

"Shaw!" Daddy shouted, and his head turned.

"Garland!" he shouted back. "See you at the house!"

Mrs. Shaw, a rare lady, quiet, poised, cordial, seated us in the book-walled drawing room and poured sherry as if she had known us all her life. Daddy went down the road to meet Shaw, who was taking his daily constitutional, and they came back in high spirits.

"A terrible man." Was it Ellen Terry who said that—or Maxine Elliott—or one of the others he fascinated and wound round his little finger? In ten minutes we all fell head over heels. In the first place he was "devilishly handsome," which he knew. In the second, there was that voice with the lilt of Ireland that could caress and bite at the same time. For instance, he said to me abruptly, "Hamlin tells me you are going on the stage."

It was true. Augustus Thomas had heard me on the platform of Town Hall and had taken me on as a lowly member of his National Theater Company, which was to begin rehearsals of *As You Like It* in the fall.[6]

Shaw didn't wait for my answer. "Don't do it," he said flatly. "You're too intelligent. I want my actors to be dummies. I don't want their ideas of how a part should be played. I want them to become what I make them."

At lunch, a gargantuan roast of beef appeared at Mrs. Shaw's end of the table, and we ate appreciatively. Shaw, quite cheerful, sat among an array of small dishes of vegetables, fruit, and nuts and was plainly having a good time. Father's companionship rather overstimulated him, and when he became too outrageous, Mrs. Shaw had only to raise her calm eyes and fix them on him.

"Now, G. B." she said quietly, and the torrent was turned off as though by a faucet.

ἐ▲ ἐ▲ ἐ▲

The more I think back on it, the more I realize what a really memorable summer it was. We were all well, united in interest, luxuriously comfortable in our London flat. For the first time Daddy could entertain as he wished to entertain and Mother could play the lady instead of the scrubwoman.

We took two short trips out of England—Mother, Connie, and I—one to Scotland, the other to Paris. I cannot remember why Daddy didn't go to Scotland with us—speaking engagement, no doubt—but I know why he did not try Paris. He had had Paris before and wanted no more of it. Mother, on the other hand, was almost pathetically eager to show us her Paris, the place where she had lived and worked through five absorbing years.

Our trip, though it had its high points, was not a success. We stayed in the Hotel de Corneille, near the Odeon, a modest hostelry built around a neglected garden with a bust of Corneille in the center. There was one bath to a floor, and one hilarious night Mother moved in and took the bath that had been drawn for another guest. She sat calmly washing herself through all the thumpings on the door, the shouts, the gesticulatings.

"I was already in," she said sweetly, emerging rosey and clean. "There seemed no reason to get out again until I had finished my bath."

We were, as usual, short of funds and had most of our meals at a little corner eatery where we leaned heavily on omelets and salad, with petits Suisses for dessert. We also had, each night, "une demi-bottaille de vin rouge," well watered, and felt Continental and dashing.

We went to the Louvre, to Versailles, to Fontainbleu, to the Paris Opera—where men in shirt sleeves and women in cotton dresses offended our esthetic taste—and we covered Montmarte thoroughly to the tune of "Look, darling! . . . There on the second floor—that long middle window—that was MacMonnies's studio!⁷ . . . And there on the corner—oh, it's still standing! How wonderful! That is the atelier where I worked for two years with. . . ."

It makes me wince now to think how bored Connie and I were and how we showed it. The enchanted hours that Mother must have been reliving, with no one to share them. I am sad to say that we failed her miserably. We hated Paris and said so, over and over. The heat, the noise, the rudeness of the people, the smells, the shock of open toilets, the reek of garlic—oh, we were a precious pair of spoiled little snobs and should have had our heads knocked together.

The only time we really came to life was when we met two American boys in the lobby of the hotel and they asked us to go to an American movie with them. I wish I were back in Paris with Mother again. What a satisfactory companion I would make now.

❧ ❧ ❧

Scotland was different—it was heavenly, if being damp and
half-frozen most of the time is to be expected in heaven. But it was
so beautiful, so everything we had hoped for. I, personally, went
around in a dream, quoting Marmion and Scotch ballads, and as we
rode around on sightseeing buses in the rain—frequently the only
passengers—we all sang "Bonnie Dundee" and "Loch Lomond" at
the tops of our voices. We got so shudderingly chilled on one trip
that, during a bus stop, Mother darted into a pub and bought a pint
of whiskey which she administered in large gulps to her teeth-chat-
tering daughters.

Melrose by moonlight, where we slept in a velvet-canopied
bed in an old house that served as a hotel and Connie said in an
awed whisper, "It's the kind of bed a King might die in." Robert
Bruce's grave, from which I daringly stole a pebble I intended to
cherish forever. Where is it now? Scott's home, Abbottsford, and
Edinburgh, that legendary city, surely one of the most dramatically
beautiful in the world. Holyrood, with its poignant associations of
Mary Queen of Scots, and the magnificent old castle on the rock
looking down on Princes Street. There is a tiny, stone-walled room
there, hardly larger than a modern closet, where Mary gave birth to
her baby and some weeks later lowered him down in a basket on a
long rope to be recovered by some of her adherents and whisked
away to safety. History is so close in the British Isles, you can
almost catch it around the next corner.

Bank Holiday closed every shop and restaurant in
Edinburgh, and we were forced to fall back on the Rutland Hotel
Grill for dinner. Mother went to bed, with hot tea and a water bottle to keep warm, but Connie and I were hungry and descended
solemnly to the Grill.

Song composed by Constance and me during an unforgettable meal:

> The Garlands went to the Rutland Grill for dinner.
> What did they have for dinner?
> A plain boiled potato.
> A badly boiled potato.
> A butterless boiled potato,

A saltless boiled potato,
An incredibly tasteless, nightmare-like potato.
That's what the Garlands had
In the Rutland Grill for dinner.

Summer ended and we were all poignantly sad to leave. I never depart from England without tears in my eyes. Something of me remains there, not to be recovered until I return.

We came down to earth, or perhaps one should say, sea, with a bump. We sailed on an American ship this time, and it was crowded with strident-voiced Americans loudly expressing their disappointment in Europe. There were almost no young men on board and what seemed like thousands of pretty girls, all far better dressed than we. Admittedly, we had been pretty badly spoiled that summer, so Connie and I elected to spend most of the voyage in our stateroom, which this time was comfortable, and read our way home.

New York was dirty and noisy, and our flat, after Albert Hall Mansions, was depressingly shabby and cramped. And we missed Mrs. Curzon, custard and all. A champagne taste can be quite easily acquired.

Notes

[1] Jean de Reszeke (1850-1925) was a Polish operatic tenor who often sang with his younger brother, Edouard de Reszke. The De Reszeke Singers included Floyd Townsley, Erwyn Mutch, Sigurd Nelson, and Hardesty Johnson (1899-1952), whom Isabel would marry in 1926.

[2] Garland had first met the immensely popular author Rudyard Kipling (1867-1936) in 1892, in Boston, after Kipling invited him to dinner.

[3] Persons Isabel refers to are Arnold Bennett (1867-1931), novelist; John Galsworthy (1867-1933), prolific novelist and playwright; St. John Greer Ervine (1883-1971), Irish playwright; Thomas Hardy (1840-1928), novelist; John Singer Sargent (1856-1925), the most celebrated portrait painter of his time; Arthur Rackham (1867-1939), illustrator of children's books; T. P. O'Connor (1848-1929), Irish journalist and Member of Parliament; Stanley Baldwin (1867-1947), Member of Parliament, elected three times as Prime Minister, beginning in 1923; Arthur Hamilton Lee (1868-1947), British politician, elevated to the peerage in 1918; and, below, [George] Post Wheeler

(1869-1956), American journalist, diplomat, and author.

⁴ A. A. Milne (1882-1956), novelist and playwright whose early works were overshadowed by the success of *Winnie-the-Pooh* (1926) and *The House at Pooh Corner* (1928).

⁵ Garland had met the playwright George Bernard Shaw (1856-1950) during his first visit to England in 1899.

⁶ Augustus Thomas (1857-1934), author of over 60 plays, was one of Garland's close friends.

⁷ Zulime may have met the sculptor Fredrick W. MacMonnies (1863-1937) in 1893, when both created sculpture for the World's Columbian Exposition in Chicago. Shortly afterwards, Zulime studied sculpture in Paris, where MacMonnies had a studio.

9. The Stage

      🙂 🙂 🙂

That fall I began my long dreamed-of career. Augustus Thomas had suggested that if I wanted to be a Shakespearean actress—which I did—I could do no better than to coach with Ada Dow, who had discovered and developed Julia Marlowe. She was said to know more about Shakespearean acting than anyone in America.[1]

She was an old lady, partially crippled, and she lived in an ugly, old-fashioned flat on Broadway in the seventies, but there was nothing old-fashioned about Ada Dow. We were fellows at once, and the hours I spent with her were some of the most valuable of my life.

I began with Portia in *The Merchant of Venice*, and Miss Dow played Nerissa with a voice as young and fresh as if she had just turned seventeen. The moment she began to act, the ungainly old body seemed to disappear and April youth took over. It was incredible. So musical and flexible was her voice that by the same token she was Romeo to my Juliet or Hamlet to my Desdemona with equal illusion. In those months I came to a clearer conception of what it meant to be a *real* actress, and though I was still resolved, a thread of doubt crept through my ambitions.

Meanwhile, I began appearing on the lecture platform with Father.[2] It relieved him of the strain of a whole evening, and the clubs and universities seemed to approve the addition. Mother had studied an old photograph of Isabelle McClintock at the time of her marriage and designed and constructed a charming costume for me of violet plaid silk, with a boned bodice over a wide hoopskirt.

Isabel and Hamlin Garland on the lecture platform, around 1922.
(*Courtesy of Victoria Doyle-Jones*)

I wore my hair parted in the middle and falling down my back in a velvet-tied snood, as my grandmother had when she was a girl. In this costume I read "The Return of the Private" from *Main-Travelled Roads*, which was the story of my grandfather's return from the Civil War. Because my voice and diction were adequate and I had been carefully coached by Miss Dow and Daddy, I found it easy to hold an audience's attention.

In my second appearance of the evening, in the "Middle Border" program we had worked out, I wore a long-trained, graceful silver crepe dress that had been part of my mother's trousseau. With my hair piled high on my head like a Gibson girl and a wide velvet dog collar, I read the story of my own youth, "The Fairy World of Childhood." In a last appearance, wearing the romantic black velvet dress, I recited a group of Father's poems. Daddy and I traveled back and forth across the country companionably. We were making pleasant money, too, and he kept asking me wistfully if I wouldn't change my mind about the stage and stay on with him. I felt guilty in disappointing him, but I was resolved.

The National Theater Company was my first engagement with a wholly professional troupe, and a liberal and raw education it turned out to be.[3] Daddy, I knew, was comforting himself with the thought that I was under the surveillance of his friend, Augustus Thomas, but he didn't realize, or had forgotten, that in a company as large as ours the director, the producer, and the stars were as remote from the rest of us as their Majesties had been in Buckingham Palace.

We had a distinguished set of leads. Marjorie Rambeau was essaying Rosalind. Ian Keith was Orlando, Margalo Gilmore, Celia. There were half a dozen other name players and then us, the riffraff, the ladies and gentlemen of the court, the peasant lads and lasses, a pretty miscellaneous lot. Not content with giving young hopefuls like myself a start, Mr. Thomas, out of the kindness of his heart, had made a place in the company for half a dozen old Shakespearean actors dating far back in his theatrical career. There were also the usual Broadway character actors, some highly-sexed young women, and a dozen or so virile, good-looking young men. In a company of that sort there was bound to be trouble, and there was. In that first week of rehearsals, I learned more of the seamy side of life than I had learned before or since.

Isabel Garland in medieval costume from her stage days, around 1923-1924.
(*Courtesy of Victoria Doyle-Jones*)

It was my first introduction, for instance, to the modern connotation of the word "fairy," and I was angry and indignant. I had never heard profanity before, nor smut, except in rough characters on the stage or screen, and the stream of language that poured from the rosy lips of some of our exquisite court ladies would have made my father's hair stand on end. As my eyes got rounder and my ears burned with disbelief, I became a figure of fun to my fellow actors.

"My God, Isabel!" one old ham exclaimed one day, "You can't be *that* innocent!"

I was—when I started rehearsals. Six weeks later I had learned "a great deal more than I cared to know."

We were to try out in Poli's Theater, Washington, D.C., and a special train took the company there, with much publicity and fanfare. The stars had drawing rooms, the featured players had parlor car seats, and the rest of us just piled on anyhow. It was the first time I had ever been anywhere alone, and I was frankly scared. I had made a friend of one of the girls, and we decided we would get a room together in Washington and cut down expenses that way. I had insisted that I was going to live on my salary and would accept nothing from Daddy. I was going to learn a good bit about money, too.

I had been in Washington before, when Daddy had led us on a personally conducted tour, and we lunched in the Senate dining room, but this was different. Poli's was a grim old place and the chorus dressing room was in approximately the third basement. There were ten girls in our room and the supporting players and extras dressed further down the dank corridor. We had a good many costume changes and a lot of running up and down stairs was going to be required, but we were resigned.

My friend and I found a cheap room in a lodging house, not too far from the theater to walk, and settled in for the duration. It was spring in Washington with the nights getting milder and the smell of blossoms on the air. I was already homesick but determined to let no one know. I had had enough teasing.

By this time my friend and I had acquired admirers, and after rehearsals we'd go for hot cakes and coffee and wander back through the empty streets to our lodging house. The production was having a hard time, what with temperament, alcohol, and sex, and there were times when it seemed it could never be pulled together, but Mr. Thomas came down from New York, soothed ruffled feelings, made the necessary decisions, and open we did.

We were all desperately tired that night, and after the final curtain, I dragged myself down the three flights to the dressing room, too exhausted to even begin to take off my makeup and change. The other girls got into their street clothes and went off with their various boy friends, but I begged off and just sat there, wondering what was wrong with me. I had never before felt such a misfit. What was I doing here in this foul old basement, among people I didn't understand and who didn't understand me? My money was slipping away. My stage appearances consisted of a few routine crosses, some conversational babble, and a noisy peasant dance in the forest of Arden. I was to understudy Audrey but no one had got around to understudy rehearsals. I was tired of the filth, actual and mental, around me, so I sat in the deserted dressing room, under the glaring lights, and wept.

I heard slow footsteps coming along the corridor, but I was too miserable to look up and only cried harder. The footsteps stopped on the doorsill and a voice as beautiful as a poem said, "My poor little girl, why are you crying?"

I looked up, saw who it was, and felt my heart give a flutter, but I was too far gone in misery to stop. Even when he came into the room and put his arms around me, I wept like Niobe into his coat sleeve. He was very quiet, very calm, stroked my hair, murmured something reassuring now and then, and gradually I came back to sanity. While I patted my nose with a powder puff and tried to restore some order to my hair, he watched me with a half smile. He had a wide, mobile mouth in a handsome Slavic face, spectacularly magnetic eyes, and a shock of dark, untidy hair. I had admired him afar, but he was a well-known actor and I only a lowly extra. At the moment he was slumming.[4]

"You know what I think you and I need," he said, moving to the dressing room door and leaning against the jamb. "Food. . . . Suppose I wait for you at the top of the stairs and then we'll go somewhere and feed the inner man—and woman."

I stared. I was being asked out to dinner by the most exciting man I had ever met—and I looked a mess! I started to stammer some excuse, but he turned and called back over his shoulder, "I'll be waiting. Don't take too long."

It was late when I emerged from the depths of Poli's. There was no one in sight, the world was empty, and for a moment my heart sank; then I saw him, leaning against the building in the dark, a graceful masculine figure with a dark overcoat hung like a cape across his shoulders. He came toward me smiling and put out his hands, gathering in both mine.

"That's a girl," he said softly. "Now—a kiss?"

There in the dark we kissed again and again and I knew that no one in the world had ever felt like this before.

                                 🙢 🙢 🙢

I remember very little about the rest of the run. Although praising the production, the critics in both Washington and New York were not kind to our leading actors. One said, "Miss Rambeau reminded me of nothing so much as a large and beautiful jockey about to ride in a heavenly steeplechase." After two weeks in New York, we folded.

In the meantime, my romance was developing. He told me, "I'd been watching you for a long time—there was something about you. But that boy was always hanging around and—what had I to offer you after all?"

"Everything!" I cried, clinging to him. "Everything I ever dreamed of!"

He was a cultivated man, well read and with a deep love of poetry, which he read to me by the hour. Apart from his dark, good looks, he was completely sure of himself, of his ability to get what he wanted out of life. He was a born actor—whatever that may be, when the training and experience are so much a part of it—and if he had doubts, he never showed them.

Each night in Washington, after we had taken off our make-up and costumes and had a bite to eat, we would go out to the Lincoln Memorial and sit there in the warm dark. His head in my lap, he would recite poetry in that low, velvet voice, and I would watch the stars and thrill with happiness.

After we closed in New York, things were not the same. The

world broke in on us. I had lecture commitments with my father, and Walter started looking for another job. I tried desperately to hang onto him but he slipped away from me. I think now that the intensity of my feeling alarmed him. I was, quite frankly, thinking of marriage, and he, equally frankly, was not. Some nights there would be excuses. Often, several days would go by when he wouldn't call me. I went through the proverbial "tortures of the damned," and one night we took a long walk around the reservoir in Central Park and talked until three in the morning. He had signed with a road company and was leaving in two weeks and suggested it might be better if we did not see each other anymore.

"It's too hard on both of us," he said, holding me for the last time. "Someday, perhaps, when we have a little more—perspective."

Stunned, I stood at the apartment window on the corner of 92nd Street and saw him cross the street and stand for a moment under the street light, looking up. Fortunately, the room was dark and he could not see me in my humiliation. I thought for one heartbroken instant that he might come back, but he turned and went off down Park Avenue and, except on the stage, I never saw him again.

≈ ≈ ≈

That summer we went again to Wyoming with the Morrises, but the West, aside from its unchanging beauty, was not the same, either. Father decided not to go this time, and Constance and I were no longer heedless young things playing tag on horseback and making fudge over a campfire. Relationships were full of undercurrents, and to ease my shattered heart I put a good bit of time and effort into trying to shatter others. I had a pseudo-romance, I am ashamed to say, with a good-looking young cowboy who felt as desperately over me as I had over my actor lover. He was good for my ego and as long as he was on horseback, silhouetted against the horizon, so to speak, I was gratified. It was fun to gallop side by side across the mesa, to have him constantly at my call, his eyes following me everywhere. When we sat together by the fire at night, he told me romantic tales of his daredevil life and the firelight etched his keen young profile, while his hard brown hands wove me a hatband made of horsehair. It was all to be expected, but when he became serious and then angry when I tried to laugh the whole thing off, I realized I had behaved shabbily and was eager to get away.

I have a letter from Daddy written at that time, and I had obviously confided in him, for his letter began,

> Your letter concerning the young forest ranger would have alarmed me greatly had it not been for the belief that all the other girls out there are quite as much interested as you seem to be. In numbers is safety so I shall not worry. . . . If it gets too worrisome out there you just come home to your cross old pop. It is always easier to bear a familiar ache. I have days of feeling pretty good natured and you ought to be here to take advantage of them. "Tip me the wink" and I'll order you home, any time. . . .

To the last, Jim couldn't believe that I was taking myself out of his life. He wrote me in New York—pathetic, ill-spelled, incoherent scrawls:

> Dear Girl
> I still feel the same. Just give me the word and I'll come and get you.
> XXXXX Kisses,
> Jim

Back in Onteora, I plunged into Little Theater work and it diverted me somewhat, but I was in a bad mood and increasingly unhappy. I seemed to have lost my lodestar, my goal, and when we returned to New York in the autumn and I started out on the theatrical agency rounds that so many other young actors were traveling, my courage oozed away completely, though I had had plenty of professional advice on how to approach agents.

"Never admit you haven't had experience. Tell them you've had a couple of years of stock, six months on the road—they'll never look it up." It was impossible for me to bluff like that—the lies would stand out all over me. Unlike Father, I was not a salesman and particularly not of myself. Gloomily, I agreed to go out on the lecture platform again.

We had some twenty engagements lined up for our first tour, and the opening one was at a boys' school in Pennsylvania. Something was wrong. We couldn't get the slightest stir of interest from the young wretches, and when we got on the Pullman at midnight, Father fell into one of his moods of black depression.

"Well, daughter, we failed. You didn't have that spark tonight. I guess you really don't want to do this after all. You can go home if you wish. I'll go on alone."

He looked so gray and tired, sitting there in his rumpled evening shirt under the harsh lights of the sleeper, that my heart turned over. On the other hand, he was unfair. I had done my best, I told him hotly. If it didn't suit him— We almost quarreled and went to our berths in bitter silence. When he saw me in the morning, we had both done a lot of thinking and he put his arm around me and brushed my cheek with his lips. We never mentioned the matter again, and that night in Canton, Ohio, where we were the guests of Orville Wright and his sister, Katherine, we had one of our greatest successes.

It was on that trip, I think, that Daddy and I went back to Wisconsin. Our friends in La Crosse had engaged us to speak in the high school auditorium and someone had done a masterly job of publicity, for as we drove up to the campus with Mrs. Easton, as far as the eye could see cars were parked fender to fender.

"You're going to have a wonderful crowd," the principal told us exultantly. "They're standing all around the walls."

That was a poignant, unforgettable evening. These were, many of them, people who had known Richard and Isabelle Garland. When I spoke of Green's Coulee in 1865, the year my grandfather returned from the Civil War, they knew just how the road curved, what farmhouses nestled in the hollows, where the red barns stood on the hillsides. They listened in a silence that was absolute till the end, then they broke into cheering, stamping applause and swarmed up to the stage.

We held what was virtually a royal levee. Everyone wanted to take our hands, to try to explain what it had meant.

"I knew your Granddad—"

"Your Aunt Jessie and I used to play dolls together—"

"I'll never forget the day your Uncle Franklin stood on his head on the roof of that barn—"

There were tears in many eyes and close behind mine. Here, too, were my old classmates from West Salem, bright, young grownups now, with attractive children to exhibit. They stood around and looked at us as if we were creatures from another planet. They wanted to take us to West Salem and show us the old house, but neither Daddy nor I could bear the idea. We had sold Mapleshade the previous summer and knew it had been turned into apartments.

"Let's keep our memory of it the way it was when your grandfather was alive," Daddy said, and I agreed with my whole heart.

&ambda; &ambda; &ambda;

Daddy wrote so well of our weekend with the Henry Fords at Dearborn that it seems superfluous to speak of it here, but it was a heartwarming time.[5] Two such nice, intelligent gentlefolk, with a name known round the world. We were friends in ten minutes.

After our lecture at the country club that Mr. Ford had built for his employees, they had one of their square dances for us, and Mrs. Ford partnered Daddy, while Mr. Ford led me out on the floor. Tall and slim and "light on his feet," as Daddy used to say, Mr. Ford was a superb dancer and arrived at the conclusion as fresh and unwearied as when we had started. I myself was flaming-cheeked and puffing, but it was fun. Later, we were to have many pleasant stays with the Fords, where Daddy was told he was welcome at any hour of the day or night.

Toward the end of November, at the conclusion of what turned out to be a very successful lecture trip, Father came back from the Players Club one afternoon on a broad beam.

"Daughtie, I have some exciting news for you."

I could do with some exciting news. I was back in the doldrums again, wasting time—except for my coaching with Ada Dow—wondering what to do and why I hadn't the drive that Emily Taft had, for instance. I had been reading aloud to Connie while she worked on some illustrations she was making for the book Daddy

had written about our English summer.[6] My sister was enormously gifted, and every available minute was spent over a drawing
board. It made a splendid excuse for getting out of household
chores, I observed, for whenever something was asked of us, Father
would be sure to say, "Don't interrupt Connie—she has an idea for
a drawing." Now, we both looked up with interest at our obviously triumphant father.

"Mary Isabel, how would you like to be a member of Walter
Hampden's Shakespearean Company?"

Connie gave a yip of excitement and I jumped to my feet.

"Daddy—what do you mean?"

Connie and I worshipped Walter Hampden,[7] had seen all
his productions, and could identify each and every member of his
company. To be a member of that company—!

"I sat with Hampden at lunch at the Club today and we
were talking shop and I was saying what a discouraging trek it is for
young people, going from agency to agency looking for a job, and
Hampden said, 'Why don't you send your daughter over to audi-
tion for me? I'm doing Brian Hooker's translation of *Cyrano
de Bergerac* this fall, and I am going to need some fresh faces and
voices.'"

That was how it happened that with trembling knees and
thudding heart I climbed several flights of stairs to Walter
Hampden's office-apartment in a shabby old building in the East
Fifties. To meet him would be thrill enough, but to be summoned
to read for him. . . . Father had sent me off with a cheery "Good
Luck—" but it was going to take more than that to steady my knees
and clear my throat. Climbing up those steep stairs, I literally
prayed.

Hampden, in a slate-gray suit, tall and dark and slender,
with magnetic eyes above a craggy nose and a wide, sensitive
mouth, met me at the door and helped me off with my coat. He
made light conversation for a few moments while I tried to pull
myself together, talking about Daddy, asking about the tour we had
been on, and volunteering an adventure or two from his own barn-
storming days. Finally, he leaned back in his chair, linked his long,
beautiful hands, and said pleasantly, "Now—what do you have for
me?"

I recited for about twenty minutes, I think—a strange

assortment: *The Trojan Women*, Swinburne's "A Forsaken Garden,"
some of Daddy's Western verses, Juliet, of course, and scene or two
from James Barrie. Mr. Hampden listened in silence, his eyes on his
desk, his face expressionless.

I stopped at last, my throat dry, my face burning. "I don't
want to—wear you out," I said helplessly.

He smiled then, a warm flashing smile. "That was good," he
said. "You have a fine, well-trained voice and you're an attractive
girl. I think you would do well in my company." He wrote down
my name and address and rose, holding out his hand. "Thank you
for coming. Get in touch with me at the end of April."

In a trance, I floated down the stairs and out into the street.
I was to meet Daddy at the Players afterward and we would go
home together on the bus. He was standing on the steps waiting for
me, and when I saw him I began to run.

"How did it go? How did it go?" He looked at me keenly
and patted my cheek. "I don't need to ask. I could tell it was victory by your walk when you turned the corner." He sighed contentedly and tucked my hand into his coat pocket as we started down
the street toward the bus stop. "Now—tell me all about it."

That was a gilded day, and the evening made it more so, for
over the soup, Daddy announced that he had decided to take us all
again to England for the summer.

"I'll go on ahead and get a flat, as I did before. I'll let
everyone know we're coming and we'll have another perfect summer. . . ."

It is very difficult to recapture a mood, an experience. That
first trip had been, as Daddy said, almost perfect. The second one
was to him a sad disappointment. It was not England that was at
fault; it was still beautiful, historic, its people gracious and cordial.
We were charmingly housed again in Sloane Square, saw most of
our friends—Shaw, Barrie, Milne—and revisited the places we had
loved. It was Hamlin Garland's daughters who had changed.
Connie and I were restless, impatient, more inclined to young men
and dancing than the most storied sightseeing. Everything Daddy
asked us to do we did reluctantly, and one day he said in frank bitterness, "I thought I was bringing over three little steam engines that
would be chugging away in all directions. Now I seem to be dragging around three sandbags."

Mother, too, had weakened, and often Father had to go off on one of his cherished expeditions alone. It gave me a pang even then to feel I was failing him, but on the other hand, the phone was ringing and there was Tony or Phil or Stephen with an idea. We house-partied, we dashed around the country in cars with the tops down, we danced far into the night and refused to get up in the morning. In fact, we were about as selfish as two over-indulged young women can be.

A few successful visits lifted Daddy's spirits momentarily. There was another Sunday luncheon with Shaw. Daddy and I went alone this time, and to round out the party, the Shaws had invited another man, a neighbor whom Shaw declared was "the most interesting young man in England." Cherry was not only handsome; he was intelligent, rich, and famous. He had just published a magnificent book which was an account of his trip to the Antarctic, and he talked as well as he wrote.[8]

Daddy fell for Cherry even harder than I did. Mother said, "Hamlin would have married Cherry in a minute," but since that did not sound reasonable, Father, for the first time, seemed quite ready to hand me over.

This was my most glamorous courtship. I was just twenty, Cherry was in his mid-thirties, sophisticated in the way money and social position bring. He called for me in a chauffeured limousine, and he himself was a vision out of high society journals—full dress, black evening cape lined with satin, high silk hat, gold-headed cane, and chamois gloves. After the theater, we went to the Savoy, where his table was always ready. There were flowers for me and champagne and caviar and pressed duck. He danced superbly, as he did everything else, and I lived in such a whirl of flattery and excitement that I hardly knew what I was doing. Father said—and though he made a joke of it, I am not too sure—that instead of finding a man who was good enough for me, I had found one who was *too* good.

That, I think, was the trouble. Cherry was so very dazzling he terrified me. There was his incredible bravery, for instance. The horrors he had been through should have left some scars on that smooth, confident face, but they had not. His worldliness, the famous names he was entitled to drop, something steely under the unfailing charm, confused and dismayed me. I felt out of my depth.

What can he find in me, I asked myself, yet when I was in his arms, everything seemed improbably possible.

At this point came a cable from Walter Hampden's manager telling me to report for rehearsals. Nothing, not even my current love, was going to stand in the way of my stage career. I couldn't have really been in love or I would not have been so arbitrary in the matter. When we parted, it was with the promise that he would come to New York at Christmas, and if things were still the same. . . . That night he kissed me with a violence that frightened me, and I resisted him. For a moment he was angry, then he laughed.

"Why, you're only a baby after all," he said teasingly. "I trust I am the man when you decide to grow up."

Looking back on it, this was one of the more mysterious episodes of my life. Daddy was as disappointed as a child. For a man who had fought tooth and nail over the years to keep his daughter, this frank desire to hand her over to a man he had known only a few weeks was almost comic. The truth was, Daddy was as dazzled by my Britisher as I was, and it was probably Shaw's fulsome introduction that did the trick.

ɘ̃ ɘ̃ ɘ̃

If my first theatrical season had been a liberal education, so was my second—but with a difference. Claude Bragdon, who designed the stage sets, said that to his knowledge it was the only production ever staged on Broadway without an oath.

Not that there was anything wishy-washy about Walter Hampden. He knew exactly what he wanted and he got it, but this was a company with a high purpose—the merest of us felt it. First and foremost, it was a fine play, translated by Brian Hooker, who kept not only the original concept and the poetry but to my mind enhanced it. Secondly, we had a gifted, carefully chosen company and a star director who was not only a accomplished actor but "a gentleman and a scholar."

During those weeks of rehearsal in the old National Theater on 41st Street, our respect and admiration for Mr. Hampden grew and deepened. Strong, intelligent, and considerate, he molded a stage full of assorted personalities into a consummate dramatic experience.

When we were not required on the stage, the members of the company sat out in the darkened theater and watched proceedings with complete concentration. No ticklings, gigglings, and gossipings for this crew. We were there to learn, and almost to a man we sat with our eyes fixed on the stage and our ears alert to Mr. Hampden's slightest word.

A line adequately delivered by a member of the cast would bring our director up on the stage.

"Just a moment, please. . . . That was very good, but it occurred to me that it might be more effective if you crossed on the line before, so that when you came to your own line . . ." and he would illustrate, saying the words so meaningfully that it was as though they sprang into light. Those who have theater in their backgrounds have an idea of the miraculous welding that takes place in a company such as ours, under a man as dynamic and inspired as Walter Hampden. No rehearsals were too long, nothing was too much trouble, just so the effect, the ultimate perfection of line and movement, came through. I know in my own case I became so caught up that I forgot my family, forgot the young men who had hitherto occupied my thoughts, and lived only for the long, absorbing hours I spent in the stale dark of the National Theater.

Mr. Hampden had chosen his company with meticulous care. Part of it was his Shakespearean touring company, and it was thrilling to meet and know the men and women I had seen as Bassanio, Jaques, Emilia, Nerissa. In the earlier days, Mrs. Hampden—a slim, lovely, gentle lady—had played all the feminine leads, but now she was cheerfully resigned to the Abbess, and Carol McComus made a vivid and endearing Roxanne. Paul Leyssac was a virile and stunning Duke, and Charles Francis our handsome, stammering Christian. It was not a play of star performances, however. We were all living together a beautiful poetic romance and our individual importance was only in becoming part of the picture.

Mr. Hampden manipulated his players as a painter does his colors, grouping, highlighting one for an instant, moving the crowd in a flow from one side of the stage to the other, never losing track of a face in the final stage picture.

"Miss Garland—" he called up to where I was sitting in one of the boxes, as a court lady attending a theatrical performance at the Hotel de Bourgoyne— "when you say that line, 'Really! Our Barro!' half rise in your seat and clutch the railing angrily with both hands. As Cyrano's speech goes on, settle down again, slowly, resentfully."

In all the crowd scenes he played with us, catcalling as lustily as any, urging the boys on to extravagant, improvised horse play. It caught his fancy that my name, "Garland," appeared in one of his speeches, and night after night, when he read the line, "Garlanded with my good name—" he would turn and make me a deep deferential bow. In truth, for all his responsibilities, he was a merry soul, and the atmosphere he evoked was warm and cooperative.

My own part in this miraculous undertaking was modest but active. As a lady of quality, a comedienne, a member of the crowd, and in the last act a nun, I had eight costume changes and a race on matinee days—buttoning and unbuttoning as I ran—of seventy-two flights of stairs. My dressing room was on the third floor, and most of my entrances were on the other side of the stage, which meant I had to go down through the basement, where the stagehands played endless games of cards, and up the stairs on the other side. It was an athletic life—the salary was forty dollars a week—but stimulation and success of the production was my reward.

For we were a success, a gratifying one. All the care and artistry and dedication that had gone into Hampden's *Cyrano* were recognized. The critics to a man approved. The public adored it, and the company settled down for a long run. *Cyrano* ran for nine months and the theater took on an air of permanence. For some of the actors it was the first security they had ever known and their dressing rooms became virtual homes. Smiles were on every face.

Except, as time passed, mine. After long years of struggle, who could wish Walter Hampden anything but success, but I had joined the company in the expectation of playing Shakespearean repertoire, and the sameness of night after night began to get on my nerves. My enthusiasm for the stage, at least this part of it, was ebbing, and there was something else.

The company being full of bright, attractive young people, before long romances were blooming on every side, and during waits, we sat two by two on the stairs and talked of the future. Yes, I was off again but this time in deadly seriousness. Another actor, naturally, but also a man worth loving and we were deeply, truly attached.

Father was a bear. He could hardly bring himself to be civil to my poor Bill who, being a handsome, charming, gifted young man, had never met such antagonism before. In his diary Daddy wrote in fierce resentment of "the commonplace young man" his daughter was "resolved to throw herself away on," but Bill was anything but commonplace. Aside from his remarkable good looks, he had a trained speaking voice of great beauty, and on Sundays when he came to lunch and spent the day, he and I would play Shakespearean scenes together to an ecstatic audience of one: my sister.

Bill brought me home each night from the theater, and we lingered later and later in the dark downstairs vestibule, unable to leave each other's arms. It was insatiable physical attraction but it was something more. We were a romantic, high-minded pair, both determined on marriage, but there were, aside from my glowering, impossible father, two big stumbling blocks: we had no money and I was dead set against marrying an actor.

It was all due to a revelation I had experienced in the first theatrical company I had joined. One of the cast was an extremely beautiful and unscrupulous woman who, despite the fact that he was recently wed, had annexed her male counterpart. The wife, there in the theater every night, would come backstage during the intermission, tense and pale, and after a futile search would be forced to ask, "Has anyone seen my husband?"

A grinning extra or stagehand would tip a thumb at the closed dressing room door of the beautiful actress. "Sure. He's in there, with her."

The wife would stand for a moment, her eyes burning with pain in her expressive face, then she would turn and slip heartbrokenly away.

Bill was a Californian. His father was in the construction business, and Bill assured me would be only too pleased to have him give up the stage and go into business with him. That sounded like a hopeful, splendid idea. "California, Here I Am" was a popular song in those days, and in my mind's eye I was already at home in a dear little orange-groved cottage on the West Coast. Bill's wife. Thrilling nights of discovery and fulfillment. Cooking. Babies. . . .

Bill bought me a small aquamarine ring that I wore with pride and delight. I felt sure that when I walked down the street people would sense that I was "engaged" and catch a bit of the glory. Mother was a darling, sad at the thought of losing me, but understanding. I overheard a portion of a conversation between Mother and Daddy at the luncheon table one day.

Mother said wistfully, "I only want her to be happy."

I can still hear Father's snort as he expressed the conviction of his soul: "Happy! There *is* no happiness except in doing the work you want to do."

Bill and I were leaving the company, he to go out to California and into business with his father, I to do one more lecture tour with my father in the fall. Bill would come back at Christmas and we would be married and I would go out to California with him. It was my constant dream, my whole life had become focused. I began collecting for a hope chest and planning my trousseau. Oh, lovely, happy days!

The night before I left the Hampden Company they gave me a farewell party in the Grill room of one of the hotels. Everyone came and it was a sweet and sentimental time. I danced with every one of the men, and there were toasts to Bill's and my happiness and it was all perfect, except that next morning I woke up with the mumps! The memories I left behind me must have been mixed. For days everyone went around apprehensively sucking lemons and fearing the worst. Bill came to see me every day, and by drawing my long hair down and under my chin I hid the ugliest of the swelling from my romantic lover.

Bill took the train for the West and I wandered around the flat like the Tragic Muse. Mother, all tender sympathy, would invite me into bed with her and listen to my plans and what Bill had said in his last letter. We were really suffering at being apart, and once a week he would phone me late at night to save money. At the first jingle of the bell, I'd be out of bed and down the hall to the phone, which was on a long cord in the dining room. You could make it stretch as far as the bathroom, and sitting on the floor, with the door closed, I would whisper and weep and send passionate kisses

across three thousand miles. Father's room was next to the bathroom. I never asked and he never mentioned whether he had listened to any of those heartrending conversations.

Bill was surveying, he reported, and a dusty, unrewarding
job it was, but he had our hopes, his father was being helpful, and
his mother was eager to welcome me. We were marking off the
days, and each night, at a specified time, I would go up on the roof
and we would look at the same star: a big W in the north, W for
William, and my heart was so full of longing and beauty that it all
but tore me apart. I was even eager to start off on the lecture tour,
for aside from the money that Bill and I so desperately needed, it
would help the time to pass. Father was a little remote with me, but
he had taken heart from Bill's absence and in general things were
going as well as could be expected.

Then in *Variety* I read it: the San Francisco Stock Company
had just signed a new leading man. . . .

Bill phoned that night. Yes, it was true.

"But Isabel, listen! It will make it all so much better. I'm getting a good salary. You can come away and we can be married—"

"I told you, I will not marry an actor."

"But darling, that isn't fair!"

"Do you think what you are doing is fair? We had an
agreement. You had no right to go back on the stage."

"Isabel, I couldn't take the construction business. I'm an
actor, not a carpenter. I'd never be any good at it. And when I got
this bid from San Francisco. . . ." His voice broke. He was as ago-
nized as I. We were really in love. "Dearest, I love you more than
life."

"But not more than the stage." In my misery, I was a
dogged, monotonous record.

He was coaxing now, trying to break me down.
"Sweetheart, think of it! We could be together right away. You'll
love San Francisco. It's a wonderful town. We could get a little
house in Sausalito—"

"Where I could stay alone night after night. Or hang around
the theater, waiting for you to get through making love to another
woman. No, Bill, I know myself. We would both be miserable."

"But Isabel, you can't mean—"

"Yes, I can. I do. Thank heaven, I can see it now and not

later. There's no other answer. You'll have to choose between the stage and me."

He chose. A few weeks later, after letters, more frantic phone calls, heartbreak, I took off the little ring and put it in its box and asked my sister to mail it to him. From the perspective of years, I regard myself with amazement. I was wise and I was right, but where did I find the strength to deny my own heart?

Notes

[1] Ada Dow Currier (d. 1926) was an actress and theatrical producer who trained the renowned Shakespearean actress Julia Marlowe (1866-1950).

[2] In November 1922, Garland and Isabel toured with a lecture program entitled "Memories of the Middle Border," in which they took turns reading excerpts from Garland's stories, poems, and autobiographies, with Isabel costumed alternately as her mother and grandmother.

[3] Isabel was an understudy for the character of Audrey, played by Hortense Alden, in a production of *As You Like It*, staged by the American National Theater Company, in April 1923.

[4] Isabel's admirer was Walter Abel (1898-1987), who played the Lord in the production.

[5] Garland describes this meeting in *Afternoon Neighbors* (New York: Macmillan, 1934), 359-368. In December 1926 Garland met the automobile magnate when he stopped in Dearborn, Michigan, to deliver lecture "Memories of the Middle Border." In Garland's account, Constance, not Isabel, performed in the lecture and danced with Ford.

[6] That is, *Back-Trailers from the Middle Border* (1928).

[7] Walter Hampden (1879-1955), noted actor and Broadway producer. In 1925 he took over the Colonial Theater and renamed it Hampden's Theater. From November 1923 to June 1924, Isabel played several minor roles in Hampden's production of *Cyrano de Bergerac*.

[8] Apsley George Benet Cherry-Gerrard (1886-1959) was a member of Robert Scott's second Antarctica expedition (1910-1913). He wrote an acclaimed account of the expedition, *The Worst Journey in the World* (1922). Garland's review of the book appeared as "The Worst Journey in the World," *Literary Digest International Book Review* 1.4 (March 1923): 12-13, 62.

10. Marriage

ð   ð   ð

Daddy and I, a silent, constrained pair, set off on our lecture travels again. Though his diary records him as jubilant at the shattered romance, he knew that I was suffering, and I could feel his sympathy. Bill's name was never spoken between us.

Night after night, I'd lie in my train berth, trying not to see into the future, which was now a long, empty tunnel. Often, I was tempted to write Bill, to call, just to hear his voice again, but I told myself over and over that it had been the right, the only, decision. Curiously, after my surge of resentment, I did not blame Bill for his choice in the matter. He had told the truth: he was an actor, and his only chance for happiness lay in practicing his trade. I saw him years later on Broadway, a poised, skillful, middle-aged actor who touched me, I am glad to say, not at all.

We were back in New York for Thanksgiving and ahead loomed the Christmas that was to have been my wedding day. I can imagine what a death's head at the feast I was and marvel at my family's quite incredible patience. In my absorption with Bill I had discarded all my other beaux, and though some came drifting back when they realized I was free again, I had a lonely time of it through the holidays.

Then, one crisp winter day, an eager male voice on the telephone said, "This is Hardesty Johnson—the de Reszke Quartet, remember? We're just over from Nice to do a concert tour with Will Rogers. May I come and see you?"

I had forgotten how attractive he was. In fact, since he was no correspondent, I had almost forgotten him completely. He came in breezily, his boyish face glowing from the cold, and in a few minutes was completely at home. Inevitably, he set his big, well-upholstered body down on the piano bench, and as he rippled off de Falla, Bach, and Chopin, the Garland family settled down contentedly to listen.

His nickname was Jimmie, from the "James" that preceded the "Hardesty," and he stayed to tea, to dinner, and, had it been possible, would obviously have stayed the night. After dinner, at Daddy's command he sat down at the piano again and sang. He had a flawless voice and diction—Jean De Reszke said he was the ideal "Lohengrin"—and now as he sat in our little drawing room the love songs of many nations poured out in a velvet flood. It was almost more than I could bear. I lay on the couch with my head turned into a pillow and wept for Bill.

Jimmie was there constantly from then on, and there was no doubt of what was in his mind. I was exposed to the most glorious musical wooing that any girl ever had—Puccini, Bach, Wagner, Verdi all had a part in it, but though I was moved, I was not won.

"None but the lonely heart can know my sadness," sang my new lover, his eyes seeking me, while I, with eyes closed, was reliving feverish, stolen hours in the dark of the downstairs hall.

My family, however, had no reservations. Father, in a complete right-about-face, was as much in favor of this match as he had been against the other, and it is easy to see why. In the first place, Jimmie was to be based in New York. I would not be transplanted to the West Coast, far from my loving family. In the second place, here was a charming, cultivated, thoroughly amiable young man, one of the sweetest souls imaginable. To Jimmie, everyone else came first; his only desire was to serve and please. And third, here was a superb voice and musicianship with clearly a brilliant career ahead. Aside from his deep love of music, Daddy was a born promoter and his imagination kindled at the idea of helping this fine, deserving tenor get ahead. Once I said the word, Father would be in there working with all that was in him. Mother was frankly devoted to Jimmie, and Connie, now romantically involved herself with my first love, Joe,[1] was all enthusiasm.

As for me, I was in a curious state. While Jimmie sang to me, I believed. I told myself it was still possible to be happy. It was impossible not to love Jimmie, and in the drawing room, after the family had tactfully withdrawn, I would sit on his lap and try to lose myself in his long worshipping kisses. Oh, I was tempted. It all seemed so right, somehow. Of all the men I had known, Jimmie was the kindest, the most generous, the most adoring. We might work together, too. After he had left the Quartet and was off on his own, why could we not do a program together, as Father and I had, a program of poetry and song interwoven in some way? We discussed it with mounting excitement as the days passed, and Father was obviously ready to take charge at once.

The Quartet was embarking on an exhausting concert tour with Will Rogers that spring,[2] and that night before he left, Jimmie's lovemaking was so intense that passion flamed in me, too. I sent him off with a half promise, and his exultant happiness twisted my heart. How fortunate I was to be so loved, so cherished.

Rapturous, boyishly naïve letters began coming. Jimmie missed me hideously. He could hardly wait till he had me in his arms again. Then for a week or more, no letters.

I began to fret, to worry, to agonize. If Jimmie had sat himself down and deliberately worked out a way to arouse my interest, it could not have been a better one. Something I had been taking for granted seemed to be slipping away from me, and I grew frantic.

I came back to the flat one dreary March twilight to find Mother and Constance bubbling with excitement, and hanging from chandelier by long yellow ribbons was the looked-for letter.

> Minneapolis, Minnesota.
> Don't worry, darling. I'm in the hospital but I'll be all right. I had to leave the tour—nervous exhaustion—and I just want you to know I release you from your promise. You shouldn't be saddled with a crock like me. Go ahead and be happy and know I'll be happy if you are and loving you with everything there is in me to the end of my days. . . . Your Jimmie.

Jimmie ill in a hospital—releasing me from my promise! But I didn't want to be released! The dam broke. All doubts were swept away. I loved him. I wanted to go out there and look after him.

"Go—" Daddy said. "I'll foot the bills." And go I did.

I could never be grateful enough to Jimmie's family. It must have been disconcerting to have a strange, slightly-hysterical young woman appear out of the blue, to have to make arrangements to put her up, feed her, drive her to the hospital, listen to her torrents of conversation. They were exceptional people, all of them, and I came to love them dearly: the lovely, slim, self-contained mother and two bright, charming sisters who took me to their generous hearts and refused to let me feel myself the nuisance that I obviously was.

We had a long, serious conversation that first night, before I went to the hospital to see Hardesty—they did not call him Jimmie. It seemed that he had always had a curiously malformed heart, one valve much smaller than the other, but it usually compensated. The tour with Will Rogers—forty-five performances in forty-four days—was so grueling, however, that Jimmie collapsed and was sent back to Minneapolis, his home town, to recuperate. After a week or so in the hospital, he could be taken home, and good food and rest were all he required. His mother had a comfortable old farm on the outskirts of Minneapolis, and there Jimmie was to stay and there I was invited also. I was wild with impatience to get him back to Dr. Turck—our patron saint, the one who had cured Daddy of arthritis and looked after us all ever since. The day before I left, Dr. Turck had called me on the phone. "You bring that young man of yours back to me and I'll fix him up as good as new," he had promised. "We'll have him in shape for a June wedding, you'll see." For the present, there was no question of Jimmie's traveling, and I was deeply grateful to my future mother-in-law for her invitation to stay at the farm.

Once there, I was back in West Salem again. Oh, the blessed silence, the complete peace! Only the wind in the trees, the cheeping of little snowbirds—it was still deep winter in Minnesota—the morning crow of the cocks. It was an almost dreamlike period. Jimmie lay there, blissfully happy and relaxed, reaching out to catch hold of me as I went by and draw me down for a kiss. Mrs. Johnson and I in the cozy old kitchen, concocting delicious meals for our patient. Quiet evenings under the lamp, while Jimmie and his mother reminisced, and I came to love and respect them more. In short, we became firm friends, and it only settled me more firmly in my resolve. I was a *family* girl, I recognized. I liked the warmth and shared interest of a family circle, and here was one that accepted me wholeheartedly.

In a few weeks, I brought Jimmie back to New York to Dr. Turck, who examined him and said crisply, "Nothing wrong with your heart. Go down to the first floor and run up the three flights to my office."

Jimmie and I looked at each other aghast. Jimmie said his first thought was that it was as good a way to end it all as any and obediently went downstairs, convinced he would not survive and only sorry he would not be able to marry me. I was in an agony of fear, but my faith in Dr. Turck was unlimited, and when my puffing husband-to-be arrived at the top floor and was pronounced in fine shape, we went joyfully into each other's arms.

We had a charming wedding in the Turck's handsome home just off Fifth Avenue, with the organ playing, me in white taffeta (made by Mother, of course) and a trailing net veil.[3] Connie was a bewitching bridesmaid, there were lots of people and champagne and some truly magnificent presents, and we rode away to a bridal suite at the Ambassador in a borrowed limousine.

There was nothing abandoned about our wedding night. I did put on my gold-satin, ostrich-trimmed negligee (my own creation and a horror if there ever was one), and Jimmie pursued me around the suite and carefully tore it off me. We had more champagne and dined expensively in our own suite and in due course went to bed. I had been armed with contraceptives, and Jimmie made love to me very gently and sweetly and, being tired, shortly went to sleep. I had experienced almost nothing and tossed and turned and finally got up and sat in a chair by the window for the rest of the night, looking out into the lights of the tall buildings and thinking in a dazed sort of way—so this is marriage. Is this all there is to it? I felt an emptiness, an ache of longing for a lost dream. I who had expected never to be lonely again was lonelier than I had ever been in my life before.

In the morning I got into bed with Jimmie again, who caressed me tenderly, and when I showed signs of responding, put me aside with a mild, "You know, darling, we mustn't make a habit of this."

At noon I phoned the family and invited ourselves to dinner. The next day we drove up to the Onteora cabin for our honeymoon.

The family came up shortly to Grey Ledge, the place we

Isabel and Hardesty Johnson on their wedding day, 1926.
(*Courtesy of Victoria Doyle-Jones*)

called the big house, a rambling, dark-red structure on an outcrop of rocks on the very top of Onteora Mountain, with a view of rare beauty.[4] It had been the property of Dr. Jones, who had built us a little theater at the back of the lot and sold the main house to Daddy. Thus the Garlands came up in the world. We all loved the place, with its deep settle-walled fireplace and the huge kitchen where a wood-burning stove kept the room cozily warm through the sharp mountain nights. Daddy had a whole wing to himself, with several doors he could close between himself and youthful bedlam. It was the first time, he said, that he was able to live with dignity.

It was an almost perfect summer, on the surface. If I was all too aware of what I was missing, no one else was, and Daddy was happier than I had ever seen him before. He had figuratively "gained a son," for Jimmie was all that a devoted son could be, and Connie and Mother were equally content. My father was deep in plans for "Hardy's" New York debut in the fall. It was to be a concert recital; he was not trying for opera at this point.

The cabin, where Jimmie and I were playing house, vibrated day and night to music. Jimmie was working on his voice and repertoire, and I was deep in poetry, trying to make a selection that could be adapted to our program of poetry and song. We dined back and forth between the two houses and swam and played tennis and picnicked, but our former group singing went by the board. When you have a consummate artist on tap, you are a bit shy of offending the cultivated ear by a lot of off-key harmony. Not that Jimmie objected; he would sing along cheerfully with anybody, but now and then an involuntary expression of pain would cross his face.

The only thing that really worried Daddy that summer was Connie's romance with Joe. She was very young, and since Joe had to spend a lot of time on his ranch in Arizona and on the West Coast with his mother, Daddy kept hoping it would all blow over. Jimmie and I were completely in my sister's confidence, and she would talk to us by the hour about Joe with whom she was madly but worriedly in love. There was something almost pathetic in the way she kept asking, "Do you think he's the right one to marry? Would a *man* like him?"

Jimmie, who was deeply fond of Joe, assured her that anyone would like him, that he was eminently suitable. In fact, we pro-

moted the match for all we were worth. We had a lot of gay trips
together, the four of us, Jimmie and I the most casual of chaperons.
We gave the old play *Rip Van Winkle* that summer, with Connie and
Joe as the beguiling young lovers. By the end of the summer, my
sister had made up her mind, and there was an autumn wedding at
Grey Ledge.[5]

Actually, it was Jimmie's wedding; he did everything but
marry the girl. What with decorating the house with branches of
autumn color, chauffeuring the guests, rushing to Albany for the
wedding bouquet, singing Connie's favorite songs, "Ich Liebe Dich"
and "Zueignung," before the ceremony, playing the wedding march,
and acting as Joe's best man, he was really, I assured him, the focal
point of the whole occasion.

I helped Connie dress in our big, many-windowed bedroom in which we had talked so many nights away, and just as she
was about to start down the stairs, we went into each other's arms
for a moment. Then, for she had inherited Mother's dread of emotional display, she set me gently aside and walked to the door.

At the head of the stairs, she looked back over her white
satin clad shoulder with a wicked smirk.

"Do I look *ethereal* enough?"

Joe's mother, a handsome, dictatorial ex-actress, was tense-
ly present, and his little sister, a poised, reserved child with a
charming heart-shaped face, and I were Connie's attendants.[6] After
the reception, at the last moment, with Connie already in the be-rib-
boned car and everyone pelting her with rice and good wishes, the
bridegroom could not be found. Jimmie finally ran him to earth in
his sobbing mother's arms, and the distracted pair departed, only to
phone a half hour later from Saugerties that one of the most important pieces of luggage had been left behind. Who do you think went
after them with it? Right.

The big old house was terrible that night. When I left, it had
only been for a few blocks from the family apartment, but our baby
was going three thousand miles away. The autumn winds mourned
around the eaves and the silence and sense of loss was excruciating.
Fortunately, Mother's brother, Lorado Taft, was there, and after dinner we drew in close together around the wide, glowing hearth and
bravely talked of other things. Daddy and Mother tried to console
themselves with the thought that Joe had promised they would

Constance Garland Harper on her wedding day, 1927.
"Do I look *ethereal* enough?"
(*Courtesy of Victoria Doyle-Jones*)

come back for Christmas, but we were glad to close up the mountain houses with their memories and return to the challenging city again.

That fall was exciting. Jimmie and I rented a flat on Eighth Street, a charming atmospheric place, and our work continued. Jimmie was teaching, and every Sunday, for a modest but helpful fee, he would be the soloist in one of the city's leading churches. I would go with him and sit in a close-up side pew and do my best, I am embarrassed to say, to break him up in the middle of his leading aria by blowing him silent kisses. We had Thanksgiving dinner with Mother and Daddy and came up on the Fifth Avenue bus carrying two hot homemade pies, one mince and one pumpkin. Their aroma filled the bus and everyone looked in our direction and grinned and sniffed enviously.

Then Christmas loomed and the first hint of trouble came from the West: Joe's mother refused to part with him for Christmas. Connie, loyal little daughter and sister, had promised to spend the holidays with us. It was a grim battle out there before Connie came East—alone. Joe said later he had been hideously hurt at her desertion, casually dismissing the idea that he was the one who had gone back on his word. Connie only stayed with us for a few days, but alas, the damage had been done.

Jimmie's debut was an unqualified success,[7] but the night of the concert I discovered for the first time what it means to be a singer on the occasion of a first public appearance. My poor husband was blue with nerves. It broke my heart to see his fingers fumbling with his shirt studs, to have his fresh young face so set and grim. I made him milk toast, it was all he dared to eat; he downed a jigger of scotch, and off he went, to do or die.

When he came out on the platform, I sat twisting my fingers in agony, understanding something of what my mother used to feel whenever Father rose to speak. Amazingly, Jimmie seemed at ease. As his accompanist arranged his music, my husband's eyes roamed the hall, found me, and a reassuring smile lifted the corners of his mouth. I blew him a kiss and the concert was on. Everything went beautifully. The distinguished audience Father had rounded up applauded with generous enthusiasm. The critics next day were unanimous in praise of his voice, his artistry. Concert dates began coming in.

It was a hard financial struggle, nevertheless. Daddy was splendid, but we were both proud and wanted to try to make our own way. Now and then some of Mother's and Father's wealthy friends would hire us for a drawing room musicale, and that was fun. We had started to try out our poetry-song program and it seemed to go well.[8] We gave it one night at the Elon Hookers' and one of their bright, charming daughters rushed up to Jimmie and me, her face alight.[9]

"Oh, that was beautiful! Tell me all about your wonderful life!"

To her we were the very incarnation of luck: newly married, a joint career, the world, ostensibly, at our feet. And we, with the monthly struggle to pay our bills, looked around at the fabulous luxury that was a commonplace to her and exchanged wry glances.

We had acquired an agent who booked us on a trip to the West Coast, where we would stay with Connie and Joe in a little house they had taken in the Hollywood hills. It was an exciting trip, for we went by way of Santa Fe and stayed as performing guests at Bishop's Lodge. Neither of us had seen this country before, and we were enamored. We rode on horseback out across the sunset desert and, traditionally, could hardly sit down the next day.

It was February when we left New York City, buried in filthy snow, garbage, and ashes, under a smutty sky. We arrived in Pasadena in a temperature of eighty degrees, birds singing, roses blooming, and Connie in an open car, wearing a brief white linen frock and tanned as brown as a berry. We lunched on a vine-shaded patio with the mocking birds going wild and a soft, caressing wind from the Pacific lifting our hair. Jimmie and I were incredulous. We fell in love with California in ten seconds flat.

"The next time we come back—we come back to live," we promised each other.

Part of it was the fact that Connie and Joe were definitely committed to the West Coast, were building a home next to Joe's mother, and were looking forward to a baby in late summer.[10] It was all too exciting to be out of, and Jimmie and I tore ourselves away with great reluctance and went back East to make arrangements to shift all our operations to the West.

Our poor parents. First, they had lost their beloved Connie; now the other young people on whom they depended so much

Constance Garland Harper, who had "gone Hollywood,"
around 1930.
(*Courtesy of Victoria Doyle-Jones*)

were preparing to abandon them. Reproach was in their eyes and their voices. However, there was the summer to look forward to, for Connie had promised to come on for a week or so and the family would be all together once more.

Her visit was disturbing. She had "gone Hollywood": hair tinted platinum, gypsy dark skin, and strange, exotic clothes that shouted money and sophistication. She was nervous and unhappy at being away from Joe—whose possessive mother's apron strings wound ever tighter and tighter—and she delivered the final blow, the one Mother and Father had dreaded: she and Joe would remain in the West from now on. She was off and on her way home before we had really time to realize she had come.

We were making plans, however. Jimmie and I were to go on in late summer and find a house big enough for all of us, and Mother and Daddy would come on for the birth of Connie's baby. Father's face was gaunt with pain as he kissed her goodbye, and Mother's eyes were blinded with tears. A shadow lay over the big house that had once comforted us all. I couldn't bear to leave Mother and Daddy there alone the night of Connie's leaving, so I made some excuse to spend the night, and my parents' gratitude was pathetic. We sat up late before the fire and Jimmie sang some of the old songs that Daddy loved, and we made it a sort of bulwark against the divided future. For the first time, I saw my mother and father as old and bereft, and it made my heart ache, yet in our self-ishness, Jimmie and I persisted in our own plans. I wanted to be near my sister, and Jimmie had studio connections and felt reason-ably assured of a profitable job.

We parted from Mother and Father as cheerily as possible, reminding them that they were to join us within a month, and I can-not remember a single pang at saying goodbye to New York City. We had our sights now on flowers and trees and eternal summer, and the excitement that New York had once offered, that still offered Daddy with his clubs, the Academy, his editors and publishers, seemed tinsel by comparison. A few friends and relatives, the peace and beauty of the Catskills, the pain of separation from Mother and Daddy: these alone provoked a backward look as we gathered our baggage and departed to greener pastures.

Those were lovely, young, carefree days in Hollywood—the four of us going everywhere together, playing tennis, swimming, dancing, trips to Santa Barbara, San Diego, San Francisco, lapping up sun and sweet air. Connie and Joe seemed as happy to see us as we were to see them, and they entertained us royally and introduced us to their circle of gay, moneyed, recently married friends. Hollywood was a simple country town in those days, as far as its Main Street went. After the motion picture theaters let out at eleven, there was nothing to do but go to the Pig and Whistle for an ice cream soda. We saw little of the studio at first, though Cecil DeMille gave me a luncheon at which were *four* famous movie stars.

We found a pleasant house not far from where Joe and Connie were building, and I think we were as happy as we had ever been. We had a concert tour lined up for fall and a job was looming for Jimmie at Twentieth Century Fox, so our future seemed secure. Jimmie was still adoring, we were popular socially, and I was too occupied to sit down and reason out what it was that took me unawares now and then, turning everything flat and meaningless.

The family arrived on schedule, approved the house, and we all sat down to wait the arrival of John Harper.[11]

I was in the hallway of the hospital with Mother and Joe when the baby was announced, and we stood stricken as Constance, unconscious and wan and bloodless as the Lily Maid of Astolot, was wheeled out of the delivery room.

"Come in—come in!" shouted Dr. Ainley, holding up a small bloody baby, much as he might have held a chicken over a butcher's counter. "Look at him! Isn't he a beauty?"

Frankly—no. I was appalled. I had never been in an operating room before, and the blood, the smell of ether, the general effect of a life and death struggle was almost too much for me. The baby had a bluish tinge and a large and curiously pointed head, and I saw Joe flinch and look away and then edge up to the doctor and ask a question.

"The head? Oh, that'll straighten out all right. A lot of them look like that at first. You can take my word for it—this is a perfect child."

Incredible, never-ending miracle. Out of the ugly welter of the delivery room emerged this little creature that within a matter of a few days was as lovely as a young prince and shortly became the focal point of all our households. Whatever the baby did was more remarkable than any child's actions before. His eyes were the bluest, his lashes the longest, his smiles the sweetest, his ways the most endearing. All day long, some of us were hanging over him, worshipping. I was permitted to come each day for his bath, to walk him and sing him to sleep. Not since I had wheeled little Ruthie Dudley in her go-cart at the age of ten had I been exposed to a baby, and something stirred in me insistently.

Jimmie shook his head. "Not now, darling—later, perhaps. We're so right as we are and I've got this new job to do and ought to give it my whole time and attention. Another couple of years, maybe." The truth was, Jimmie didn't care for children, hadn't seen much of them, was a bit apprehensive about them.

Daddy had commitments in the East and finally he managed to tear Mother away. That was a beastly year for them. Their letters were one surge of longing for their children, though they had a few good times: nice visits with Frank Seaman at Yama Farms,[12] and in the early summer, Mother had her heart's wish, which was to see Greece, Egypt, and Italy with her artist brother. Uncle Lorado was taking over a University group and Mother and Aunt Juliet were included. Daddy was so lonely rattling around in the Big house in Onteora that he came out to spend the summer with us, bringing Blinkie with him.

Jimmie and Connie and I met the train in Pasadena, and I saw with a pang that Daddy didn't swing down the steps the way he used to but came down slowly and carefully. His hug was still strong, however, and his face shone with affection. Blinkie was in a travel basket in the baggage car, and Father explained that he had left the train at every ten minute stop and gone up and taken her out for a stroll along the tracks. They must have made an amusing picture to the other passengers: the white-mustached old gentleman, the cavorting, little white mop. White! What am I saying? The apparition that came streaking to us along the Pasadena platform, uttering her shrill, rapturous yelps, was almost coal black, matted of hair, and incredibly smelly. But she was ours—and she loved us. An hour later, once again her snowy self, she was happily taking over our new rented house.

Daddy enjoyed his stay with us. He had a big, sunny study-bedroom and bath all his own, and he basked in our firelight, with Blinkie on his knees, or sat contentedly in the patio looking out over the hills of Griffith Park and doing, I could see, some pretty concentrated thinking. One morning when he and I were breakfasting out in the patio alone, I heard what it was.

We had been talking about Connie's lovely Spanish house into which they had just moved and were happily and expensively furnishing. Daddy had enjoyed superintending the building of it and now, after a little silence, while his eyes roamed the line of hills and the wind lifted his white hair, he said slowly, "Daughtie, your mother and I need you. We need you like—hell." Daddy never used profanity and the word came out with a wry smile. "You don't know what it's like getting old, with no young people around to give you a stake in the future. I've been thinking. . . . You and Jimmie have been renting around long enough. It's time you had a home of your own, started raising a family. I'm prepared to buy the lot next to Connie and build you a house *provided*—" he emphasized the word with a smile and an emphatic finger— "provided you set aside a wing for your mother and me, when we get tired of the cold and loneliness back East and decide we need to visit our children."

"Oh, Daddy!" I had my arms around his neck. "It's too wonderful—"

"Wait a minute, now. Don't decide in a hurry. We're not getting any younger, your mother and I. Old people are inclined to be cranky and set in their ways. Not—" he added hurriedly— "that we're proposing to *live* with you. I've got my work and responsibilities in New York, and your mother has her friends there. It would just be for Christmas, say, and the worst part of the winter. They tell me you don't have any winter out here. . . . Well, what do you think about it?"

"I think you're the most generous and thoughtful father who ever lived! I'll have to talk to Jimmie, of course, but you know how he feels about you and Mother. We'd love to have you for as long as you'll stay. . . . Oh, Daddy is it really true? Am I going to have a home of my own?"

Notes

1 That is, Joseph Harper.
2 In April 1925 the humorist Will Rogers (1879-1935), whose early

performances were noted for his trick roping accompanied by satire on current events, left the Ziegfeld Follies to begin a series of concert performances accompanied by the de Reszke Singers. Later, he became a film star and served as toastmaster at a dinner to celebrate Garland's 73rd birthday.

3 Isabel and Hardesty were married on May 12, 1926.

4 In August 1925 Garland bought a house in the Onteora community, now able to afford the $4,000 price—and the yearly association dues—from royalties from the sale of rights to a film version of *Cavanagh, Forest Ranger*, filmed as *The Ranger of the Big Pines* (1925). Isabel and Hardesty are honeymooning at Camp Neshonoc.

5 Constance and Joseph Wesley Harper were married on September 12, 1927.

6 Joe Harper's mother is Olive Grismer (b. 1878). She had married William Armitage Harper in 1898. Biographical records are incomplete, but census records show that she was still married to Harper in 1910 but by 1920 had married the actor Joseph R. Grismer, who died in 1922. In 1910 she had a role in a Lillian Russell play in Indiana, *In Search of a Sinner*; and she may have acted under the name "Olive Harper Thorne" in four plays between 1912 and 1922 (*Internet Broadway Database*). Joe's sister is also named Olive Grismer (b. 1916).

7 Hardesty gave a solo recital at New York's Steinway Hall on October 26, 1926, in a program that included Purcell, Elgar, Grieg, Duparc, and Strauss. See "Hardesty Johnson Heard," *New York Times*, October 27, 1926, 25.

8 On January 11, 1927, Isabel and Hardesty gave a combined program of song and poetry at Chickering Hall, introduced by Garland.

9 Elon Huntington Hooker (1869-1938) was the founder of the Hooker Electrochemical Company.

10 The houses are in the 2000 block of DeMille Drive, a gated community in Hollywood overlooked by the mansion of film director Cecil B. DeMille.

11 John Wesley Harper was born on September 6, 1929.

12 Frank Seaman (1858-1939) was a former advertising executive who founded Yama Farms Inn at Napanach, New York, in 1913. The Inn was famous for its Japanese-inspired architecture and was a well-known resort.

11. Home

❧ ❧ ❧

Father, as he himself expressed it, was a "do-er." The next morning he was over consulting with Joe's mother, Aunt Olive, who had designed her house and Joe's and Connie's and was now to see that ours would be harmonious with the others. It was all most exciting and Daddy was in his element. Things were well underway by the time Mother returned from her Greek trip, and a wan lady she was. She had contracted some kind of fever that hung on and left her weak and shaky, but she was so glad to be back with her children and grandson that we told ourselves she would be all right before long. She loved the idea of the new house, and we all went around in a state of high enthusiasm.

The plans were ready and the foundations laid before Mother and Daddy left for the East in the spring. The lot was a hillside one, bowered in olive trees, looking out over the mountains of Griffith Park and the Planetarium, with Old Baldy's range to the east. Daddy had become more and more extravagant as the plans progressed. Every room had to be three feet longer. There was to be a fireplace in Jimmie's and my bedroom and one in Daddy's study, as well as in the drawing room. More and bigger windows. Hand-wrought iron for the decorative balcony that ran, in the New Orleans style, the full length of the house. Handmade Spanish tiles for the long, low roofline. He was spending money like a drunken sailor, he admitted, and he was enjoying every minute of it. Aside from rebuilding Mapleshade and the improvements to the Onteora cabin, he had never built a house for himself before, never started with anything new and fresh and exactly as he wanted it. He was so caught up in the venture that he could hardly bear to tear himself away, but there were the usual lecture dates in the East, and Mother was eager to stop off in Chicago and see the Taft family.

"Good luck, daughtie!" Daddy called from the train steps. "Let us know when our suite is ready and we'll come and occupy it. Hurry them up, so that we can be in the new house for Christmas!" Jimmie and I were also carried away. This was to be our first real home—all the others had been furnished rentals—and we began designing custom-made furniture and haunting auctions and Barker's bargain basement. Jimmie was doing well at Fox as a singing-actor and assistant choral director, and we were living handsomely, too handsomely, to tell the truth. Our new California friends were all better off than we were and could afford to lose fifty dollars or so at cards each night, or spend the weekend at Catalina or the Santa Barbara Biltmore. We were included in most of the invitations, and now and then, feeling guilty, we went. About this time we started drinking too much, too. It was Prohibition and it was smart to have your bootlegger drive up in a sedan with his wife and baby and leave off a vastly overpriced case of contraband. It was Jimmie who introduced me to the "dressing drink," the one you have in your bedroom while you are getting ready to go out and not feeling sanguine about the prospect. It most certainly helps, but the trouble is that you get started that much earlier.

Aside from planning for the house, I was leading a cushy life. My mornings were usually spent on the tennis court, either the DeMilles' or one in Beverly Hills, with luncheon and bridge to follow. At six my husband returned home and we went out to cocktails and dinner or had people in, followed by more bridge and poker. In our new house, Father said, we were to have a permanent cook-housekeeper, in return for which I would contribute my secretarial services. He was working on his literary reminiscences, and Connie took time off from little John—another baby was on the way—to do skillful pen and ink illustrations for the book. We were young and fairly prosperous and should have spent our time counting our blessings, except that we did not.

In fact, Connie and I were not behaving very well. From the first, she had had a mother-in-law problem and it did not improve with time. Hurt with her husband's abject devotion to his mother,

Illustration for *Back-Trailers from the Middle Border* (p. 357), by
Constance Garland. Represented are Hardesty Johnson and Isabel
during their stage performance.
(*Courtesy of Keith Newlin*)

Connie tried to get back at him by flirting foolishly with other men. Joe tried the same technique and hurt piled upon hurt.

In my own case, I had discovered early in our married life that my nice husband was a hypochondriac. The consciousness of his malformed heart made it inevitable but he reached the point where he was afraid of any exertion. A concert was a matter of dread and his interest shifted to teaching, which required much less physical and nervous effort. Love-making, too, it seemed, was dangerous, and though he continued to woo me with words and music, our nights were merely for sleeping. I became tense and restless. I flirted, too, and was on occasion short-tempered, but no one could really be angry with Jimmie—he was so darned *good*.

We managed it. We all had Christmas in the new house, and Father's pride and satisfaction in it were beyond words. He all but went about patting it. Connie's little daughter, Constance, was born by arrangement on New Year's Eve.[1] Jimmie and I were down at the hospital, but I phoned the news home and Aunt Olive came over with champagne for the other grandparents. Joe went to an all-night party.

Mother and Daddy and Jimmie and I were pretty luxuriously bestowed, with a pretty Swedish maid to bring up hot homemade sweet rolls on our breakfast trays in bed. I gave a few hours at the typewriter to Daddy every morning, but what he really wanted me to do, had always been urging me to do, was to try my hand at writing. In England, he had insisted I keep a diary and gave me a handsome one in which I wrote a few banal pages and then gave up. Now and then I made a half-hearted start and had finally worked out an idea for a mystery novel based on the people and situations I had been observing in Hollywood.

Every Sunday morning, for instance, we all went down to spend the day at the Santa Monica Beach Club: babies, nurse, Joe, Connie, Jimmie, and I, with now and then a reluctant parent as well. The crowds and glare troubled mother, who was not making the recovery we had hoped for from the Egyptian fever, and Father frankly detested the beach and hated the sight of scantily-clad people playing volley ball or romping boisterously in the sand. It became somewhat of an ordeal for me, too. I was not a strong swimmer, and having been caught once in a Pacific rip tide, I was wary about going into the water. I am also a heliophobe, for too much sun is sickening to me and I was no good at volley ball, so I would get myself an umbrella and a book and lie looking out at the sea and the merry little ones in the surf and wishing I was back in the cool comfort of our home again. Part of the time, I planned my mystery, which was to start with a murder at the Beach Club, among the giddy motion picture and society characters with whom I was thrown.

Father, who had recently discovered Edgar Wallace and was avidly reading the whole list, was delighted to hear of my project. He bought me a new typewriter and boxes of fine bond and carbon paper and waited hopefully for progress. Each morning after he had finished his own stint, I'd hear him come out in the hall and listen at my door. Eventually, he would tap lightly.

"I don't hear any typewriter keys clattering in there, Mary Isabel," he would call out. "What's the matter? Old Subconscious not working?"

"Old S.C." was his name for the mysterious inner wellspring that every creative person knows about, the power that can, without warning, take over and turn the most dogged drudgery into a singing flood. I had not had much experience with it at this time and was mostly glad to give up any pretence of writing and go into the big, sunny study and type letters and revised manuscript. It was a sweet and valuable companionship we had in those days, my father and I.

Daddy continued to delight in the new house. I was always having to drive him and Mother to the May Company or Barker's or Sloane's for just the right piece of furniture to fit this corner or that. "We've had enough shabby things. You and your mother deserve the best we can afford," he would say, but it was Daddy who took the most joy in them.

Both my parents loved to motor. Mother was more relaxed in a car than anywhere else, and at the wheel of Daddy's new car (he proudly bought a new one each year, and it had to go up the hill at the Planetarium in high or it was no deal) we went all over California. In the season, we would drive out to visit friends in Arcadia and come home with lugs of huge, delicious navel oranges. We explored the Missions, the mountains, and the coastline, toured museums and universities, but the thing we all liked most of all was the Sunday afternoon polo game at the Riviera Club. It was balm to your soul to sit out under that flawless sky, the sea wind fresh on your cheek, watching the charge of superb Argentine, British, and American ponies up and down the emerald green field. Even the drive out and back was charming, through Beverly Hills' finest residential district, and our favorite radio station, KFAC, had the inspiration to put on a Bach program every afternoon at four, so that we came home on the wings of music. Through Jimmie, who had toured with him, we came to know Will Rogers, and Daddy and he became good friends. Often, of an afternoon, we would drive out to the Rogers ranch and oversee a practice game, with Will captaining a team consisting of his two young sons, Will Jr. and Jim, and the motion picture director Hal Roach. There was scant style to Will's riding, but he was a hell-bent-for-leather polo player.

It was a peaceful, almost idyllic life, but with the coming of spring in the East, Father would grow restless again, line up lecture dates to pay the cost of the trip, scoop up Mother—who was enthralled with her grandchildren and would far rather have stayed with us—and off they'd go, back to the Big Town and the intellectual stimulation that was the breath of life to Father.

Much as we loved our family, after they had gone it was a relief to have our new house to ourselves. We could entertain anyone we liked, stay up all night playing symphonic records, do or not do whatever we pleased. Jimmie started writing songs for an operetta that his friend, John Boles,[2] was considering doing for the motion pictures, and I wrote the lyrics. It was fun and brought us together in a way we had not known since we worked on our concerts together. I needed something like that. My mystery novel was hopelessly bogged down and my creative energy was demanding an outlet. It would have been the ideal time to have children, except that Jimmie didn't want them. Neither, at this point, did I.

Early in the summer, there was a phone call from Mrs. Frank Vanderlip, whose three-thousand-acre estate at Palos Verdes we had visited several times.[3]

"Frank and I are going to Europe for three months and we wondered if you young people might like to occupy our guest house during that time. It would be a great comfort to know that there was someone in residence while we're away."

Jimmie and I were all but speechless with joy. The guest house was a lovely eight-room Italian villa at the foot of a long line of cypresses. It overlooked a tennis court and far below were three miles of romantic private beach. There were riding horses at our command and a handyman to lay the fires and attend to the garden, and Jimmie and I took possession with rapture. It had a Mediterranean beauty. All day I found myself going about singing "Come Back to Sorrento"—the sea was so deep a blue, the air so fresh, Catalina Island a low-lying violet presence on the horizon.

The trouble was we wanted to share it with everyone, and in those three months we never spent a night alone, and I got pretty tired of cooking for a houseful of guests, but it was worth it. We were all in swimming one afternoon off Portugeese Bend when Jimmie spied a large, mysterious object washing back and forth under the oncoming waves. Bravely, he investigated, to find it was a case of scotch whiskey wrapped in burlap, apparently dropped off by a rum-runner during a midnight sortie. Jimmie had the scotch analyzed by a chemist, and it was pure, uncut, and in every way admirable. From that time on, our male guests spent most of their time hopefully combing the waves, but the experience was not repeated.

Back in Hollywood, Connie's winsome children were a constant joy, and at first she shared them with me wholeheartedly; but gradually, as her own emotional resentment grew, it seemed to be directed at me. She called me less often, there were fewer evenings that the four of us spent together, and she seemed distant and impatient when I did see her. Finally, I decided to have it out with her.

"Well, frankly," she said, "Joe thinks we've been seeing too much of you and Jimmie and says we should devote more time to our other friends."

Later, Joe told the same story, only differently. "Connie has decided we have been seeing too much of you and Jimmie and should give more time to our other friends."

This was known as "passing the buck," and I don't know where the truth lay, but I was, naturally, hurt beyond measure. I decided not to call or invite them to anything, and after a few weeks, Connie invited us to dinner. There is nothing more fruitless than a grudge with one's only sister, so we went and they came to us occasionally after that, but the old happy intimacy was gone. I had no clear idea of what Connie was going through, nor she of me, but it was a disillusioning, unhappy time that I prefer to forget.

That fall there was a big change in our lives. Father's letters from Onteora, where Mother and he had been spending the summer in Grey Ledge, grew more and more forlorn. Mother was not improving; she was getting worse and was, in fact, nearly helpless. It was impossible for her to live in the big house with inadequate care. There was only one solution.

"Mother needs her daughters," Father wrote in bitter surrender. "I have taken her away for the last time. I'll continue to come East when I can, but from now on your mother will make her home with you and Jimmie."

What were we to say? The original agreement was that they would be three or four months' visitors. Fond as we were of them and grateful for their generosity, it was impossible to lead any life of our own while they were there. Guests had to be carefully screened to please our parents, early hours observed, menus adjusted to their needs and likes. Perhaps the hardest thing of all was their unhappiness every time we went out. They wanted us there all the time, and I was quite sick with sympathy, mixed, I am afraid, with a little resentment at the change in their faces when I said, "We're not going to be here for dinner tonight." Each time we drove away, it was with the picture of two silent figures on each side of the fireplace, and the wistful appeal on their eyes haunted me though the gayest evening.

Our first impulse was to cut and run, but how could we do that? How could you walk out on a frail, sick darling, whose love was twined around and around you like a vine? Father had built the house for me, for my happiness. What kind of ungrateful children would we be who could walk out on responsibility like that?

Jimmie was quite desperate, but the more we talked it over, the more we realized where our path lay. We must never let them know that we felt anything but joy and satisfaction in their company. Having no children, they became, in a curious roundabout way, our children, and the future was gray with duty and self-sacrifice.

We met them with open arms at the train, and on the surface life resumed itself smoothly and pleasantly, but underneath was real tragedy. Mother was now in the ugly grip of Parkinson's disease. Her hands and feet shook constantly, and she was in morbid dread that in time her head would shake, too. Thank God, it

Hamlin Garland in his Hollywood home.
(*Courtesy of Victoria Doyle-Jones*)

never did, and strangely, after Father died, the shaking all but disappeared; she was once more able to hold a cup and a fork and her beautifully modeled face took on an unearthly beauty.

At this time, she refused to see anyone and would stay in her room when we had anyone to tea or dinner. Father was bewildered, miserable. He haunted her bedroom, sitting by her hour after hour, sometimes reading aloud or listening with her to symphonic music on her bedside radio that was never turned off, day or night. Often he would lean forward and take her poor, quivering hand in his big paw, holding it for as long as she would permit him. In her own wretchedness Mother was cool, almost unkind to Father. In the car, when Jimmie and I took them on long drives up and down and across California, Father always sought Mother's hand, humbly, almost pleadingly, as if in shame for some past injustice, yet I knew that Father—stubborn, unreasonable, emotionally mercurial—was at the core all warmth and tenderness.

Oh, but the poor man was lonely! Separated by three thousand miles from his familiar world of the Century Club, the Academy of Arts and Letters, and his literary and editorial friends, he tried gallantly to find comfort on our quiet, olive-treed hillside. Unable to drive a car, with no bus or other transportation available, he was marooned, unless Connie or Jimmie or I drove him somewhere. Then where was he to go? Los Angeles was not a literary town, with congenial groups of literary craftsmen to draw on. The University people were life-savers. Once or twice a month, Dr. Baxter or Dr. Cooke or Dr. Greever would make the long trip out to have coffee and cakes on our back patio or in front of the drawing room fire.[4] Often they would bring a group of students with them, and for an hour or two Father would expand and become his old glowing self again, only to drop back into gloom after the guests were gone. Yet he loved our fine new home, the trees, the birds, the flowers, the warmth. One of his favorite expeditions was to Armstrong Nurseries, where he would buy blooming potted plants with prodigal abandon.

"I'm too old to wait for them to grow," he said. "I want color and bloom around me *now*."

He always maintained, however, that California should not be for young people. "They haven't earned it. It should come as the reward of a long, hard life spent somewhere else." By his faraway look, I could tell that he was momentarily back on the Dakota plains, or fighting his way along Chicago's bitter, winter streets.

Now and then a brief lecture tour, winding up in New York, would be arranged, and off he would go, alone. Each time I saw him off my heart ached, for I knew he would find fewer familiar faces at the Century Club and the Academy because so many of his closest friends had been laid low by disabilities or death. Each trip grew shorter and he came back to us in a sort of desperation, fleeing from painful memories, trying to lose himself in the stimulation of his children and the peace and beauty of his last home.

Daddy still kept his writing habits, rising at dawn to brew his powerful coffee, taking his place at his desk, but the work went slowly and he was glad to "knock off" and come out and sit in the sun and wait for his morning's mail. That, too, had tapered off, but most days there would be a letter or two from a reader who had discovered—or rediscovered—Hamlin Garland. It was touching the pleasure they gave him.

"There! You see I'm not forgotten after all. There's life in the old gentleman yet."

Indeed there was. Up to almost the very end, Father was as vital as an April wind. The trick was to keep him amused. "For your mother's sake—" he explained, as they went several times a week to the motion pictures, and Jimmie and I were with them the night Father saw Greta Garbo for the first time.

Up to then, he had become virulent at the very name, seeing "that woman" as a female fiend, dedicated to corrupting men's souls, but this time, with malice aforethought, Jimmie and I took Mother and Father to a film called *Victory*, the story of Marie Waleska, Napoleon's Polish love.[5] Within ten minutes, to Mother's and our delighted amusement, Daddy capitulated. In short, he fell in love.

"That is the most magnificent actress I have ever seen!" he announced on the way home, recalling the countless actresses he had seen: Duse, Bernhardt, Ellen Terry, the best of the American and British stage. "This girl has it all over them. She is—I hate the overworked word but there is no other adequate—she is glorious!" Thereafter, Father saw every picture Garbo ever made, some of them over and over. It's fun to see a man in his seventies so stirred, so enraptured.

Father had always preferred the company of good looking women—he and Lorado Taft were together in that. I remember Father once saying to Mother, "Zulime, don't ask any more *plain* women to this house. I do not care for plain women."

This applied to housekeepers as well; the competent but unattractive were passed over for a comely face and a soft lilting voice. Our Astrid was a young Swedish beauty who pleased everybody. She had a soul as endearing as her face and figure and a quick skillful hand with pastry, pots, and pans. In fact, she was a jewel without peer, as all too soon some fortunate young man found out. Her successor was a darling but incontestably plain, and for several days Daddy almost sulked until Anna, in her own way, succeeded in insinuating herself in his regard.

It was due to the kitten we were given by Mother's Chicago friend, Dora Drane.[6] It was a tiny orange Persian, and it was ailing and alive with pet shop fleas. Anna fell upon it with cries of pity, took it into her room, bathed and brushed it, and within a few weeks had transformed it into a healthy, gloriously-coated show cat. Father named it "Ectoplasm," after his interest in psychic research, but its nickname was "Hector," and it was the only cat I have ever seen who would retrieve, just as a dog does. You threw a walnut shell and Hector would bring it back to you time after time, one evening choosing to place it deliberately in the outstretched hand of my big doll, Rosalie, who had been brought down from the attic to sit nostalgically under our Christmas tree.

We were all caught up in psychic investigation at this time, and to this day I marvel at the evenings in Father's study. Mrs. Drane was an extraordinary medium. With the best of humor, she would sit for us night after night, go promptly into a trance in the small armchair Daddy set for her, and around her slumped figure would stir and move and sound incredible, inexplicable things. The room was darkened but not so dark that we could not see each other against the drawn window shades, and there was not one of us—including Mrs. Drane—who could be discerned taking a hand in anything that happened. The cone out of which the voices came had been made by my husband out of a big sheet of drawing paper. Mrs. Drane had not even seen it until the first night, yet it floated around Daddy's study on an even keel like a zeppelin, and the phosphorescent paint Jimmie had applied to both ends made the small end remarkably like an open mouth as it came slowly but unhesitatingly to our ears.

Many personalities "came through": friends of Daddy's, Henry B. Fuller repeatedly, as well as voices claiming to be long-dead relatives. It was all absorbing and breathtaking but inconclusive. Mrs. Drane, who was a spiritualist, would have liked us to believe, but we could not, any of us. Father maintained that psychic manifestation was "unexplored biology" and that one day, along with the rest of the scientific marvels, its secrets would be probed. Nearing the end himself, he said he would like to be convinced, but nothing he had experienced in his forty years of psychic research had given him the slightest conviction of life after death. He was to have one more exciting psychic experience before the book closed.

ঌ   ঌ   ঌ

In the meantime, Jimmie and I, comfortably blurred by alcohol, were leading pretty shallow lives, unable to find each other in the merry-go-round we were on. We had a few comforting friends. One of the De Reszke Quartet, the bass, Harold Kellogg, and his bright, musical wife, Maxine, lived near, and we played bridge back and forth with musical evenings in between. Mother and Father liked the Kelloggs and made them welcome. Others for whom Mother would leave her lonely bedroom were Frank and Gertrude Tresselt.[7] Frank had been Jimmie's boss at Fox and was a handsome, brilliant pianist, and Gertrude was a lovely little Dresden doll with a merry, irrepressible spirit.

There were also the Walter Pidgeons.[8] Daddy said Walter was the handsomest man he had ever seen, and Father was a judge. Ruth and Walter became our close friends. Walter had a beautiful deep, natural voice and studied singing with Jimmie, while Ruth and I used to play gin rummy in the bedroom overhead. Though they lived in a handsome home in Beverly Hills and were in social demand everywhere, Walter's dramatic career was in a suspended state and he was bitter and resentful. Waiting around for opportunity to knock in Hollywood is one of the world's most humiliating experiences.

Our most rewarding friends were Dolores and Jack Barrymore.[9]

We met the Barrymores through Mr. and Mrs. Thomas Patten, who, with their adorable "Jakie," kept open house on Upper Vine Street.[10] I don't know what Father would have done without Uncle Tom to talk to, and his two women were as merry as crickets. From the day we arrived in Hollywood, they had adopted us and their home became a second home to us. Cultivated, wise, witty, and incurably hospitable, the Pattens' afternoon tea became an institution. Henrietta Patten's sister had married Maurice Barrymore, and they had known all the Barrymore children since they were small. Jack was especially close and devoted to Uncle Tom, which was how it happened that one evening we all met for a picnic at a rustic site called the Uplifters Club. It is now, alas, a tract site, but in those days, with its great live oaks, it was a near approach to the wilds, and you could build a fire and fancy yourself far from mundane cares.

Jimmie and I, wildly excited at the prospect of meeting the famous Barrymores, were late in arriving, and our first sight of Dolores was of a slim figure, in an expensive white linen frock, propped against a tree, a large bowl of onions in her lap. These she was industriously peeling and slicing. Her heavy gold hair was a sloppy crown, her eyes were huge and as blue as gentians, and despite the onion-induced tears streaming down her lovely face, she was a princess straight out of a fairy tale.

"Hi!" she called, waving her paring knife gayly. "Forgive me if I don't get up. Steak with fried onions tonight—yum!"

Jack, who had been reclining at Uncle Tom's feet under an ancient oak, sprang to his feet and made a graceful bow.

"Mebbs, isn't it?" he said in that inimitable voice, using the childish nickname that my family and friends sometimes gave me. "And Jimmie." He looked from one to the other of us with a whimsical smile, then turned with a nod to Uncle Tom. "You know, I think I am going to like them."

John Barrymore. How to describe him? Without exception—not forgetting George Bernard Shaw—the most fascinating man I have ever met. Jack was more than a good looking actor. He struck sparks from everyone he encountered. There was nothing of the poseur about Jack. He had too wicked a sense of humor to take himself or anyone else seriously, though at this time he was deeply in love with his beautiful wife. There was a small Dolores, too, as spoiled and imperious as I had been in my babyhood, and the whole Barrymore household on Tower Road, including a pack of equally spoiled dogs, revolved around the little one.

Their home was the most picturesque place imaginable, and as we became good friends, Jimmie and I were in and out of it several times a week. High up in the hills overlooking Beverly Hills and the sea, it was really two separate tile-roofed buildings joined by a long stone cloister. In the center was a large, irregularly shaped swimming pool surrounding an Italian marble fountain. Jack and Dolores had their bedroom in the high building—a round tower that seemed to have no part in this day and age. Jack had built the tower for Dolores without having her see it until it was completely finished and furnished and he could carry her over the threshold in his arms. It was wildly romantic but somewhat inconvenient, and to practical Dolores, who was an adoring mother, it was too far from her child and nurse, who lived in the front house with the servants and the dogs.

Night after night we dined with Jack and Dolores out on the broad front terrace, with a million stars over our heads and a million more at our feet, drinking heavenly wine out of frail Venetian glass and talking of a thousand things. Jack was amazingly well-read and informed on music and art, and though he often came home exhausted from a day's shooting, after a short nap, a swim, and a drink and he was his spectacular self again. I'll not soon forget the night he loomed up in the doorway, makeup still on, superbly turned out in full evening dress, with a red satin-lined cape swirling behind him the breeze. With an ardent "Ah!" and a leap, he scooped up Dolores and held her to him in a long swooning kiss that was as graceful as a pas de deux.

One night he was too fagged to play our usual bridge and after dinner disappeared into his cluttered study, which was jam-packed with rare and exotic treasures from all parts of the world. It was a hot night, even on the Barrymore hilltop, and Dolores, who was one of the most natural and unassuming of girls, decided to shed a too-tight girdle. She left it on a chair in the little library adjoining the dining-sitting room where we usually spent the evening.

An hour or so later, Jack, in a dark red dressing gown, his hair tousled from sleep, appeared dramatically in the doorway, holding the girdle like a tray on his outstretched hands. Gliding across the room to me, he dropped with infinite grace to one knee and proffered his burden.

"Yours, I believe, Madame?" he purred.

Jack and I both loved poetry, and I had fun reciting aloud two of my favorites: Swinburne's "Forsaken Garden" and Chesterton's "Lepanto," both of which aroused in him such blazing enthusiasm that he must dig out the books and read them back to me. It was a thrilling experience: that voice, so rich, so flexible, so sure. He adored music, too, and often Jimmie would sing, while Jack lay stretched out on the couch, Dolores in his arms, looking down at a world that was all his.

There was no problem in those days of his drinking too much. We never saw him any way but in complete control of himself, but rumors were going around. Later, as we read of his roaring back and forth across the country in drunken idiocy, with a greedy, young female in pursuit, it was hard to reconcile it with the gracious host and warm friend who had meant so much to Jimmie and me.

One day we persuaded Father to call on the Barrymores. His reluctance stemmed from an earlier period in New York when, as chairman of the Pulitzer Prize committee he had attended a performance of *The Jest*. Essentially a gentle, honorable man, Father had been shocked right out of his boots, and as in the case of Garbo, he had mistaken the character for the man. Still, Tom Patten's love and respect for Jack were frequently expressed, Jimmie and I frankly doted on both Dolores and Jack, and Father finally accepted an invitation to tea.

Again, as with Garbo, Father succumbed. When Jack set out to charm, there was no one who could withstand him, and Dolores, her golden hair blowing in the wind, her elfin baby in her arms, was a picture Madonna.

"You know," Father said reflectively on the way home. "I have never before seen anyone who seemed to have everything—but those two."

I am glad he did not live to see the ugly ending.[11]

Speaking of beautiful women, through Ruth Pidgeon, herself an exquisite person, I met Madeleine Carroll.[12] I had admired her ever since *The Prisoner of Zenda,* and when Ruth asked me to lunch with them at the Beverly Hills Brown Derby, I was almost as excited as I had been over the interview with Walter Hampden. Ruth and I were early and sat at a table looking up Wilshire Boulevard, and suddenly Ruth said, "There she is," and I could feel my heart leap.

I don't know what I had expected, possibly the coiffed, queenly beauty of the film, but what I saw was a slight, fresh-faced, fair-haired English girl, in a brown tweed suit and low-heeled walking shoes, striding swiftly and gracefully toward us. She had a wide-brimmed, slouch hat crushed in her right hand, and her hair was blowing in the wind. Even under the blazing California sun she was flawless—skin, hair, eyes, features, figure, everything—and when she greeted us, her lovely, low-pitched voice was part of the whole. She was as simple and gracious as Dolores Barrymore, and not only I but everyone in the restaurant sat watching her in a trance of enjoyment. "I have just seen the most beautiful woman in the world," I told Daddy, though he put up a stubborn fight for Greta Garbo.

Father had one social occasion in Los Angeles that was completely satisfactory. A loyal longtime friend, Gaylord Beaman, conceived a seventy-third birthday dinner for Hamlin Garland and worked like a demon to make it a success.[13] Over Father's worried protests, he wrote friends and fellow writers in England and America, and a flood of letters and wires from those who could not be present came pouring in. They were eventually all collected in a large volume which my sister still has today.

The dinner was splendid. The pity was that mother could not go, but she would have hated it anyway. All the rest of us were there, the family, the University people, and other admirers rallied round, and Father was feted and toasted within an inch of his life. Dr. Robert Millikan was the chairman and Will Rogers the principal speaker.[14] Father had a few misgivings lest Mr. Rogers might become *too* funny, but there was no need to worry. Will Rogers was exactly right.

We have such a happy photograph of Father taken at the dinner: handsome, modest, but radiant with pleasure. He had not had such accolades since he was elected to the American Academy of Arts and Letters, and though he often spoke sadly about being forgotten, here was a man who was obviously *not* forgotten. As the warm, heartfelt tributes were read out from Shaw, Barrie, Kipling, Edith Wharton, Gifford Pinchot, Hoover, and a myriad of others, including a large group of the younger men expressing their gratitude for his help and encouragement in the early days of their climb, I could see that Father was deeply moved.

ða ða ða

Early in December, my husband came home from the studio one night in what was obviously a high state of excitement. During our dressing drink—in those days I changed into long, trailing hostess gowns every night and presided at the end of the long table opposite Daddy—Jimmie attempted to be elaborately casual, but his high color gave him away.

"Uh—darling. . . ." He was getting into a brown velvet dinner jacket in which he looked like an operatic tenor, handsome but plump. "You remember I studied with Jean de Reszke?"

"Of course." I might have shown more interest, but as a matter of fact I was thinking about a rowdy Malibu party of the night before and of an insistent young actor with whom I had gone for a long walk along the sand. There had been the usual kisses and a half promise on my part to go for a drive into the desert in his new sports car, but now I felt only reluctance at the prospect. I was bored with everything, I told myself, but that might have been because I was still sober. Grimly, I applied myself to the gin and grapefruit juice.

Jimmie, his back to me, was working on his necktie. "I had no idea she was in this country. When I last heard, she was singing in some musical in London."

"Who was singing in some musical in London?"

He swung round. "Haven't you been listening? Why, Mari, of course."

"Mari who?"

He said her last name then and a light broke. Oh, I knew about Mari. She had been a pupil of de Reszke's in Nice when Jimmie was studying there. From all accounts, she was a fascining, gifted, dramatic soprano, some years older than Jimmie, but I

Marguerite Namara ("Mari") in 1910.
(Courtesy of Library of Congress, Prints & Photographs Division, LC-B2-1234)

gathered there had been more than a flutter in my husband's susceptible heart. She had been married to various people at one time or another, but at this point, Jimmie told me, she was living in Hollywood with a new husband.

"A *new* husband! Good heavens! . . . How does she look?"

"Wonderful! I mean. . . ." Jimmie was blushing. "I mean, she looks well and it was fun talking about Nice and Monte Carlo and the old days. She has a lot of important friends out here and she's hoping to get a break in the movies." He visibly braced himself. "Look, would it be all right if we invited them to dinner?"

He looked so eager and self conscious that I almost laughed. I suppose I might have been miffed at this interest in an old flame, but all I felt was a curiosity to see the siren myself. In the ten years of our married life I had never had occasion to question my husband's interest in another, and it rather intrigued me.

"Why not?" I said promptly. "Say when."

He still looked uneasy. "I haven't met her husband. He's a writer of some kind and someone told me he drinks."

"Who doesn't?" I drained my glass. "Come on, dear, it's time to go down." I paused at the door. "He's presentable, I assume? Not the fighting Irish type, or the falling-down drunk?"

"Oh, no. They say he's a brilliant, attractive guy. She wouldn't have married him if he wasn't, but he's supposed to like his liquor."

"Then he shall have his liquor. We'll fill him up on cocktails and put the wine carafe right at his elbow and if he disgraces himself, you'll have to remove him."

My husband grinned. "Righto. I'll call Mari after dinner."

I was introduced to the lady over the telephone, and unlike so many professional singers, her speaking voice, too, was lovely. She was part French, so there was a bit of an accent, and she was plainly high-spirited and fun.

"It was charming to run into Jeemie yesterday! You must be food for him, he looks so big and healthy. Did he tell you how we used to sing duets together half the night in Nice? His voice—it is so beautiful!"

"I know. Will next Friday at seven-thirty be all right for you and your husband?"

"Oh, everything's all right with Jon," she said airily. "I will tell him we are coming. Au revoir, then, till Friday."

(In this story, told with all the honesty of which I am capable, I might use actual names, but though there is almost no one now to be concerned, I have chosen to use pseudonyms, and Mari and Jon these two people will be to the end of my tale.)[15]

Notes

[1] Constance Garland Harper was born on December 31, 1930.

[2] The actor John Boles (1895-1969) began in silent films; his singing ability enabled him to make an easy transition to the new fad of musicals.

[3] Narcissa Cox Vanderlip (1879-1966) wife of Frank A. Vanderlip (1894-1937), former Assistant Secretary of the U.S. Treasury (1897-1901) and then vice-president and president of New York's National City Bank (from 1901-1919). Vanderlip purchased 16,000 acres at Palos Verdes in 1913.

[4] Frank C. Baxter, John D. Cooke and Garland Greever were members of the English Department at the University of Southern California.

[5] Isabel refers to the movie *Conquest* (1937), which starred Greta Garbo as Marie Waleska.

[6] Dora Drane was a psychic. Beginning in January 1933, Garland recorded many séances with Drane in his diary. He describes the sittings—with Drane renamed "Delia Drake"—in *Forty Years of Psychic Research* (New York: Macmillan, 1936), 333-361.

[7] Frank Tresselt (b. 1895) was the choral director for the film *Are You There?* (1930), also known as *Exit Laughing*.

[8] The actor Walter Pidgeon (1897-1984) had trained as a singer and acted in a number of musicals, but his career had stagnated. In 1935, he decided to return to Broadway to reestablish his career, and he and wife Ruth drove East with Isabel and Hardesty to economize on expenses; after he returned to Hollywood in 1936, he soon became one of Hollywood's leading stars.

[9] The actor John Barrymore (1882-1942) and his second wife, the actress Delores Costello (1903-1979). Barrymore was widely regarded as one of the handsomest actors of his generation and had achieved considerable acclaim for his stage performances of Shakespeare's plays, especially *Hamlet*.

[10] Thomas Patten (b. 1862) was the former postmaster for New York City. As a youth, he had been a member of the acting company of Augustin Daly.

[11] Isabel refers to John Barrymore's decline, which involved drunken and profane ad-libbing in his acting and public drunkenness, widely cov-

ered by the press. He died of cirrhosis of the liver and pneumonia.

[12] British actress Madeleine Carroll (1906-1987) attained considerable celebrity in Alfred Hitchcock's *The 39 Steps* (1935). Isabel is mistaking the later *The Prisoner of Zenda* (1939), a box-office hit, for one of Carroll's earlier films.

[13] Alexander Gaylord Beaman (1889-1943), Los Angeles businessman and Garland's financial advisor. Garland describes the celebratory dinner in *Afternoon Neighbors*, 554-557. The collection of birthday tributes are now part of the Hamlin Garland Papers at USC (item 711d).

[14] Robert A. Millikan (1869-1953) was president of Caltech and the winner of the 1923 Nobel Prize for physics.

[15] "Jon" is the writer Mindret Lord (1903-1955); "Mari" is the singer Marguerite Namara (1888-1974).

12. A Meeting

      ટ   ટ   ટ

We did our best that Friday evening. The cook was on her mettle, and there were flowers, candles, chilled wine, and firelight. Father and Jimmie were in dinner jackets, and I wore my most dramatic dinner gown: floor-length black velvet with long, tight sleeves embroidered with silver beads, a gown in which Father said I looked like Beatrice D'Esté. He had always been interested in women's clothes and liked to go shopping with Mother and me. Mother was not coming down to dinner, but she felt the general excitement and made me promise to come up and report at the first opportunity.

I was surprised to find myself nervous as the hour neared. It was not the thought of entertaining two complete strangers—I had faced hundreds of them in my life—it was a nagging apprehension of what Jimmie had hinted about Mari's husband. I had always loathed and abominated drunkenness and was smug in the fact that Jimmie and I rarely overdid. I had been at Hollywood dinner parties where the cocktails were so frequent and so potent that out of a company of twenty guests only four or five had been able to make the dinner table. In my case, there was just one night I remembered with horror. It had been a long tennis-cocktails-lunch-bridge-cocktails day, and I arrived home to the realization that we were due at a large formal dinner party that night. Moaning, I flung myself on the bed. "I can't! Jimmie, I'm tight! I can't get up and dress and go out again!"

He was understanding and helpful, administered alka-seltzer, and later, judiciously, more alcohol, helped me in and out of the shower, and handed me things while I dressed. He assured me later that I came through the whole evening with flying colors, that no one had the slightest idea that anything was wrong.

When I awoke next morning, the thing that terrified me was that I didn't remember one moment of the night before! From the time we left for the party to seven-thirty the next morning my mind was a blank sheet of paper. Yet apparently I had wined and dined and laughed and flirted just as usual, came home under my own steam, brushed my teeth, and gone to bed, and no recollection of it remained with me. What one might have done during those lost hours! It was a shivery and sobering experience.

That night, however, the stage set was perfect. The house looked charming, the fire glowed, the roses drooped prettily, and Hector was an endearing little ball on the hearth. When the bell rang, Daddy and Jimmie were deep in conversation and Astrid occupied in the kitchen, so I went to the door myself.

Mari was the operatic prima donna incarnate. She was a dark, theatrically beautiful woman in her forties, with aquiline features and dark, smoldering eyes. She was wrapped in an atrociously ugly cape of monkey fur, and from her elaborate coiffure glittering rhinestone earrings dangled to her shoulders.

"I'm Mari—and you're Isabel!" she exclaimed happily and made a little gamin gesture with her thumb over her shoulder. "And this is—" At which point, my husband came up and she made a rush for him. "Jeemie, my sweet!" Flinging both arms around his neck, she kissed him on both cheeks in the Continental manner. Father, amused, stood waiting, and Mari disengaged herself and extended a pretty, jeweled hand. I was left facing the tall, masculine figure lounging patiently on the door step.

"I'm Jon," he said, smiling. "Sporting of you to take us on. I trust you know what you are in for." He had a nice low-pitched voice with a trace of British accent that fell pleasantly on my ears.

So this was the drinking husband. He was disconcertingly good-looking, almost motion-picture actor handsome, with wide, clear brown eyes and a head of thick, dark hair that had the sheen of a bird wing. In contrast to Daddy and Jimmie, he wore a worn and somewhat rumpled brown tweed jacket, flannel trousers, with a yellow wool scarf knotted casually around his throat. His shoes,

Mindret Lord ("Jon"). "I was left facing the tall, masculine figure
lounging patiently on the door step."
(*Courtesy of Victoria Doyle-Jones*)

I observed, had not been recently polished, but he was plainly a
gentleman—and sober.

I put out my hand. "It's nice to have you. Come in and meet my father and my husband."

Our dinner party went swimmingly. Mari sat on Father's right and prattled entertainingly. Jon was on my right, with the wine decanter close at hand, but so far as I had seen he seemed to have very little interest in alcohol. His conversation was a joy, witty, sophisticated, never lacking in taste. Jimmie and I exchanged congratulatory glances on occasion, but it was plain that my husband's attention was directed to the other end of the table and Mari's sparkling face. Now and then I caught the hint of a smile on Jon's lips, a knowing quirk that indicated he had been through this sort of thing before. He had, I noted, a beautiful mouth, wide and sensuously modeled, and his hands, like those of Jimmie, were the hands of an artist—strong and sensitive.

There was no trouble in finding something to talk about. Jimmie had lived abroad for five years, I had made two trips to England, and Jon was just back from London, where he had had some sketches in a successful review. Jimmie asked him what he was doing now, and he shrugged. "Pot boiling," he said without bitterness, but there was a tension that showed itself in his incessant smoking. Father glanced his way in disapproval now and then— Jimmie and I smoked as little as possible with my parents, who did not smoke at all and were vaguely troubled by it—and before long I saw that Jon had become conscious of the situation and was making a brave effort to abstain.

After dinner, in the drawing room, with the arrival of coffee and liquors, Mari took charge. "Can't we have some windows open?" she demanded. "It's so smoky in here and it's bad for Jeemie's and my voice."

Her accusing look sought out her husband, on the point of lighting a fresh cigarette, which he calmly crushed out and went to assist Jimmie in pulling back the drapes and setting wide the French windows. Mari was already sitting on the piano bench, skilled fingers running up and down the keys.

"What a lovely instrument. . . . Jeemie, come and play for me."

He crossed to the piano and she slid along the bench to make room. "You know, I'm no pianist but I'll accompany you if you'll sing."

"After all that dinner!" She patted her tight little stomach and there was no doubt about it: for all her seductive figure, Mari was a real trencherwoman. "I'll sing if you'll sing with me," she coaxed, cuddling up to him like a kitten. "Oh, Jeemie, it's like old times, isn't it? . . . What shall we sing?"

In the end, we had a full concert, Daddy, Jon and I, and Mother as well, for the celestial sounds went floating off up the stairwell. They were professionals and perfectly matched, those two: Jimmie's pure, exquisite tenor, Mari's dazzling coloratura. They gave us one love duet after another, and Father, sitting with closed eyes as he usually did when he listened to music, seemed supremely content. Jon, one leg thrown over the arm of his chair, listened critically, with the quick, right word of appreciation after each number.

"Bravo!" he said at one point. "I never heard that sung better by any tenor. Jimmie, you're a real artist."

My husband flushed with pleasure, and Mari nodded smugly. "Didn't I tell you? Jon knows what he's talking about, Jeemie. He wouldn't just say that."

"Do you sing too, Jon?" I asked.

"Good lord, no!" He sat up abruptly, felt for a cigarette, then abandoned the idea. "I've just done a little composing now and then."

"Jon wrote a beautiful barcarole that I sing for an encore at my concerts." She made a face. "His favorite composer is Bach— ugh." She turned back to Jimmie. "How about some Grieg? In Monte Carlo—remember?"

Their eyes held for a moment, then he set his hands on the keys again. "How about this one?" The opening bars of "Ich Liebe Dich" filled the room.

Mari caught hold of his arm and squeezed it. "Oh, you pet! You *do* remember! . . ."

About eleven, Jimmie brought in whiskey and soda, but Mari refused and Jon could only be persuaded to accept a highball after considerable urging. It was midnight before they left. Father had, he used to phrase it, "sloped" some time earlier, and when the door closed on our guests, Jimmie mixed us both a nightcap and we settled down to enjoy the last of the fire and talk it over.

Jimmie put his head back and yawned. "Good party, darling. Everything was fine. I know they enjoyed themselves."

"I enjoyed myself. The singing was heavenly."

"It was fun getting back in the old groove again." There was a little pause. "What did you think of them?"

I had no reservations. "I think they are both fascinating. Mari's so beautiful and alive. I could hardly take my eyes off her."

"And what about Jon?" He grinned. "We certainly didn't have to sop him up off the carpet. He didn't drink as much as I did. He's quite a guy, I'd say."

"So would I. How many years older is she, would you say?"

He frowned. "Oh, I don't know—ten or so, I suppose. It doesn't matter with a woman like that. She's—timeless." He was staring into the coals, and I knew he was back on the Riviera in a world of music and moonlight and high ambition.

I got up to turn out the lights. "Mari asked us to dinner next Thursday. They've rented a little place up a canyon somewhere. She says it's very simple and Jon does the cooking."

Jimmie laughed indulgently. "That's Mari for you. I doubt if she knows how to cook. You can't be a prima donna and a slavey at the same time. You accepted, I hope?"

"Of course. I wouldn't miss it for the world."

Mother was still awake, as I knew she would be, and her eyes were bright with interest. "Darling, what a treat that was! It was like being at the opera in Chicago or New York. What are they like?"

It was easy describing Mari—almost the typical stage opera star—but Jon. . . . There was something strange and—special—about Jon. I couldn't get him out of my mind. The grace, the poise, the quick mind, a certain—acceptance of life. I had to know more about him.

"Her husband's awfully attractive, too." I bent to kiss her. "You'll like them both. Goodnight, darling."

It was about ten-thirty the next morning when the phone rang. I had been sitting at my typewriter for an hour or two, doing nothing. I simply could not drag up one word to put after another, and the pile of typewriter paper loomed accusingly. It was a relief to be interrupted.

"Good morning. I hope I didn't wake you. This is Jon."

I had recognized that warm, pleasant voice. "No, of course

you didn't. I'm no loller-in-bed. Jimmie has to leave by eight-thirty, so I get up and start the day, too."

"Same here. . . . Mari asked me to call and thank you for last night. She's tied up at the studio all day but she wanted you to know what a delightful time we had."

"I'm glad. We liked it, too—and we're looking forward to Thursday."

He laughed shortly. "I hope you like spaghetti."

"Adore it—both of us."

"That's good." He sounded a bit grim. "Because that's what you'll get. You see, to be frank, we're sort of strapped at this point—"

"I know all about that. Things aren't too rosy for Jimmie and me, either."

"You!" he exclaimed. "In that great big house, with four-course dinners and maids—"

"Oh, we enjoy it but it isn't really ours. At least, the house is supposed to be mine, Daddy built it for me, but the trimmings are all his contributions. On our own, Jimmie and I could just about afford a two-room walkup."

"Really? It's hard to take in. You had me worried last night in all that trailing velvet—you looked so unapproachable, 'daughter of a thousand earls' effect."

"Have you ever read Daddy's *Son of the Middle Border*?"

"Afraid not."

"Well, do and see what I come from: a long line of unsuccessful farmers. Daddy was the most unsuccessful of the lot, so he turned to writing. You're a writer, too, I know—"

"The hackiest of the hacks. At the moment, I'm trying to earn a dishonest dollar by writing horror stories."

"What are horror stories?"

He laughed. "You mean you really don't know? You're lucky. The point is, they sell."

"Then why aren't you writing one this minute?"

"Why aren't you? Writing, I mean."

I could hear Father's fond voice the night before holding forth at some length about the mystery novel his daughter was embarked on, and I felt myself squirm. "Oh, I don't know. It just isn't—going well today."

"Neither's mine. . . . Look here, I heard you saying something about tennis last night. You play, don't you?"

"Very badly, but I love it."

"Ditto. And in case you haven't noticed, it's one of the better days. What do you say we get out and bat a few balls, clear our brains, start our imaginations working?"

There was really no reason why I shouldn't. Jimmie was at the studio all day and I'd been playing off and on with Walter—John Boles—Joe. We had a tennis court close at hand on the DeMille property with permission to play at any time. It was all quite simple. Why then did I hesitate, as if this was somehow—momentous?

Suddenly, I made up my mind. "I'd love to. I have to go out to luncheon at one, but there's no reason why we can't get in an hour or so." I was giving directions about how to find the court when I heard two light taps at my bedroom door—Daddy's private signal—and I cut short the conversation. "I have to go now. I'll see you at eleven-thirty."

"Come in, Daddy," I called.

He had a sheaf of hen-tracked typescript in his hand—nobody could mess up a nice, clean sheet of typed manuscript as thoroughly as my father—and he looked bright-eyed and cheerful.

"Well, that was quite a party you had last night, daughtie." He patted my shoulder. "Congratulations. You make a charming hostess."

"Thank you, Daddy. You liked Mari and Jon, then?"

"Very much. She's a bright, attractive woman with a very beautifully trained voice and her husband has a brain. I hope we see more of them." He shook the papers in his hand. "Now, if you can give me a couple of hours—"

"Oh, Daddy, I'm—sorry," I stammered. "It's just that I have had this engagement to play tennis for—over a week and you hadn't told me that there was anything important—"

"Tennis?" His face cleared. He had loved the game himself and highly approved of the exercise for a daughter who was, to put it mildly, not athletic. "Run along, then. This can wait till tomorrow. I wouldn't have brought it up except that I didn't hear your type-writer—"

"No, I—there's something I have to think out before I begin

on the next chapter. I'll be glad to work for you tomorrow." I jumped up. "I'd better get dressed. Isn't it a lovely day?"

"Perfect." He lingered. "Proud of your home last night, daughtie?" he asked gently. "Did it satisfy you?"

I knew how much it meant to him, and I put my arms around him and kissed him. "It's beautiful—exactly right. You've been so good to us, Daddy."

He hugged me close to him for a moment. "Well, daughtie," he said with a half smile, "as the old New England saying goes, 'It's not all on one side like the handle of a jug.' You and Jimmie have been pretty good to *us*." At the door he turned back. "Who did you say you were playing tennis with?"

"Ah—Josephine. Josephine Thomas."

It was a spontaneous, easy lie. I was lunching with Josephine and we often played tennis beforehand, but why had I lied at all? Daddy went away satisfied, and with a curious sense of guilt, I went into the dressing room to get out my tennis clothes.

The court was empty when I arrived, and I settled myself, racket, and balls on a bench that stood in a sort of arbor covered with jasmine. The flower scent was almost overpowering, and a light, clean wind played with my hair and cooled my flushed cheeks. I was not feeling myself at all, and when I tried to analyze it, those touching words of Father's in my bedroom kept returning over and over. They *had* done so much for us and we had returned comparatively little. This morning, for instance—what was I doing out here on the tennis court waiting to play tennis with a perfectly strange man, when I should be at home taking dictation in Daddy's—

At that moment, I heard the chug-chug of an ancient motor and saw through the screen of vines a small, shabby open car coming to a halt outside the entrance to the court.

"Hello—" I called. "I'm here."

He slid over the top of the door—it wouldn't stay closed, so was tied up with string—collected his racket and tin of balls, and came, half running, across the court toward me. He was really astoundingly good-looking in white duck and a bright blue pullover, his shining hair fluffed by the wind. He was full of apologies.

"Mari had a whole list of errands I was supposed to do—

take the clothes to the laundry—get her watch fixed—you know the kind of thing. And then the pup got sick and I had to drop her off at the vet's." He sat down beside me. "Mind if I have a cigarette while I catch my breath?"

"Of course not. I'd like one, too."

He looked at me quizzically. "Well, another surprise. I realized I was pretty unpopular last night, what with your father's disapproval and singers' throats and all, but I did try to be good."

"I saw you trying."

"It's a damn silly habit, of course." He lit both our cigarettes and settled back. "I don't usually smoke like a chimney, but when things aren't going right, it seems to help."

"I'm sorry."

"About what?"

"That things aren't going right."

He shrugged. "Oh, hell. We're not going to sit here and talk about my troubles. Tell me about your writing."

We finally got around to playing a set of tennis, in which I was soundly licked, and I just managed to get home and dressed and out to Beverly Hills on time. Everyone at the luncheon told me I looked particularly well, and I knew I did—nothing like tennis to set the blood racing—but I was also conscious of a sense of well-being, of feeling young and vital, and, yes, even happy, something I had not felt for some time.

"We must play again," Jon had said, as we collected our paraphernalia and left the court. "And don't forget you promised to let me see the first chapters of your book."

"I want to see what you are doing, too."

"I wouldn't waste your time on it," he said curtly. Then his face brightened. "But I have a start on a *New Yorker* sketch that might interest you. We'll talk about it on Thursday."

❧ ❧ ❧

It was a very simple little house; more than rustic, it was almost falling down the steep canyon hillside where it clung. Jimmie was shocked. "I can't picture Mari living in a dump like this," he said, frowning up at the ungainly structure about fifty feet

above us. "You should have seen her in Monte Carlo. She was living high, wide, and handsome then. They must be having a hard
time."

I was about to say, "Yes, Jon told me about it the day we
played tennis," but I broke off in mid-phrase. I really had not
intended to conceal anything. Jimmie would have been delighted
to hear that Jon and I had played tennis. It was just that it was a sort
of private something I liked to keep inside me and mull over. We
had had such a good talk there that day in the sun and wind. I felt
I was coming to know Jon and he, me. It was a different relationship from any I had had before. We were both omnivorous readers
and theater and music lovers, moved by so many of the same
things. Tonight I had brought the first two chapters of my mystery
story with me, as Jon had asked, and hoped to have a chance to
show them privately to him at some point.

Jon met us at the door in slacks and a striped T shirt, a dish
towel in his hand. "Welcome to Toad Hall." He grinned, indicating
the cluttered little living room whose chief features were a huge sagging divan and a battered grand piano. "Simple, but it's home. Pick
a chair. Mari will be down in a minute. I'll get a drink."

He disappeared into what was obviously the kitchen from
the alluring Italian smells issuing therefrom, and a second later
Mari made her entrance.

I say "entrance" deliberately. Nothing could have been
more incongruous within that drab room than the vision in crimson
brocade and high-heeled gold mules, with a gaudy, embroidered
Spanish shawl flung dramatically around her shoulders. She was
enraptured to see us.

"My sweets! How angelic of you to come. Jeemie—" she
looked at him languishingly. "How is that beautiful, beautiful
voice?"

He had no chance to answer, for Jon appeared with a tray
on which was an assortment of unmatched, slightly-chipped glasses and a large carafe of red wine.

"It's cheap and slightly alcoholic," he announced. "There's a
half gallon on the back porch, so drink deep." There were potato
chips and peanuts and eventually a huge platter of spaghetti, awash
in an inspired garlic sauce, and a bowl of superb mixed green salad.
That was it and who could possibly want more?

Inevitably, after dinner, Jimmie drifted to the piano, where Mari joined him, and soon the room vibrated to Verdi, Puccini, Mozart. In the occasional lulls, Jon and I exchanged brief remarks, but even that interruption became too much for Mari.

"Why don't you two go somewhere else?" she suggested. "You are distracting Jeemie and me. Take Isabel upstairs, Jon, and entertain her there. She can look at my scrapbook."

Jon gathered up two glasses and hooked a finger through the handle of the wine jug. "They want to get rid of us. Follow me."

He led the way up a slightly unsteady flight of stairs to a bed-sitting room, with windows on three sides opening out on the dark hillside. The room was obviously Mari's and was at the moment a shambles. Feminine garments were strewn every-where—on the floor, the chairs, the unmade bed. Dusty costume jewelry was heaped in piles on the dressing table, already crowded with half-empty perfume bottles, makeup, hair brushes, and combs and dirty powder puffs. Magazines and newspapers and the rem-nants of boxes of chocolates added to the general unholy mess.

Jon looked around and shook his head. "Don't let it fright-en you; it always looks like this. I'll see what I can do." He applied himself to clearing off the bed and straightening the stained antique velvet spread that was intended to cover it. In a cut-down carton in the corner, a small brown head lifted, and big dark eyes regarded us dully. Jon smoothed the long, silky ears with a gentle hand.

"This is Victoria Regina—Vicki. At the moment, she is not feeling very well, but she's going to be all right, aren't you, girl? The little dog licked his hand a time or two and, reassured, lowered her head again. Jon drew out an old, wooden rocking chair. "Here—this is your safest bet. And here is the scrapbook Mari wanted you to look at."

He put a huge photograph album on my knees and filled our wine glasses. As I turned the pages, I saw that all the pictures were of Mari, from the age of one to the present day. She was cer-tainly photogenic. By the age of six, the prima donna was already in evidence, and in her wedding dress, at seventeen, even in grace-less white taffeta, a short, stiff veil bound tightly to her head by a wide, unflattering bandeau, the dramatic beauty had emerged. There were publicity pictures of Mari in numerous dramatic roles and moods—tragic, flirtatious, languishing—but the ones that held

my interest the longest were the ones taken in Nice and Monte
Carlo. Mari was young then and consciously alluring, and in
almost every photograph, my tall, boyish-faced husband was in
close attendance. Jon looked over my shoulder.

"Quite a case, it seems."

The first act duet from *Tosca* came soaring to us up the
stairs, and we both paused to listen.

I went back to the book. "She wasn't married to anyone,
then?"

"Not that I know of. It's pretty hard to keep track. Mari has
been a busy girl."

I wanted to know when Jon met her and how, but I
restrained myself. It was really none of my business, and anyhow,
Jon had other ideas. He stretched himself out on the bed, piled a
mound of pillows behind his head, and looked at me lazily.

"Did you bring the chapters I asked you to?"

"Yes, but—"

"Good. Read them to me." Feeling shy, I opened my mouth
to protest, but he said reassuringly, "We have lots of time. They'll be
at it down there for another couple of hours at least. Come on, let's
have it. You said you were stuck. I might be able to help you out."

In the end, I did read about twenty pages aloud, and I had
to admit to myself that they were effective, very atmospheric, with
a dark, deserted old house, night and the wind in the trees, banging
shutters, stealthy footsteps, and a young, quaking heroine in the
middle of it all. Jon listened in silence, his eyes half-closed,
wreathed in cigarette smoke and looking in profile like a Crusader
Knight on an ancient tomb. As I laid down the pages and looked at
him nervously, he opened his eyes and sat up.

"Good—" he said briskly. "Damn good." He crushed out his
cigarette in a tarnished silver bowl and felt for another. "Of course,"
he went on thoughtfully, "you're going to have to explain all that."

"All what?"

He waved his hand. "All those goings-on: the creaks, the
bangs, the shrieks, the footsteps—"

"But—but they are just in Sheila's imagination! She finds
herself in this deserted house and thinks she hears—"

"No, you don't. Good lord, girl, don't you know the first
thing about writing a mystery story? The point is that everything

you put in has to be accounted for at one point or another before the thing is wound up. If you have a stealthy footstep, you have to say *whose* stealthy footstep, and why. The same for the creaks, the banging shutter, etc. Mere imaginings won't go. The thing has to be as intricately put together as a spider's web, everything conforming to a pattern—"

"Oh, I couldn't do that!"

"Sure you could, if I helped you. I've got a head for these things, if I do say so."

"Oh, would you? Help me, I mean?" I was blazing with hope, with excitement. I was seeing a light at the end of a long, dark tunnel. "Daddy gives me advice, but he doesn't know much about writing mysteries, and I just get more confused all the time. Sometimes I'm tempted to give the whole thing up."

"Don't. You've got the flair. All you need is a lot more work and my fine Italian hand for plot. Take the start of Chapter Two, for instance—" And we were off.

It was several hours later that we suddenly realized the concert was over. Only the sound of low-pitched conversation came to us from downstairs, and Jon got up reluctantly.

"Good lord, do you know what time it is? Ten minutes of one and Mari has an eight o'clock call! I'm supposed to see she gets to bed at a decent hour every night. She'll kick me for this."

He held out his hand and I put mine in it.

"Come on," he said gently. "We have to go down."

13. Work

≈ ≈ ≈

Late as it had been the night before, I was up early and clicking away furiously. I wanted to get down all Jon's suggestions while they were fresh in my mind, and it was thrilling the way things seemed to fall into place. What had been a lot of dangling loose ends were becoming a skein, and I was so hard at work that at first I did not hear the familiar tap-tap at my door. I looked at the clock—after eleven! I was an hour late for my secretarial duties.

"Oh, Daddy, I'm sorry! I was so lost in what I was doing—"

Far from being resentful, he was all approval. "That's the way—that's the way! Go to it. I've been listening to those keys pounding and it was music to my ears. Old Subconscious take over?"

"Yes. I mean—" I was about to tell him of Jon's help but decided to leave that till later. "I'll be right in."

"I don't want to break in on—"

"No, I was just stopping anyway." A feeling of power swept me. "Oh, Daddy, isn't it fun when it goes right!"

Christmas was particularly satisfactory that year. Mother seemed definitely better, Connie's children were our constant delight, and Jimmie, giving up the treadmill of the studio, now had all the pupils he could handle and was happier than he had been in a long time. I was happier, too, writing and sensing a professional book growing under my hand. By this time Daddy knew of the assistance Jon was giving me and was keenly interested. Each

The Harper family: Joseph, Connie, John, and Constance.
(*Courtesy of Victoria Doyle-Jones*)

morning, when I finished my own stint, I would go into Father's study and read what I had written and we would discuss it and speculate as to what Jon would have to say. By this time, I also had read some of Jon's serious stories and was deeply impressed. There was no doubt that he was a born writer, though his method was completely different from Daddy's and mine. It would take Jon all day to write three pages; every word had to be exactly right before he went on to the next. Father and I, on the other hand, would dash off fifteen or twenty pages and spend an immense amount of time later paring it down to six or eight. Father was a great believer in rewriting. "Polish it, daughtie—polish it," he would charge me, making me aware of too many adjectives and adverbs, of superfluous dialogue and a tendency to lose track of the plot. Between Jon and Daddy, it was a wonderful "course of sprouts" that I was getting, and Daddy was as absorbed in my progress as I was. Except for the late hours we were keeping, he had no word of criticism.

"They're a bright pair," he said often of our new friends. "You and Jimmie are in luck to have them."

We were in luck, certainly, but as Mari and Jon became all-absorbing, our other friends gradually fell away. People got tired of calling us for dinner, only to be told that we had a previous engagement. We had exposed all our former friends to our new ones, but it did not seem to "take," as it had with Jimmie and me. Lack of money had a lot to do with. Mari was reluctant to invite people to their shabby little house, and while they, themselves, had a horde of wealthy, socially important friends, it was a matter of going to Beverly Hills homes instead of offering hospitality in their own. Jimmie and I had become members of the family.

One night Mari announced that they simply had to give some kind of a party to repay studio and social obligations. Various friends in the motion picture business had been giving her small roles from time to time, and it was essential that she show her appreciation.

"I hate—hate—HATE this place!" she said viciously. "I'm sick to death of being poor. Why can't Jon sell things the way other people do?"

She was unfair, as I knew. Jon was selling things. He had sold a story to a pulp magazine the week before for fifty dollars, twenty of which went into a new permanent for Mari, who had only the foggiest conception of the value of money. But I also knew that Jon had set his sights on the slicks and was clearly going to get there someday. In the meantime, there was no doubt that times were lean. Each time Jimmie and I were asked to dinner, we came with our arms full of provender: cold meats and spaghetti, cheeses and pickles, half gallon jugs of red wine, but Mari, being Mari, made only the slightest pretense of being grateful. If we had been able to take her to dine at Chasen's, now—but she was "fed up with pigging it in this disgusting little hole."

"Oh, Mari, you're worrying too much," I said about the party. "If people are having a good time, they don't pay much attention to their surroundings. They'll just think it's cute and rustic. Jimmie and I will help and it will be a vast success, you'll see."

When Jimmie and I arrived at seven on the night of the party with our contribution—a large Michael's cheesecake and two bottles of bourbon, which we could ill afford—we walked into utter confusion. Jon was grimly cleaning the living room, Mari was upstairs having hysterics, and nothing, nothing whatever had been done about the dinner.

In short, clipped phrases, Jon explained. I had never seen him angry before, but this time his eyes were murderous. He had been called to an important studio interview and took the car. Mari had a rich, idiotic woman friend who volunteered to drive her to market, and Jon had left ten dollars—the only ten dollars—with a list of what was absolutely essential to buy. When he got back at six, nothing had been done about straightening the house, no groceries were lined up on the kitchen table, and it developed that Mari and friend had had a happy shopping spree, in the course of which Mari had spent the major part of the ten dollars and then had come back home to sleep it off.

"I'm afraid I gave it to her," Jon said savagely. "Now I don't know what the hell to do. They'll start coming in half an hour. Most of them we couldn't reach, if we tried to head them off. If you have any suggestions, let's hear them."

I looked at Jimmie. "How much money have you?"

He dug into his pockets. "Not very much—six or seven dollars."

"That'll do—it has to. Jon, give Jimmie your list and he can go to market. In the meantime, let's get into that kitchen."

We pulled it off, I'll never know how, except that Jon was terrific. In no time, he had sauces simmering, while I dug into the cupboards for plates and glasses and silverware. There was a lot of hand-embroidered linen, and with greens placed here and there and candles lighted, the room looked almost artistic by the time the first guests arrived.

Mari made her usual late dramatic appearance, elaborately gowned and coiffed, showing no sign of the emotional crisis she had been through. Later, after the last of the meatballs, spaghetti, and salad had disappeared with the red wine down a dozen or so gullets, Jimmie was sent to the piano and he and Mari sang like angels. The party was a roaring success, and when the last guest had gone, Mari swept back upstairs, ordering Jimmie to follow and talk to her while she "unwound."

Jon and I, in the midst of the debris—the guttering candles, cigarette smoke, dirty dishes and glasses, and an unfortunate mess in the corner where the puppy had been sick—met each other's eyes and began to laugh.

He caught both my hands and drew me, still laughing, up against him. "Isabel—Isabel—" he said against my hair, "what did I ever do without you?"

As suddenly as he had seized me, he let me go, and as we stood apart I thought surely he could hear my heart beating, so loud it sounded to my own ears.

"Well—" I managed, after a long, shaken silence, "how about getting to work?"

Without a word, he turned and began gathering up over-flowing ashtrays and crumpled paper napkins, and as I followed, my own hands full, into the kitchen, I was thinking in terror that nothing would ever be the same again.

Yet, oddly enough, it was—or seemed so. Neither Jon nor I ever made any reference to what had happened, and it came as strange, as remote, as last night's dream. We still had our tennis, and now and then Mother and Daddy would stroll over to watch us, calling out words of applause or cheerful derision. Work on my book continued, and Jon was his amiable, helpful, hardworking self, but there was a difference, a subtle one. When, on our usual evenings together, Mari sent Jon and me away so that she and Jimmie could sing undisturbed, we went upstairs silently and fell almost feverishly into literary discussion. Gone were our former personal conversations, the light-hearted teasing. What Jon was thinking under it all, I could not guess. I only knew that my own mind was in a turmoil, darting this way and that like a fish, unwilling to put a name or a reason to anything. I was just living each day as it came but with the definitely nerve-wracking sensation of seeming to be holding my breath.

On New Year's Eve, Father and Mother had decided not to wait up for the traditional midnight on the West Coast. Jimmie and I dined with them, and at nine-o'clock—midnight New York time—we all had a glass of champagne and they said goodnight and went up to bed, while Jimmie and I took off in a pouring rain to see the California New Year in with Jon and Mari. Daddy had donated a bottle of champagne and we had our usual other offerings, but we were anything but lighthearted as we started. In the first place, it was raining *very* hard and Mother was apprehensive and had kept asking us not to go.

"You know what California rains can be. I hear all sorts of ominous reports on the radio—"

I kissed her. "We'll be all right. It's not far, after all, and we'll come home early. Happy New Year, darling."

"Happy New Year, my dear." Her eyes followed me, and I could imagine her listening with a sinking heart to the sound of the car's motor.

It was a perilous trip. Cars were stalled in the fast running floods at the cross streets, and the rain beat so hard against the windshield that it was almost impossible to see out, even with the wipers working at full tilt. However, we made it and struggled up the rough, slippery path with our umbrellas and our bundles.

The house was snug and warm and smelled of the pine branches that Jon was burning on the hearth, and for an hour or two we were safe and gay. We had the radio tuned to KFAC and at intervals newscasters would cut in with bulletins about the storm and warnings of impassable roads, but it wasn't until almost midnight that we noticed the first leak. It was in the south wall and shortly thereafter another appeared, and soon a small stream of water was running across the floor, where Jon and Jimmie tried to contain it with barricades of newspapers.

Mari was furious. "Just wait till I call up that landlord! We pay enough for this dump without having it leak like a sieve. Jon, roll the rug back, so that at least it won't get any wetter. Not that it's worth saving, but it's going to be damp enough in here without a sodden rug under our feet." She put a dramatic hand to her throat. "I feel a cold coming on, already. . . . Jon, put more wood on the fire and get the champagne ready. As soon as we celebrate the New Year, I am going to bed. I only hope the bedroom does not leak, also."

The champagne cork popped satisfactorily. Above the pounding of the rain on the roof, we heard New Year's bells and clamor on the radio and voices shouting "Happy New Year, everybody!" followed by the strains of "Auld Lang Syne."

We clicked glasses, said "Happy New Year" to each other, and drank, then Mari set down her glass and held out her arms.

"Come kiss me, Jeemie. Wish me happiness and good luck—"

As Jimmie's arms went around her, Jon turned to me.

"Happy New Year, Isabel," he said, and kissed me lightly on the cheek.

The next moment my husband was back and taking me in his arms. "Happy New Year, sweetheart," he murmured, and though he held me warmly, reassuringly, waves of Mari's heavy perfume floated up from his coat front.

Jon had crossed to Mari and was bending over her, but she put out an impatient hand.

"Look out, you'll spill my champagne." She made herself comfortable against the couch pillows again. "Well, let's all hope this New Year will be a better one. Anyone who wants this last one—he can have it." She emptied her glass. "A leetle more champagne, Jeemie, my sweet. I'm going to get a bit swacked tonight." She rolled her big eyes at him impishly. "Remember that last New Year's in Nice. I thought you were never going to—" She stiffened and sat upright, listening. "What in God's name is *that*?"

We heard a long, ominous shudder that built to a climax in a thundering roar. With one accord, we leaped to the front window in time to see half of the hill across the canyon road from us peel off and come crashing down on the floor of the canyon. Mari screamed and covered her eyes. In the dark and the downpour there was little we could see but flying debris and dislodged rocks bouncing on the pavement. Suddenly, after all the uproar, there was complete silence.

"Oh, God—" Mari whimpered. "Do you think this house will go, too?"

Jon laid a hand on her shoulder. "It'll be all right. This place has good foundations."

I was peering out into the dark. "Oh, Jimmie—the car!" Daddy's handsome new car, of which he was so proud—I could see it buried under tons of debris.

He snatched up his overcoat. "I'll go see—"

"I'll go with you." Jon took a flashlight from the table drawer, and the two men went out into the dark.

Mari was huddled up on the couch, her face white and terror-stricken. "Now the rest of the hill will fall down on them and we will have no men anymore! Oh, I hate this California! I should never have come back here."

In spite of the wind and the rain, I went out on the front porch to look and listen. It seemed ages before Jimmie and Jon came back, soaked and wind-whipped, but with reasonably good news.

"The car's all right—" Jimmie called, as he caught sight of me. "The slide missed it by about two feet, but the whole road is blocked off. It'll be a long time before we can get out of here. I doubt if they can do anything much before daylight."

"Daylight!" I thought of my poor mother and went in hurriedly and tried the phone. The line was dead, of course. Jon reported the telephone poles were lying across the road like discarded match sticks.

I looked at my husband despairingly. "Oh, Jimmie, what will we do? Mother and Daddy will be frantic."

"There's nothing we can do, till the equipment comes and digs us out. We're just lucky that we—"

I had a hideous thought. "Jon, does anyone live on that hill across the road? I mean, might there be someone buried under—"

He shook his head. "No, thank God. I thought of that, too, but the nearest house is about two blocks away and the road is clear beyond the slide."

Mari drew a long, shuddery breath. "So we are not to die tonight, then? Mon Dieu, what a terrible country this is! You roast—you freeze—you drown! And in between, you are *bored* to death. . . ." She shrugged. "Well since there is nothing we can do till daylight, why not make ourselves comfortable. I said I was going to bed and I am. I will go upstairs and when I am ready I will call, and you, Jeemie, will come up and talk to me. You two—" she waved a casual hand, "can go on with your writing or something. There is one thing certain: no one is going to forget *this* New Year very soon." Her high heels clattered up the bare stairway.

I caught at my husband's arm. "Is there really no way of getting the car out?"

"Not a chance. It will take all kinds of bulldozers and men."

The radio, which had fallen silent, now suddenly and mysteriously came on again full force with a tense voice saying, "Special News Bulletin! A landslide in Carter Canyon has blocked all roads but so far as is known there are no casualties. The storm, which has already dropped six inches of rain on the city, is expected to taper off toward morning—"

I gave a sigh of relief. "Mother will be listening and she'll hear that. At least, she'll know we're not dead. Oh, dear." I sat down limply. "I feel as if I'd been run over by a ten-ton truck."

Jon looked at me sympathetically. "Would you like some coffee or a drink?"

"Oh, yes—a drink, please. I'm so cold and shaky."

I shivered convulsively, and Jon produced a worn sweater and laid it around my shoulders. "Pull in close to the fire—I'll build it up a little—and Jimmie and I will see what we can find in the spirituous liquor line. There was some brandy put away somewhere, I seem to remember."

I crouched as close to the fire as I could, teeth chattering, worrying. It was obviously stupid to worry. We had to wait for rescue, and the thing to do was be sporting about it, but I couldn't get the picture of my parents out of my mind. They'd be up walking the floor, straining their ears for every radio report. Thank heaven, Connie and Joe lived right next door and could reassure them.

"Here you are." Jon put a glass in my hand and knelt to adjust the new logs he and Jimmie had brought for the fire. My husband was about to install himself in the big old club chair by the hearth when Mari's plaintive voice floated down the stairs to us.

"Jeemie! . . . I'm lonesome. Come up and talk to me."

"Coming—" With his drink in one hand and a glass of milk for Mari in the other, he left us.

Jon was still on one knee by the fire, and I stole a quick glance at him. Etched in firelight, he was as romantic as a young prince in a fairy tale. He was wearing a tawny, high-necked sport shirt, and his hair shone like a burnished helmet. He was there, silent, motionless so long that I found myself asking, "Thinking—or dreaming?"

"A little of both." He got up smiling. "And very poor company, I'm afraid." He took a sip of his drink from the glass on the mantel and bent to rub his hands in the warmth of the fire glow. "Well, here we are and here, it appears, we stay. How about it? Shall we do as Mari suggested and get to work?"

Ordinarily, I would have agreed at once, but something—the brandy, possibly—made me reckless. "No. Let's talk instead."

His eyebrows lifted. "Talk about what?"

"You."

"Me?" He considered this unsmilingly, watching the smoke from his cigarette drifting lazily toward the chimney opening. "What is there to say about me?"

"Everything!" The word burst out and I felt myself flushing. "I mean, I know so little about you."

"What would you like to know?"

I decided he was enjoying this sparring, and so was I. It was the first time we had talked together of anything but plot sequence, motivation, or atmosphere since the night of the party, and I was conscious of a stir of inner excitement.

"Oh—where you were born, what your mother and father were like, everything you did up to the time we—met."

"Phew!" He let out a long, amused whistle. "You don't want to know much, do you?

"And how you met Mari and your life together."

His smile faded. There was a long silence, while the rain continued to thunder on the roof and Debussy's "Nuages" drifted down from the upstairs radio. Fool! I told myself, panic-stricken. What made you say that? You have no right to—

Jon was looking into the fire, and after a moment or two he said deliberately, "Mari and I have no life together."

"But—"

He shook his head. "That sounds pretty melodramatic, doesn't it? After all, we've been together twelve or thirteen years— if you call occupying the same establishment 'being together.' We're—ah—useful to each other, let us say. Mari took me on when I was a callow copywriter for an advertising agency. She has done a lot for me, opened doors I never could have opened for myself."

"You have been useful to her, too," I said hotly. "You support her, wait on her hand and foot, act as an—"

"Escort," he broke in. "That's the most important. A woman like Mari, especially as she grows older, must have an ever-present escort, some more or less presentable male who will demonstrate to the world that she is still sought-after, desirable. Mari has never loved me, has never loved anyone but her own devastating self."

He smiled wryly. "That's a bitchy thing to say, isn't it? Still, it's true."

"But you—"

He leaned back, his arms folded behind his head. "Oh, I thought I was madly in love, at first. Glamorous prima donna condescending to poor, little, commonplace me. I couldn't believe my luck. . . . It didn't take long, though. You know, in marriage there has to be a lot of give and take, and to coin a cliché, in Mari's case it was all take." He shrugged. "What the hell. It's all water over the dam."

"But you're still together?"

"Together?" He said the word curtly. "Well, why not? Life is no bed of roses, but I've never found anything better until. . . ."

He went down on the floor before me and took both my hands.

"This is pretty dangerous conversation, you know," he said, under his breath. "Are you sure you want me to go on?"

We were very close together and his eyes were searching my face. Before I could even try to answer, he bent forward and laid his warm lips on mine. My arms went around his neck. . . .

14. Love

❖ ❖ ❖

I don't know how long we were alone there by the fire, wrapped in each other's arms, living only in the moment. All I had glimpsed before in my life was as nothing to the realization that I loved Jon and he loved me. I could have sung anthems on the mountain tops.

Gradually, we became aware that the storm had ceased, the world was quiet, and wan, gray light was stealing into the room. Lingeringly, we drew apart to look into each other's eyes for a long, questioning moment before we were back together again.

"Jon, it's almost morning!"

He turned my face up to his. "Is it different—in the morning?"

"No! Oh, no, it's even more real. The only real thing I have ever known in my life. Jon, what has happened to us?"

"Some kind of . . . miracle." He kissed me slowly, tenderly, then, being Jon, turned practical. "How about bacon and eggs?"

"Oh, darling, yes!"

We were sitting opposite each other at the kitchen table, as if we had been there before, as if we were *meant* to be there, when we heard the others on the stairs. Jon released my hand with a swift parting grip that said, "Remember. No matter what happens, remember."

It was late afternoon before the road crews managed to clear the way for us to get out. The telephone was still dead, but the radio reports were reassuring and the family would know by now that we were safe. The Kelloggs had been invited to New Year's

Day dinner, and I was glad to think of them there, cheerful and diverting.

That was a strange day. Jon got food for all of us, and we were elaborately chatty, but the undercurrents were strong. For me, there was too much to think about, or rather there was only one thing I wanted to think about. All the others I tried to put way back in my consciousness. All I wanted in life was to be alone with Jon again, and that I could not be.

"When will we see each other again?" I asked under my breath as Jon helped me down the hill to the car.

"Soon, very soon," he said, but there was desolation in our parting. Jimmie and I said not a word to each other on the drive home.

The Kelloggs, kind people, were still with Mother and Daddy when we arrived, and we were welcomed like returned voyagers. It was a dramatic and truthful story we had to tell, but I was conscious of a question in Mother's eyes. The fever that was burning in me must have somehow communicated itself to her, though she did not ask nor comment either then or in the days that followed. Jon and Mari were going to Palm Springs with some wealthy friends for a week, and lonely as it made me, I was almost glad of the chance to relax, to take stock of what had happened to me, and to try to think my way through to a solution.

The day after they got back, Jon called me. Mari was at the studio and Jimmie at his teaching, and Jon asked if I would go for a drive with him. His own car was in the shop, so I agreed to pick him up on a certain corner, and as I turned off the boulevard and saw him standing there, something like a frantic bird began to flutter inside me. I drew up to the curb and he was beside me, laying his hand for a moment hard over mine.

"Where to, Jon?"

"Oh, anywhere. How about Mulholland? There are a lot of wide open spaces up there."

"Do you need wide open spaces?"

He drew a deep breath. "God, yes. Wide open spaces with you, that is." He bent forward and brushed my cheek. "How are you, darling? It happened, didn't it? You're not just something I've dreamed up?"

I tried to keep my eyes on the road. "It happened. . . . Oh, Jon, what are we going to do?"

"Do you have to think of that, now? Do you know how I have missed you? That week in Palm Springs was a living hell."

"I know."

"Do you? I wonder. You can't possibly love me as much as I love you."

I gave a rueful laugh. If it were only true. Where was the poise, the self control I had been carefully building up over the years? I was trembling, my heart was pounding, but I managed to turn the car off the main road and onto a slightly leveled hilltop that looked south and west, with no human habitation in sight. I stopped the car, Jon took me in his arms, and the miracle reasserted itself. There, in the sun and wind, with the world spread out before us, I knew that for good or ill I was linked to this man for the rest of my days.

We drew apart at last, and Jon lit cigarettes for both of us. I tried, shakily, to make conversation. "You didn't have a good time in Palm Springs, then?"

"I told you, it was bloody awful. Even if they weren't all nitwits, how could I be expected to enjoy myself with the main part of me missing!"

I said again, "Jon what are we going to do?" He was silent and I went on desperately, "There's Mari and Jimmie. And Mother and Daddy. . . ."

"Oh, yes—your father." He spoke carefully. "You care a lot about your father, don't you?"

"Of course."

"And he worships you, that's obvious. He wouldn't like this, would he?" Now I was silent, and he went on slowly, "Do you really think it is necessary to *do* anything? The important thing is that we have found each other. Can't we just live for that, for the time being?"

He was right. It was all so new, so overwhelming. What was I doing trying to make sense out of something that was glorious insanity? Live for the moment, live for this moment. My head on his shoulder, I let the hour drift by till I happened to glance at his wrist watch and sat upright.

"Jon, I've got to go!"

"No—" He held me fiercely and it was wonderful, but I had promised to drive Daddy down to the University for a literary tea, and I must not fail him.

"Let me go, darling— No, I mean it." I held him away and stepped on the starter. As the car swung back onto the road, I asked, despairingly, "Oh, Jon, when will I see you again?"

"Whenever you wish. How about tennis tomorrow?"

"You mean—go on just as we used to?"

"What else are we to do? The world must wag, my dearest girl, no matter what's inside us. If I can't have you to myself, at least I want whatever part of you I can have."

"But they'll—see!"

His laughter was a shout. "Do you think it is shining out all around you like a halo?" He turned to examine me closely. "You know, I think you're right. There does seem to be a sort of nimbus—"

"Jon, don't tease!" I laughed but I wanted to cry. What he had suggested seemed so far beyond my powers. "I think Mother suspects already—"

"That may well be. She is a very intuitive woman. Are you afraid that she will give us away?"

"Mother? Never. I heard her telling Daddy one day that all she wants is my happiness—"

"*Are* you happy?"

I might have said the obvious, "Happy and miserable at the same time," for there was a depth in me I had never known before. Everything was in sharp focus: the hills, the sun, the dashboard of the car, Jon's hands, a gray cat skimming across the road. Where I had trained myself to be indifferent for so long, now everything in life, by keeping me from Jon, seemed to have the power to destroy me. I hated them all: Jimmie, who had brought all this on by his insistence on an old romance; Mari, who took for granted what I would have given my soul to possess; my mother, who would wish me well but hadn't the physical or emotional strength to fight for me; and Father, who would fight me, I knew, to the last ditch. Oh, to be out of it all! To be lifted up, somehow, Jon and I, and transported to a simple, empty place that we would fill with nothing but our love.

"*Are* you happy?" he repeated and his face was grave. "If it isn't—right, it isn't worth all the wear and tear. There's bound, eventually, to be wear and tear. The longer we can stave it off, the better. That's why I say that for the moment we carry on as matter-of-factly as possible. Despite our joint halos, I claim we look like perfectly normal citizens, and I suggest we maintain that role until—"

"Until—what?"

"We'll cross that bridge when we come to it. . . . Here—let me off at the next corner." He was out and standing beside the car, both hands gripping the window sill. "I love you," he said with deliberate slowness. "I love you now—and forever."

↊ ↊ ↊

The days went by in an empty jangle. On the surface, nothing was changed. Jon and I played tennis two mornings a week, usually with Mother and Daddy watching us. We talked over the book at intervals, and I sat at my desk in the mornings and tried to write, but the stream was damned up again and nothing came. Instead, my chin on my fist, I sat staring out over the olive trees at the hills beyond, seeing only Jon's face, hearing only his voice. We had had no more time alone since that afternoon in the car, and when we dined back and forth between the two houses, Mari did not plead her usual exhaustion but became, instead, excessively gay. At her command, we went in for dancing, movies, new restaurants, friends' houses. No longer were Jon and I banished to the "writing room."

Jimmie and I, too, were in a curious suspended state. We had neither of us made any reference to New Year's Eve and, indeed, what was there to say? Jimmie was his usual pleasant, undemanding self, absorbed in his teaching and coming home weary at the end of a long day. If the dressing drink came up a bit quicker and stronger than it used to, who could blame him?

At the dinner table, as spring wore on, we had plenty to talk about. Mother was a good deal better, and Father had decided to take her East for another summer in Onteora. He was eager to get back to his friends, to the center of things, and she bravely agreed to accompany him. They would be leaving about the middle of May.

In the meantime, we took them on long scenic drives, saw that they had their movies several times a week, and tried to keep things as comfortable and normal as possible, but I knew that I was not deceiving my mother. In unguarded moments I would catch her studying me, and though we always exchanged loving smiles when our eyes met, I could feel her silent questioning.

There were times when I felt that if I did not see Jon alone, even for five minutes, I would die. I remember one Sunday afternoon, listening with the others to the Philharmonic broadcast of *Romeo and Juliet*, and though we sat across from each other, apparently absorbed in the music, the undercurrent of communication between Jon and me was surely as visible as a taut wire. A quick glance, a slight brush of hands, a whispered "Darling—" was all we had to sustain us through those long spring weeks. Even the telephone was denied us, for Mari's was in her bedroom and ours within hearing distance of everyone in the upper and lower halls.

At last the day came when we put Mother and Father on the train for the East. Mother held me closely for a moment but did not speak, and I felt relieved and guilty at the same time. Daddy was buoyant and waved his hat as usual off the back platform for as long as the train was in sight. Jimmie and I drew deep breaths as we went back to the house that had become ours again.

A week or so later, Mari and Jon came for a visit. They had given up the hillside house and were moving to an apartment which would not be ready for them for another ten days. It was Mari's idea to spend the interval with us.

"You have all that room, now your Mama and Daddy are away, and we would pay something and we could all have fun together."

It sounded reasonable, though knowing their financial situation, Jimmie and I agreed that we would not accept any payment. I was outwardly calm as I made the arrangements. Our cherished Anna had left us to be married, and we would do nothing about another housekeeper until Mother and Father returned in September. Inside, I was a cyclone of joy and apprehension. To have Jon in the same house, sleeping in Daddy's study—Mari was to have Mother's room—would it be bliss or agony? Wild excitement raced through me as I made the beds and ordered in the necessary groceries. At least, there must *some* opportunity to see Jon alone. Mari was starting a new picture; Jimmie went every day to his teaching studio. With no one else in the house but our beloved little Blinkie, getting very old now but still in charge. . . . At which point each time I turned my brain off. Jon had said we must wait to cross our bridge. I had done my best to carry out my part of the bargain, even though I felt torn apart in the process. Something was going to have to be decided—soon.

Our first evening with our new boarders was easy and gay. I cooked a splendid dinner and conversation went pleasantly. After dinner, Mari and Jimmie went directly to the piano, while Jon and I elected to wash up. As soon as the swinging door to the kitchen closed behind us, Jon held out his arms and I went into them. Holding each other, we heard in the distance Mari's voice soaring, and a second later Jimmie joined her.

"My love. . . . My own love. . . ." Jon kissed my ear, my chin, my mouth. "Have you missed me? Have you missed—this?"

"Jon, I can't stand it! To go on day after day, pretending—with nothing to look forward to—to plan for—"

"Hush." He laid his finger on my lips. "I've been thinking, and tomorrow we'll talk about it. For tonight, let's just try to be happy."

For a few hours, I told myself, I was. After we came back to the drawing room, Jon and I lounged peacefully on the couch, while Mari and Jimmie filled our world with music. We had all decided on early bed, and as I went around turning out lights and plumping pillows, my heart was saying over and over, "Jon's here! He's only a few feet away from me, looking up into Daddy's olive trees and thinking of me. Jon's here!"

Next morning, Jimmie went off as usual and Jon took Mari to the studio, arranging to meet me on the tennis court at eleven. The whole rest of the day, until Mari and Jimmie returned at six, would be ours, time to look into each other's faces, to say over and over again those all-important words, to plan. Jon had been thinking, he said. Surely, if we directed our whole minds to it we could work out some way in which, without hurting anyone too much, we could manage to be together for the rest of our lives.

We played a little tennis for the appearance of the thing, then wandered back across the grass to the house, where Jon made us a cocktail and I put together roast beef sandwiches and a salad.

We had lunch out on the patio on a day of supreme beauty, and
though we were circumspect, for Connie's bedroom windows overlooked the terrace, we were in such a daze of content that it seemed
one could ask nothing better than to just stay this way forever. Here
we were, two people who truly loved each other, and there was no
hurry, nothing dark or looming, just sunshine and bird songs and a
few, rare, snatched hours. It would be better if I was in his arms, but
that would come later.

"Jon, I'm so happy!"

"Beloved. . . ."

"You haven't said *you* were happy."

"I'm stunned. This is too much to take in all at once. Do you
mean that nobody's going to walk in on us?"

"Nobody." I glanced up at the house next door. "Another
day it might have been my sister, but they all went to Coronado for
the weekend."

"Would I like your sister?"

Oddly, they had never met. Connie was playing her own
games these days, and aside from doing her duty to her mother and
father, we saw very little of her. I considered. Would you like
Connie, if you didn't love her? She had become very brittle of late.
I knew something of what she was going through, but not all. I
knew she was playing too fast and too hard and that something was
bound to break.

"You'd like the *real* Connie. But let's not talk about her. Let's
talk about—"

"Let me guess." He smiled through his cigarette smoke.
"Us?"

I asked it again, I had to. "Jon, what are we going to do?"

He turned the question back on me. "What do you want to
do? . . . You love Jimmie, don't you?"

"I will always love Jimmie. And you love Mari."

"Yes," he said slowly. "For what she meant to me at one
time, I love Mari. But things change. We're not meant to stay in one
place. What it all boils down to is—how much are you prepared to
go through?"

"Anything!"

"It's easier for me, no children, no parents. Hurt feelings on
Mari's part, but not too bad. She's half in love with Jimmie, in love,

frankly, with any man who will give her the admiration she lives by. I've become old hat. She'll raise Cain, but not for long." He bent forward and his face was sober. "Look, darling, I'm prepared to go the whole way, if you are. . . . I thought, as a first step, I'll move out, take a room somewhere. I can support myself now, and as soon as Mari and Jimmie agree to a divorce—"

There it was, out in the open. Divorce. Such an ugly word, a closing door, but also an opening one. My heart began to pound.

"The big problem is going to be yours," he went on. "I don't imagine Jimmie will stand in your way. He's a good sort, and besides he's in pretty deep with Mari. Where you are going to be up against it is with your father."

"I . . . know that."

"Think it over—think it over—carefully."

I didn't have to think, I knew. Father was devoted to Jimmie, detested the whole idea of divorce, had fought it with Aunt Turbie and with various of his friends who had taken, to his mind, the cheap and dishonorable way out. He could be expected to fight it ruthlessly with me, too. I loved my father, owed him so much, and cringed at the thought of what I would be doing to him, but there, a foot or two away from me, the sun on his shining black hair, was the most important thing in life.

I put out my hand. "I have. It's no matter. It's worth it, everything's worth it if in the end you and I can—"

"Live happily ever after?" He took my hand and held it to his lips. "We'll talk of this again. In the meantime, say that you love me."

"Aren't you tired of hearing it?"

"Am I tired of breathing? This is the very foundation of life, sweetheart. From this moment on, I dedicate all that I am to you."

That was the moment, that Friday afternoon, that Mari came home unexpectedly from the studio and found me in Jon's arms on the terrace. Jon had said she would "raise Cain," but the scene was beyond my wildest imaginings. Actress that she was, she pulled out all the stops. She wept, she screamed, she jerked open bureau drawers and flung their contents into suitcases. She called me ugly names, she cast herself on the bed and beat the pillows in a frenzy, calling on God to witness her wrongs. Jon and I stood by, for the most part in silence, though I did manage to mention that she seemed to have found a certain amount of consolation in my husband's company.

"Jeemie!" she shrieked. "Wait till he hears of this! He will kill you!"

Jimmie, coming in at this juncture, was understandably dazed as Mari leaped at him. "Jeemie, look at those two! They say they are in love!"

Over Mari's untidy head, I saw my husband's face freeze. He made no reply, and trying to bridge the dreadful moment, I said, quickly, "Will you come into our room, Jimmie, please? I would like to talk with you alone."

"Yes, go with her!" Mari commanded. "And I am going, too. My husband and I will never come into this house again!" She pointed at the half-filled suitcases. "Jon, finish my packing and get your own things. We are leaving. Never, never did I have such a false friend!" She looked at me with blazing eyes. "I was a fool. From the first, you were after Jon."

There were many things I might have said, but I have always hated unpleasantness, and unlike Mari I was no fighter with words. I went into my bedroom, expecting Jimmie to follow, but he did not. A few minutes later, I heard him carrying Mari's bags down to the car. She followed, slamming the front door dramatically behind her, and I came out into the upper hall as Jon emerged from Father's study with his own luggage.

He gave me a rueful smile. "Perhaps it's better this way. Don't worry. You'll hear from me."

"Jon!" Mari shouted fiercely out of the car window.

Jimmie came slowly back into the house, and I heard him go out to the kitchen and take out a tray of ice cubes. I was shaking so that I had to sit down at my desk and hang on with both hands for fear of falling. When he came up to our bedroom with the cocktail shaker and glasses, he looked so gray and set that my heart twisted. As he poured out our drinks, I saw that his hand, too, was shaking, and when he brought me my drink, I looked up at him pleadingly.

"Jimmie, I'm sorry. . . ."

He touched my shoulder lightly. "Don't be. And anyhow I don't think this is the time to talk about it, do you? We've both been through a rather nasty scene, and I doubt if we'd make much sense.

Let's have a drink or two and then I'll take you out to dinner. I think we could both do with some diversion."

"But I owe you—"

"Nothing," he said flatly. "And if you don't mind, I'd rather not go into it tonight. By tomorrow, we may have acquired a different point of view. Come along. Drink up and I'll fix us another."

With nothing more said, Jimmie left as usual at nine the next morning, and all that long day I sat within sound of the phone, waiting for a call from Jon. It was late afternoon when it came, and his voice sounded deathly tired.

"Well, I've done it, moved out, as I said I would. I'm at the Westland Hotel, in case you want to reach me. No one else knows where I am."

"Jon!" I was swept with a sudden wild happiness. Jon had meant it! He had taken the first step on the long, hard road that would bring us to ultimate happiness. "Mari—?" I asked fearfully.

"She's with Kitty Bales, having hysterics, as you can imagine. She'll come out of it, all right. Kitty's an ass, but having sloughed off four husbands, she's the right person for Mari at this time. Have you a pencil? I'll give you the hotel phone and my room number."

I wanted to say, "Oh, my beloved, come to me," but Jimmie would be arriving at any moment, so I asked forlornly, "What are you going to do tonight?"

"Go to bed and get some sleep. She had me up all night, in case you're interested, and I'm a wreck. I'll try to get my strength and energy back so that I can be of some use to you tomorrow. Tennis at eleven?"

I told myself that tomorrow everything would be all right again, that there was just one thing to concentrate on: Jon had kept his promise. Tomorrow, whether we played tennis or not, we would be together, able to talk things over honestly and bravely. But how could I live until tomorrow?

I heard Jimmie's car stopping outside the house, and I put my mouth close to the phone. "Good night, my dearest. And thank you!"

"I love you, don't forget that. I love you." With a click the connection was broken.

There was an ordeal ahead for Jimmie and me. I scarcely

knew this grim man who, without a word of blame for Jon or me, took the whole burden of responsibility on himself.

"It was bound to happen." Jimmie was walking the floor, his hands deep in his dressing gown pockets. "Mari and I were having our fun and it threw you two together. You had the same interests—"

"Oh, Jimmie, it's more than that." It was wonderful to be able to talk like this, to pour it all out to this kind, understanding person who seemed to have not a single thought for himself. "Jon is—the other part of me."

"As I never was." He stopped and faced me. "How did I fail? I tried so hard."

"I know you did. And you didn't fail. You've been the nicest, dearest husband in the world, and I'll be grateful to you the rest of my life."

"Except you don't want to live with me." The bitterness came through now, twisting his mouth, choking his voice. I had hurt Jimmie, and it made my heart ache.

"There's Mari—" I stammered. "You're in love with her."

"No. I've been smitten with her for years and I've had a kick out of seeing her again, but I want you to understand there's only been one woman for me and there will never be another. That's where I blame myself again. I wanted you so much that I didn't stop to consider if I was the right one for *you.* We seemed to have so much in common that I told myself I could make you as happy as the next man."

"And you did. I don't think you ever knowingly gave me an unhappy moment. But this is something else, Jimmie, can't you see? Everything is involved in this, heart, soul, body—"

"Yes," he said slowly, "I can see that. I was never—man enough for you."

"Jimmie, please. . . ."

"I was never man enough in anything. I should never have agreed to live with your parents, for instance, fond as I am of them. If we had had a home of our own, this might never have happened."

"Darling, don't. You're just torturing yourself, and what good does it do? All that matters—"

"Is that you love Jon and he loves you." My husband drew a long breath. "All right," he said after a moment. "I can take it if it is going to make you happy. That's been my one thought all these years. I won't stand in your way. Whatever you decide to do, you can count of me to back you up."

I went to him. "Please hold me."

He took me very gently, drawing me down on the bed, brushing back my hair, kissing away the tears. "Just promise me one thing: that you won't leave me until you have to. I won't take advantage of it, I swear. I only want to stay with you and look after you."

We slept together in peace and trust for the first time in many long months.

                   ᔰ ᔰ ᔰ

I had hoped that Jon would phone me in the morning after Jimmie had gone. After all, he was in a hotel with a private phone, and I was hungry to hear his voice, to know he was only a few blocks away and would be with me before long, but he didn't phone, and I told myself he must have a hundred things to attend to and he had said he would see me at eleven.

In my new happiness, I called a very close friend, the only other person in the world who had a suspicion of what was happening. In a few words, I told her of Jon's and my secret, and my voice singing along the wire alarmed her.

"Isabel, be careful! Don't rush into anything. You and Jimmie have been—"

"We still are!" I flung back at her triumphantly. "He understands. We're closer today than we have ever been."

"But your father—"

Nothing had the power to frighten me this morning. "Oh, he'll come round in time—and Mother, I know, will be on our side. Oh, darling, I'm so happy!"

Happy indeed I was as I took my way to the tennis court, fifteen minutes ahead of time, and there I waited . . . and waited. By eleven-thirty, doubt was creeping in. At twelve, trembling and terrified, I went back to the house and phoned Jon's hotel.

The hotel clerk repeated the name after me doubtfully. "Who? Oh, him. . . . He checked out last night about midnight."

"Checked out?" My brain was whirling. "Where did he go?"

"How should I know? He didn't leave a forwarding address. This woman called for him in a taxi, and off they went."

"This—woman. . . ." I repeated carefully. "What did she look like?"

He laughed, knowingly. "Oh—oh, I can see trouble brewing. Would it mean anything to you if I said she was dark and good-looking and wore a kind of checked black and yellow coat?"

I hung up the phone.

Mari! I knew that coat so well. A slow, sick tide began creeping through my body. I tried to think, but thoughts and emotions were circling like butterflies. Mari had come for Jon and he had gone with her. But why? What had happened? How had she known where to find him? Jon had told me that no one knew where he was. Where had they gone? What I was feeling might have been the approach of death itself.

I knew only one possible way of finding him—through Kitty Bales—and I fought to keep from dialing her telephone number. Don't! Don't! I charged myself. You'll just be humiliated. There must be a reasonable explanation, an emergency of some kind. Jon will call you as soon as it's possible.

All the endless afternoon, I wandered the house from one room to another, standing unseeingly for long periods at the windows, rehearsing every word Jon had said to me the day before. Trying to make sense out of it, I worked out a dozen stories, but none rang true. The fact remained that my love, the man who twenty-four hours before had dedicated his whole future to me, was gone without a word, an explanation. I would not wish any living soul to have to go through what I went through.

As night came on and the time for Jimmie's return, I think I went a little off my head. No matter what it all meant, I had to know, and the only thing I could think to do was to call Kitty Bales.

Somehow, I managed to make the connection, and a cheerful Southern voice answered.

"No, ma'am, there's no one here now. Mrs. Bales is in San Francisco and the other folks went to Catalina."

To Catalina! "The other folks" could have been anyone. I tried to keep my voice even. "You mean—"

"Miss Mari and her husband. They stayed here last night, and when Mrs. Bales had to leave for San Francisco, they decided they'd go to Catalina."

"For . . . how long?" That strange little croak, was it mine?

The maid was helpful. "I think they said something about two weeks. Anyhow, they won't be coming here when they get back. I heard them say they were moving into a new apartment the first of the month."

15. Flight

&. &. &.

It was a nightmare so savage that my mind refused to accept. Jon had vanished out of my life as completely as if he had never been there, but aside from the apparent reason—that he had gone back to Mari, which I would not let myself consider—there had to be some understandable explanation. Perhaps there had been an accident, some unexpected family tragedy. It reminded me of how little I really knew of Jon when the only actual place of reference I had was the phone number of Kitty Bales.

Uncertainty is a particularly vicious hell. As the days passed and the phone rang only from friends with invitations to tennis or bridge or dinner and the mail brought no familiar handwriting, I found myself turning into somebody I had never known before. I forgot my pride. I tried everything. I wrote to the old hillside address, praying the letter would be forwarded. I called all our slightly mutual friends, fishing for a clue. I inquired at the studio where Mari had been working, but in every case I drew a blank.

Eventually, to my shame and regret, I called Kitty Bales, who was so crisp and dismissive that I knew at once she was lying.

"Mari and Jon?" she repeated vaguely. "I haven't the slightest idea. They went to Catalina, I know, but I've been out of town and haven't heard a thing since I got back."

I tried to match her offhandedness. "Did they take that apartment they were thinking of?"

"The one on Rodney? No, they found something else, I believe, out in Westwood or somewhere."

And so the nightmare went on. I could hardly bring myself

to leave the house for fear Jon might call, and I finally reached such a state that it was impossible to hide it any longer.

One night after dinner, when Jimmie and I were sitting by the fire, ostensibly listening to a symphony concert, my husband got up suddenly and came and sat beside me on the couch.

"What is it, Isabel?" he said, taking my hand and holding it gently. "What can I do to help you?"

"No one can help me!" The words burst from me, and the next minute I was sobbing wildly. "Forgive me. . . . I didn't mean that. It's good of you to care."

"It's Jon, isn't it?" he asked soberly. "I've been wondering. Has something gone wrong?"

"I don't know," I said dully. "That's the trouble. I don't know." A sudden flare of hope made me ask, "Have you seen Mari lately?"

"Not since that melodramatic departure. It seemed wiser to let things drift. Why do you ask?"

"Because they've disappeared."

"They? You mean Mari and Jon?"

"Yes. I've tried everywhere, and no one knows where they are."

"But I thought you and Jon—"

"So did I." I forgot this was my husband, forgot everything but my own torment. "Jimmie, I think I'll go mad!"

"No, you won't." His hand gripped mine fiercely. "You're too much of—a person for that. Did you and Jon have a quarrel?"

"No! The last I heard from him he had moved to a hotel and was coming up the next morning to talk things over. He's just gone! Jimmie, what shall I do? I can't go on not knowing."

"Of course not. Give me till tomorrow. I'll see what I can find out."

He called me during the morning. "They're living in a flat on Alomar." He gave me the address and the phone number and hung up quickly.

I sat by the phone a long time, fighting a battle with myself. To dial, to hear the phone ring, and then a voice—Jon's voice? What could I say to him and what would he say to me? He made the decision; he had taken himself out of my life. How could I come crawling, begging for an explanation? Yet I had to know. I had to.

Mari answered the phone. I tried to disguise my voice. "May I speak to Jon, please," I asked politely, but she banged down the receiver. When I tried again a few minutes later, the operator reported the phone out of order. Obviously, Mari had left it off the hook.

Then I would write the letter I had been writing and rewriting in my mind for days. I mailed it and there was no answer. Doggedly, I wrote another, telling myself that the first one might have gone astray. Still no answer. Now, anyhow, I knew where I stood. Only a fool would try anymore.

That night my self-control broke and I told Jimmie the whole story. "Jimmie, I have to go away! I can't go on living here now. Take me away somewhere. Take me away!"

He nodded. "I think that's a good idea. . . . What would you say to our driving East and surprising your mother and father in Onteora? There's plenty of room in the big house, and you know they'd be happy to see you." He smiled crookedly. "That is, if you can bear the prospect of going off on a trip with me."

"If you can bear to put up with me. Oh, Jimmie, yes, let's go! Let's leave right away!"

A week later we set off. Ruth and Walter also wanted to go East, and money was a problem with all of us.[1] Since our car would be going, they elected to go with us, and we planned to take off at night, hoping to get over the worst of the desert before the heat became unbearable.

Before we left, however, there was a bitter duty we had to discharge. Our poor little Blinkie was at the end of her days. The veterinarian said it could only be a short time, and neither Jimmie, Connie, nor I could face the ordeal of having her put away. To this day I bless the kindness and courage of my brother-in-law, Joe Harper, who gently gathered the doomed little shadow in his arms and drove away with her.

I had left the house, too emotionally wrought up to watch her go, and when Connie and Joe came to dinner, Joe was as stricken as a man could be.

"God! She rested her little chin on my wrist and looked up at me so trustingly! I hope I never have to go through anything like that again."

After dinner, Connie and I went upstairs, and perhaps

because we were leaving, we were nearer to each other than we had been for a long time, so near that I opened my heart and told her the story of Jon and me. I can see her sober face now under the lamp and hear the sympathy in her voice as she said, "You poor girl, what you have been through! I'm so sorry. I always thought you and Jimmie were happy."

"We were, comparatively. But the love that Jon and I had for each other, the love I *thought* we had for each other, was the difference between artificial light and sunlight. For the first time in my life I felt I was living with every bit of me, that I would never be afraid or unhappy again. Until you have found it, you can't guess what it's like."

My sister moved restlessly. "I suppose that is what is known as Romantic Love. I never met it and I never expect to. It sounds pretty—uncomfortable." But when we said goodnight and goodbye, she put her arms around me, a rare thing for her to do. "Try to be happy. And if ever there is anything I can do, let me know. Good luck."

For an instant, with my little sister in my arms, the years revolved and took us back to other times when we had been close and dear to each other.

We picked up Ruth and Walter in Beverly Hills, and as we drove away into the pre-dawn dark, I was numb, past feeling anything. Only a few weeks ago life had held vistas of such dazzling joy that I was dizzy at the prospect. Now, nothing lay ahead but day after empty day.

> None but the lonely heart can know my sadness,
> Alone and parted far from joy and gladness. . . .

Jimmie used to sing the poignant Tchaikovsky song, and now the words kept repeating themselves in my brain: "None but the lonely heart can know my sadness. . . . None but the lonely heart can know my sadness. . . ." Over and over with the turn of the wheels that were carrying me three thousand miles from my lost dream.

That was not a light-hearted trip for any of us. Ruth and Walter were themselves going through a difficult time. It was a hundred and twenty in the shade at Boulder Dam. A rock struck the

windshield and shattered it, just missing Walter, who was riding in
the front seat with me. Our money was running low and we could
afford to stay in only the cheapest and drabbest places. The one
who could be counted on to keep his sense and good humor was
Jimmie. What a magnificent sport was my husband, a bulwark to
the tense, despairing female who sat beside him in virtual silence
mile after endless mile.

We left Ruth and Walter off with friends in Chicago and
went on our weary way, relieved. It is hard to keep up a pretence
in front of other people, but between Jimmie and me there was no
pretence. He knew the agony I was in and gave me in return only
sympathy and consideration. We didn't speak of the past, just of
New York and what we would do there. For the first time, Jimmie
suggested that we might stay on in New York, at least through the
winter, and already dreading my return to Hollywood, I almost
agreed with him. We decided to say nothing about it for the present, however, knowing how alarmed and unhappy it would make
my parents.

Mother and Daddy were in New York, occupying a friend's
apartment. The loneliness and responsibilities of the house in
Onteora had proved too much for Mother. "We were like two
ancient peas rattling around in a trunk," Father said. They were on
their way back to California, waiting only for a few days with
Jimmie and me. New York was going through one of its infernal
heat waves, and both my parents looked thin and old and exhausted. It was all we could do to break the tragic news to them.

"Blinkie . . . gone!" Mother whispered, slow tears welling.
"Oh, I shall miss her!"

Father's face was gray. "That strange little creature. What a
place she made for herself in our lives. . . . There's going to be a
lonely feeling around DeMille Drive. You children had better wind
up your visit here in a hurry and come back and cheer us up."

Jimmie and I exchanged brief, unhappy glances. After they
were back home, with Constance nearby and a new little dog, perhaps we might write and tell them. They thought we were only in
New York for a few weeks, to see old friends and go to theaters and
concerts.

Mother and I had a private talk. "I'm worried about you,
dear," she said. "You don't look well."

"Oh, I'm all right," I said quickly. "It's just this heat."

"Your eyes are dull and you look feverish. For some time I have thought that something was wrong. Are you sure—"

"Perfectly sure." I got her off the track by adding, "Your grandchildren are blooming and will be awfully glad to have you home. Let's go down to Schwarz's tomorrow and pick out some thrilling presents for them."

I assured her that Connie, too, was well and was careful not to hint of any trouble in that direction. It seemed as if we had arrived at some sort of turning point in our lives, my sister and I, and our poor parents were invariably going to be hurt. I tried not to think about it, to think of nothing but the decisions of the present.

Father also had a talk with me. "Daughtie, I want you to have a good time in New York. You've been cooped up with dreary old people too long and you're entitled to some fun. It's no fun in New York without money, so I want you to take this." He put a packet of bills in my hand. "Your allowance will continue and if you get into difficulties," he smiled, "you know who to call on."

"Daddy, you're so splendid."

"You and Jimmie 'whoop it up' a bit and then come back and see what a welcome awaits you at home."

Jimmie and I didn't go up to Onteora after all. With Mother and Daddy gone, the house would have seemed too big, and neither of us wanted to live with painful memories. At this time, as at several other times in our lives, we had a great piece of luck.

My beautiful friend, Edith, had married a tall Irish stockbroker, strangely reminiscent of my Uncle Angus, and as he was vastly successful, they were occupying a penthouse on the 13th floor of a smart Madison Avenue apartment building.[2] Pat adored his lovely princess and would have liked to see her draped from head to toe in diamonds, rubies, and emeralds. He had made a pretty good start on it, and one night after dinner with them, Jimmie and I were fascinated by the picture of Edith, in a trailing, white chiffon evening gown, half a dozen inch-wide diamond bracelets on each arm, changing the diapers on their brand new baby, while Pat heated the formula on a little electric plate.

A few days later, Edith called. She and Pat were farming out the baby with his nurse and grandparents and were going to

Europe for three months. Would Jimmie and I like to take over the penthouse while they were gone?

Would we! It was an answer to prayer in more ways than one. In the first place, it was high up and reasonably cool. In the second, it was a glamorous spot, luxuriously furnished and completely surrounded by a wide brick terrace that was dotted with trees and fountains and shut off from the mundane world below by a high box hedge. It was an ideal place to entertain, and Jimmie and I, taking Father's advice, had become hectically social. Here was a way of impressing our friends and conserving our capital at the same time, and we joyfully accepted Edith's offer and moved into our Shangri-la two weeks later.

That was a pretty gaudy summer. I had scarcely time to breathe and I was glad not to. By going every minute during the day and piling into bed tight and exhausted at night, I didn't have time to think, but now and then such waves of misery and loss would sweep over me that I played morbidly with the idea of flinging myself off the roof. Then I would take another drink or an extra sleeping pill and concentrate on plans for the next day.

Lying awake one night I remembered an entry in one of Daddy's diaries: "Mary Isabel will never be happy, she has too much of me in her." Oh, Daddy, I thought, swept with pity for him and for me, did you ever go *this* low? How did you fight it? How did you bring yourself back to sanity again?

Jimmie and I entertained constantly. As with the Vanderlip place, we wanted to share our luck, and friends brought their friends and before long our terrace became the focal point for a lot of expensive, pleasure-bent people. Ruth and Walter turned up. He had been offered the lead in a Broadway production and his success story was starting. Lawrence Tibbett came and so did Gladys Swarthout and her husband, Frank Chapman. Through my friend Julie we met the well-known columnist Hedda Hopper, who found our penthouse a convenient place to stop by in the late afternoon or evening with one of her more important contacts.[3] I would rather not think what our liquor bills were, but I know I kept the refrigerator stocked and ready at all times for gala meals.

I had known Julie in Hollywood, where she and her bright, positive mother attended some of the Drane séances.[4] Julie was a rare creature, a delight to look at, flawlessly chic, with a quicksilver mind. She had been a dancer and was as graceful as a flower in the wind. The motion pictures had snapped her up, and after a tremendous success in her first leading role and with the most brilliant of futures assured for her, she had suddenly signed a contract to make pictures in Europe and left America for five years.

When she returned, such is the way of Hollywood that she found herself completely forgotten, and with no motion picture offers, she went back to dancing. When Jimmie and I ran into her in New York, she was dancing in a smart supper club with two attractive young men partners. Jimmie and I went several times to see them, invited them to the penthouse, and Julie and I became fast friends.

I remember going one day to the Algonquin, where Julie and her columnist friend, both short of funds at the time, were staying. They had a small, dark room, and it was festooned with laundry lines strung from corner to corner, from which dangled all manner of feminine lingerie. As the newswoman said, it was the address that mattered, but it all seemed so bleak and sordid to me that I had an inspiration.

"Jimmie, why don't we ask Julie up here to stay with us? We have an extra bedroom and she's such a darling I'd love to have her."

Jimmie looked at me oddly. "Can't take being alone with me anymore?"

"Jimmie, don't be ridiculous. It isn't that and you know it. Have you any objection to my asking Julie?"

He was contrite. "Of course not. She's a wonderful girl and would brighten our lives no end. I just wondered. . . ." His voice changed, and he said gently, "How is it going, darling? We seem to have no time to talk nowadays. You're happy some of the time, aren't you?"

What could I say? That I would never know happiness again? That day and night I was something going about in a hollow shell? Why should I burden my kind man with that? He wanted to believe that I was being diverted, recovering. Let him believe it.

"Oh, lots of times," I told him, and changed the subject.

I am not proud of that period of my life. Inevitably, I tried to find romance again. I set out one night quite deliberately to take a man, in whom I had only a slight interest, away from a girl who worshipped him. There was obviously some decency in me, for I stopped in time, but I can still see the girl's white face, her frightened, desperate eyes. It was that that brought me up with a jolt. For the moment, I was back in the National Theater Company in Washington, watching the poor wife in the backstage corridor, turning, heartbroken, away from the closed door of the other woman's dressing room. Despite what Mari had said of me, I did not play that kind of game.

When Julie came, it was like having a sister again, the kind of sister I had not had for many years. We were completely at ease with each other, and my love and admiration grew from day to day. She was so brave, so uncomplaining, so infectiously gay. We cooked together, entertained together, washed our hair together, and in the process learned a great many things about each other.

Julie was beset by suitors, turning up at all hours bringing gifts, but the one we almost accepted as good enough was David. He was a sturdy, brown-eyed, good-looking, well-to-do Midwesterner, and he worshipped our Julie. On him we wined and dined handsomely night after night. Our favorite haunt was Tony's on 53rd Street, and often we would gather there for eleven o'clock breakfast—those of us who were able to make it. Breakfast was in the kitchen, a cozy spot on a gray day, and after a drink or two (did we ever stop drinking in those days?), ravioli and coffee tasted just right, and the day began to wear, dream-like, away. We had some other favorite restaurants on Second and Third Avenues, places of simple decor but where the steaks were two-inches thick and the drinks flowed freely. In fact, David was such a determined host that there were times when the drinks were lined up two and three ahead of us as we waited for our dinner. It never seemed to occur to us that we didn't need all that alcohol. It was the thing one did.

Julie was deeply fond of David, but she was not sure that she loved him. We were sitting out on the penthouse terrace one morning, both drying our hair and shelling peas, and we were talking very confidentially. Suddenly, something in me seemed to be released and out came the whole bitter story of Jon. Julie's sparkling, piquant face grew grave, and the slim, lovely hands among the peapods moved faster and faster. There was a tension building up in her that seemed to match mine, and when I had finished in a storm of tears, she bent forward and kissed me gently.

"Now I would like to tell *you* something," she said slowly.
"It's something I swore I would never tell anyone in the world. It's
because you are almost exactly where I was five or six years ago,
and perhaps what I have to say might help you. I know how
unhappy you are—I think I almost guessed—and I would so like to
help. Think over what I am saying very carefully, please."

Her story, too, was a tragic one. On the very crest of her
motion picture triumph, there had been a man with whom she fell
deeply in love. As in my case, he was tied to but estranged from
another woman, and it all seemed quite hopeless.

"But, oh, Isabel, for what I had I was grateful. Life, for the
first time, was full of meaning and richness—as it was with you and
Jon. I asked only that I might go on seeing him.

"Then one day he didn't call. Days went by and still he
didn't call. I know what you went through. I couldn't believe it.
One moment we were everything to each other; the next, the world
ended. I wrote. I called his home and was told that Mr. and Mrs.
'Smith' had left the city and it was not known when they would
return. I felt I couldn't bear to go on living in Hollywood where
everything reminded me of him, so when I was offered a contract to
make pictures abroad, I took it.

"It wasn't until I came back, five years later, that I knew
what had really happened. He had become desperately ill and was
taken to a hospital and it was weeks before he was able to try to
reach me. All that time, not hearing from me—his wife had intercepted my letters—he thought that I had stopped caring, and when
he was well enough to make enquiries, I had left for Europe and
that seemed to be the proof of it."

With that swift, dancer's grace of hers she was on her feet.
"I'm sorry to bore you with this—" she shrugged. "It was all a long
time ago, but it does have a moral—*never take anything for granted*.
Find out the truth, no matter how grim it may be. Discover by some
means or other what happened, or you'll never know a moment's
peace the rest of your life. This is Aunt Julie speaking, and Aunt
Julie knows."

I sat a long time alone on the terrace after she had gone, one
of the few times I had dared be alone since that dreadful day in
Hollywood, and I was thinking clearly, almost dispassionately.
Julie was right. As long as there was this uncertainty, I would

Julanne Johnston ("Julie"), in a publicity still from
The Thief of Baghdad (1924). Julie told Isabel, "Find out the truth,
no matter how grim it may be."
(*Courtesy of Andrea Evans*)

continue to drift, to throw my life away. Jimmie had said I was "too much of a person to fall apart," but wasn't that what I was really doing now? I must find out, once and for all, the direction my life was to take.

Then how? . . . Julie's words came back to me, and an explanation flashed into my mind. My letters to Jon, written in Hollywood in my own unmistakable scrawl, could easily have been intercepted and destroyed. Perhaps Jon had been taken ill, and when he was well enough to try to reach me, it was to find that the phone had been disconnected and that Jimmie and I had gone East. Wouldn't he have been justified in thinking that our romance was over, that I had decided to remain with my husband? *Find out*, Julie had insisted, and I thought I saw a way to do it.

I wrote a letter to my sister, reminding her of her parting offer: "If ever there is anything I can do, let me know." In the envelope I enclosed another one containing a single sheet of paper. On it I had set down the words I had written and rewritten a thousand times in my mind.

> Jon—when we last talked, you said, 'From now on I dedicate all that I am—to you.' After that—nothing. Don't you think that I am entitled to an explanation, at least?
> Yours always,
> Isabel

To Connie I wrote,

> Will you please put the enclosed envelope in another one and address it to Jon at this number on Alomar? I would suggest a typewriter, though I am sure she does not know your handwriting. . . . No matter what comes of this, I shall be grateful to you forever.
> Your
> Sister

Notes

[1] That is, Ruth and Walter Pidgeon, who was returning to New York to act in the play *Something Gay* (1935).

[2] Edith Shearn married Arthur ("Pat") Kerrigan, one of the original partners of Merrill Lynch, in 1927.

[3] Persons not previously identified are the actor Lawrence Tibbett (1896-1970), the actress Gladys Swarthout (1900-1969), the actor Frank Chapman (1844-1940), and the actress and, later, gossip columnist Hedda Hopper (1885-1966).

[4] "Julie" is the dancer and actress Julanne Johnston (1900-1988), who starred in a number of silent films. Her most notable role was that of the Princess in *The Thief of Baghdad* (1924). She retired in 1935 and married David Rust.

16. An Answer

ప్ ప్ ప్

Jimmie and I had been out of the city for the weekend, and while he went to put the car away, I went on up to the penthouse. There was a bundle of mail in the box beside the door, and my heart sank as I saw the usual letters from Daddy. He wrote every day or so, and while I was touched and grateful, today I felt that I could not bear the gentle but insistent reminder that it was time we came home. I sorted through the pile listlessly, and on the bottom came upon an envelope addressed in a beautiful, familiar hand. Jon!

For a moment, I stood frozen, conscious of the sudden wild pounding of my heart. Jimmie would be up in a minute. Clutching the envelope, I flew to the bathroom and locked myself in. I could hardly manage to tear open the envelope, and I read the few lines in one hungry, disbelieving glance:

> My own love. Mari begged me to try it once again
> but it was no use. I am all yours and will do what-
> ever you want me to do. Jon

I went down on my knees beside the bathtub. "Thank you, God," I said aloud. "Thank you, God."

I stayed there so long on the floor, my head buried in my arms, weeping, reading the words over and over, blinded by the glory of a future once more, that Jimmie became anxious and rapped on the door.

"Isabel, are you all right? You're not ill?"

"No. I'll be out in a minute," I called back. It was several minutes before I could pull myself together, comb my hair, and put makeup and powder over the marks of tears. When I emerged, I tried to pretend that everything was just as usual, but Jimmie was not fooled.

He took one look at me. "You've heard from Jon."

"How did you know?"

"It's written all over you. Have you any idea how your eyes shine? And the pile of mail on the floor of the hall was a give-away. . . . It's good news, isn't it?" he asked gently.

I tried to smile, but the tears came first. "Very good news. Jon still—loves me."

"Of course he does. I never doubted it. Did he explain?"

"Yes, very briefly. He said that Mari had begged him to come back and try again but that it wasn't—any use." Now that my waiting was ended, in some strange way I was proud of Jon, proud that he had been fair enough to give Mari the chance that she asked for. In fact, the world had become so right that I could hardly find a flaw in anything. Then I looked at my husband and saw such misery in his face and eyes that my own happiness shamed me.

"Jimmie, don't look like that—please!"

"Do you want me to go now?"

"No! Why should I want you to go? You are my—true friend and husband. I love you very much, Jimmie."

"What is Jon going to do? He'll be coming here, of course."

"I suppose so. I pray so. He says he will do whatever I wish. We will have to decide."

"May I stay till he comes?"

"Of course." It was as quick and simple as that—my decision. For ten years Jimmie had stood by me through everything, and my love and gratitude to him was very deep. My love for Jon, overwhelming as it was, had not changed my feeling for Jimmie. Jon would understand. I wanted Jimmie to understand. I put my arms around his neck and kissed him. "Please stay with me. I need you."

His face flushed with relief and he held me tightly for a moment, then let me go. "You're going to have a lot to decide, I'm afraid. Remember what I told you in Hollywood: whatever and however you work it out, I am standing behind you. I will do everything I can to help. May I make a suggestion?

"Do, please."

"Don't tell your mother and father anything about this, for the present. Let them go on thinking you and I are—together, till the practical side of the thing has been worked out. They have no suspicion, have they?"

"I don't think so. At least, Mother may have suspected at one time, but our going away must have relieved her mind. Daddy knows nothing."

"Then let him go on knowing nothing. What is to be gained by breaking his heart? That's what it will mean, you know."

I clasped my hands. "I know—I know! Jimmie, what can I do?"

"Take first things first. I imagine now the first thing you want to do is write to Jon. I'll go out and put the groceries away and make us a drink."

With Connie as intermediary, the letters flew back and forth between New York and the West Coast. I had written her about what had happened and was about to happen, but I begged her not to say a word to anyone. One day my sister asked Jon to come in and see her and wrote to me, impressed and approving:

> Your Jon came in to tea today. I took the liberty of asking him straight out if he was as serious about this as you are, and he said that he was, that his dearest wish was to marry you as soon as possible. He is attractive, I must say, and I liked his directness and honesty. It looks to me as if you are a very lucky girl.

I had written Mother and Daddy saying that some concerts had come up for Jimmie, which was true, and that we were staying on in the East for a while longer. Daddy's return letter set the absolute deadline as Christmas:

> Your mother needs you, Mary Isabel, and your poor old father would like his secretary back again. I am writing each day, but the book goes slowly and my state of mind is pretty low. It will be a joyful day when we have our elder daughter back again.

I was happy, I was sad, I was guilty, I was radiant. I was full of dreams, plans, and practicalities. Jon had very little money, and Jimmie and I, in our crazy extravagance, had spent almost all we had. My hundred dollar monthly check from Daddy came regularly, but it could not begin to cover our expenses. The big immediate question was where to find the money to finance Jon's trip to New York. With my pride in my pocket, I went to a wealthy family friend and asked to borrow five hundred dollars. He was tact itself, asked no questions, and told me to take my time about paying him back.

Rapturously, I wrote to Jon:

> Here it is, dear love—our Open Sesame to heaven! Oh, come, come quickly! We have two more weeks in the penthouse, then Jimmie goes and Julie and I are taking a little apartment together. We'll find you a room nearby, and when you are here, we will be able to make further plans.
>
> Oh, Jon, I'm so frightened! Suppose when you see me again you decide I'm not the right one after all? Remember Portia? . . . 'I would be a thousand times more fair, ten thousand times more rich. That only to stand high in your account. . . .' We have a long, hard pull ahead of us, darling, but we'll be together, that's all that matters. I love you, love you, love you!

A few days before we were to leave the penthouse, Jon telephoned. Jimmie heard my ecstatic cry, "Jon!" and tactfully took himself to the farthest corner of the terrace. Julie was in her room with the door closed and I could talk freely. Jon said he was leaving the next night and his voice was as shaken as mine.

"Are you sure you want me, dearest? It's going to be hard on you. I wish I could feel I was worth the sacrifice—"

"Sacrifice! Jon, it's my life! I only breathe because you are in the world and coming to me. . . . I won't try to meet the train. I might faint from ecstasy and disgrace you. Come straight to the penthouse, beloved. I'll be waiting for you. Oh, Jon! . . ."

Julie moved the next day into the little apartment I was to share with her on 53rd Street, not far from Tony's. We had found a room for Jon in the next block, and while it was going to be a come-down from penthouse living for all of us, I was too happy to be daunted. Jimmie had rented a small apartment and a teaching studio in Steinway Hall and was making plans for the winter, but our last night together we spent alone in the penthouse.

We sat out on the terrace very late that night, so occupied with our own thoughts that we said little. Both of us, I think, were reliving our lives together, and there had been so much that was good and sweet and right that I wanted to talk about, but shyness held me back, and in the end it was Jimmie who began.

Looking out over the hedge at the city's towers, he said slowly, "I never thought it would end this way. I had high hopes for us."

"Some of them were realized, weren't they?" My voice trembled. "We have a great deal to be proud of, to be grateful for, Jimmie. Can't we just try to remember that?"

"I suppose we'll have to." He turned his head and I saw his twisted, half-smile. "Don't be afraid. I'm not going to go maudlin on you. You and I both hate scenes, and you're going to have enough to contend with without that, but I do have to say that once again I'm not being much of a man."

"What do you mean?" I didn't want to ask but it slipped out. He swung round in his chair to face me, his head and broad shoulders silhouetted against the night sky.

"I mean—" his voice was rough with self contempt, "that a *man* would be putting up a fight. What am I doing handing you over to Jon when I want to keep you? Oh, I told you I'd go along, and I will, but something inside me is saying, 'You're a fool. She still loves you—a little. Get in there and fight for what is yours.'"

Disturbingly, a little thrill of fear ran through me. Jimmie had been drinking, as usual, but I could not help noticing he was drinking more heavily than usual. This was his last night as my husband. What if the alcohol released some strain of ugliness, of sadism? I had never known anything but kindness and care from my husband, but tonight was surely more than a man might be expected to take in patience.

"You're wrong," I said quickly. "I think you're more of a man than anyone I know."

His head lifted sharply. Now it was his turn to say, "What do you mean?"

"Jimmie—" I held out my hand and after a brief hesitation, he accepted it. "What you are doing has a courage that many a man might envy. You have always said you wanted me to be happy. Now, when you have the right to be bitter, to stand in my way, you have chosen to be generous and brave. I love and admire you."

"More than Jon?"

I ignored the childishness. "I love Jon. Someday I may admire him—as I do you."

"More than your father?"

Were there years of hurt in that question? Yes, I admitted to myself, until the appearance of Jon, no man had loomed so large on my horizon as my father. Subconsciously, most of my decisions had been made in deference to his. It was Daddy, really, who had chosen Jimmie for me: someone easy, good-humored, someone he could mold. With Jon, on the other hand. . . . I turned my thoughts off. That was tomorrow's problem, not tonight's.

"Yes," I said truthfully. "More than Father. He would never do what you are doing. Mother once told me that it was impossible for Father to apologize. You have no need for an apology. You are behaving—" I tried to say it lightly, "as 'an officer and a gentleman.'"

Suddenly he was down beside me on the couch.

"Would 'an officer and a gentleman' do this?"

ૐ   ૐ   ૐ

Why can't I remember the exact circumstances of Jon's arrival? I know that I was still in the penthouse, alone, shivering with anticipation and fear; I know that everything was all right from the first moment—but how he looked or what he wore, or what I wore, or what the first things we said to each other were— everything was lost in the blazing joy of being together again.

I do remember, and will to my last breath, the way we went silently, hand in hand, into the darkened bedroom and lay down together like tired children. Harbor at last, I told myself. Let me just stay here forever with his arms around me, my head on his shoulder. In my mind there were no questions, no feeling of guilt, of right or wrong. Nothing existed but Jon's lips and hands wooing me to an urgency that matched his. All that I had known before of sexual response was swept away in the tide that brought us together. Jon was a wonderful lover, strong, insistent, considerate. Not that consideration was needed. I was his as he was mine. Body and soul soared limitlessly together.

We had a few hours on the terrace before we must come down from the heights and settle into our drab, little cells on a midtown side street. There was much to say but we had a lifetime for that and little really that needed to be said in those first hours. Except to consider briefly the misunderstanding that had kept us apart.

"I wonder what you would have done." Jon was watching the smoke of his cigarette. "I mean, if someone had come to you in the state Mari was in. It was horrifying. She begged me, almost literally on her knees, to come back, to give it one more chance. She brought up everything that had been between us, all she had done for me and what she had given up for my sake. She said if I would come back for just a month and promise not to see you again during that time, or call or write you; if it didn't work, she would agree to let me go. She went on for hours, Isabel, until I was worn out. Finally, to get her out of the hotel, I said I would think it over and persuaded her to go back to Kitty's."

"When we got there, she began again, threatening suicide this time. Kitty had to leave in the morning and I couldn't walk out on Mari in that condition, so I agreed on two weeks in Catalina. I was sick thinking what it would look like to you, but it seemed to be worth the gamble. Only two weeks—and when I was able to explain to you that half the battle was won. . . ."

"Didn't it work at all?" I didn't want to ask it but I had to.

"No," he said curtly. "I gave it every honest chance. I have nothing to reproach myself with, and when we finally broke up, Mari admitted as much and . . . thanked me." He moved restlessly. "Well, what the hell. All that matters is what we do now."

There was one more thing I had to know and then I was as glad to drop the curtain as he was.

"Jon, how did Mari find out where you had gone?"

His mouth was grim. "Your so-called friend told her. After her talk with you, she got on the phone to Mari. I had an interesting little talk with your friend later, when I found out. She claimed

she did it for your sake, that you really loved Jimmie and were
going back to him."

"You believed her!"

"Why wouldn't I? You had left, you didn't write—"

"I did write."

"I know, now. Mari admitted holding up your letters, after
she saw that we weren't going to be able to work it out together
again. Since then she has been fine, Isabel. We can see our way
clear now. And Jimmie?"

"Has been fine, too. Oh, Jon, there are just two big problems. One is money, the other is—"

"Your father."

I shivered and crept closer into his arms. "Not now. Let's
not think of anything more tonight except—"

"I love you," he said and his mouth sought mine once more.

❧ ❧ ❧

David had invited us all out to dinner that night. Jon and I
said a wistful farewell to the penthouse, which I left in perfect order,
and in a taxi full of our luggage, we made our way to West 53rd
Street. Once my things were installed in the apartment I was to
share with Julie, we went in a body to inspect Jon's quarters: a cheap
but not dismal furnished room at the back of an old brownstone. At
least it would be quiet and now and then sunny, and there was a
small gas stove and a minute icebox in the bathroom.

"All the comforts of home," Julie jibed gently. "Isabel, are
we going to miss that penthouse!"

Jon seemed satisfied. "That's a good table for my typewriter," he said cheerfully, "and I don't intend to look out the window much, anyway. I shall keep my nose to the grindstone till I can
support my girl in the luxury to which she has unfortunately
become accustomed." He grinned. "And to which I rather take,
myself."

Our eyes met and we were back in that lovely shadowed
bedroom with all the stars in heaven whirling about us.

We had one of our gay, alcoholic dinners in a steak house on
Second Avenue, and it was amazing how many drinks Jon could

hold without showing any signs of it. I overdid a bit myself, but after all, this was a celebration beyond peer. Jon and I held hands at every available moment, and I was so brimming with happiness that I stammered like a child. Just for an instant now and then I blinked my eyes to realize it was not Jimmie sitting beside me on the bench. It made me fleetingly sad to think of him off alone somewhere, but Jimmie had a great many warm friends and an unattached, attractive male is always sure of a welcome.

What mattered was that Jon had found an immediate place in Julie's and David's regard. He had changed since I saw him last, but his striking, almost Oriental good looks were rather increased than otherwise. He had told me once, laughing, that a famous East Indian poet was reportedly in his family background, and there was a definite Arabian Nights atmosphere about him. I was wildly proud of him, of his wit and charm and intelligence, and in the light of his frank adoration I basked like a petted cat. We all walked home across town from the restaurant, and, clinging tightly to Jon's arm, trying to match my steps to his easy, graceful stride, I told myself that no one in the whole wide wonderful world had ever been as blessed as we.

While Julie and David went up to the apartment, Jon and I lingered in the downstairs hall, unable to tear ourselves apart. We were both deathly tired and had agreed on an early bedtime, but now it seemed literally impossible to part.

"Are you sure you won't disappear before morning?" I whispered into his coat sleeve.

"Don't you think you had better come with me and make sure?"

I wanted to. How I wanted to, but there was iron in me, too. This was the man I had chosen, and one day I would be his wife. I wanted nothing that looked cheap and tawdry in our relationship. Jon and I would live as circumspectly as possible in our separate establishments until we could come out and proudly proclaim to the world our own home. Jon knew my thoughts, and though to his sophisticated soul it all seemed a little over-elaborate, inconvenient, and arbitrary, he agreed that the decision was mine.

As I involuntarily stiffened, he laughed and drew me closer. "Oh, I know, sweetheart," he said gently, kissing me goodnight. "We have to do this thing right, don't we?"

As the fire mounted and we clung dizzily together again, he added in muffled tones into my hair, "But it does seem such a damn waste of time."

I woke to a gray morning in a bleak, unfamiliar room and for a moment was bewildered and frightened. Then I caught sight of Julie curled up like a kitten in the bed across from me, and the whole incredible reality came surging back. How was it possible to *bear* such happiness! It was far too early to call him, and so there was nothing to do but lie there in a half dream, counting the minutes till I could see Jon's face again, hear his voice, feel his hand. An eternity of bliss stretched out before me like a shining plain.

It had turned cold during the night, and when we all met for breakfast in Tony's kitchen, the savory smells and the fire glow only added to my satisfaction. It also gave me an idea.

"I know!" I said joyfully. "Let's all go up to Onteora! It should be glorious with the autumn coloring, and I so want Jon to see it." I wanted Jon to see, to know everything I loved. Jimmie had turned the car over to me, and all four of us were for the moment footloose and fancy free. In a few hours we were off.

I am afraid that I chattered every inch of the way. Jon drove, beautifully, as he did everything else, and I sat cuddled up close beside him, and when I could take my gaze from his handsome profile, I was pointing out and explaining the scenery. I went way back to the story of our first trip up to the Catskills on the Hudson River Day Boat, and as we turned from the lovely rolling riverside country into the mountains, the landscape became an enchantment that matched my mood, an explosion of flame and salmon, cerise and gold that made your eyes ache with color.

We had decided to stay in the little house instead of the big one, and as we turned off the Onteora Road and jolted down the rutty track to the cabin, I was wild with excitement.

"There it is! Isn't it sweet? Isn't it beautiful?"

Julie and David exchanged amused glances. It was a very plain little frame cabin on a rough hillside, but today it was bowered in glory.

Jon's arm went around me. "It is very beautiful, my love," he said gravely.

I did not sleep much that night. The evening had been perfect: a great, roaring fire in the native stone fireplace, lamb chop broiled over the coals, long soothing highballs always at hand. The firelight flickered on the Navajo rugs and the walls still lined with the books I remembered from childhood, books we had not yet removed to the big house. Pictures came and went in my mind; a myriad memories hung in the air. And over and above all, there was the presence of Daddy.

Our reading evenings, Daddy lying on the couch, Mother with her knitting under the kerosene lamp. Daddy hated to have her knit while he read aloud. "Zulime," he would command dramatically, "Stop that *twiddling*!" Connie was usually on her stomach in front of the fire, playing with the kitten or intent on her drawing board, her charming, absorbed face half-hidden by a fall of tawny hair. I was always close beside the couch where Daddy lay stretched out full length, reading aloud from Howells or Mark Twain, John Burroughs or Joe Lincoln. Once we laughed so hard at Joe Lincoln's *The Postmaster* that Connie and I actually hurt and Daddy rolled right off the couch onto the floor. It was the same couch, covered with the same Indian blanket, where Jon and I had spent the evening, my head on his shoulder, our hands linked.

Now, upstairs in the little open-walled bedroom my sister and I had shared for so many years, beside a sleeping Julie, I looked out on the Catskills, dreaming under the frosty stars, and in spite of my great joy knew that my soul was troubled. I had come a long way from the romantic young girl who had "huddled up" in this bed with her little sister, who had wept passionately and thrilled and yearned over fleeting, half-glimpsed dreams. I was a long way too from the bewildered, unsatisfied bride who had lain here sleepless night after night beside an unconscious husband and looked into the future in desperation.

Heretofore in my life my father had been my bulwark, my rock. His pride in me, his gratification in my accomplishments had warmed my soul and spurred me on to great effort. This night, there in the dark, I faced the enormity of what I was doing. For a stranger, a man I scarcely knew, I was tossing away everything I had been taught to believe in, cutting myself off from the warmth and tenderness that had surrounded me all the days of my life. I knew too well what Father would think of this: the shock, the horror, the deep, dazed hurt. What was this incredible power that so filled me that I knew nothing of shame nor regret, only a tumultuous happiness and a savage resolve to keep what I had found at any price?

Downstairs, in the dying firelight, the man I loved lay sleeping. Everything in me cried out to be there beside him, gathering courage from his strength, his warmth. I sat up in bed. Almost I went down to him. Something like a cold wind seemed to be blowing through me, threatening everything I was planning to build my life on. I fought against it fiercely. I must manage to shut out everything in the world but the thought of Jon and the life we would make together. All these memories calling me back had no place in my life now. We would not come to this place again until Jon and I had accomplished what we had set out to do.

&ak; &ak; &ak;

Back in the city, we settled quickly into a routine. Since the most important thing was to make money, Jon and I both turned to. I installed my typewriter at the other end of the long table that held his, and each morning at nine we doggedly went at it. With Jon's presence and professional advice, my creative stream began to flow again, and abandoning my novel, I wrote short story after short story and at last sold one. It was a Christmas sketch and it sold, almost too late for the Christmas issue, to a Canadian magazine called *Chatelaine* for the sum of $75.[1] I was giddy with triumph, ordered half a dozen copies, and sent the first one to Father, whose pride and satisfaction were expressed at once.

"I knew you could do it, daughtie! It's a good story, well told. There's something about New York. I've recognized it for years, but don't let it get a hold on you now. Your place is back here with your two wistful old parents. There will be time later for 'The Big Town.'"

Jon, too, was selling, slowly, small checks in return, but along with the pulp stuff he was writing brief, highly original blackouts aimed at the *New Yorker*. Each time one came back, crushing as it seemed at the moment, it would be accompanied by a scribbled note, "Our kind of stuff. Let us see more." Oh, ambition was high in our drab little office on 53rd Street, but each day also brought its tide of low.

One of the hardest things I had to face was my twice weekly letters to Mother and Daddy. I have reread some of them since
(my parents kept every letter I had ever written to them), and these
are miracles of camouflage. I had taken Jimmie's advice, and as far
as Mother and Daddy knew, Jimmie and I had a flat on 53rd Street
and Julie was still with us. They both knew Julie and liked her, and
it was some satisfaction to know that I was at least telling a half-
truth. While I spent all day with Jon in his little flat, each night I tore
myself away and went back to Julie and—respectability.

Since I only saw Jimmie for cocktails occasionally, I was
hard put to fill my letters with accounts of our supposed doings, but
I drew on my imagination, and it seemed to work. However, as we
continued to remain in the East, my parents became understandably
hurt and impatient. A few days before Christmas, Father wrote me
a curt note that was to haunt me. I had just written to say that we
were not coming.

> Dear Mary Isabel,
>   I consider that we have been fair to you and
> Jimmie, but are you being fair to us? You know
> your mother is very ill. She is fretting for you. Do
> you feel you have the right to ignore her? . . . As
> for me, I make no claims on you. You are young
> and self-centered. That is the way youth accom-
> plishes, I suppose. If you feel what you are doing
> is worth the loneliness and heartache of your
> mother and father that is your decision, but I
> admit to a great disappointment in you and
> Jimmie. This will be a sorry Christmas for your
> old
>   Daddy

I showed the letter to Jimmie when I had a drink with him
one blizzardy afternoon at the Savoy Plaza, and his face grew sad.
He, too, had changed. The boyishness had gone, and though he
professed good cheer whenever we spoke, I could see that things
were not well with him. Yes, he said, his teaching was picking up.
Yes, he was still soloing in church every Sunday, and now and then
a concert or an oratorio came up, but as I knew, concert singing was
a strain and he was doing as little as possible.

"I get by," he said briefly. "But Isabel, I hate to have your parents think of me that way." He read the letter through again and slowly put it back in its envelope. "They were always so good to me. I don't like them thinking I am the one who is keeping you here."

"It was you who advised me not to tell them," I reminded him. "I hate it, Jimmie, as much as you do."

"Oh, I admit it was my idea. I thought I was being very wily at the time."

"Wily?"

"Yes. The point was, if no one knew we were separated, one day you might change your mind and come back to me. It was like—not closing a door."

"Oh, Jimmie, I'm sorry."

"Jon's still the one, then?"

"Now and for always." I laid my hand for a moment on his. "May I say again how splendid you have been? As soon as we get this divorce thing settled, I hope you'll find someone perfectly love-ly and marry again."

He smiled slightly and removed his hand. "I told you my answer to that our last night on the penthouse terrace, remember? Well, will you have another drink, or shall we go?"

My "divorce thing" was looming larger and larger. Through friends, we had heard of a lawyer who specialized in Mexican divorces, and as that seemed to be the only possible solution, Jon consulted him and came back to the apartment deep in gloom.

"These things are so damned expensive! How long before we have that kind of money? What do we make—forty lousy bucks here, seventy-five there, and it's all gone before we know what's happened to it. We're going to need some kind of a miracle. Well, what the hell." He put out his arms and drew me to him. "We had a miracle once," he said huskily. "It can happen again."

That was one of our blackest hours. It was true about the money. Daddy still sent me the hundred dollars a month, but I had to pay my share of the apartment rent with Julie and help out Jon when he got behind, and everything in New York was so dear. Our drinking, except when we were taken out by David, had dwindled to a glass or two of cheap sherry before dinner, but even that was more than we should afford. Gone were the restaurant days, the theater days, the dancing days. We were down to bare bones, but we were together. Something would break soon. It had to.

Sometime after Jon arrived in New York, Mari sent a big, old theatrical trunk of his clothes after him. I arrived just as he was opening it, groaning at the heavy charges he had had to pay, and as he lifted the lid, I saw, artfully arranged across the top of a jumbled mass of clothing, manuscripts, and unmated shoes, a long line of photographs. Every one was of Mari, all her glamour and press photographs down the years, and the big one in the center was a large studio portrait of Mari and Jon, their cheeks pressed together, wearing bright, improbable smiles.

Jon cursed. "God damn!"

I looked at the array with distaste. "When was that big one taken?"

"Oh, some anniversary or other. I hated the whole deal, but Mari needed some new publicity pictures and the guy insisted on that idiotic pose. Wouldn't you know she'd do a thing like this!"

He picked up the photograph and started to tear it across, but I snatched it. "No. I want to study it. You look awfully young. You were very good looking, but you're even better looking now."

He kissed the top of my head. "That's because of your influence, your home cooking." He began scrabbling around in the depths of the trunk. "No wonder I had to pay out all that dough. She's sent *everything*, everything I discarded years ago. Look at this!" This was a mangy raccoon coat, smelling very strongly, and with reason. "The dogs used to sleep on that . . . but she had to pack it up and send it along. . . . Books that mean nothing to me . . . moth-eaten sweaters . . . cologne bottles she once gave me . . . worn-out tennis shoes . . . at least fifty pounds of worthless manuscript, written on both sides so I can't even use it for seconds!"

He began to laugh, angrily, helplessly, and there was nothing to do but laugh with him, though it really was not very funny.

Note

[1] Isabel's story has not been located.

17. Christmas

&. &. &.

Our first Christmas together was approaching, and I tried to turn my mind off from others I had known. Jon was a skillful amateur photographer, and one afternoon I put on my silver brocade evening gown, and he took some stunning photographs of me to send to my relatives and friends. He also took one that I still find appealing: a silhouette of my wistful profile against the small back window of our work room. I remember standing there quietly in an Indian print dress and telling myself how happy I was but how far from the beloved ones on the West Coast.

Jon sensed my heartache and, when the session was over, took me in his arms and held me for a long time.

"Next year," he said softly, "we'll have our own home. And a Christmas tree. And, please God, we'll be just as happy then as we are now."

Julie and I had a tree in our apartment, a gift from David, and my sister had shipped a lavish collection of gifts from herself and Mother and Daddy. Because a large number of them bore Jimmie's name, I asked him to stop by for a drink on Christmas afternoon, and as the hour neared, Jon pleaded a story to finish and tactfully withdrew to his own lodgings.

Jimmie's call was not a success. At my insistence, Julie and David were there, but the old camaraderie was gone, and it was an effort to make conversation. There was embarrassment, too, in the joint gifts to Jimmie and me, and Jimmie would obviously have liked to skip the whole matter, but he had to know what had been sent in order to write the proper thank-you notes. Mother and

Daddy and Connie had been wonderfully generous with us, and there was an extra hundred dollar check from Daddy, "To help keep the wolf from the door." The check was made out to me, and I said, hurriedly, "I'll cash it tomorrow and then if you'll invite me for a drink, I'll give you your half of it."

"I don't want it," Jimmie said abruptly, almost rudely, and stood up. He had brought me red roses, and they glowed like a flame on the table behind him. He was so unlike the Jimmie I knew that I felt confused and miserable, and I was miserable enough already. I was missing Jon. Ever since he had left to go to his room I was feeling as though the most essential part of me had been torn away. I kept seeing him sitting there before his typewriter and wishing I was across from him. Was he really writing, or was he lying on the bed thinking of me, feeling bereft, too? Perhaps he imagined the four of us having a roaring good time. I hoped he was a bit jealous, and I could hardly wait for Jimmie to go so that I could dash to the phone and summon Jon back again. In the meantime, I persuaded Jimmie to take some of the handsome books Daddy had sent, the shirts and socks and ties that had been carefully selected by Connie, and a large box of California candied fruit and nuts.

Thus burdened, he paused in the doorway for a last, forced "Merry Christmas," and moved off down the hall in the direction of the stairs, walking slowly, his shoulders drooping. I wanted to run after him, to catch him by the arm and say, "Jimmie, don't be so unhappy. Someday, when you've found the right person, you'll be glad, too." And in my utter selfishness I thought resentfully, How can I let myself be happy when you look like that?

Julie and David were both silent when I came back into the room and went straight for the telephone. I didn't pick it up at once as I had intended, for I felt, or thought I felt, a wave of unspoken reproach. I was wrong, for they had both accepted Jimmie's and my parting as inevitable, but seeing him again, so changed and thin of face, had been a shock to all of us.

Julie broke the uncomfortable pause. "I don't think Jim's eating enough," she said practically. "We'll have to invite him out to dinner, David, and feed him up."

"Let's do that," David said warmly, adding the usual, "Who is ready for a dividend?"

Jon's present to me was a tiny box that I was forbidden to

open until we were alone. Julie and David were going to a cocktail party and would not be home until late, so Jon and I had the apartment and the whole evening to ourselves. We cooked dinner together in the inadequate kitchenette, and he was pained at our meager collection of herbs and spices.

"That is something I must remedy at once," he said, shaking his head over the lack of sweet basil. "I'll lay in a supply tomorrow, also a mortar and pestle. That's the only way to get the real savor out of herbs, crush them freshly yourself. Which, by the way," he reached for me, "applies to lips. Crush them freshly and frequently. . . ."

When he finally released me, I had just breath enough to ask, "Now may I see my present?"

"You're changing the subject."

"I think I'd better. And you did say that when we were alone—"

"So I did. You have a one-track mind. All right, greedy girl, hand it over."

We were both flushed and shaken as we sat down on the couch together, and I brought out the little packet from my coat pocket and handed it to him.

"I'll open it for you. Close your eyes." I heard the rustle of the tissue paper, a tiny click, and the next instant a ring was sliding into place on my left hand. Jon said, "Open your eyes," and I gave a happy cry. It was my engagement ring, a small square topaz like a chunk of sunlight, and it meant more than any ring had ever meant since the beginning of time.

Jon looked at it disparagingly. "I'll get you a better one someday." Father told me he had said those very words when he put his first modest ring on Mother's finger.

"There isn't a better one." I held it to my lips. "I love it for the pretty thing it is and for what it means. I shall wear it forever."

He took my hand, turning it from side to side so that the golden stone caught the light. "Before long, there will be another one next to it, a wedding band, in case you're interested."

"Jon! Do I ever think of anything else? But you really shouldn't have spent all that money."

His face darkened. "It wasn't 'all that money.' It was dirt cheap, if you must know. Someday, wait and see, you'll glitter like that Christmas tree, and it won't be tinsel, either. But about that ring, I decided it was time I had something to bind you with."

"As if I needed binding. Surely by now you know that I am yours forever and a day."

The quaint old expression caught his interest. "Why that "and a day" business, do you suppose? It sounds suspiciously like an out for somebody."

"If you ever want an out—"

"Idiot. Precious idiot." I was back in his arms again, and time and the world were no longer important.

At dinner he hinted mysteriously, "I have another present for you, but you won't get it till tomorrow."

"Oh, Jon, what? You mustn't spend any more money."

"I won't be spending money for this, I promise you. It's by nature of a deal, and I'm only hoping you'll be as pleased as I am."

"If it makes you happy, I know I will be."

"We have a date, then, tomorrow afternoon at five o'clock. I want you to wear your best clothes and make an impression."

"Impression on who?" I demanded, but he refused to say another word.

Getting dressed the next afternoon, I hummed happily as I laid out my fur coat. It was, by now, a slightly shabby gray squirrel, but it was light and warm, and as the New York winter winds began to blow, I was grateful for it. I had acquired it one hot autumn day in Hollywood, where fur coats are really an anachronism, and it had been Daddy's Christmas present to me. I had come running down the street from the fur shop to the parked car where Mother and Daddy were waiting, and I twirled and posed on the sidewalk in my new garment, completely oblivious of passersby.

"This is the one I like, Daddy! Isn't it handsome. Don't you think I chose well?"

Daddy's face wore a look of fond amusement as he got out of the car and came around to run his hand over the soft fur, to turn me around consideringly. This must have been a fine moment for a one-time Wisconsin farm boy. In the early years of their marriage, Father had told me, he had purchased my mother a fur coat, something called a "pony coat." As a child, I was horrified to discover that "pony" actually meant "horse."

"It's squirrel, Daddy. Isn't it luxurious?"

"It's pretty and it becomes you," Father said calmly. "Tell them to put it in a box and we'll take it home."

I hesitated. "But Daddy, it costs—"

He held up a hand. "I said up to five hundred dollars, remember. If it is under that—"

"Oh, it is!"

"Good. Send the salesman out to me and I'll give him a check." He did not wish to leave Mother alone, so I kissed them both rapturously and raced back to the shop.

I was thinking of Daddy that afternoon as I walked down the street with Jon, warm and snug in Father's Christmas gift, his hundred dollar check in my pocketbook. "Jon, I'm very lucky."

"*We're* very lucky," he corrected, putting my hand into his overcoat pocket as Daddy used to. "We only need one thing, aside from a divorce, that is."

"What do we need?"

"You'll see in a minute."

We rounded the corner of Madison Avenue and turned north, and knowing the neighborhood and the various shops we were about to pass, I had a sudden, sinking feeling. "Jon! No!"

I began to hold back. We were about half a block from a pet shop, outside whose windows Jon would invariably stop and linger. The last time there had been Scotty puppies in the window, and I had seen the tenderness in Jon's face and eyes as he watched the rowdy, tumbling little devils. Jon was going to give me a dog, the last thing in the world I needed or wanted!

"What are you stopping for? Come in." He held my arm firmly.

"Jon, you mustn't!" I stood stock-still and fixed an imploring look on him. We had reached the pet shop, the windows were full of poodles this time, but I absolutely refused to go in.

"Jon, I mean it. You're going to give me a dog and I *do not want one*. It's sweet of you and I know how you feel, but I absolutely refuse."

"Oh, come on," he urged. "Just step inside. You don't have to have a dog it you don't want one. You're probably right. I have to go in, anyhow. There's something I want to talk to the owner about, so just come in with me for a minute."

Like a mother propelling home a reluctant child, he pushed

me ahead of him into the shop. Inside was bedlam. At our arrival, in cages all around the walls, dogs yipped and yelped and leaped and bayed. I put my hands hard over my ears and turned to flee, but at that moment I caught sight of her.

She was not in a cage. She was wearing a collar, but she was not tied and was sitting quietly on a dark cushion, small forepaws neatly together, an utterly charming, foxy, little black face under crisp, silver ears turned inquiringly far to one side. She was almost the color of my squirrel coat, and she made my heart miss a beat.

It was too noisy to speak, but Jon, smiling, went over to her and pointed. I followed him and went down on my knees beside her. She reached out and gave my hand a small, polite lick, then sat back composedly again.

"Oh, if you mean this one!" I breathed and picked her up and held her under my chin. She snuggled against my shoulder, relaxed, completely happy.

Jon gave a shout of laughter. "That's the one! That's the one! Oh, darling, are you hooked!"

Jon had told the truth: he didn't have to give any money for her, though she was a valuable Cairn, three years old, with an impressive pedigree. The pet shop owner had sold some puppies Jon had bred and owed him money, and the transfer of the little dog would wind up the transaction.

I had some remnant of sense remaining, and I tried to summon it. "She's adorable, but how do we know what she's like? She may not be housebroken or—"

"Take her out for a walk," the owner suggested. "She goes on a lead just great. Take her around the block, see how she looks at you."

In the end we did that. There was a bar we knew around the corner, and with the little creature walking sedately between us, we headed in that direction. When we came to the revolving door, she marched ahead and, with her nose pressed to the partition pushed through like an old habitué, entered the bar with all the dignity in the world.

"That's a girl," Jon chuckled. "You know the ropes, don't you. . . . Let's sit over here and see what happens."

We sat at a little table in a dark corner, and while the bartender was taking our order, our new friend went under the table, curled herself into a small, gray ball between our feet, and went philosophically to sleep. Jon and I exchanged glances. This *was* what we had been needing all along.

Her name was Lassie, too banal for my imaginative husband-to-be, so she became Molasses, Lasses for short, and never was there a better bargain. For the rest of her life she went with us everywhere, always a lady, never objectionable in any way. Just so she was within sniffing distance of one of us was all she asked. The only thing that unsettled her poise was an elevated train. At the first far-off sound, she would flatten herself out on the sidewalk like a gray, quivering pancake and someone would have to pick her up and cuddle her till the menacing monster had passed. She was at home in elevators, restaurants, hotels, department stores, and cars, and even met rude dogs with equanimity. It seemed that she had played "Flush" in *The Barretts of Wimpole Street* with a road company, and I am sure she was splendid. No need to dope this darling, for she was composure itself, until. . . . But that comes later.

The other thing we needed so desperately—a divorce—haunted us night and day. The friend who had lent me the money to bring Jon to New York was in Europe, and in any case, not being able to pay back the first loan, I would not have presumed to ask for another. I might have lied to my father, pleading illness or some other emergency, but I couldn't do it. Except for just enough for our daily living, Jon and I were without resource. We were both writing doggedly, but sales were few and far between. Gradually, we pawned or sold everything of value we possessed: jewelry, silver, watches, cameras. Father had left me a charge card at Bloomingdales, and it was, literally, a life saver. In the grocery department we could buy tinned things, spaghetti, rice, crackers, jam, tea, and coffee, but I was careful to use the account sparingly, and we were definitely not living "high on the hog." It was fortunate, perhaps, that the store had no liquor department. Jon and I, except when guests, were on very short alcoholic rations. It was, in fact, a period to challenge the most dedicated love, and looking back on it, I am both proud—and wondering. Depressed we were, frequently, but every day seemed only to strengthen our love, our resolve. I cannot remember a quarrel in all that time, harried over money matters though we were. As I told Jon, it had to be true love. Why else put up with something so frustrating and uncomfortable?

In the midst of this happy-wretched period came a wire from my sister. "Arriving Friday for two weeks. Engage hotel room near you. Will explain when I see you."

It was wonderful to think of seeing Connie again. In spite of my preoccupation with Jon, I missed my family sorely, and Daddy's letters, growing increasingly reproachful, wrung my heart. Such was my conviction, however, that this was the right, the *only* thing to do that I did not waver for a moment. Miraculous to be so sure of something. From the moment Jon had said, "I am all yours and will do whatever you want me to do," I had had no thought but our eventual marriage. I wanted Connie to come; I wanted her to see for herself that I had chosen the one, if appallingly difficult road. She was deeply fond of Jimmie, and despite the help she had given me, I knew that underneath there must be criticism and doubt. Now she would come to know Jon and the rock on which my life was built.

Jon and I met Connie at the train and at first I hardly recognized her.

She was very chic and expensively turned out, but her face was strained and the look in her eyes so desperate that it frightened me. She was excessively gay and entertaining, and she and Jon got along beautifully, as I knew they would. Connie was well supplied with money, and we did gourmet restaurants and theaters, things we had not been able to afford for ourselves. Being Connie, she made no attempt during the first part of her visit to confide in me. All she said was that she needed a change, and as she had always loved New York, she decided to come and look in on me. She was restless as a butterfly, drinking too much, worrying about her children, but it wasn't until almost the end of her stay that she broke down and told me the truth.

"Mother and Daddy don't know it, but Joe wants a divorce."

"Connie!"

If my first thought was for her, my second was for Father. One of the things he hated most in the world was the idea of divorce, and now with both daughters. . . . I had known things were not going well in my sister's life, but thinking of the two beautiful children, their lovely home, her statement shocked me to the core.

"But—but he can't! What—"

Her voice was full of weary resignation. "Another woman, naturally, one who 'understands him.' Not, this time, his mother."[1]

"Have you agreed?"

"I am supposed to be thinking it over. Joe had already seen a lawyer. When I get back, I'll have to find one, too."

That part of it would be easy enough for them, I thought, with a wave of bitterness of my own. Joe was well-to-do, it would all be worked out in a civilized manner, but little John and Constance—what would it do to them? All the tragedies I had heard of broken homes came flooding in on me. It didn't seem possible it could happen to that home, those little ones. In the end, I knew that my sister would be all right. She was immensely charming; men were drawn to her. After a few months of emptiness, of feeling "the woman scorned," she would find someone else, but what would it mean to her children—to Mother and Daddy?

"Connie, I don't know what to say—"

"Don't say it, then," she said sharply, then put her hand briefly on mine. "I'm sorry. I'm not making much sense these days, I'm afraid, and seeing you and Jon has not helped either. You seem so happy.

"We are, in each other. And someday we'll work things out the way we want them. In the meantime—"

"In the meantime," Connie repeated, "I go back and face the music. I'm not going to tell Mother and Daddy till the very last minute. With you gone, they depend more and more on me. Remember how Daddy used to call us 'Tempest and Sunshine?' Well, I'm still supposed to be their Little Sunshine, and I'll try to act the part as long as I can. . . . Where's that man of yours? Isn't it time somebody fixed me a drink?"

It was about a week after Connie left that the letter came. I opened it with the usual guilty uneasiness that always accompanied the arrival of a letter from Daddy, but this one was different. It was a sheet of paper with only a few lines on it in longhand, and they stabbed, as they had been meant to do:

> Mary Isabel,
>   Your sister tells me you have left your hus-
> band and are involved with another man. I need
> not tell you what this means to me but I want to

say I will never see this man or take him by the
hand. Your monthly allowance will continue but
do not expect anything else from me.
  Father

Connie had given me away! The thing I had dreaded most
had come about. I had wanted to come to my parents with the
problem solved, to say proudly, "Mother and Daddy, this is my husband. We love each other very much and have worked hard to
prove it. Jimmie understands and has given us his blessing. Won't
you?"

My sister had undone us. The love and trust Daddy had
had in me was swept away. I could see him sitting at his desk, his
head in his hands, a tide of pain and despair sweeping through him.
"Oh, Daddy—" my heart cried out to him, "I haven't really failed
you! Nothing has changed my love for you and Mother. I have
found the other part of my life, that's all. One day we'll come back
to you and you'll see and we'll all be happy again. Please try not to
hate me."

To my sister I wrote a scorching letter, which brought a
quick reply. "What could I do? They were bound to hear it from
someone before long. Jimmie's friends knew you were separated,
and when I heard Daddy talking about you and Jimmie to the
Kelloggs and saying you were expected home shortly, the only
thing I could think was that Daddy must hear the truth from me and
not from some outsider. I softened the shock as best I could by
telling them I knew and liked Jon, that you were deeply in love and
meant for each other, that Jimmie was satisfied about it, and that
you were both writing and earning the money for a divorce, but
there is no denying the fact that Daddy is shattered. He told me
never to mention the matter to him again, and for the moment I
agreed. Mother, of course, is wonderful. She cried a little and held
my hand, and then she asked me to tell her everything about you
and Jon and what your plans were. When I had finished, she said
'Send them my love. And tell my daughter that I wish for her happiness more than anything in the world.'"

"I am sorry you are so angry with me," my sister's letter
went on, "but I really feel I did the only thing I could do. It would
have been humiliating for Daddy to find out the whole thing

through casual gossip. If you think it over, I am sure you and Jon will understand."

When the first resentment had passed, we did understand. The wonder was, really, that Mother and Daddy had not heard it before. All our friends knew, but my parents lived such circumscribed social lives that they were not exposed to the ordinary channels of chit-chat. Friends like the Kelloggs would never have mentioned so disturbing a matter. In the end, Jon and I agreed that Connie had been right: it was best that they heard the worst from her. Poor Connie, who along with her own problems had to bear the brunt of the following emotional weeks.

I wrote Father at once, pouring my heart out, trying to make him understand the supreme importance of this love in my life, but his only answer was another curt note: "I understand that you are contemplating divorce. You will have no help from me in this matter. I have always stood for honesty and decency and I wish no part in this dangerous venture you are embarked on. From now on, the subject is closed between us."

His letters, however, continued, brief and impersonal, concerned mainly with Mother's health and the development of the grandchildren. Never again did he make reference to either Jimmie or Jon or suggest as he had in every letter heretofore that the time had come for my return. Except for the monthly check, he seemed to have no more concern for me, and it was a constant loneliness inside me.

Jon was incredibly patient. He knew I was suffering, but only once did he really express himself. It was one afternoon when he had come in and found me, face down on the couch, crying my heart out. Daddy's letter about the divorce was lying beside me on the floor, and Jon read it, then he swore.

"God damn it! What's your father trying to do? This isn't the end of the world. It isn't as though we had murdered somebody—or set out to starve little children—or kicked cripples! We're just two wrongly-mated adults trying our best to get straightened out."

"Do you think we'll ever get straightened out?" I asked woefully.

"Of course." He drew me up against him. "And for a starter—I had a break today. A man I know is putting on a revue and he wanted some dramatic sketches. I submitted five and he took them all."

"Darling, that's wonderful!" I struggled up, flooded with hope. Jon was so clever, such a gifted writer—all he needed was the right opening, and perhaps this was it.

That spring and early summer we spent a large part of our time in a darkened, off-Broadway theater watching the production of a musical revue. It was my third encounter with the professional theater, and a completely different one, but as absorbingly interesting as the others had been. In the company were three or four top-flight comedians, and to our satisfaction, Jon's sketches were played to the hilt. The director-producer was a temperamental, autocratic, little man who managed to establish feuds with most of the writers, composers, and members of the cast, but he had a flair for this sort of thing, and the production opened to complimentary notices, many of them calling attention to the "exceptionally witty sketches."

Eventually, Jon's personal battle with the producer reached such an impasse that four out of the five sketches were removed from the production, but Jon took his appeal to Equity, which ruled that Jon had a run-of-the-play contract for five sketches. Though the four removed sketches were not put back, each Friday night throughout that hot New York summer, Jon and I appeared bright and early at the box office and under the baleful glare of the producer collected the money for all five sketches. It was a windfall to us and Jon promptly made the first payment on a Mexican divorce.

Shortly afterward, a wealthy New York society woman called Jon. She had written a play she wanted "doctored" and Jon's agent had recommended him. She would pay one thousand dollars.

"Whee!" Jon hung up the phone and flung his arms around me. "We're in, darling—we're in! Kiss me quick, my blessed bride-to-be—and find me the phone number of that divorce lawyer!"

A few days later, he brought the play home and we read it together. It was incredibly amateur, no construction, a fantastic plot, some scenes three minutes long, others would have played for an hour. Jon groaned and became understandably profane.

"Believe me, I'm going to earn every cent of that thousand before I am through," he said grimly.

I earned it, too. Equally grimly, I tried to keep my sights on the ultimate goal, but I did not enjoy the next month. Every afternoon at five, Jon would report at the lavish Park Avenue apartment where his co-author resided, with the revisions he had made since the day before. The sessions lasted two to three hours, and I am frank to admit that I was sick with jealously. I had not met the lady, but Jon admitted she was young and good-looking, and there was no doubt that she was filthy rich. As the sessions began to lengthen, I suddenly boiled over.

"Here I am, doing the very thing I swore I would never do—walking the floor, waiting for some man to come home! That's why I would never marry an actor. Must I go through the same thing because I am marrying a writer?"

"I can't help it, darling," Jon said ruefully. "She's paying out the money, the money that we have to have. There's always one more scene that she wants to talk about."

"There will be one more scene that she won't want to talk about," I said, trying to be funny but actually as mad as a wet hen. "I know I sound like a jealous wife, and I guess I am, almost." Repentant, I flung my arms around his neck. "Oh, Jon, will we ever have any *peace*?"

Note

[1] Joe Harper had entered into an affair with Cecilia DeMille Calvin. Constance and Joe were divorced on January 18, 1937. One year later, on January 21, 1938, Joe and Cecilia married—and moved across the street into the DeMille mansion.

18. Peace

ॐ ॐ ॐ

That summer Julie decided to marry her David. It was so obviously right that Jon and I rejoiced almost as much as if the wedding had been our own. Julie's adored mother came in from the West Coast, and Jon and I were the ones who drove her out to the small white New England church in Old Greenwich, where the ceremony took place. They leased a delightful penthouse on East 57th Street, and with Julie's mother comfortably installed not far away, they became New York householders, and our companionable times continued.

I needed a roommate, and a charming actress friend of Julie's and I took an apartment together for a brief time. We were merely perching, for the lawyer assured us that the divorce decree would be coming through at any minute.

Jon and I had one special dream to which we were holding fast. We were neither of us city people. The peace I was so yearning for was not to be found on a pulsing street in Manhattan, and though Jon had been born and brought up in Chicago, his heart, as well as mine, longed for the country. As soon as we were legally one, we planned to leave the city and find a small, remote place where there would be trees, birds, fresh air, and blessed silence.

Through a friend, we heard of a possible spot, only an hour and a half drive from New York, on the borderline of New Jersey. It was part of an original Colonial grant and still belonged to the first family, in the person of a tall, pleasant, easygoing bachelor in his early forties. In vast excitement, we drove up to talk to him.

If we had created the place ourselves it could not have suit-

ed us better. In the center of several thousand acres of young tim-
ber, on the shore of a small, private lake, stood a log cabin that the
owner had built for himself. The nearest town was seven miles
away, the nearest neighbor, two. The owner himself lived in the big
family homestead some twenty miles away but used the cabin as a
summer retreat and for hunting and fishing. There was nothing visible from any window in the house but gentle wilderness and water.
While our own little lake was better for frogs and fishing, there was
a large, clear swimming lake only a few miles away, over a rutted
country road that was traveled at the most only two or three times
a week.

We liked Douglas and he liked us, and when we drove
away in the dusk we had a receipt for the first month's rent—a
minute sum, considering we had leased a hold on Paradise. There
were certain drawbacks, of course, but we dismissed them. No
water, except the lake. No heat, except the big, native stone fireplace and a wood-burning stove in the tiny kitchen. No lights,
except for kerosene lamps and candles. No plumbing, only a rustic
outhouse, demurely concealed behind a lath screen. But it was
beautiful and wild and quiet, and it was ours as soon as we could
claim it.

Our wedding day—only a few days before Christmas—
came at last.[1] Jon went down to the lawyer's office for the long-
delayed papers, and I met him "under the clock at the Biltmore"
at noon. There are no words to describe what I felt, but I was wearing, as I recall, a singularly unattractive outfit: a bargain suit of forest green wool with a matching turban that kept threatening to blow
off as we crossed on the ferry to Jersey to a justice of the peace who
kept his office open to marry us at one o'clock on a Saturday afternoon.

Except for the little golden wedding ring, it was a brief,
unromantic ceremony, with two of the office staff called as witnesses, and we climbed back on the ferry in a daze and stood clinging to
each other, and the rail, in the cutting wind and repeating over and
over incredulously, "We're married! We did it! We did it!"

If our wedding was merely practical, our lavish reception
was not. Julie and David gave it for us in their lovely high-ceilinged
penthouse, and one of Julie's gifts to me had been a gold silk cocktail dress. Jon had bought me white orchids, and I was a pretty daz-

zling sight as we climbed the steep, iron outside staircase that led to the penthouse door.

All the family friends and relatives we could round up were there, including my beloved cousin, Jessie Louise Taft, and it began to snow, so that everyone coming into the fire-lit, flower-filled room was powdered with white. The very air seemed to vibrate with our triumphant happiness, for this was something that against all odds we had brought to be.

Dressing for the reception, in the hotel where we were to stay for a few days while looking for an apartment, I had sent off a telegram to Mother and Father and Connie:

> Jon and I were married today. Please be as glad as
> we are. Love always, Isabel

There was an answering telegram waiting for us in the hotel when we returned late that night:

> Mother and I so happy for you. Letter follows.
> Love, Connie

No mention of Father. It was a hurt, but I had not expected otherwise, and tonight there was nothing in my soul but soaring gratitude. Out of everyone in the world, we alone knew perfect content. All that I had dreamed of was realized, and it was not just for tonight—it was for all time.

꒰ ꒰ ꒰

We found a pleasant little furnished place that we could afford and moved into it on Christmas Eve, complete with Lasses and a Christmas tree. My throat aches, remembering the ecstatic happiness of that time. It seemed that nothing of evil or woe could ever touch us again.

Then, a few days after Christmas, came an unhappy letter from my sister. She had embarked on the preliminaries of her own divorce and had been forced, at last, to tell Mother and Father.

> Mother was shocked and sad but understanding,
> but Father was wild. Both daughters getting
> divorces! How could God sit up in his heaven

and let this happen to him! He went on so that at
last I came right back at him. 'Do you think this is
easy for *me*?' I asked. 'So you think I'm *enjoying*
this? If you can't say something kind and helpful,
don't say anything at all.' He looked at me for a
moment, then said quietly, 'Very well, Constance,'
and went into his study and shut the door. . . . I
suppose it was terrible of me, but I had taken all
my nerves could stand, not only in my own life,
but with Daddy's constant ranting about you and
Jon, how you were flinging your life away, and so
on. I showed him the wedding telegram and he
froze but said not a word. He is hideously hurt
but perhaps time will soften the blow. In the
meantime, Mother and I couldn't be prouder of
you. She is pining to see you, but I know you
want to stay in the East for the present and I'll do
my best to hold the fort. I must say I feel a little
bit like Daddy: how can God sit in his heaven and
let this happen to *me*!
   Your loving,
   Sister

Two days later, there was another letter from Connie.

I take it all back—Father is being simply wonderful! There have been no more tirades. I can feel
his love and sympathy, and this morning *he offered
to go down to the lawyer's office with me*! I was so
touched I cried, for the first time, in front of him,
and he put his arms around me. He is made of
rare stuff, our father. I can't tell you what it means
to know he is behind me. There has been no
recent mention of you and Jon so I can only
assume he is doing some thinking there, too. . . .
Mother, I am sorry to say, is failing very badly, but
she still talks happily of your marriage. Do let us
hear your plans.

Our plans, naturally, were centered on the little cabin on the
lake, but it was still too early to go up, and we tried to curb our
impatience and pass the time with assembling things that would be
useful there. Since there was no electricity in the cabin and Jon and

I were both dedicated music lovers, we invested in a battery radio and record player that would assure us of music wherever we went, and as soon as the road to Onteora was clear of snow, we planned to go up and raid Camp Neshonoc of kerosene heaters, down quilts, Navajo blankets, books, dishes, and pots and pans. It was glorious fun planning our own home, though admittedly on a different scale from the one Jimmie and I had had in Hollywood.

My allowance arrived as usual on the first, but there was no letter to accompany it. I wondered if I would ever hear from Daddy again, and in the midst of my happiness, I was conscious of a sick pang. For thirty-five years my life had been secure in the thought of my father's love. Was it possible that the confidence and tenderness were at an end between us? I would not let myself believe it. I wrote every two or three days, as usual, to both Mother and Father, detailing our daily activities, our progress in writing, and one triumphant day I was able to buy a copy of the *New Yorker* and mail it to Connie with a scrawl saying "see page 35." Yes, Jon had made the magazine at last, and his creative powers seemed to move into high gear.[2] Money troubles would now begin to fade. We could go dancing now and then—one of our chief delights, for Jon was a perfect dancer, and we moved together as if in a dream. There would be theaters and concerts, and we would be able to take Julie and David out to dinner. I was so proud of Jon, of what he was, of what he could do, that it seemed some echo of my confidence must percolate into my father's doggedly closed brain.

Late in February, there was a telegram.[3]

> Your mother very ill. If you want to hear her voice
> again, you must come at once. Father

I cried all that night in Jon's arms. There was no question but that I must go, but how could we bear to be separated? We talked of Jon's coming with me, but aside from the expense and a doubtful welcome, Jon was deeply involved with an idea he had had for using printed cellophane sheets in a sort of booklet that could be used for maps, charts, and all manner of advertising schemes. The Washington patent attorney who was in charge of the project was sure we were going to make a fortune out of it, and in his enthusiasm was personally defraying all expenses. We both agreed: it would be unwise for Jon to go away at this point, but at the thought of three thousand miles between us again, the old horror and insecurity came flooding back. Jon soothed and comforted and reassured, and in the morning I wired that I would be leaving two days later.

"But only for a week," I kept promising Jon and myself over and over. "I'll go out and see Mother and tell her about us and she'll understand. Oh, darling, how can I bear to leave you?"

There was no flying in those days, so it was three almost unendurable days and nights on a swaying, jolting train. I have never been able to sleep on a train, and listening to the crossing bells, watching the sleeping villages flash by in the dark, I relived in memory many a train trip, beginning with the one I had taken alone with Daddy to West Salem. That happy little girl was still in me somewhere, but it was a tense, exhausted woman who disembarked at Pasadena.

Connie met me at the train and on the way home told me about Mother. "We've tried everything—injections, diet, sedation, even snake venom that someone told us about, but she gets steadily worse. I don't think she wants to live. She just lies there with her eyes closed, and when we ask her questions, her voice is almost inaudible. She has rallied a bit since she knew you were coming, but I am afraid you must be prepared for a shock."

Daddy opened the door for us, and I went into his arms in the old way. He patted my shoulder as he released me and turned to the stairs.

"Your mother is awake and waiting for you," he said in a voice that was harsh with feeling. His face was gray and drawn. He looked like an old, old man. "She has been counting the hours."

Mother's eyes were huge and bright with tears in her pale, wasted face, and the arms that went around my neck shook pitifully, but she managed a smile, "Oh darling . . . darling," she whispered, drawing back and searching my face. "You're happy now, aren't you? Yes, I can see it in your eyes. Oh, my precious little girl, I am so glad for you."

Her voice miraculously strengthened, and we talked and talked during that week, Mother and I. It was during this time that she told me the story of her own great love, and for the first time we were two women together. She improved visibly during my stay, and we all took heart. I told her about the cabin on the lake and our plans for the summer and fall. "Later, perhaps Jon and I can both come out for a while," I promised her, with an inner resolve never to leave my husband again. It was an ordeal to be back in this house, to lie awake at night in that familiar bedroom and feel the shadows of the old nightmare gather around me.

Mother clung to my hand. "I know, I know. You must go back to him—but you'll come soon, won't you?"

Father and I had no private talks. On the surface, he was just as usual, alert, interested, affectionate. He, himself, never mentioned Jon's name, but I used it frequently, when I wasn't proudly referring to "my husband." I had brought a sheaf of short stories Jon and I had written, and the first morning, without comment, I laid them on Daddy's desk. By night they were back on my desk, without comment, but I knew he had read them, for at dinner he had several valuable suggestions to make about mine. As we said goodnight that first night, I asked Father if he would like the use of my secretarial services for a few hours each morning while I was there.

For a moment, his face expressionless, he made no answer, then he said, "Why, yes, Mary Isabel, if you can spare the time. Constance has been helping me out now and then, but she is pretty occupied these days."

Next morning I took my accustomed seat before Daddy's big, old Royal, and though I had rather dreaded the prospect, all went smoothly and well. Daddy dictated a handful of letters and laid out a couple of hideously corrected chapters of the new book for me to type,[4] and everything was so pleasant and matter of fact that something impelled me to say, "It's like old times, isn't it, Daddy?"

He stood motionless for second, looking past me into the olive trees, and under the whitening mustache, his mouth was a grim line. Then, with an effort, he said remotely, courteously, "Yes, daughtie, it is. Quite like old times." And went out of the room and left me alone.

Connie was indeed "occupied these days." Not only did she have her home, her two lively, picture-book-beautiful children—who seemed quite oblivious of the ferment around them—her social life, and her ever-looming divorce problem, but as I had foreseen, the suitors had begun to gather. In fact, she was going a frantic pace, and I wondered how she survived. To add to the confusion, Joe was in and out of his mother's house next door at any hour of the day or night and was more than likely to stop in at Connie's for a romp with his children. Connie never knew when she would come home and find him there, and the added nervous strain was telling on her.

"If I could only get away for a while!" she said in desperation. "I'd give anything to be able to take the children and get out of here, but it's so expensive to go to a hotel—"

"I know! Onteora!"

I think the idea struck both of us at the same time, but I said it aloud.

For a moment my sister looked almost happy. "Onteora—"

"Why not? It's not more than an hour or two drive from the cabin where Jon and I are going to be. We could visit back and forth and have fun. The children would adore it. Oh, Connie, come East this summer—do!"

She said she would think it over, and when she took me to the train in Pasadena a few days later—heartsick for mother, I had stayed on three extra days, though I was frantic to be off—I could see Connie was half convinced.

"It will depend on a lot of things, but mainly Mother. She has been so much better since you were here that I've started hoping again. Thanks for coming, Sis. I can imagine what a wrench it must have been for you." She looked at me reflectively. "You know, I don't think I would ever want to love anyone that much. It makes you too—vulnerable."

Vulnerable, yes, but, ah, the rewards!

≋ ≋ ≋

Three more endless nights and days and I was racing down the Grand Central platform into Jon's arms, with Lasses executing little shrimp-like wriggles of welcome around our ankles.

"Oh, darling!" I cried from the depths of my being. "I've come home! I've come home!"

"Home" was our little forty-dollar-a-month apartment.

Though pleasant enough, it admitted sunlight for only twenty minutes out of the day. As spring started to come on, a thin, knife-like band of pallid sun would come in the side window and lie across the carpet briefly before it vanished behind a jutting commercial building. One of our amusements was to watch Lasses in her basket beside the radiator. Though she appeared to be sleeping, we could tell by the quiver of her ears and her eyelashes that she was counting the seconds, and as the first tiny blade of sunlight entered the room, she would leap from her bed and ensconce herself in it, and there she would stay till the last lingering ray withdrew. Then she would rise dejectedly and make her way back to her basket again.

"Just think—" Jon told her one day, ruffling her thick, silvery coat, laying his cheek against the top of her head. "Before long you're going to have three thousand acres of sunlight! How will you like that, my girl? How will you like that?"

The passionate promise in his voice communicated itself to her, and Lasses gave a short, rapturous bark. Jon and I looked into each other's eyes and laughed from pure joy.

A week later, early in March, we took off in a car piled to the roof with provisions, clothing, and household necessities. On the very top of the load, reclining in state in Jon's old raccoon coat, was Lasses, ears alert, ready for any adventure we had in mind. The weather was still pretty bitter, but we absolutely could not wait a minute longer.

Our landlord was waiting for us at the cabin when we reached there about twilight. He had a royal fire going in the fireplace and the woodstove in the kitchen glowed comfortingly. Lasses was out of the car first and off on a thrilling tour of inspection. Poor little city dog, this was Paradise for her, too. Douglas helped us unload and stayed for a drink. We had bought a steak for our first dinner, and Douglas volunteered to cook it for us while we went on with our unpacking and stowing away. To our horror, he took out a pan and *fried* the priceless thing that we had intended to grill lovingly over wood coals, but his good intent was so obvious that we didn't say a word.

Eventually, he tore himself away, and as soon as the door closed, we shot the bolt, dragged the couch up closer to the fire, tuned our radio to the symphonic music station in New York,

Mindret Lord at the cabin by the lake, 1936.
(*Courtesy of the University of California,
on behalf of USC Libraries Special Collections*)

drained our glasses once again, and in the utter silence and peace of our kingdom slept in each other's arms the night through.

Awakening to an icy March dawn was somewhat less idyllic. Both fires had gone out, and though we had covered ourselves sometime during the night with a down quilt, our teeth—and Lasses, who had crawled in under the down quilt with us—were chattering, but it was fun!

We splashed water on our faces, ice-cold water from the bucket Jon brought up from the lake, built up the fires, put water on to boil for our coffee, and got out the frying pan, the bread, and the bacon and eggs. Our two typewriters sat companionably together on the long oak table, glorious music was pouring out of our battery radio, and Lasses, stretched full length in a six-foot square of blazing sunlight, gave a bottomless sigh of satisfaction that might have been ours.

This was Spartan living and we gloried in every moment of it. Jon had always been the soul of efficiency around the house, but it made me amazed and proud to see how skillfully he could split logs, how sure he was with fires and heaters and lamps. He was a carpenter, too. Douglas said we might put up bookshelves for our books and manuscripts, and Jon had them squared and nailed and installed in no time. The main room of the cabin, with its chinked logs, was as picturesque as a stage set, and the Indian rugs we had brought from the Catskills gave just the right note of color. The huge, hand-hewn bed, which we got around to trying the next night, was as hard as the floor, but it did not daunt us.

"Just think how beneficial it will be." I maintained. "We will have the straightest spines in Christendom."

The big drawback—and it was that—was the lack of water and toilet facilities. It was hard to go out on a sleety night in March to a grim little outhouse half-full of snow. And bathing, until it grew warm enough for swimming, was a problem. We used to take turns, standing and shivering, in the wash boiler, while one or the other poured water over our already soaped bodies. Lasses, too, became a problem. She had turned into a wanderer, a country dog, coming home from her travels with strange, distasteful smells clinging to her heavy coat. There was one time when we were going in to spend the weekend with Julie and David. We had just washed Lasses and she was at her beguiling best, when somehow she slipped away from us and I could see her far down the road rolling joyously in some unspeakable mess.

"Stop her!" I shouted to Jon, who was shouting the same thing to me, but when we both arrived on the scene she had accomplished her purpose on the remains of a dead snake, far, far gone in the road. There was nothing to do but hold our noses and wash her all over again.

Our friends were wildly curious over our lake and log cabin, and we had them up in relays. Julie and David came frequently and sportingly. I am afraid they did not like the rustic life quite as much as we did. In any case, there was what turned out to be a new little David on the way.

Anya Seton and her husband came for a weekend. As a naturalist's daughter, one would have thought Anya would be overjoyed by the primitive life, but Anya, though charming about it all, was a girl who liked her comforts. In return, they invited us to a curious house they had rented on the beach somewhere, P. T. Barnum's seaside horror. By some strange chance, from Friday night to Sunday night we drank nothing but rum, and I have never cared for rum since. It was during this visit, incidentally, that Anya first broke down and confessed to me that she had taken up writing.

"I have a story I've been working on," she said diffidently. "I wonder if you and Jon would read it and see if it has anything."

We read it in bed that night and both became wildly enthused. She was a born story-teller. It was all there in that first tentative, uneven effort. "Good lord, girl," Jon told her the next morning. "Whether you like it or not, your work's cut out for you. All you have to do from now on is sit down and write."

Apropos of alcohol, when we first came to the lake, Jon and I made a thrilling discovery. It was possible, in the little town seven miles away where we did our marketing, to go to the back basement window of a certain shop, rap three times on the glass, murmur a password, and out would be passed to you a brown paper sack containing a quart of local applejack—all quite illegal, of course, but the price for this treasure was seventy-five cents!

Also it tasted good, fruity and smoky, and its pleasant effect in our stomachs was comparable to that of the best imported scotch. Ah! we told ourselves, our liquor problem was solved. We were all set for the duration. For several days we sipped and congratulated ourselves and smugly discussed the economy, and then I awoke one morning with a most peculiar sensation.

My tongue was numb, inert. I couldn't move it, it just lay there, and when I tried to talk, I couldn't form the words. Jon sat up in bed, wild-eyed, and mumbled something and pointed to his mouth, indicating a similar situation. Within minutes we had arrived at a sorrowful discovery: our lovely, deceptive applejack was as raw and strong as a wild mule and we had, almost literally, burned out the inside of our mouths. Back to sherry and red wine for us.

That was the spring of springs. Aside from our personal contentment, neither of us had ever watched spring creep across the country before. Always, when Connie and I went to West Salem or Onteora, it was with summer in full bloom, and this slow unfolding, day by day, of the plants and grasses and trees around us was something that Jon and I watched with passionate interest.

Some time before, in Hollywood, Father had read aloud Donald Culross Peattie's nature journal *Almanac for Moderns* to us, and I had so loved the book and longed to share it with Jon that I purchased a copy in New York and took it up to the lake with us.[5]

We did not devour it in one gulp but severely rationed ourselves. Each day, on the exact date of the journal excerpts, we read one page aloud to each other, one and one only, though the wish to read on was almost irresistible.

Take the following excerpt, for instance.

> (Donald Culross Peattie) April 2nd. Each year, and above all each spring, raises up for Nature a new generation of lovers. As I write this, a boy is going out to the marshes to watch with field glasses the mating of the red-winged blackbirds, rising up in airy spirals and clouds. . . . And at the same time there will be a man who all his life has put away this call or never heard it before . . . and he goes out in the woods to collect his first botanical specimen and to learn that he has much to learn, for all his years.

My husband was that boy, that man. On April 2nd, outside our snug little cabin, the reawakening was taking place again. Through the alders on the lakeside the faintest tinge of green was creeping, and the earth, swollen by spring rains, seemed to grow, expand. We could scarcely bring ourselves to sit before our typewriters, there was so much to observe and study and marvel at in the world we inhabited. Jon's binoculars were never more than a few inches from his hand. In rough farming boots he squelched around the muddy rim of the lake, coming back with shining eyes to exhibit minute treasures of plant and insect life. He was an insatiable bird lover, identifying the migrants, teaching me the characteristics of the local residents. The next book I gave him was Peattie's *Singing in the Wilderness*, a life of Audubon, and we read it aloud each night, identifying our wilderness with his to our soul's satisfaction.

As spring came on, an absorbing domestic drama was played out on the back and front porches of the cabin. A wren, surely one of the most charmingly designed of little birds with his round body and long, flirty tail, decided that our front porch, the one overlooking the lake, was a satisfactory place to establish a nest. He and his mate worked slavishly for days with twigs and grass and some pieces of string that Jon provided to construct a safe, comfortable home for the mother-to-be and the babies. When the nest was finished and the eggs laid, the mother settled herself upon them, and father began his duty of supplying her with the proper food during her long vigil.

BUT—and here the drama reached fever pitch—not content with a wife and family on the front porch, our wren friend shortly thereafter established another lady and another nest on the *back* porch!

At first we couldn't believe it, but as the days passed the poor little bigamist found himself working harder and harder to keep both front and back porch beaks filled. We would see him swoop in under the roof with a moth in his beak, lady number one would make a grab for it, tear away perhaps half; and then, with a flirt of his tail the perfidious wretch would swing around the house and deposit the remaining tidbit in the open beak of his other love. Since both ladies were sitting firmly on their eggs, neither, presumably, knew of the existence of the other, and watching the harassed provider, Jon and I could not resist a wave of sympathy for him. This was only the start of the trouble. What was he going to do when all the eggs were hatched and two nests crowded with gaping mouths were waiting his arrival?

To end the suspense, I will say that he did a super-human— super-bird job. Both families were fed, raised, trained, and launched without a casualty. I can only hope he felt twice the satisfaction.

This and much more went into my letters to the West Coast, and eventually it had its effect. Most of my communications had been from my sister, with a few brief ones dictated by Mother, but one memorable day I saw Daddy's characteristic handwriting on an envelope, and my heart leaped. The letter was short and impersonal, but it told me that I was not banished forever.

> Dear Mary Isabel,
>   Your sister is talking of taking the children to Onteora this summer. I think it is probably a good idea. There is too much confusion and emotional upset here. I know you will do what you can to help her. I understand that you are living not too far away and I want you to know that you can count on me in this matter. Go and fix up Camp Neshonoc, make it look welcoming and nice, and I will foot the bills.
>   Father

What a *good* man, I thought proudly. Stubborn, childishly unreasonable, passionate, inconsiderate at times, but under it all, how basically true. It had cost him something to write that letter, but now I knew that in the warm, strong circle of his love I would still be held.

Notes

[1] Isabel and Mindret were married on December 21, 1936.

[2] There is no record of Mindret publishing in the *New Yorker* prior to 1942, though he may have contributed pieces that were unsigned or published under another name. His *New Yorker* stories include "So Bright! So

Beautiful!" July 25, 1942, 52-55; "Heaven Will Protect the Working Girl," September 26, 1942, 37-38; "Our Daily Bread," December 12, 1942, 94-96; "Lorenzo," July 24, 1943, 40-44.

[3] The letter is dated December 25 [1936]. Isabel arrived on January 11, 1937. See *Selected Letters of Hamlin Garland*, edited by Keith Newlin and Joseph B. McCullough (Lincoln: University of Nebraska Press, 1998), 385.

[4] That is, the manuscript of "The Fortunate Exiles," which remains unpublished.

[5] The son of Garland's friend of his Chicago days, the journalist Elia Peattie, Donald Culross Peattie (1898-1964) was a naturalist whose works include *An Almanac for Moderns* (1935), *Singing in the Wilderness* (1935), and *The Lives and Achievements of the Great Naturalists* (1937), among many others. *An Almanac for Moderns* grew out of Peattie's daily journal in which he recorded detailed observations of the natural word that became the inspiration for philosophical musings. In the next two chapters, Isabel imitates Peattie's technique.

19. The Journal

 ⩜ ⩜ ⩜

As spring moved into summer, the countryside became ever busier and more exciting, and inspired by the example of Donald Peattie, Jon and I began to keep a daily journal. My entries were personal, domestic, bemused with happiness; Jon's, a blend of scientific knowledge, discovery, and poetry. The truth was, I am sorry to say, that the journal was about the only thing we did write. Our world was so new and thrilling that the temptation was merely to sit and observe, and we yielded to temptation. It was almost impossible to drive Jon to his typewriter; there was so much to be attended to outdoors. He had to identify every bird and bird call, for instance. He had to supply us with fish for dinner. He had to find out all there was to know about wild mushrooms. But here the journal may speak for itself. This is the first entry:

July 20th (Jon): "Until about two o'clock yesterday afternoon I think we both wondered if we would live through the day or die in agony. The day before we walked through the woods (the Appalachian Trail) and gathered mushrooms. Having learned to distinguish the amanitas from Ernest Thompson Seton's book, I felt comparatively safe in choosing the mushrooms I did.[1] This is, till after I had eaten them. One kind was a perfectly formed upright affair with a light mauve cap, and instead of the usual sort of gills, something like a white sponge underneath. The stem was solid and without a ring, a cup, or a veil. I took a spore print of it, and the print was dark brown. This mushroom I cleaned and sliced, and Isabel broiled it in butter, and it turned out to be one of the best-tasting things that ever I ate. We thought it was like a very delicate and exotic roast pork. Like a suckling pig grown in outer space."

July 20th (Isabel): "This is the first time in months that I have seen Jon at his typewriter, and I am delighted beyond measure. There has been so much of confusion in our lives these last few months, but now this heavenly spot is beginning to smooth us both out and make us long to do something creative again. There is no question in my mind but that something extraordinarily subtle and rich will come out of Jon's original brain before long. I can see it fermenting already, and this first page of our mutual diary is the sign of it.

"This morning when we awakened very early, after our long, hard day in the roaring, hellish city yesterday, we were wrapped in white mist that completely hid the lake, the hills, even the young oaks and chestnuts that surround our little log house. By the time we took our coffee out on the east porch the mist had lifted, but the skies were still in gray turmoil. I asked, 'What kind of a day do you think it is going to be?' and Jon said, 'Whatever kind it is will suit me.' It is dangerous to be so completely content. Somewhere back in my stern ancestry is a curious strain of fear that will never permit me to 'gloat' very long. I have so much—so much more than I ever dreamed life could offer—that I can't help feeling the blow must fall somewhere. Our lack of money is our only trial, and here in this remote place money and all it represents seems so unnecessary. Enough to buy groceries and cigarettes and gasoline for our trips to the lovely, wind-swept lake where we swim—what else would one use money for? Jon writes of mushrooms, I write of content, and they are both one and the same."

July 21st (Jon): "A while ago I had an idea that it might be fun to cook a dinner on brochettes, like that Turkish or Armenian dish called shashlik. I didn't have any wire, so I straightened out a coat hanger and cut it in two. Last night it was cool enough to have a fire in the woodstove, so we tried out the brochettes. On them we put chunks of squash, tomato, Bermuda onion, bacon, and lamb. Isabel seasoned it and brushed the whole thing with melted butter. I forgot—we picked a mushroom and added that, too. Then we broiled the whole thing over the glowing coals, and when it was black on all sides, we ate it with rice. Isabel said, 'How rare it is that anything turns out to be as good as it's planned.' But the fact is, you couldn't have planned anything to be so good. We made pigs of ourselves, as usual, and then sat about, stuffed and happy, until bedtime, which was later than ordinary because we waited to hear the Wallenstein Simphonietta.

"Judging from the way the wrens acted a few days ago, I am convinced that she is laying eggs. Such a hullabaloo! Jumping up and down on the rafters and constant conversation—nothing at all like their songs. First one would look into the nest, then the other, then both together. Sometimes, when the sight— whatever it was—seemed to overcome them, they'd jump down to the back of a chair and sing. I said, 'If she hasn't laid eggs, I'll never believe another wren as long as I live.' Standing on tiptoe, I managed to get my two fingers inside the nest, and it was rather like an electric shock to feel a smooth little egg rolling at my finger tips. It was a joyful moment, and I was inclined to crow. In fact, I did crow. 'At least,' said I, 'no one can deny I have learned some bird language.' But even that was an understatement. I felt I'd learned it all."

July 21st (Isabel): "It does seem idiotic, on a day of such surpassing beauty, to be concerned over the fit of a cheap, little, red-and-white polka-dotted bathing suit. Why can't I just say 'the heck with it' and go out and wander around and absorb, the way Jon does?

"We had planned to swim today, but in the shadows the wind is cool and we shall go blueberrying again. Whatever we do seems to be the very thing we had wanted most to do, so deep is our satisfaction with each other and our surroundings. Connie's children said of their cook-housekeeper, 'She thinks too much of herself,' and I fear the same applies to us. Too much of ourselves and our dog and our cooking and our landscape and our capability of living the only kind of life that is worth anything at all. People must find us very objectionable, though we do our best to conceal our sense of superiority and listen as patiently as possible to the stories of our city friends' incredibly trivial doings.

"After dinner, the full moon came up slowly over the lake, adding the last touch of theatricality to our landscape. What with fireflies and drifting mist, a phosphorescent tree stump, bird calls, and wooded hills against a pale yellow sky, it was all a little *too* beautiful. Feeling we ought to do something about it, we walked to the top of the hill and tried to drown ourselves in it, but suddenly, as the stars appeared one by one in the fading sky, panic overcame us. We hurried home, built a fire, and sat about it and finally decided that the only way to treat a night like that was to shut all the doors and windows, pull the curtains, stuff our ears with cotton, and spray Flit everywhere."

Shortly before we started the journal, my sister and her children had come on from California, and once we had seen them safely bestowed, we hurried back up to our lake again.

July 23rd (Isabel): "Now we must come down from our hilltop and face life again—the life being my distracted sister and her two handsome but strenuous little darlings. We come away from our visits there in a state of mental and physical exhaustion, and yet we love them dearly and are glad to do what we can to help. I marvel at my husband's patience. He seems to have the same life-saving gift of withdrawal that Uncle Irving Bacheller has. I envy him."

Our summer, which we had dedicated to contemplation and literary effort, turned into a kind of mad steeplechase. One day a week in New York on business affairs, two or three with Connie and the children in Onteora, with the result that we were perpetually on the road. Jon was wonderful with Connie's children. He had had very little to do with children before, and their quick minds, their enthusiasm, their warm affection brought a wholehearted response from him. He was the ringleader in all their doings, and they came to adore him with a fervor that he confessed made him uneasy: "I shouldn't let those children get too fond of me. It isn't fair to them—or to the man Connie will inevitably marry. I'll miss them like hell when they go, but it's better that they find their 'father-image' or whatever in the man who's going to have to do the job."

While it lasted, though, the three of us and the children had a riotous time. We swam and boated and picnicked and played hide-and-seek around the cabin in the dusk, and Jon and Connie drew for them and I made pies and cakes and fudge and taffy, and we all sat around the fire after dinner and told ghost stories. We taught Sister to cut out paper dolls and Uncle Jon instructed little John in fly-casting and the art of making a figure-four trap, in which they managed to catch—a snail.

The high point of the summer was the visit of Connie and her children to our log cabin on the lake. To the ordinary child, the place would be a thrilling land of discovery, but John and little Constance, who we called Sister, were poor-little-rich-children, in constant need of diversion, and their reaction to the simple life was unpredictable. As a matter of fact, we need not have worried. The visit was a howling success. After inspecting it carefully, the only thing the children did not like, they said frankly, was the outhouse, and as we admitted that we did not either but that it seemed to be indispensable, the matter was disposed of and there was not another word of criticism.

Jon taught his new nephew to row the boat, and one afternoon John elected to take his sister and her favorite doll and stuffed animal out on the lake. They got to the middle of the lake right enough, but when he decided to turn for home, John found himself unable to do anything but go round and round in a circle. They were a quaint sight out there in the lily pads, but Connie began to get nervous and implored my husband to go to the rescue. Jon only laughed. Unseen by the children, we were watching from the window, and he explained to the worried mother that the lake was only two feet deep at that point, and if anything happened, he could save both children in a minute.

"Let John work it out his own way," he said comfortably. "He's been doing a good job. Let him finish it."

Eventually, John caught on, straightened out his course, and made a neat, professional landing, to our united applause.

"Did you see that, Mommy?" he demanded proudly. "Did you see me row that boat? I'm a very good rower, aren't I, Uncle?"

"A very good rower," my husband assented, with no refer-

ence to the unfortunate splashings and circlings of a short time
before.

Our landlord, who was highly impressed with my pretty,
giddy sister, joined us one day for a picnic on the big lake. It was
a day to conjure with. We rowed out to a little island in the middle
of the lake, Douglas in charge of one boat, John proudly assisting
his uncle in the other, and tied up under some willows at the
water's edge. The little beach was clean, white sand, and a warm,
shelving rock ran out into the crystal-clear water. We lazed and
swam and ate and lazed and swam in a state of such supreme
satisfaction that it remains one of the enchanted times of our lives to
this day.

July 31st (Isabel): "A radio announcer said cheerily last night, 'Well,
    folks, the summer's half over,' and it sent a chill through me.
    This summer that was to mean peace and production has
    slipped by in a flurry of travel, worry, work, and exasperation,
    and we have written nothing. Jon has learned about birds and
    trees and mushrooms. We have both been well, have eaten
    magnificently, have reveled in sun and shade and water, and
    have listened to glorious music and made love and watched
    sunrise and midday and sunset over our small, dreaming lake,
    and the days have flashed by with incredible speed—but where,
    oh, where is literature? Jon is wary as a bird about settling
    down to his typewriter, but someday I shall drive him to finish
    his novel. I say *drive*, for I know that he will never do it by him-
    self. He's not exactly lazy—or is he? My problem seems to be
    quite the reverse of Mother's. Father was and is a besom of
    energy."

July 31st (Jon): "Isabel and I have everything in the world we want
    but about four hundred dollars, and the lack of that makes us
    intermittently miserable. We have love, health, beauty, hope,
    and what we call comfort. We can count our blessings and add
    them up to an impressive total, and nothing is sillier in the
    world. Counted blessings are forlorn things. All in all, the
    important thing, the only important thing, is that which one has
    not. . . . I think if I had to choose from among all human attrib-
    utes, it would be the capacity for enjoyment. To be able to take

pleasure in what there is—in what you have—even in what you want."

August 1st (Isabel): "We did our morning chores to Rachmaninoff's *Rhapsody on a Theme of Paganini* and hardly suffered at all in consequence. The house is now in readiness for the arrival of our guests—a longtime friend of Jon's and his current lady friend—and while my housewifely eye sees spider webs under the radio and dust under the couch, which is Lasses's hideaway, I can but hope to a visiting eye that the house will seem as bright and cheerful as it really is. It is quaint, the difference in male and female. A man would have made no preparation at all for this visit, aside from ordering a few more packages of cigarettes and a quart of gin, but I find myself thinking nervously, 'Now I must black the stove—and polish the brass ashtrays.' Who really gives a darn when the lake glitters outside the windows and our lovely wooded, moss-covered point looks like a setting for *A Midsummer Night's Dream*? Tonight I shall feed them shashlik and a peach shortcake and wash my hands of the entire matter—if I can."

August 3rd (Isabel): "This morning as I came out on the porch, broom in hand, a slim, slithering, unconcerned mink, holding his head high and carrying in his mouth a dead bird, strolled by not ten feet from me. It was like something out of a storybook, a fantastic illustration of an animal. Later, when Jon and I were sitting in the living room, I happened to glance over my shoulder, and there he was again, standing on his hind legs just outside the screen door, warm-brown, bright-eyed, extremely handsome, staring brazenly in at us. I gave a little cry, and he slipped away. A moment later, Jon espied a baby rabbit cowering under some leaves at the foot of a tree, thinking himself completely hidden. Jon got so near he could almost touch him, when the rabbit leaped into the air and disappeared, too."

August 4th (Isabel): "There being a brief lull in the entertaining business, Jon and I are hurriedly writing in our journal—he getting rid of a bit of more or less suppressed venom, I copying some

poems he contributed to our poetry contest last night.　Here
they are:

> The heron cries in surprise,
> The black snake strikes—in vain.
> And with the flash of gentian lightning through the trees,
> Frogs and startled ducklings leap.
> We sleep.

> Go fetch me an azure egg from a swallow's nest.
> Fly to the salt marshes and bring reeds.
> Pluck down from the morning dove.
> Gather light, soft things.
> This creature sings.

> The red-winged blackbird's flash
> Is not like cash.
> The lily's frond
> Is not a bond.
> The lovely weeds are rank—
> And I have nothing in the bank.

My own attempt was less poetic, but it expressed the occasional exasperation I felt with my adored, absent-minded husband:

> What are you going to do
> With someone who remembers hardly anything?
> I remember a night of stars—
> A summer wind that touched your heart with tears—
> A tree that, fire-smitten, still endured—
> And the smug, silent security of our faith.
> But he. . . .
> There was someone he loved and he forgot the hour.
> There was a tryst to keep and he forgot the name.
> And still he knew the title to each flower.
> The multitudinous birds were not the same.
> What shall you do with one who strays
> In such disturbing, vari-colored ways?
> Lady, I say—for I am woman, too—
> If such a one do such a thing to you
> Forswear him!
> For the game's not worth the playing
> When he who should be constant goes astraying.

August 5th (Isabel): "This is a morning of acute exasperation.　Our
guests have gone, leaving us all—including Lasses, who has
had too much cuddling—in a state of collapse.　They have also

left us an icebox full of expensive food, which my frugal soul will not permit me to toss into the flames. What do you do with the major part of a five-dollar steak? A big pan full of fricasseed veal? A large parcel of sliced ham and Swiss cheese and sausage? A dozen rapidly decomposing pears? A dozen passé cupcakes? The problem is driving me mad, for we are leaving directly after lunch for Onteora and won't be able to dispose of anything.

"We have just completed a towering mound of dishes, and now I must make beds, press clothes, and pack. We have been occupied every minute for the last five days, and the extra work, combined with the necessity of being charming, sympathetic, and gay every waking moment, has left its mark on us. It will be a long time before we take on such a task again.

"'If ever,' my husband says grimly."

August 4th (Jon): "While we were having breakfast on the porch, the Least Bittern came and perched on a stump in the water not twenty feet from us. Bitterns have an aura of mystery about them that it is hard to define—they are so silent, such swift, strong flyers, and once they land among the reeds, they disappear so completely.

"They've just played Brahm's *First Piano Concerto*, and now they're beginning on Bizet, which seems an odd sort of program to make. But imagine having to make up an intelligent program every day of the year. If it were up to me, I don't suppose I'd get farther than the 18th Century, and certainly only one of the three B's would be much represented. Bach, Vivaldi, Monteverdi, Scarlatti, Purcell, Rameau, Couperin. . . . After all, program-making might not be too difficult. At least, they'd satisfy me.

"It is strange and probably unexampled that two people can be so happy as we—and *know* it. People look back and say, 'We were happy then.' They say, 'If we had only known how happy we were, how happy we could have been.'"

August 14th (Isabel): "Jon is launched on one of his strange, imaginative stories, and I am bitterly jealous. It took a great deal of effort on my part to get him started, but in the end he wrote four masterly pages, and his eyes shone as he said, 'I'd forgotten what fun writing is!' I haven't. That's why I am wandering around like a lost chicken.

"The moon is on its way again, and last night when we walked out to look at the phosphorescent tree and couldn't see it because of the flooding mistiness of the moonlight, I remembered what Aunt Juliet once said to me: 'Nothing fixes moonlight like marriage. It will never make you miserable again.' I see what she meant now, for with my husband's arm around me, I can look at all that beauty quite impersonally and go home cheerfully to stack up the dinner dishes and cold cream my face, feeling, if anything, more romantic than ever before but not suffering over it. It is quite marvelous to get out of the restless unhappiness my poor sister's in into fresh, clear, smooth water. Jon and I were wondering idly what we would do if we were rich, and all that we could think of that we wanted at the moment was to redeem the camera from pawn, put in a sink and a septic tank, and perhaps buy a reliable car. Oh, and I *would* like to send the sheets to the laundry."

August 15th (Jon): "I think I'll call my story 'A Special Gift.' It's one of the most dismal bits I've ever written, and unless I'm mistaken, there's no market for it anywhere. So, just possibly, it's a good story."

August 15th (Isabel): "Autumn is in the air today—in the air and the drying grasses and the changing color of the sumac. I welcome it, but it is a little frightening too to realize the relentless march of the seasons. It is something I had forgotten after ten years of California. For a month now it will be so lovely that it hurts. Then suddenly a strong wind and gray skies and bare branches.

"Jon finished his dreadful little story, which he wrote with magnificent restraint and subtlety, scaring even himself by its macabre significance, and I, praise God, managed to force *myself* to the typewriter and turn out several very poor pages of a story based on Connie's wretched mix-up. I've been making a blooming nuisance of myself lately, moping about, doing a lot of unnecessary household chores, so when an idea finally came to me, I said to myself, sternly, 'Woman, trot in there and write

those words down. You've been wanting to write; now write.'
Jon's relief was almost pathetic."

August 18th (Jon): "About midnight a storm blew up from the
    south, and while Isabel and I were out on the porch watching it,
    a lightning bolt about five feet wide landed on the hill across the
    lake. We were scared half to death and went in and sat on the
    guest room bed, trying to comfort Lasses. A second later, there
    was a river of white fire in front of our eyes and a hissing noise
    and an earth-shattering report. Isabel and I said together, 'It got
    us that time!' We listened for a moment, but there was only the
    storm to hear. Then Isabel said, 'Smell it!' The house was full of
    burning sulfur, so strong it was almost choking. We wondered
    whether the house was on fire, but it had been too wet and there
    was too much rain for that.

    "By now, the worst of the storm seemed to have passed, so
    I put Lasses back in her bed and we all went to sleep and didn't
    wake again for several hours. This time the storm was just as
    fierce, in another way. The wind hit the house like something
    alive and tangible. It was as if the wind was making a steady,
    intelligent effort to push the house into the lake. But the house
    is as strong and heavy as the rock on which it stands, and you
    could tell that nothing was going to happen. The wind would
    push until it grew tired. I was afraid, though, that one of the
    trees might be shot through the roof."

August 18th (Isabel): "We are two languid individuals this morning,
    after a long, hot drive back from Onteora yesterday afternoon
    and a night of too much drama. With daylight, we found that
    the lightning bolt *had* struck our house, shattering first a huge
    rock just outside the front door, then going on to gouge a deep
    channel in the heavy front door and tearing up a gash in the
    floor to a place under the couch where it apparently grounded.
    I felt at the time it was too close for comfort, but I hadn't known
    how close. Suppose we had been sitting on that couch, as we
    had a few minutes earlier, with Lasses in her basket just beside
    us? Having been conditioned by Daddy not to be unduly con-
    cerned about thunder storms, what really frightened me was
    the tremendous wind that followed and bent our trees as

though they were weeds in a field. Jon and I wandered around half the night, closing and opening doors and windows and battling the mosquitoes, which were ferocious. The lightning flashed, the thunder crashed, the trees lashed, and at intervals the full moon came out and made the whole thing pretty preposterous. And after all that rumpus, it is still warm and sticky.

"We had hoped to have a few days to ourselves now, but I find letters from Daddy asking me to go to town and see about the book, and of course I must go.[2] Also, a wistful little note from Mother that made my heart ache. We'll simply have to go west this fall. Perhaps we will be able to find a remote little place, within a short drive of Hollywood, so that I can be of some comfort to my mother and father without being absorbed by them, as I have always been until I met Jon. This place is so lovely, we are so happy, so self-sufficient—yet I can't forget how my parents live in their children. This summer, with both daughters—not to mention the adored grandchildren—away, I can imagine how empty life must seem to them.

"Connie leaves for home in two weeks. Summer is nearly ended, and aside from Jon's short story and this journal, we have created—nothing."

August 19th (Isabel): "Jon has turned on the news commentator on the radio, and he is telling us of frightful bombardments in Spain and China and of thousands fleeing for their lives from Japanese guns, and we sit here, concerned with personal and domestic matters, and let the reports drift by. It is a blessed comfort to be out of the swarming city, the logical center of attack, and up here in the wooded hills, which are of no concern to anyone save us and their land-poor owner. Originally a Colonial grant of 80,000 acres, the holding has shrunk to a few thousand acres of exquisite beauty, crowded with wild animals, birds and fish, flowers, and fruit and nut trees. Yet poor Douglas must beg his scant pocket money from a wealthy uncle and wait patiently for us to pay the rent. His one dream is to sail, and he is tied hand and foot till the healthy, formidable woman who is his mother dies. It is a mournful drama to watch from the vantage point of our ecstatic enjoyment of our landlord's inheritance.

"This is our eight months' anniversary, and aside from a change in the weather, we can't think of a more perfect place to be. Thank God for these months of joy.

"Jon is being heckled by an invisible bird and is slowly going mad. For three days the air has been full of celestial melody, but never once has he been able to catch sight of the singer, who spends all his time in the highest treetops and seems to take malicious joy in the hunt for him."

August 20th (Jon): "At last I found one of the singers! As I had at times suspected, it was a goldfinch, and what a beautiful, fat little bird he is. Well, that solves one mystery. The next time I hear him, I'll know. He'll never give me a crick in the neck again.

"Next week we have the family. God bless us all and make me a better boy. Amen."

August 21st (Isabel): "The radio has just told of a record heat wave, and we are ready to believe it. I don't feel a bit like a glamour girl today. After a long, mosquito-bitten, sleepless night, my hair is like a nest of wires, my feet are hot and swollen, I am dripping with perspiration, and frankly I could do with a bath. I suppose the *Ladies' Home Journal* could take me in hand and turn out something, and I'd like to see them try—with the thermometer and the humidity at 88 and all the garbage to burn before we start for Onteora. And yet I long to be attractive for my husband, and somehow toilet water and a swipe with a powder puff seem inadequate."

August 29th (Isabel): "We have been racing about like insane insects for days—Onteora, the lake, New York, the lake, Onteora, the lake. Now for three days of solitude before we go back up to Onteora for Connie's last week. The children had another rapturous time here with us, with the boat and fishing and swimming and eating. They will never forget this place as long as they live—nor will we. . . . Today is not only a deliriously lovely day, it is also a good day for drying clothes, praise God. What with all the company and travel, we are down to the last shreds of our wardrobes.

"It is hard to collect my thoughts today. My brain is as skittery as a mouse, and I find myself doing all sorts of unexpected things. At one moment I am packing summer hats away—then I clean the ice box—then I start a letter to my parents—then I darn a pair of Jon's socks and look for spots on his best suit. It's all pretty futile, but it must be done and there's no one to do it but me.

"From where I sit, I see our disgustingly dirty car. I must go out and wipe it off. And then there's the matter of lunch."

The little Harpers had not only had a "fabulous" time with us, they had painstakingly collected a bucketful of small fish and tadpoles, which they insisted they were going to transport back to the West Coast with them. Connie, in desperation, appealed to my husband, and he, as usual, was equal to the situation. When John and Sister came out the last morning to inspect their treasures, they were aghast to find the bucket overturned and all its fishy contents missing. Their yells of anguish brought us to the scene, which their new uncle studied with a grave eye.

"A bear," he pronounced at length.

"A—bear!" The children's eyes were like saucers.

"It has to be. . . . See these large tracks in the mud? Those are bear tracks. Bears love fish, and there are quite a few bears in this neighborhood. Yes, that is undoubtedly what it was—a bear."

His pronouncement was very convincing, and the drama of it all almost made up for the loss of the fish. I never did find out how Jon manage to produce bear tracks. They looked entirely authentic, even to me.

August 30th (Isabel): "Yesterday noon, in the midst of my domestic labors, inadequately clothed in an old print dress and torn stockings and ankle deep in soap suds, Douglas arrived with his pretty girl friend. Gladys wore a gay, little pink play suit and had a ribbon around her head, where every curl was in place. And there I stood, my lank hair streaming, glossy with perspiration, wringing out shorts, surrounded by flapping pajamas and dripping socks. It was quite a picture. I loathe being caught this way. Nobody has a right to slovenliness, even when doing the weekly laundry.

"Hair washing day again, and dog washing, as well. Lasses

and I both detest it, but we must arrive at Onteora looking our best, confronted by a week of revelry. Jon has a haunted look already at the mere mention of it, but it will be only a week. Then back here to, I hope, work—and peace. I'll find it hard, I imagine, until I settle on something to write."

Our last few days with Connie and her children alternated between wild gayety and poignant anticipation of parting. We played all the children's favorite games, and they hung on their uncle like desperate little monkeys, hardly to be shaken off. Connie still had her champagne glass in her hand when we loaded them into the car for the trip to Albany, where they were to catch the train for Chicago. With my head against Jon's shoulder, I sobbed softly most of the way home. Only a very remarkable man could have come through all this with the patience he showed.

September 12th (Jon): "Back again to our cottage and to each other and possibly to work. While we were in Onteora, Isabel's Aunt Juliet sold one of the stories I had collaborated with her on for $600, of which I will get $250. That will be very nice indeed, but I wish the sale had the same effect on me that it had on her. While she plunges into work on another story I gave her, I sit and wonder what to do next."

September 12th (Isabel): "So much has happened. Connie and the babies have gone. Jon and Aunt Juliet sold a story (in the nick of time). We have closed up Camp Neshonoc, where we had so many happy, hectic hours. My husband has been sick and is well again. We have brought all our possessions to the cabin where we expect to stay till we decide what we are to do this winter. None of it sounds very dramatic, but there was plenty of drama for all that.

"The Onteora house was still and forlorn when we came back from seeing them off that day. As we worked at putting it in closing order, my heart ached at every little reminder of them. Connie's discarded lipstick. The paper doll cuttings on Sister's bedroom floor. The forgotten flag in John's room. I was glad to come away from there—where no one hung head-down from the bar or raced up and down the creaking old stairs. What a trial they have been to us—and how we miss them.

"We came home to a house draped in cobwebs and worked furiously to put it in order for a dinner party for Douglas and his mother. At seven, we dined off embroidered linen in fire and candle light and felt ourselves take root again in our own soil. We slept softly, too, for we had brought a splendid mattress from Onteora."

September 13th (Isabel): "It is a gray, chill day, and we are luxuriating in our fire and our snug little home. Yesterday was so distractingly lovely that we did nothing but wander around in the sunlight—and scrape mildew off our clothing that had hung too long in the back of the closet. But today, with the wind racing across the lake and the rain beating on the windows, we are shut in with our dog and our typewriters, and something should come of it. Jon has donned his country boots again and is stomping impressively around the room, looking like the 'Black Villain of the Bogs' or something. There is enough food for today, but next morning we must go down to the village to send a birthday telegram to my father who will be seventy-seven tomorrow."

September 15th (Isabel): "Letters came today from Connie and the children, letters that warmed your heart and made your throat tighten. Connie wrote that Sister suddenly said, 'I have such a sad feeling—up here,' putting her hand to her forehead. 'It is about Anini and Uncle. I think they are here—and they are not here.' John said, 'You know, Anini and Uncle have given us things you can never repay.' We have had our reward for all the trials and tribulations of the summer. Sister said, 'Weren't they marvelous to us!' I hope my husband feels as I do, for of course it has been doubly hard on him, but he spent half an hour today on a stunning pair of illustrated letters to his niece and nephew, so I assumed he was as moved as I was by their loving little notes."

Notes

[1] Probably a reference to Seton's *The Book of Woodcraft* (1921), which includes a section on identifying edible mushrooms.

[2] Isabel refers to the manuscript of *The Mystery of the Buried Crosses*. Garland had sent the manuscript to Harold Latham, his long-time editor at the Macmillan Company, who declined the book.

20. Autumn

ॐ   ॐ   ॐ

September 15th (Jon): "One of the attractions of this lake is that
   although it is on top of a hill, there is no 'view.' We are in the
   approximate center of a circle not more than half a mile in
   diameter, and the circle itself is an unbroken line of trees beyond
   which we cannot see. Thus our horizon is close to us and the
   world seems intimate. Even the section of sky that is above our
   circle is small—so small that every change in the heavens is a
   surprise. We cannot watch an approaching cloud, nor can we
   know that a storm is gathering in the distance. When clouds
   appear they are already near us and a storm may be upon us in
   the very moment that we are prophesying the weather will continue fine. Changes when they come are dramatic and sudden.
       "It has often occurred to me that I have never tried to write
   anything beautiful. It seems to me that few modern writers *do*
   try. Whether it is because there is something embarrassing in
   beauty, or whether we today feel ourselves incapable of captur-
   ing it and creating it, I do not know. Perhaps we are all afraid,
   miserably afraid. It is all right today to recognize beauty in a
   dung heap or even in a shining contraption of steel that serves
   some apparently useful purpose. No matter how badly you do
   it, if you can manage to identify humanity with nature in some
   way, it makes the auditor vaguely apprehensive that there is
   beauty in it somewhere. It's easy to do it badly and almost
   impossible to do it well, but what the hell! Is that any reason for
   trying to find the universe in the crankcase sludge of a motor
   car?"

One of our chief topics of conversation during Connie's visit had been psychic research. From Daddy's excited letters, which were increasing in number and content, we knew he was off on another psychic quest, the result of which was to be his *Mystery of the Buried Crosses*. As Father's interest mounted, so did ours. The story of the earlier Parent discoveries was intriguing enough, but to add to it, Father was working with a medium—a very intelligent woman, by all accounts—who seemed to be able to "call up" long-gone Indians and Spanish padres, and a highly-colored historical canvas began to unfold.[1] Connie attended some of the sittings before she left and was impressed but skeptical. Mother and Father, however, for the first time seemed to be wavering.

September 16th (Isabel): "Last night Jon and I sat and talked for a long time about our parents and our childhood and the apparent near conversion of my father to a life after death. After forty years of doubt, he writes that he is now convinced of the survival of personality, but timid souls are reluctant to have him come out and say so. If he were younger, what a fight he could put up. Mother writes that it has completely changed her attitude toward death. 'It all seems so friendly.' If these psychic experiences have done that for my mother and father, isn't it their duty to give it to the world just as it came to them?"

September 17th (Isabel): "A trip to the city brought us racing back to our lake, our silence, and our fire. The city was hot, full of Legionnaires, appalling in its confusion. On my way to an appointment with Dr. John Finley, editor of the *New York Times*,[2] I rode on the subway and found I was almost frightened. In four months I have become a countryman, and to have anyone shove against me and force me out of the way is intolerable. And the smell, the dirt, the hopeless faces!

"It is a strange feeling to sit discussing the Fourth Dimension in an office twenty stories above the New York pavements. When I told John Finley of the people who had advised Daddy to tone down his book, to make it a mystery instead of a conviction, he said, 'He shouldn't do that. He should tell it just as it came to him.' But sitting in the outer office of Scribner's, running over in my mind the bewildering story, I felt how hopeless is the whole thing. Out of thousands, perhaps ten will believe in the honesty of the author and his psychic. Daddy speaks of astronomy as 'the hopeless science,' but psychic investigation is a thousand times more hopeless. After forty years of disbelief, why should Hamlin Garland suddenly come to 'believe?' Scoffers will call it senility."

September 18th (Isabel): "Days like this are always a problem: are we to close the doors and windows and light a fire, shutting out the bright, cold, glorious day, or leave the house open to the winds of heaven and go around with numbed fingers and snuffling noses? It is not quite fifty degrees and for the moment we are still in favor of open air, but when we settle down to work, I imagine the fire will win out."

September 19th (Jon): "Let me write down that our young oaks grow straight and sway in the wind like the masts of tall ships in a crowded harbor. That although the wind is strong today, the hills lie hushed and strangely silent under the dark sky. The summer birds have gone and the winter birds ruffle gray feathers in the shrubbery . . . acorns and dead leaves patter on the roof . . . the bright, sharp pickerel wood is sinking into the lake . . . the sumac glows blood-red in the twilight. . . . Let me write it down for the very reason that I love it dumbly. I am not above it, nor beneath it, nor of it. I cannot find a parallel in me for the change in the leaves, nor for the songs of the birds. Neither can I find in Nature either reflection or expression of man. Since I am not of religious mind, I cannot convince myself that sentient God made me and the little black and yellow caterpillar that Isabel says looks like a French poodle. Or if we are all descendents of a primeval ooze. I understand the fringed gentian none the more for that. But I can wonder."

September 19th (Isabel): "My husband said to me the other night when I was complaining of our continued poverty, 'Of course, you realize that life will never be completely right. We are worrying about money now. Later, it will be something else—your father's health, for instance.' Now comes a letter from Connie saying that Father has a cataract in his eye. She tells me not to be concerned, that he is being treated by the best eye man they could find, but when you are three thousand miles away such a report stops your breath for a moment. My father is seventy-seven and my mother is an invalid. I must be near when they need me.

"I wonder what is in store for us. There are so many things that threaten the happiness of people in our position. I suppose in later years we will remember this as our perfect time, shut away from the world and happily dependent on each other for everything. Having been poor most of my life, I count the thinning wad of bills in my wallet, while Jon, who knows how easily money can come as well as go, shrugs his shoulders and refuses to despair. Thank God, there is this difference between us. It is a wondrous thing to live with someone who is not afraid of life."

September 20th (Isabel): "I've just finished a large washing, and as I hung it on the line my hands were stiff with cold, as they used to be in New York when I hung the family washing up on the rooftop of 71 East 93rd Street. . . . Yesterday afternoon, we took a long walk up the road and came home with baskets of apples, real spicy-smelling country apples from a forgotten tree on the deserted farm at the top of the hill. City apples have a faintly disgusting odor, but these little gnarly things are as fresh as the wind. It is disturbing to see them rotting there under the trees. All that goodness that one cannot save."

September 21st (Jon): "I wish to God I could get to work. I think one reason why it's so much harder than it has ever been is the thought of the possible success of my invention. If it should make money, then I won't have to write the sort of thing I should be writing at this moment."

(My work, too, was at a standstill. Having shelved mystery novels as taking too long, I could not find a short story idea that attracted me. The urge, the necessity to write was stronger every day, but it seemed impossible to lay hold on "old S.C." anymore. Hence the next entry.)

September 21st (Isabel): "One day I am going to get to work and clean this house, not just think about it with a broom and cloth, but really get down to brass tacks. I loathe dirt and disorder, but I am afraid I loathe cleaning more. I hate dust in my nose and in my hair and getting my fingers into grime. Washing and ironing and cooking and dishwashing I rather enjoy because nothing gets on or in me that I don't elect to have there, but clouds of dust, cobwebs, and fuzz on a broom disgust me.

"The wind has shifted again, this time to the north, and it keeps Lasses on the jump. She has various favorite basking places. When the wind is in the north, the front of the garage is perfect. From the south, the lee side of the point seems quite right. From the west, she lies for hours close beside the chimney, blinking with sensuous pleasure, wagging her tail languidly whenever you speak to her. She will rouse herself immediately, however, if a walk is in prospect and lead the way up the road, growling with pleasure, looking back over her shoulder to be sure we are coming. From the moment that we pass the garage, she is another animal: a hunting dog, alert to every sound and movement. Having cornered a small frog, she jumped about it for fifteen minutes, unwilling to touch it but determined not to let it go. Jon said she reminded him of a frolicsome bull, awkward but agile. She is an adorable little companion, endlessly interesting and responsive. A large part of our joy in this place is due to her delight in it."

September 23rd (Jon): "We've just finished dinner. Lamb chops broiled over the coals, eggplant and, my God, fresh pumpkin pie! Its like will never be again. To eat such a pie is to take communion with the woods, small aromatic gardens, and the vanishing America we love.

"This small place, this lovely, small place with the cool, dark outside and the mist rising through the reeds . . . the yellow soft light of our oil lamps . . . the hum of insects and the high, sweet song of tree toads. . . . My wife here with me . . . and Lasses . . . the three of us together."

September 24th (Isabel): "This morning is really too much. I am dizzy with beauty. Every window frames a picture of water and sky and sunlight on leaves turning rose and flame and amber. And we are listening to Rachmaninoff. The combination is almost frightening.

"I had a distressing letter from my sister concerning the honesty of the medium with whom my father has been working these past six months.[3] I hope with all my heart that it isn't true. It will be a tragic blow to Daddy, with the book already in the hands of the publishers. I almost dread going to town for the mail.

"It seems a miserable thing to start off through the golden haze of this perfect morning, leaving our lake and our birds and our peace behind. All the other trips were bad enough, but this one—with nothing at the Onteora end but two cold, empty houses—seems a useless ordeal. However, it must be done."

September 26th (Isabel): "We saw that both Onteora houses were as ready for winter as we could make them, and at two o'clock we climbed into our laden car and started for home. Aunt Juliet said, 'I think that if I had what you two have, I'd just say good-bye to all the rest of the world.' She doesn't really mean it, for she is hopelessly social, but it was a pleasant tribute to our married success.

"We found some delightful letters from the children when we got back, in which we were variously depicted as fairies cavorting on leaping fish and angels with halos ascending heavenward, clutching each other's hands. Mother writes that John wears Jon's hat with a 'reverential air' and that they talk of us constantly. 'The reward of virtue,' Aunt Juliet says."

September 30th (Jon): "{I firmly intended to get started on the story today but, my God, what can you do with a day like this! I don't think I have ever seen anything so beautiful. Isabel and I took a long walk and came home with quantities of hickory nuts, apples, autumn leaves, and flowers.

"Tonight we heard Hitler and Mussolini tell each other what great guys they were. Also, it turns out that Germany and Italy are the only true democracies in Europe. The Japanese are bombing nothing but military objectives. The Italians in Spain are volunteers. Gee, it just seems almost impossible to believe."

September 30th (Isabel): "The last day of September and a day so
glorious that to stay indoors is impossible. What a magnificent
contrast to yesterday in that rotten, crowded city, where to be
without money means to be without self-respect. I felt myself
crawling—in spirit—along the avenues, knowing I had only
three dollars in my purse. Here, today, I can forget it, for
Daddy's faithful check should come tomorrow, and for the
moment we have no need of money. Yesterday was a nightmare. We came home, too tired to speak, finding the house icy
and dark. Jon built a fire in the kitchen range, we moved Lasses
in her basket in under it, and sat there in the sudden warmth,
sipping a drink, broiling a slice of ham, and thinking ourselves
the most fortunate of humans. I had purchased a hot water bottle at Macy's, and we crawled into a luxuriously comfortable
bed in complete contentment."

October 1st (Isabel): "Last night's sunset, which Jon called 'a sunset
with marabou,' outdid even the day in splendor. It was so perfect that we stayed outside to watch it till the last trace of coral
pink feathers had faded from sky and lake and one star came
out. With the mist creeping up from the reeds and the wild
ducks arriving in little bands to land noisily on the still-shad-
owed waters, it was another one of the theatrical effects that
modern stage designers would go to any length to avoid. The
color was too glowing, the outline too sharp, the rising mist too
frankly an effect. As for those ducks—with the gobbling and
complaining and chit-chat that went on each time a party flew
in from the north—they were, if anything, a bit faker than the
rest. It was rather a relief to go into our stage-set cabin and find
it cozy with firelight and the smell of crabmeat Creole and
baked potatoes.

   "We listened to *Back to Methuselah* on the radio, and I was
startled to find I can remember almost every line of the Garden
of Eden episode. It is fifteen years since I played Eve in the first
American reading, yet I can reproduce every inflection. I have
a newspaper photograph of me in a short, leafy garment, with
long streaming hair, bending over the dead faun. Our Adam
was somewhat of a trial, I recall. He was a bit on the sissy side
and never did completely learn his lines. This first production

of a new Shaw play had been so ballyhooed that the hall was packed to the gunwales for both performances."[4]

October 2nd (Isabel): "This is a queer day, neither flesh, fowl, nor good red herring, now hot, now cold, now bright, now gray. And queer things are in the air, too, according to a frantic letter that came today from Connie. She seems to think that at last she's found it—the one love—and confides that she thinks Daddy would approve. From the vantage point of complete content with my own love, I can look down on poor, scurrying, seeking, little people with deep pity. I hope with all my heart that Connie does find the right man soon. If she makes up her mind, she'll fight for it through any amount of confusion and disapproval. I did. Thank God I had the sense to. I would give a lot to be out there now, giving her what help I can, if only by listening to her. I am frightfully curious about the man.[5] I have no mental picture of him, about ten or fifteen years older, I would say, and I have a vague impression that he wears glasses. It is a strange sensation to have one's much-loved little sister interested in a completely unknown male. I imagine Connie felt somewhat the same way about me, though she had at least met Jon and knew how attractive he was. I wonder if anything will come of this."

October 3rd (Isabel): "Last night we had an enchanting experience. I saw in the radio section of the paper that a play was being broadcast from Edinburgh and London, and when we tuned in, it turned out to be one of the most beautiful and moving poetic dramas I had ever heard. It was the story of Bonnie Prince Charlie's invasion of Scotland and England, written especially for radio, with a musical background that included the sounds of bugles at dawn from Edinburgh Castle, horses neighing, hooves clattering on the frosty earth, the clank of swords, a harpsichord tinkling in a great stone hall, the cheering of crowds in the streets, and all through it, like a scarlet thread, the high-hearted marching song of 'The Forty-five'—the Clans that rose in support of the young pretender. For an hour we sat entranced, moved to tears by the account of that brave, absurd, foredoomed march. A cold wind was sweeping across our lake, and the darkness shut us in while we listened to the wind wailing across the actual Scottish moors and heard the whispers of men crossing a treacherous swamp in the midnight fog. . . . The cast was enormous. One superb voice after another took up the tale, now from London, now from Edinburgh. At moments we were eavesdropping on poignant bits of tense dialogue; at others the narrators were chanting of Preston Pans, of the surrender of Carlisle, of the early snowfall and the long, lonely roads. To me it was almost unbearably moving, and I thought, as I do so many times, what it would have meant to Daddy. How much of the background for this he gave me. How much we have shared, he and I.

"It is cold and gray again today, but I am baking my first pot of homemade beans from a recipe Douglas gave me, and I think Jon is at last writing. It must be nice to write. I might try it sometime."

October 4th (Isabel): "The beans were a great success, so that's that. I can bake beans with the best of them. . . . Down to the city again tomorrow. I start feeling a bit insane the minute I sight the bridge, and I go on feeling hectic and unreal the whole time I am there. In contrast to Daddy, who loved New York and needed it for his life's blood, there seems to be no place for me in the midst of that frenzied competition. I am a dead leaf—a speck of dust—a worm.

"I am tired of planning economical meals. If I could just walk into a market and order a couple of squabs, a porterhouse steak, a lobster, and so on, it might be fun, but after all, there is a certain satisfaction in making something edible and good out of an end of ham, half an onion, and some stale bread. Nothing makes me more cocky than turning out two ounces of cottage cheese from half a bottle of sour milk. I'm just made to be poor, I'm afraid, for I am efficient. Feeling depressed and meager last night, I had a sudden vision of the fun it would be to loll in a hot bath, put on fresh, new clothes, drink one or two champagne cocktails, and sit down to an interesting dinner that someone else had planned. Then our own simple meal was good and I was proud of myself and forgot about the vision."

October 7th (Jon): "We've been thinking and talking about Mr. Garland's book, which we have just read.[6] The manuscript itself is completely unconvincing, and yet the impression we got from his letters was very convincing. Beyond doubt, the manner of the investigation was haphazard, and I wonder whether it is too late to salvage anything useful from the whole thing. It does seem to me that a more thorough attempt should have been made in the first place to explain the mystery by normal, physical means. It is not enough, for instance, to know what the alloy was that was found in the crosses. Where did the various metals come from? Where were they mined? By whom? When? How much heat was required to make the alloy? Was the same alloy used for any other known purpose? It is stated that Adam Smith had a workshop. What did he do in it? He didn't need a workshop to make the crosses, for that all that was necessary was a fire and a pot in which to melt his metal. Then the question of Arabs and Moors in America before the Tenth Century. It would be ridiculous to say it isn't possible, but when Cortez arrived the Indians had no memory of ever having seen a white person."

October 11th (Jon): "Let's see—Thursday was the night of the Aurora Borealis, a spectacular display covering half the heavens with streaks of rose and pale blue light. Friday we went to town. Saturday and Sunday Anya Seton and Chan were here.[7] Today is my birthday, and I am quietly, smugly happy that we can be alone together. That is a present of which I never tire."

October 11th (Isabel): "Thirty-four years ago today a very lovely lady, I have seen her photographs, brought into the world all that life holds of peace and joy for me. It is strange to think how, through we never met, our lives paralleled each other. Both our mothers were born in small Illinois towns. In Chicago our families lived a block apart. Jon and I went to the same school, the same concerts, opera, the South Shore Country Club children's parties. I left Chicago when I was twelve. Jon, at fifteen, went into advertising and started making his own life that, after a wide, exotic circle, brought him back to me. . . . For a celebration today there is a tiny collection of presents: a blanket robe, some caviar, and Peattie's *Book of Hours*. I will bake a pumpkin pie. It isn't what one would call lavish, but it is very pleasant and sweet.

"Anya and Chan spent two days and nights with us, and all went well. This time they seemed to love our little house and didn't mind the weather, which was cold and foggy. I don't think either of us had ever been more tired than we were last night. I felt as if I had been beaten. We sat about in a stupor till nine-thirty, too weary to do anything but tell each other how blissful it was to realize that nothing, absolutely nothing, was expected of us. . . . As they were leaving, Chan said to me wistfully, 'I'd give anything to get Anya off alone with me in a place like this.'"

October 16th (Isabel): "These last few days have been anything but jolly, with Jon incapacitated by a lame back and in pain, and cold weather setting in. I have been in a panic. Day before yesterday I was ready to pack up and go back to the city, but today, now that my husband has recovered, I find myself brave once more. I don't mind hardship and cold and work, but I do mind anything being wrong with Jon. He scoffs at me for worrying, but if I were ill, I would be rushed to town and a doctor in record time. The trouble is that we are normally so disgustingly healthy that we are unprepared for ailments and imagine the most appalling consequences.

"It is so cold that we have to keep the bedroom closed off, and when I step into it, it takes my breath away. . . . We are reading aloud *A Book of Hours*, such exquisite prose that it makes you sick at heart to realize your own lack of craftsmanship. Jon could write such delicate, imaginative stuff if he could forget agents, markets, popular magazines, and the need of making a living. Tomorrow we are starting on the *Collected Works of Jon Burroughs*, which Jon, with his passion for nature study, is bound to love. In a wily fashion, I am writing Father of our literary experiences, of Jon's reactions and comments. Father has never yet referred to my husband by name, but once or twice he has spoken of 'you two,' which I take to be a hopeful sign."

October 17ᵗʰ (Jon): "There was a white frost this morning and thin ice around the edge of the lake, but the sun is hot in a cloudless sky. The temperature has risen to fifty, and probably such a day has never before been seen on this inclement earth.

"Isabel glares at me from across the fireplace and says, 'That isn't work!' It isn't. Isabel says she doesn't glare. She says she's not a glarer and she doesn't 'give a good Goddamn spit' whether I work or not. (Isabel: In my Chicago childhood, this was considered by the younger element the most profane expression you could use.) I guess it was my conscience glaring at me. But now I think it over, I'm not sure it was a glare, anyway; it was more like a beam."

October 18ᵗʰ (Isabel): "For the first time, we were cold as we slept last night, and Douglas told us the temperature dropped to twenty-seven and froze the radiator in his car. Tonight we will add another down quilt to our assortment of bedding and build a bigger fire for Lasses to sleep by. When we awoke, the countryside was powdered with frost and the lake was incredibly smooth and beautiful. Jon rowed across to get spring water, and behind the boat the ripples spread and spread, shattering the perfect reflections in the quiet water."

It was that day, or the next, in the late afternoon, that we were startled by the sound of an approaching motorcycle, and Jon went to the door to receive a telegram, which he handed to me. It was addressed, for the first time, to both of us, and it was from my father. Stunned, I read it aloud.

> Your mother and I would like you to come home
> for Thanksgiving and spend the winter with us.
> Wire collect when to expect you. Father

Jon and I exchanged long, incredulous looks; then he held out his arms, and with tears streaming, I went into them.

He held me strongly but let me cry, and when the worst was over, kissed me gently.

"It would appear, my girl," he said whimsically, "all bets to the contrary—we've won."

I clung to him. "Jon, I'm afraid!"

"Afraid of what?"

"I don't know. Life, I guess. Of what it can do to us."

"It's done pretty well up to now, wouldn't you say?"

I drew a deep breath. "It's been too good to be true. Here, alone together, surrounded by beauty—"

"Eating well, sleeping well." He smiled into my troubled eyes. "Don't look so tragic, sweetheart. You want to go, don't you?"

"Yes—no! Oh, Jon, I don't want this to change, ever!"

I flung out my arms, embracing the cabin, the lake, the hilltop, our whole enchanted world, and I saw his eyes following mine. Lasses, who had been disturbed by my tears, came to stand in front of us, looking anxious. Holding me closely with one arm, Jon laid his hand on her head.

"Shall we put it up to Lasses? What do you say, old girl? Shall we stay or—go?"

At the magic word "Go," Lasses gave a short, sharp yelp of enthusiasm and made for the door.

Jon smiled ruefully. "That was a mistake. . . . Well, how about it? The decision is up to you. I only want to say one thing—" His eyes held mine and there was a steely note in his voice I had never heard before. "I know you are worrying about your parents, that you should go back and be near them, and I understand and admire you for it. But something must be established now and for all time. I will go back with you. I will do my level best to fit in, to make your father and mother like me, but one thing I will not do: I will not live with them."

"Jon. . . ."

"No, wait a minute." He put his hand over my mouth. "We can find a little place of our own not too far away. You can be with your parents as much as you like. I'll never say a word, but when you come home, you must come home—to me."

"Oh, my darling!" I flung my arms around his neck. "That's just what I was going to say! We'll have a home of our own, our peaceful, happy times alone together!" All that we were giving up, all that awaited us of adjustment and heartache at the end of the three-thousand mile road back, welled up in me in a great wave, and out of the depths of my soul I cried, "Promise me that no mat-

ter what happens you'll go on loving me! Promise me that you will
love me forever!"

Notes

[1] In 1932 a man named Gregory Parent had written Garland to
explain that his wife, Violet, a psychic who had died five years before, had
discovered many hidden objects at the direction of spirits and had taken a
number of spirit photographs. Was Garland interested in examining the collection? Always interested in psychic problems, Garland called on Parent
and surveyed his collection of ectoplasmic photographs. He was intrigued
but was unable to investigate further because of a looming deadline for
Afternoon Neighbors. But in the fall of 1936, with *Forty Years of Psychic Research*
published and looking for a new project, Garland remembered Parent's collection and decided to take up the investigation. But Parent had since died.
When he succeeded in locating Parent's sister and the collection of photographs and more than 1,500 objects, Garland enlisted the aid of a medium
named Sophia Williams in an attempt to verify the legitimacy of the Parent
collection, an investigation that was to culminate in his last book—*The
Mystery of the Buried Crosses*—and which was to become an obsession that
consumed his final years. Isabel discusses the making of the book in more
detail in chapter 22.

[2] John H. Finley (1863-1940), formerly president of the College of the
City of New York from 1903 to 1913, became associate editor of the *New York
Times* in 1921 and editor in 1937. As a long-time friend, Garland wanted
Finley's advice concerning *The Mystery of the Buried Crosses*.

[3] "I am so convinced Mrs. Williams is a fraud—in part at least,"
Constance began her letter to Isabel, "that my comment will necessarily be
biased." She described her discovery of the medium's fraudulent production
of whispers and her suspicion that Williams had to have an accomplice who
planted the crosses. As for her father's credulity: "Daddy asks leading questions. He has trusted her so that he has unconsciously given her all the help
in the world"; during one séance when Constance wouldn't let her father ask
the questions, "we got nothing" (Constance Garland Harper to Isabel
Garland Lord, undated [marked "Saturday"], USC).

[4] Isabel played Eve in George Bernard Shaw's *Back to Methuselah* at
the Lenox Little Theater on January 26 and 27, 1922, as a fundraiser for the
Vassar College Endowment Fund. See "Adam, Eve and the Serpent to
Appear in Costume at Vassar College Benefit, *New York Times*, January 22,
1922, 25.

[5] Isabel refers to George Palmer Putnam II (1887-1950), the husband

of Amelia Earhart, whom Garland had invited to attend a séance to speak with the missing aviator, whose last radio transmission was on July 2, 1937. As letters between the sisters and Garland's diary reveal, Putnam soon developed a romantic interest in Constance.

  [6] That is, the manuscript of *The Mystery of the Buried Crosses*.

  [7] Hamilton (Chan) Chase, was Anya Seton's second husband.

21. Goodbye

&. &. &.

My return telegram said, "Will be with you for
Thanksgiving. Letter follows. Love and gratitude." Then I had to
sit down and compose one of the hardest letters of my life.

I could see them as I wrote. Mother in her pretty bedroom,
sitting in the armchair in the bay window, the sun on the beautiful,
silvery head, holding her shaking hands tightly together, watching,
listening, waiting for the steps, the voices that meant so much to her.
And Father, at his desk in the study that over-looked the treetops,
getting up every few minutes to go in and "see if Zulime is all right,"
going down to sit in the sunlight by the front door with his morning mail, out to the kitchen to brew his precious cup of coffee. They
were thinking of us constantly, I knew, but how to let them know
our decision without having it seem like a blow in the face? In the
end, I put it to them honestly and simply:

> Jon and I are deeply touched by your invitation. It
> is good to feel so welcomed, and we are counting
> the days till Thanksgiving, but dearest Mother
> and Father, it would not be wise or right for us to
> attempt to live with you. Jon and I have a special
> routine, a way of life that we must maintain if we
> are to go on creating. Our hours, our tastes, our
> thinking are necessarily different from yours. Our
> idea is to look for a small, simple house not far
> from you, where we can live our own life, while
> sharing yours. I am writing Connie to look
> around for us. She knows the sort of country-liv-
> ing we prefer. Of course, it will be wonderful to

spend a few days with you in the luxury we have not known in all these months, and you must know that we are grateful beyond measure for your generosity. Just think! In a little over a month we will all be together again!

October 18th (Isabel): "We are beginning to be involved with the problem of our belongings again as we face the prospect of a drive across the continent to a winter home in California. We go about murmuring 'two trunks . . . two typewriters . . . two radios . . . seven suitcases . . . books, manuscripts, records, pillows, bedding . . . not counting our dog and her beloved basket.' I have a dreadful fear that at the last moment Jon will insist on taking our fine inner-spring mattress. . . . I am baking beans again, a job I enjoy immensely. Along about four o'clock the whole house will be full of the most heavenly odor, and at dinner, accompanied by homemade coleslaw and pickles and brown bread—dear, dear.

"A friend, after reading a few pages of our journal, said, 'I like Isabel's pages best. You tell everything. Jon's are so—impersonal.' It was meant to be a compliment, but it gave me quite a turn. Is that all there is to me—a gossip? Have I no deep, significant thoughts? Can't I even *observe*? It is true I write mainly of domestic matters, but I like to think that I could dwell in lofty intellectual realms—if I wished."

October 18th (Jon): "Most of the day the wind has blown boisterously, and tonight it is colder and swifter and the leaves mingle with it intimately. The pattern of the thinly clothed trees is lacy against the indigo sky. . . . I can remember when neither a star nor a single patch of blue was visible through those branches. I can remember when the wrens sang and scolded, when the warm water was full of small, iridescent fish, when the roadside was lined with tiny, confused rabbits and chipmunks. I remember so much that was young then and bright and brave. We are older now, but only by the measure of the joy we have taken in these things that now we remember. So be it. Let us age like this, each year adding the memory of another spring, summer, fall, and winter lived in full. Shall we be gay when the year's first soft breeze scatters the white sheep of heaven across a sky of new, warm blue? And shall we be well and strong and brown again under the hot sun of another summer? And in another year, when we have seen the drama through once more, shall we again be gravely happy in our love that knows no season and no death? I think the wrens will be back next year."

October 19th (Isabel): "Each evening we stroll about our estate, picking up stray hickory nuts and twigs for kindling and watching the sunset light fade out of the water. Last evening was gray and gusty, but today is just plain wet. Lasses is so disgusted that she won't step off the back porch, and even her bed is not satisfactory today, for the fire flares up occasionally and scares her out of her basket and under the couch. Lasses wants no surprises in her life. Things are to go along according to form and custom. Biscuit at eight, lunch at twelve, afternoon walk, warm, steady glow of firelight—with no sparks—an after-dinner walk, nap between us on the couch in preparation for a good night's sleep. No loud voices, no visitors, no cars passing on the road, no doors slamming in the house across the lake. Everything ordered, peaceful, centered around the wishes of a small, stubborn, black and gray Cairn who has more personality than a hundred other dogs put together."

October 22nd (Jon): "It's a black night and the high wind sounds like surf running on a long beach. I've been thinking that it's hard not to invest the birds and other wild things with the emotions and the senses we possess, and I wonder if it's true that they think only of eating and breeding and keeping alive. How differently would birds act, constructed as they are, if they felt and thought as we do? What would they do on a black, windy night like this? I think of the Towhees huddling in crevices in the stone fences. The juncos are all together, a hundred or more of them, in the thick brush of a little hollow. The blue jays are clever, and they and the crows have found four separate woods, each one in the lee of a hill. Tonight they'll be in the woods behind the south hill. The sparrows are in the roadside thickets, and God alone knows where the chickadees are. Perhaps they are sitting with the nuthatches and kinglets in old woodpecker holes. . . . Oh, well, it's an old argument, and I can't add anything to it. I don't even know what I feel myself—whether creatures lower in our scale feel a part of what we feel or whether we get maudlin about it and think they do. . . . But here am I with my mate, sheltered from the wind. I hope they are."

October 24th (Isabel): "In the kitchen, my lord and master is engaged in shaving off three days' whiskers, for which I thank heaven. Anya says she likes her man to look primitive, atavistic, but I object violently. Whiskers do strange things to Jon: he becomes a cross between a Messiah and a hobo and a disconcerting companion. Here he comes, smooth and shining and fully conscious of the improvement. Oh, I love him so much and must be sure never, never to let him know. All the love experts agree on that."

October 25th (Isabel): "We broke the ice in the pail in the kitchen to get water for washing and it has grown much warmer all day. Jon has become so skillful at fire-making that we have scarcely any chance to suffer. Getting up is a bit of an effort, but within ten minutes there is a comfortable crackle in the fireplace and the stove. Of course, he cheats and uses kerosene, but it works and who cares.

"Douglas and his mother have gone and we are alone on our lake tonight, and there's no use pretending I don't mind, because I do. So many things could happen to Jon—or the car. Well, at least there are the Poles at the other end of the lake. I don't want to see or hear the people in the other house, but I cling to the thought of someone there—in case. I'm not afraid of the dark, or tramps, or animals, but I'm afraid of something going wrong with my husband. In that case, I would probably run the two miles to the Dunays' and hardly realize I was doing it. Nothing must ever happen to Jon. We must stay always young and well and in love, he confident, I trusting in him. We won't, of course, but if we are together and able to lock hands and smile, I shall count myself blessed among women. I think that perhaps I have found the one man in the entire universe."

October 28th (Jon): "I should be worrying now—I have so little. The earth is barren, the fog is here, and the cold is coming—yet my heart sings an echo of its summer song: We are here together. We are here together, still! . . . A paragraph is so neat. It is quarantined within a wall of sanitary white. Each paragraph should represent a different thought. I should write on specially watermarked paper—paper which, when held up to the light, would show through the printed words the legend, 'I love you, my darling!' But watermarked or not, it is there."

October 28th (Isabel): "No getting around it, this is a very damp day. And before long, we must climb into the poor, sodden old Auburn and skid and slide down to the village. One of these days we aren't going to make it, and somebody with a team of horses is going to be several dollars richer. After all, we can't expect to be lucky forever, and the car is ancient and tired and the road abominable.

"I have been gorging on fiction lately, and I don't think the diet is good for me. I am restless and apprehensive and confused, and the hectic introspection of the last few novels I've read has been anything but soothing: everyone frustrated, wretched, seething with venom. Jon is wiser than I. When we read together on the couch in the evening, he is deep in bird lore and dipping into anthologies. He refuses to read modern fiction, and I am about to follow his example.

"At the moment, my husband is clumping around the kitchen in his muddy boots, intensely engaged in concocting a beef stew. It is now at the garlic-smelling stage, but I don't doubt that it will be a creation. From where I sit, I can see him in silhouette, frowning over the sizzling mess in the frying pan, his pipe clenched between his beautiful white teeth. Oh, my lord, here he comes with the pan. He has elected to finish it over the open fire."

October 29th (Isabel): "Last night we were wrapped in silence, and a fog that was like warm chiffon drifted past the window. I had a wretched night with a strained back that bothered me, but as I lay awake in the darkness, my heart was singing hymns of gratitude. I am loved and I love. We are content with so little;

we find joy in every hour of the day. To walk under an October sky, to stand in the fragrant kitchen while we cook our dinner, to dine by lamplight, to sit side by side on the couch reading, growing warmer and more sleepy, and at last to be in each other's arms in a soft, cold bed and to feel the fire between us mounting, mounting, till we are swept into that final conflagration that is the supreme reward of being a man and a woman. Then we know nothing more till we wake and see dawn breaking over our still, little lake and hear the chorus of the birds. This is my almost perfect life. To it I would add only some sort of financial security, no matter how small, the ability to write again, my parents and my sister and her children within an hour's drive."

November 1st (Jon): "Very few trees have any leaves left, and the wind has a new sound. Each approaching gust can be heard for perhaps a mile before it arrives. The day of our departure for California comes closer. If we had money we would be happier about it, but I doubt if we would be very happy."

November 1st (Isabel): "We are talking of starting on our drive to California on the 10th, which leaves us only a little more than a week. We have been so happy here that I almost dread to go for fear. . . . But it is cowardly and stupid to feel that our love, our companionship, depends on environment. I shall like any place where we are together, and Connie writes of a charming little house waiting for us in California. So, penniless but still hopeful, off we go in the faithful old car to cover the continent."

November 3rd (Jon): "Sometimes when you have to do a physical thing you do it emotionally first, and then when you come to doing it actually, it doesn't mean very much. Maybe that's the way it will be when we go to California. Maybe that's the way it is right now. I left this place several days ago. In the old days when I used to worry I always ended in a fit of utter despondency, but that hasn't happened since we've been together. I'll live, I'm afraid."

"November 3rd (Isabel): "We've been trying to get our things in order. We spent yesterday afternoon and this morning sorting and burning manuscripts, and a more melancholy job cannot be imagined. What hopes they represent and what a jumble! I have three novels and uncounted short stories, as well as a lot of radio scripts. Jon has a novel and a play and innumerable sketches and short stories that have been tried and found wanting. I'd burn the whole collection, but Jon won't let me. . . . I wish I knew what to do about going west. To be wise, we should stay right here till we are independent. I suppose we are utter fools to rush off half-cocked in a rackety old car, with only borrowed money in our pockets and nothing sure ahead, yet the family pull is strong, and how can I refuse my mother and father?"

We made one last trip to New York, Jon to see about business matters, I to say goodbye to my beloved Julie and her brown-eyed cherub son, and, with some apprehension, to have a parting drink with my former husband.

To my relief, Jimmie was looking well and cheerful. I told him of our plans, and when I spoke of the house Connie had found for us, he said, quickly, "Good, good. I'd hoped you'd do something like that."

On an impulse, I said, "Jimmie, I hope you'll marry again. You were such a *nice* husband. There surely must be some girl—"

He flushed and twisted his glass. "Well," he said slowly, "as a matter of fact, there is."

"Oh, Jimmie, wonderful! Who is she?"

"My accompanist."[1]

"How thrifty!" The word slipped out, but we both laughed and I added hurriedly, "I meant, how ideal. I could follow you only so far along the musical road, and she'll be able to go the whole way. Oh, I am so glad!"

He showed me her picture, an attractive, intelligent girl. Years later, on a trip to New York, I met her and found her charming, with a fine motherly streak that was just what Jimmie needed.

(After his death, at fifty,[2] I came home one night to my flat in Sutton Place and found a large manila envelope pushed under the door. In it were half a dozen pictures of me and a note: "Hardesty always cherished these very much. I think you should have them back." There they were: the first snapshot I had given him in England, a studio portrait of me in medieval costume, publicity pictures of us together on the concert platform, me with Connie's children in my arms, and my wedding photograph. It was late at night and I was tired and frayed. I sat there for an hour or more, weeping for the old, lost days.)

November 7th (Jon): "The last entry. Tomorrow and tomorrow and Wednesday we start for the Coast. It will be a long road.

"Because we have been so happy here, it is a bitter thing to leave this place, but after all, the happiness that there was we brought to it and we can bring it again. There is a high tree here from which a goldfinch used to sing his enthusiastic joy. The beam is there on which our wren perched to announce his parenthood. The lake reflected the shining glory of the young herons, and around us the hills echoed the cries of the timid grebes. . . . They have gone, all of them, and now we go, leaving this house and this country, where we too have sung our happiness, behind us.

"The young birds learned their songs here and practiced them during the summer. In the south they will sing like masters. Hell, so shall we."

It was a professional job of packing that Jon did on the old Auburn. Time and again, I would have sworn that it could not be done, that we would have to abandon something, but aside from the Onteora equipment, which Douglas promised to return for us in the spring, we managed to get everything and ourselves aboard. Once again, Lasses was to lie luxuriously on the cushion on the top of everything, little knowing that she would be saying goodbye to her favorite spot in the world forever.

In one of my letters to the family, I had written a humorous description of the car and its probable appearance as we started west, and the picture alarmed my father.

"They will think you are 'Okies' and stop you at the border," he protested. "If you have any trouble, just call us collect and we'll pull wires and get you released. I hate to think of your coming all that way in a secondhand car. Drive carefully. Your mother and I won't have an easy moment until you get here."

Our last night was, inevitably, a tense, melancholy affair, but we were so exhausted by a day of frenzied domestic activity that we got into bed as soon as possible and fell asleep almost at once. With my head on my love's shoulder and his arm holding me close, I was able to say above the ache in my heart, "At least, we're going together. No matter what happens, we will be together."

It was a gray, chill morning, no color anywhere, as we turned the key in the lock for the last time and hoisted Lasses to her queenly perch in the back. Jon slowed the car at the top of the hill, and we looked back on the beloved world we were leaving. The smoke from our carefully banked fires rose slowly into the still air. A fox sparrow—Jon told me it was—sang a lovely, soft, warbling phrase from the hedge. A red-tailed hawk swung in wide circles above the lake. Oh, the silence, the peace!

Jon's face was blurred for me through my tears, but he bent to me and his mouth on mine was warm and strong. Neither of us said a word as he put the car in gear, and we rolled off down the hill for our three-thousand-mile quest.

After a few minutes, Jon asked casually, "Care to light me a cigarette?" and the curtain had come down.

It is not my intention to recreate that drive, which had many high spots and some vicissitudes, but there is one thing I must say in all gratitude: aside from a flat tire or two, our faithful old car never faltered. Perhaps it knew it was going home, back to the green pastures of the West Coast.

Because of the lateness of the season, we had decided on the southern route, and hour after hour we moved steadily down into and across the Deep South, sleeping and eating at the cheapest decent places we could find. Our first motel—the hour was so late that we hadn't noticed—was located only a few feet from the main railway line, and every train that tore down the track that night seemed to come right through our little hovel. Lasses, with her phobia about the sound of approaching trains, was in an agony of fear, and we put her in bed between us and felt her shudder and shake the whole night through. We were a spent trio the next morning as we took the road again in a pouring rain, but sometime during the day the clouds moved off and we were able to find a quiet place beside a cheerful little mountain brook for our next night's stop.

Neither of us had ever come this way before, though Jon had made several visits to Palm Beach and I had stayed with the Irving Bachellers in Winter Park during my concert platform days, but we were unprepared for the dismal poverty, for the ugliness of the swamplands, the desolation of the tiny, tumbledown cabins, with their gaunt, blank-faced inhabitants. It wasn't until we crossed the Mississippi that we grew resigned to the scenery and the accommodations. Everything in the South seemed so slipshod, so dirty, the food so poor. No one cared about your comfort or made the least effort to be civil. We decided this was because we were staying in the cheapest places, trying to save money, but as soon as we crossed into the Southwest, the whole picture changed. Though we were still traveling cheaply, everyone smiled. The motels were clean and neat, the food was freshly cooked, the very air took on a sparkle. Suddenly, we were enjoying our trip.

All this time, Lasses—the little stoic—had been lying uncomplainingly on her pillow atop the mound of luggage. We would stop at intervals and give her a run, and we took her for a real walk when we paused for the night, but it was always a walk on a lead and my heart ached for her, with the wistful memories she must be revolving of country lanes, exciting smells, intriguing woodland animal life.

I forget just where it was, but it was the first glimpse we had of the desert. We emerged from a gap in some low-lying hills, and ahead, as far as the eye could see, was—nothing. No one on the straight, wide highway, no trees, no houses, no barns, no human thing. Jon stopped the car and drew Lasses down from her perch.

"What do you say we let her have a real run? She's been so good all this way and there's certainly nothing here to worry about." We both got out to stretch our legs, and Jon set Lasses on the ground and gave her an encouraging pat.

"There you go. Have a little run, old girl. See if you can scare up a rabbit."

With a shrill ecstatic yip, Lasses set off across the desert, running for all she was worth, but a second later she gave a wail of anguish, dropped to the ground, and rolled over on her back, all four legs thrust straight up in the air. Jon and I raced after her and found her whimpering piteously.

"What the—" Jon began as he bent over her and then we saw. Her paws were literally stuck through with those scourges of the dry country—cactus barbs and foxtails. Never having had any first-hand experience with the desert, Jon and I had no idea of what was waiting for our poor little Eastern country dog, used to innocent grass, soft drifted leaves, or the mossy margins of the lake. We spent the next hour painstakingly removing dozens of cruel little needles, but the result of the episode was that never afterward could Lasses be persuaded to go off on a run by herself. If we put a lead on and took her along a sidewalk she would go; otherwise, she would lie on her pillow and look at us through narrowed, disillusioned eyes. I don't think she felt we had actually planned the torment for her, but her faith in our judgment was permanently shaken. Lasses never set foot on wild land again.

As we neared California, on the last stretch of our journey, we found ourselves going slower and slower, starting later in the morning, stopping earlier at night, taking side trips to see local beauty spots. One of these was the Carlsbad Caverns.

I knew about the Caverns. Mother and Daddy had gone there with my sculptor uncle, Lorado Taft, who had been asked to supervise the lighting of the miles and miles of breathtaking underground beauty, and they had all gone down into the depths in the workman's open elevator and come back up transported with what they had seen. "If you ever have a chance to see the Caverns," Father had said, "do it, by all means. They are superb."

So here we were, in the neighborhood of several hundred miles, and the temptation was strong.

"It will cost us two days," Jon said, warningly, "but if you really want to do it—"

He longed to go, I knew, and my "Oh, I do," came promptly.

Two more days. . . . Two more days alone together before we had to face—whatever it was we were to face. As the miles had rolled behind me, dread was building up of the meeting between Father and Jon. In his own words, Father had declared, "I will not meet this man. I will never take him by the hand." Granted, he had had time to think it over. Here were two strong, quick-tempered personalities, each cherishing a justified grudge. The wrong word, the wrong inflection, could undo the patient buildup of two long years. Why not postpone it as long as we could, even if it meant adding two days to the trip we had come to enjoy so much? Besides, Father had said I must see the Caverns.

It was one of life's memorable experiences: miles of lofty, fairytale caverns, so beautifully lighted under my uncle's suggestions that not a bare light bulb was visible anywhere. All you were conscious of was soft, glowing folds of Grecian drapery, delicately elaborate carvings, huge, symmetrical pillars seemingly supporting crystal ceilings of incalculable height. I had been somewhat apprehensive. In the first place, going through the Caverns required a five-mile walk, and my feet are not always reliable. I also had claustrophobia, and the thought of being eight hundred feet underground was daunting, but when we were finally inside, the air was fresh and cool, the sand under our feet crisp and white, there were numerous places to rest, and each chamber we entered was a marvel of imaginative beauty. We came out to our car and our patiently waiting dog in a sort of trance.

We took ten days for the trip across country, which we could have made in seven or eight. There was no trouble at the border—they had seen rattier caravans than ours—and at least we were heading for a known address. We spent our last night out among the orange groves and under a full moon at Claremont. We could easily have reached Hollywood that night, but we told ourselves, guiltily, that we were too tired, that we would disturb people by coming in late, and that it would be more sensible to do it in the morning.

For our last evening of freedom, we found a bright little coffee shop not far from our motel, and after dinner, with Lasses on her lead, we wandered along a country road, sniffing orange blossoms and so full of emotional heaviness that it was hard to find anything to say. Jon held my hand tightly, and I knew he was thinking, as I was, about tomorrow. At least, I knew to what I was returning. To Jon it was a whole new and difficult world, and yet for my sake he was facing it bravely. I prayed I had made the right decision, at the same time knowing that I could not have done otherwise and face the days coming on. Let them be good days, I repeated to myself over and over. Let them be good days.

At last, turning us about for our walk back to the motel, my husband spoke. "That house, the one Connie found for us, where did she say it was?"

"In the San Fernando Valley, in Encino." At the memory of Connie's letter, hope came flooding back. She had acquired a new man, and this one had a ranch house at the foot of the Encino hills. The grounds were quite extensive and contained a guest house.

"Wayne took me out to see it and it's adorable," she had written, "surrounded by trees, backing up on a quiet country road and not visible from any other house. It's very small but it has a living room, bedroom and bath, and a tiny, modern kitchen. It's pine-paneled and has a fireplace and it's cheap. I should think you and Jon would love it. I can hardly wait to show it to you."

"It sounds like an answer to prayer," I said.

Jon nodded. "Particularly the 'cheap' bit," he said grimly. "Oh, God, darling, why am I such a failure?"

"You're not a failure!" I seized his arm and shook it. He was brooding off and on over the patent, I knew. Just before we left New York the lawyer had written discouragingly of something similar filed a great many years earlier and now come to light, and my husband's dream of getting rich quick was dimming. "You just haven't found yourself yet. When you do—"

"Let's talk about that house." We walked in silence for a moment, then he said, more to himself than me, "I like the idea of all those trees. That will mean birds, of course. There aren't as many varieties on the West Coast, but there are always migrants."

"And there's a fireplace, remember. And no one can see us from the road." Excitement was mounting in me and with it a glimpse of continuing joy. We were not "trapped," as I had felt before. There was another charmed circle to be established, another refuge from the ugly turmoil of the world. And with Mother and Daddy only a short drive away, my conscience would not ride me as it had been doing these many months.

We were back at the motel now, and as the door closed behind us, Jon took me in his arms.

"We'll make it, darling," he said almost fiercely. "All we have to do is hold fast to what we have and we'll make it."

Our lovemaking that night had an almost desperate quality,

as though it might be for the last time. But that was absurd. We were we and the rest of the world was still outside.

It was about noon of a clear, beautiful California day that we drove down Los Feliz Boulevard and turned left onto DeMille Drive.

"The tennis court!" I exclaimed, as we passed it. "Oh, Jon, we can play tennis again!"

He sent me a swift, sidelong glance, but his face was set. There was a cold weight in the pit of my stomach, and I was shaking as we rounded the corner house and came in sight of Connie's pretty low-lying place. Then came the long wrought-iron balcony that I knew so well.

Jon stopped the car and I said softly but for all time, "I love you."

"I love you."

We were halfway down the long flight of steps when the front door opened and my father stood there.

"So you got here at last!" he called, and as we reached the bottom step, he smiled and, holding out his hand, said in that warm, vibrant voice that carried no hint of reservation, "Welcome, Jon."

"Daddy!" I ran into his arms and they were still strong, at seventy-seven.

"Welcome, my daughter."

Nothing more was said, nothing more ever would be said, but I knew that we were a family once more.

Notes

[1] Hardesty married his accompanist, Beverley Peck (1904-2001), in 1940. Both became teachers at the Julliard School of Music.

[2] Hardesty died on April 23, 1952, at age fifty-three, after an extended and unnamed illness, according to his obituary ("Hardesty Johnson," *New York Times*, April 24, 1952, 31).

22. Return

ク↝ ク↝ ク↝

Whatever awkwardness there might have been, though there was none, was broken by the shouts of the little Harpers, who had spotted us from a window next door and now came charging across the grass to fling themselves on us. Connie followed, and we all went up together to see Mother. She was very white and thin but her face was luminous.

"Oh, it's so wonderful to see you!"

She held out a hand to Jon and me, and as I put my arms around her, Jon gently kissed the hand he held. Lasses was introduced and admired, the children danced and screamed, everyone but Mother turned to and helped us unpack the car, and within a few minutes we were standing among our shabby, travel-stained possessions in the big bedroom where I had wept so many nights away, and this time I was weeping again but in my husband's arms and for joy.

We all lunched together, even Mother came down, and John and Sister insisted on being seated on either side of their uncle. Daddy uncorked his most cherished wine, and the talk was a merry flood of reminiscences about Onteora and the lake, to which my parents listened with smiling interest. Lasses was at home at once and promptly took her stand in the kitchen, where she was about to be thoroughly spoiled by Mother's and Father's nice, bright housekeeper.

It was after the dessert—there was always a choice of two, and Daddy and the children settled for both—when I saw Jon's hand go involuntarily to his pocket, only to be swiftly withdrawn again. I sent him a grateful look, but my sister had had the same idea.

"I need a cigarette. Jon, have you got one?"

He presented his pack, lighted her cigarette, and was about to put the cigarettes back in his pocket when I said, impulsively, "I'll have one too, dear, if Mother and Father don't mind."

Mother merely smiled, but Father said briefly, "No, no, go ahead. All you young people smoke nowadays, I know. I don't approve of it, but after all, it's your decision."

Lighting my cigarette and his own, Jon agreed amiably. "It's a stupid and expensive habit, I admit. For myself, I prefer a pipe."

Father nodded. "A pipe I respect, though I have never tried one. Many of my literary friends smoke pipes. They say it helps them to concentrate."

"You should read J. M. Barrie on the subject," Jon said. "I don't suppose you know *My Lady Nicotine*?"

"Of course I know it. You don't have to be a smoker to appreciate a masterpiece like that."

Mother spoke up suddenly. "I wish Hamlin *had* learned to smoke a pipe. I think it would have been a comfort to him."

"Grandfather smoking a pipe!" John and Sister whooped with amusement, and on that note luncheon ended.

We had coffee out on the terrace. At my insistence, Daddy himself had made it, and I saw him watching intently to see that Jon and I showed the proper appreciation. It was not hard. We had not had coffee like that—even our own—for many months.

I saw Jon wander over to Connie and say something in a low tone. I knew he was asking about the house, and on some pretext, I went to him and said in an undertone, "Darling, please—not yet. We'll get to that later. For the weekend, we're house guests—"

Connie agreed. "We'll talk about it tomorrow. I can take you out any time. It's there, waiting for you."

That afternoon, while Mother and Daddy rested, Jon and I worked at unpacking and sorting our mountain of possessions. The bedroom door was closed, but instinctively we talked in low voices. The worst of the confusion coped with, Jon lay down on one of the twin beds and folded his arms behind his head. "Am I doing all right?" he asked.

"You're perfect. Bringing Barrie in was inspired."

He looked surprised. "That wasn't put on—I love that book. I was tempted to draw out your father on Shaw, but that can wait. What I really want to get started on is the psychic business."

"Jon, no—not yet. Remember what Connie wrote us. If Daddy wants to talk about it, he'll bring it up. According to her, he was pretty badly shaken."

"Then maybe he ought to be shaken a bit more," my husband said practically. "I want to be in on one of those sittings."

"So do I and I hope we will, but I gather it's a rather touchy subject right now and it's wiser to wait."

"All right." There was a little silence, and then Jon said slowly, "He's a damn good sport, your father. I wonder if I would have been, in the circumstances."

We had both been thinking of Daddy's surrender, and I was full of wonder. This man who had been bitterly hurt, my father who never apologized, had in one wholehearted moment erased the ugliness of two long years. It is interesting that in his diary this dramatic and all important moment sets down only the fact of our arrival and the comment that Jon "looked as if he needed a new suit."

As for me, my soul was overflowing with gratitude, not only to my father but to my husband who had the sensitivity and the generosity to appreciate the gesture for what it was.

"You would have done the same thing," I assured him ardently, and knowing the next most important thing that was possessing his mind, I said: "About the house, I'm as frantic to get out and see it as you are, but I haven't mentioned the matter yet to Father, and frankly, I dread to. We'll have to be tactful about it."

"This breaking into family life takes a lot of tact, I observe," Jon said lightly, and at my look of alarm, he laughed. "You poor little kitten, you're one bundle of nerves, aren't you? Come over here and lie in my arms for a while. I need strengthening."

Dinner without Connie and the children might have been difficult, but Mother bravely came downstairs again, and after Jon and I had described our trip and the Carlsbad Caverns had been thoroughly discussed, the talk turned to Thanksgiving.

"Mary Isabel," Daddy demanded, "Have you forgotten how to make a pumpkin pie?"

Before I could answer, Jon did, vehemently. "Has she forgotten how to make a pumpkin pie! Your daughter makes the best
pie in the world. In fact, she's one of the best cooks."

"Then thank Mother," I said quickly. "She taught me."

Jon turned to her and bowed gravely. "Madam, I thank you.
For a long line of superlative meals, I thank you."

Mother flushed and laughed and I leaned over and took her
hand. "When we get our own house—" I began, then stopped
abruptly. I had been about to say, "We'll entertain you and Daddy
frequently at dinner," but fortunately Daddy was engaged in a conversation with the housekeeper and had not heard. Jon sent me a
mischievous, mock-reproachful look, and I took a sip of wine and
tried to look unconcerned.

"We miss our polo games, daughtie," Father said tentative-
ly. "Connie is too busy and disinterested to take us. I don't know if
you—"

"Isabel's told me about your Sunday afternoon polo," Jon
said with immediate interest. "I used to go a lot in England. I have
never been to a game out here."

"There's one tomorrow afternoon." Father's eyes shone.
"The Argentines are up and some good men are playing. If you and
Mary Isabel—"

"Count us in. I don't ride but I like to look at horses in
action, and I think polo is one of the most picturesque games I
know."

Father leaned back in his chair. "That will be very nice," he
said.

After dinner, we had music. There was a Philharmonic
broadcast, and the four of us sat before the fire in the drawing room
in relaxed silence. Music soothed Mother, and she was not shaking
at all as she lay back in her chair in her pretty lace gown, her chin
cupped in her hand. She was at peace, I could see, and so it seemed
we all were. It was a rare and beautiful time.

When I went up with Mother to help her to bed, she pulled
me down beside her and kissed me. "He's very handsome," she
whispered, "and very nice. You must be good to him."

I was halfway between tears and laughter. "I'll try."

"I think Father likes him, too," she went on, "but he has been
angry with you for so long that it will take time."

"Father is magnificent. I could ask for nothing better. You're both wonderful and we're so glad we're here."

She looked at me wistfully. "I know you are eager to get into your own house—"

"Wouldn't you be—if you were in my place?"

She drew a quick breath. "Of course. . . . Connie says the place is small but charming. Why don't you have her take you out to see it in the morning? You don't want to run the risk of losing it."

What a rare, understanding person she was! I kissed her. "Bless you, dearest. I'm so proud of my mother."

On the pretext of errands to be done, Jon and I and Connie and the children drove out to the San Fernando Valley the next morning. Oddly enough, though I had lived all those years in Hollywood, the Valley had never before entered my life, and as we drove along, flanked by walnut and almond groves, I found it stimulating. The main boulevard was lined with shacky little stores, gas stations, and deplorable domestic architecture, but to the northeast was the noble wall of the San Bernardino Mountains and to the south the romantic, wooded Santa Monica Range, both dust-brown now but soon to turn green with the first rain. It had a kind of country feel, and Jon and I, holding hands excitedly, missed nothing.

At Encino, a tastefully planned little settlement, we turned south and headed directly for the mountains where, at the dead end of a road, a ranch house nestled under great eucalyptus trees.

"Here it is," Connie said, as we came to a halt. "And there comes your new landlord."

He was a big, broad-shouldered, extremely handsome man, with crisp, graying hair and friendly brown eyes. As the children rushed for "Uncle Wayne," Jon and I exchanged glances. This one had definite possibilities.

The cottage was ours at once. Compared to the log cabin it was the height of luxury. Only a shower, to be sure, but there was running water and electricity, and Connie had not misled us: though it was on Wayne's property, it was so far in the back and so shielded by trees as to be completely hidden from the casual passer-by. The little drawing room was delightful, with big windows opening out into fruit trees and flowers, and behind, a high cypress hedge cut us off from a rarely traveled road that wandered up a gentle hill.

Garland with his grandchildren,
John and Constance ("Sister") Harper.
*(Courtesy of the University of Southern California,
on behalf of USC Libraries Special Collections)*

"What a perfect place for Lasses's evening walk!" Jon exulted. "And here—" He laid his hand on the sill of the window that
opened out of the dining area, "here is where I am going to have my
bird feeding station. We can sit and watch them while we are having our coffee." He turned toward Wayne who, eyes on my sister,
was paying little attention to anything else.

Jon lifted his voice. "All right with you?"

Wayne started. "All right with what?"

"All right if I put a shelf outside this window for the birds?"

"Do anything you want. You can't hurt anything." He
looked smilingly back and forth between us. "Do I gather then that
you have decided to take it?

"Good lord, yes!" Jon exploded. We all laughed and the
children squealed with excitement.

Our mistake was in not warning them. When we returned, Father was reading the Sunday paper in the sunlight beside the front door, and bursting with important news, John and Sister rushed to him.

"Oh, Grandfather, you should see it! Anini and Uncle have the sweetest little house! It's almost like a doll's house, except it's big enough for them and Lasses—"

My father looked back and forth between Jon and me, then he began to get up slowly. Connie had gone to put her car in the garage, so we had no mediator and something told me we were going to need one.

"What's this about a house?" My father's voice was level and controlled, but I was not deceived.

The children were about to launch into a detailed account, but their mother's voice called them home, and Jon and Father and I were left alone. I began to stammer an explanation, but my father cut me off.

"There's no necessity of anything like that, Mary Isabel," he said curtly. "This place has enough room for all of us. Your mother needs you. We expect you to make your home with us."

He made a move as if to go, but Jon stepped in front of him. "Just a minute, Mr. Garland—" he said pleasantly. "Aren't you forgetting something?"

The eyes beneath the bushy eyebrows were cold. "What?"

"Our agreement. I remember every word of that letter Isabel wrote you. She said that we would be glad to come out and spend Thanksgiving with you, but that it was imperative we have a home of our own. Today we found that home—not far away, so she will be with you frequently—and the day after Thanksgiving we intend to move into it. It's not that we're ungrateful for all you've done for us. It's just a matter of—" he shrugged and smiled, "well, call it commonsense."

Father stood his ground for a minute, then he turned, flung open the front door, and went heavily into the house.

Jon and I stood there in the flooding sunlight and looked at each other.

"Oh, Jon, he's so—hurt," I whispered in misery.

He looked haunted. "I know. I tried not to say too much. I haven't forgotten how big he's been about the whole thing since we got here, but God damn it—" his fists clenched. "He doesn't own you anymore! He doesn't own either of us. He'll just have to take things as they are and knuckle under."

The front door had opened again, and Father said, "Mary Isabel, your mother wants you."

When I went to our bedroom a little later, Jon was lying on the bed, reading.

"What's happened?" I asked fearfully.

He sat up and ran his hands through his hair in a confused sort of way. "Why—nothing. Your father picked up the paper again and started reading. I waited around for him to give me hell, but when he didn't, I decided to go in, too. I had my hand on the door when he called me back and said, 'Look at this—' and showed me a book review or something. Just then the housekeeper came out and said he was wanted on the phone, and that was the end of that."

Amazingly, it was. The children were lunching with us and going to the polo game, and conversation at the table was turned over to them. Father was quiet but genial as we got into the car. Jon drove well and not too fast, and my parents settled back in relaxation.

It was a lovely afternoon at the Riviera Club. A handsome game, polo—agreeable to all the senses. At intervals during the afternoon, Jon and I exchanged secret glances that said, "We have a home!" but there was no real chance to talk about it until we were in the kitchen alone, preparing dinner. It was the housekeeper's evening off, and we were assembling the food she had prepared and talking excitedly.

"The thing we need most," Jon was saying, "is a long refectory table to go in front of the window seat—one big enough to seat the whole family but one that's light and won't take up too much room. I can make one easily—and when I put up some extra bookshelves on each side of the fireplace—"

The swinging door to the dining room opened, and Father came in briskly. "I'm after a glass of sherry for your mother and me." As I got out the bottle and glasses, he went on conversationally, "Talking about your new home, I imagine. Where is it exactly? The children didn't have time to tell me." While we were gathering ourselves together, he went on. "Your mother and I have been talking. She says it's right for you to have your own home, and I guess I must agree. It's hard for old people not to think of themselves first. We were all happy here together for so many years that I sort of imagined it could go on. Don't let what I said worry you." He picked up a glass of sherry and held it out to Jon. "Will you take this up to Mrs. Garland, please. I'll stay here and keep my daughter company till you get back."

When Jon had gone, Father looked at me soberly. "How are you off for money, daughtie? If you need any—"

"Oh, Daddy—" I put my arms around his neck and buried my face against his shoulder. "You're the kindest—"

"There, there." He patted me and I dried my eyes and managed to smile.

"We're all right for the moment. We've already paid our first month's rent, but unless something happens—"

"I'll help you out if you need it. Just let me know." He picked up his own sherry glass and departed.

In the mail next morning was a check for Jon from the *New Yorker* for $300, and to see my husband's face was sheer delight.

Daddy, too, was impressed. "Well, now, that's fine—fine," he said warmly. "Which story was it? Any of those I read?" It was the macabre little tale Jon had written at the lake, and what it did for his morale was incalculable. It's a good feeling for a man to know he's able to take care of his own wife.

Now that the secret of the house was out in the open, we talked of little else. Daddy and Mother wanted to inspect it, and we drove them out the next day. It was amusing to watch my father going around opening cupboards and peering into closets, and when we got back in the car he said, doubtfully, "I don't know, daughtie. It's pretty small. I admit it has a certain charm, but do you think you'll be able to—"

"Oh, Daddy, you should see some of the places in the East! This will be absolutely perfect. Wait till Jon puts up more bookshelves and makes us a nice, big, family-size table—"

"Are you interested in carpentering, Jon?" asked Father.

"Very much. I understand that you're a professional."

Daddy snorted in amusement. "Oh, I'm a dabster—I'm a dabster, all right. A dab here and a dab there—eh, Zulime?"

"You're a very good carpenter," my mother said calmly, "until something distracts you."

"All I can say," I exclaimed happily, "is that we're in luck that Connie has Wayne hitched to her cart."

Father's face darkened. "I don't care for that young man. He's getting too serious about your sister."

"Would you want him to be un-serious, Daddy? After all, Connie's going to have to look to the future, and Wayne is a great success with her children."

Father was stubborn. "Your sister doesn't have to marry the first man who presents himself. She is an exceptional girl, Constance. I shall do my utmost to prevent her marrying the wrong man."

Jon's mouth twisted wickedly, and I was in mortal terror he might make some dangerous comment, so I reached over and pinched him surreptitiously. Fortunately, Mother came in with a remark about the new house, and the moment passed safely.

That night, Father embarked on the psychic business. He was at this point, he admitted frankly, troubled in his mind, and he gave us the whole story from the beginning.

In condensed form, it seemed that in 1904 a woman named Violet Parent, a resident of Southern California, claiming to have clairvoyant powers, announced that she had established communication with the founding California padres and that they had told her there were, lying buried in various natural spots in California, small crosses and other metal artifacts made by the early Indians and hidden by them for safekeeping. So convincing was her tale and the evidence she had to substantiate it that a large group of friends—and skeptics—formed into search parties, and under the direction of Mrs. Parent's "voices" went out into the field and began digging up the crosses she had described. They also located various caches of money in widely separated places. Many of the crosses and artifacts were concealed in balls of hard dried mud that could only be opened with a hammer and often were deep under several feet of packed earth and rock that had plainly not been disturbed for many years.

In 1932, Gregory Parent, the husband—Violet had died some time previously—came to Father with some of the crosses and his extraordinary tale and asked him to write it as proof of the spirit hypothesis. As a psychic investigator, Father was intrigued and spent much time mulling over the story, the careful journals that reported all the circumstances of the finds, and the mysterious little objects themselves, but it wasn't until Father himself happened on a medium who claimed that she, too, could tune in on the padres that he became actively involved.

Father's medium was, apparently, telling the truth. On various expeditions, with the small, faint "psychic voices" of the padres speaking in the car or out on the hillsides, giving detailed directions, Father himself dug up metal crosses and curious little artifacts that he was assured had been hidden there by the Indians many years before. Naturally, he became highly excited and, as he wrote us in the East, told himself that here *might* be the actual, physical proof of the survival of personality.

The Parent story was fascinating, and Jon and I were enthralled with it. It was so full of "whys." One could assume that the Parents made the crosses themselves and planted them in an area covering many hundreds of miles—their only transportation in those days was a horse and buggy—but why wait for them to be dug up by someone else many years later? Where did the caches of money come from? Mr. Parent was a thirty-dollar-a-month grocery clerk. What about the signed statements of witnesses attesting to the authenticity of the finds and the fact that before each mud ball was opened, the "voices" would give a detailed and accurate description of what it contained? And how to explain the mysterious, paper-doll-like photographs that reliable citizens maintain Violet took with her Brownie camera of a living room table covered with a sheet and set about with nothing but bits of greenery and rocks?

Constance had told us of the advent of the new medium in Daddy's life and the further interest that she provided. My sister had been on some of the expeditions and had herself unearthed a cross out of the solid earth at the base of an old tree. She was deeply impressed at first, she admitted, but gradually doubt crept in. Father had set up a sort of intercom system between his study and his bedroom, and while the medium sat in one room, Father addressed questions to the voices from another. Presumably, the medium could not hear the questions, but Connie inadvertently found out that by standing close to the door, everything said in the study was perfectly audible. By this time she was convinced that the medium was "having Daddy on," as she expressed it, but there was still the matter of the crosses to be explained.

Retelling the story that night to Jon and me, Daddy produced a half a dozen or so of the artifacts, and I saw my husband examining them carefully. The questions he asked were shrewd and, from Father's point of view, disturbing.

And there was the great disappointment. Jon and I had been eager to be in on some of the sittings, and Jon had worked out a series of clever tests, but unfortunately, just two or three days before our arrival, the medium's powers failed. No voices came through. She was ill, she claimed, weak and dizzy and unable to "project." To Jon and me, it was all a bit too coincidental. There were, however, Father said, some previously indicated locations where there were still crosses to be discovered, and we set a date for an expedition.

Over cocktails at Connie's house the next afternoon—just the three of us—Jon expressed himself firmly.

"*Anyone* could make those things," he maintained. "I could—you could. All you need is the right alloy, an iron pan, a hot fire, a tray of sand, and a number of small figures or bas-reliefs. I have a hunch your medium has been taking advantage of Mr. Garland's interest in the Parent story and has been manufacturing and planting a few crosses on her own. Or she could have pinched some of the Parent ones, though your father maintains she has never had access to them."

Connie was sitting up straight. "You mean that we—the three of us—could go to work and turn out an actual cross?"

"As easy as cake. Lend me your kitchen some afternoon and I'll prove it to you."

"We'll try it this weekend."

A day or two later, we went out on a cross-hunting field trip. There is a round, picturesque mountain looming up out of the earth at Chatsworth, and it is quite a struggle to the top, but the "voices" had insisted that there were buried artifacts there, so up we went, Jon, Connie, and I. It was rough going and hot and exhausting—and a complete failure. With no psychic to direct us, we poked about aimlessly among the rocks and bushes, ate our picnic lunch, and were glad to give up.

Connie told us a delightfully humorous story of being on one of these expeditions with Daddy and seeing him lose his footing and start sliding down a steep hillside. As he passed her in a cloud of dirt, rocks, and uprooted shrubbery, he grinned and called out cheerfully, "*Some* old gentleman play golf!"

The truth was that this had been an engrossing experience for Father. Coming toward the close of his life, when the days had begun to seem long and empty, the Parent puzzle fired his imagination. He was talking less and less of the spiritualistic angle, so perhaps it was not quite the shock we anticipated when Connie went over to his study one afternoon with a completely authentic-looking cross on a pie tin. Jon had rubbed it with dirt and charcoal to darken it, and we had used tiny doll heads and the raised fruit and flower border of a piece of Italian pottery to make the designs. To almost any eye, it was interchangeable with the Parent finds.

Connie had wanted us to go with her to confront Daddy, but I was reluctant and Jon refused flatly.

"I've done enough damage already by making the damn thing. I don't want to be around when the bubble bursts."

Connie, dauntless girl, went on her mission alone. When she came back, she was flushed and triumphant but curiously subdued at the same time.

We were wild with excitement to hear her report. "What did he say? How did he act? Tell us everything that happened!"

She had gone into his study and said, "Daddy, I want to show you something—" and held out the tin with its contents.

He glanced at it absently, then at her. "What is it?"

She summoned all her courage and got it out. "Do you see this cross?"

"Yes, certainly, but I don't—"

"This . . . isn't a Parent cross. We made it—Jon and Isabel and I."

"*You* made it?"

"Yes. Jon got the alloy and we poured it into wet sand that we had already marked with the design. It's as easy as—anything. Jon maintained that it was possible for anyone to make these things and now we—proved it."

"Then what happened?" I demanded.

My sister shook her head. "I don't know what I expected.

All Father did was to pick up the cross and examine it minutely. Then he laid it back in the pan and brushed some sand off his hands."

"In that case," he said thoughtfully, "I guess I'll just have to call it *The Mystery of the Buried Crosses* and let it go at that."

23. The Valley

ᔥ ᔥ ᔥ

We all made a valiant effort to be happy on Thanksgiving Day, but not all of us succeeded. The children were worried about their father's absence, and my tense sister made only the briefest appearance and then was off and away with one of her various admirers. My pies, however, were good, Daddy admitted, and ate a large section of both the mince and the pumpkin to prove it, adding the remark that I remembered his making from childhood, "It will never be so good again." After dinner, we asked Daddy to read some Robert Benchley aloud to us, and Connie's children rolled on the floor in laughter, as Connie and I used to do with Joe Lincoln.

Jon and I, though certainly happy, were hardly present. Our thoughts were focused on settling into the guest house, to which we were moving in the morning. We were up and away at the break of dawn, thus avoiding the reproachful glances that would be sure to accompany our departure. However, we had promised to return that night for dinner and cold turkey, so it was not really desertion.

From the first, the house was all we had hoped for. Small it was, but glorying in its privacy, the country effect from every window, neither of us was about to complain. No sooner were we unpacked than Jon was on his way to a lumber yard and came home in triumph with a six-foot length of nicely grained plywood. Expertly and at the hardly extravagant sum of $2.25, he constructed a trestle table that survives and serves faithfully to this day. The table was our first requirement, for we had invited the whole fami-

ly to a housewarming luncheon the next Sunday before the polo
game—a custom that continued during the next two years.

   The next most important construction was the bird feeding
station outside the back window, and from the moment it was set
up it was in constant use. Our local birds—white crowns, thrashers,
mocking birds, bluejays—took over at once, but it was the migrat-
ing birds that delighted my husband.

   "Isabel—come here—" he would command softly, and I
would creep to the window to be shown and informed about some
handsome visitor on his long way to and from Mexico or South
America. The food we put out was of all kinds, and the free-load-
ers seemed to enjoy everything. One time it was a large piece of
strawberry shortcake topped with whipped cream, and all our
greedy, crowding visitors turned into clowns, with wide bands of
white fluff around their beaks. The hours my husband wasted
before that window—hours that he had sworn were to be devoted
to writing.

   Our pattern for living was quickly established. Twice a
week we dined with Mother and Daddy. On Sundays, they came to
lunch and the polo game, often with Connie's children, who soon
laid down the law that it had to mean lemon meringue pie. During
the week, I went in every other day to act as Daddy's secretary and
stay on for lunch with Mother. My parents seemed to be content,
and while I found that once again all this traveling back and forth
left me little time for literary activity of my own, I was relieved to
be doing my duty by my parents and taking some of the strain off
Constance.

   In his "Afterword" to *Back-Trailers from the Middle Border*—a
book which Connie illustrated most charmingly—Daddy had, he
declared, closed the series. "My story is told. I drop my pen and
turn my face to the fire." However, with *The Mystery of the Buried
Crosses* off his mind, Father had begun work on a book he was
calling "The Fortunate Exiles," a fifth volume to the chronicle of
the Garland family that began with *Trail-Makers*.[1] Father could not
exist without writing, and having lost all interest in fiction, a sequel
to his autobiography was the logical choice. It was, necessarily, a
somber tale, and as I worked at copying it, I wondered if it would
ever be finished or published. Daddy's former full life, crowded
with distinguished people and interesting ideas, had thinned down

to a pleasant, uneventful existence among the trees and flowers of what, to him, was an alien land. Now and then a fellow writer would pass through Los Angeles, and psychic talk filled the air again when the Stewart Edward Whites came down from Burlingame,[2] but in the main, Father was dependent for entertainment on the family, the loyal University people, the Pattens, and his brother, Franklin.

I am shocked that thus far I have said nothing about my Garland uncle. As a child, the comings and goings of Uncle Frank— he was a touring actor—were occasions of wild excitement, for along with his good looks and natural charm, he was deft at sleight-of-hand and could pluck quarters out of your hair bows or even out of your toes. Some years younger than Daddy, he was a complete contrast. Where Father was burly and broad-shouldered, Uncle Frank was slight, delicate, a dandy in dress and manner. He was never without a flower in his buttonhole, and he moved with a relaxed grace that was very attractive.[3]

When Uncle Frank and his second wife moved to California, Father was delighted. He loved his only brother and hoped that Frank's wife might prove a companion for Mother, but Mrs. Garland, an extraordinarily handsome woman who doted on her husband, carried a chip on her shoulder. An ex-nurse, limited in education, she decided that the Hamlin Garlands intended to patronize her, and she would have none of it. Invited to dine, Frank's wife refused to come. She made no effort to be kind to my poor mother, and her feeling toward Father was vitriolic. It was a disappointment to my father and a great bewilderment, too. Mother and I talked it over and we agreed that Daddy hadn't the least idea why the woman hated him so. Nor, indeed, have I— unless it was her inherent jealousy of the affection between the two brothers. Father was not always the soul of tact, but, basically, he was warm and generous. Toward the end of his life, my uncle became very feeble, and we would drive Daddy down to call on him. Mrs. Garland ostentatiously left the house each time Father came. She did not wish to see or speak to "that man." Sad—and absurd.

There were also the occasional and welcome visits of my mother's brother, Lorado Taft, now and then accompanied by his gentle, charming wife, Ada. For some years, my uncle had been burning with a really tremendous idea: an art museum that was to consist entirely of superb casts and laid out in cross sections, so that walking from east to west you would be cutting through the centuries, and walking from north to south you would be following the continuous artistic and architectural history of each particular country.

Father was so fired by the idea that he did his utmost to promote it for Los Angeles and succeeded to the extent that the city presented Lorado Taft with a building site on the hill next to the one on which the Planetarium is situated in Griffith Park, Hollywood. There was a civic ceremony, where my uncle was photographed turning over the first shovelful of earth. Uncle Lorado, whose life-long dream this had been, was transported with joy. It was a question, ultimately, of raising the money, but various rich and influential people were interested, and the thing might well have come into being except that my inspired uncle died, and with him the whole project. It is good to know that he died happy, however. I have some of his last letters to Father, and they are overflowing with gratitude and affection to "you, Hamlin, who have brought this to pass—the biggest thing in my life." In his mind, my uncle could see that majestic reproduction of the Parthenon up against the wide, blue California sky.[4]

With the arrival of Jon and me from the East, a new and stimulating change took place in Father's life. He had a phrase he liked to use in approval: "He has a lively mind," and now he came upon it, incarnate, in the form of my husband. It was not long before Daddy was inviting Jon up to his study after dinner, "to thrash this idea out, without the womenfolk interrupting." With forty years between them, literary craftsmanship was their shared interest, and night after night as we left for home, Jon would be laden down with volumes that Father had pressed upon him for his verdict. "The brain" that Father had recognized the evening of our first dinner party was still in evidence and deepening and broadening, and the satisfaction Father began to take in his new son-in-law was almost comical. In fact, I became a little resentful. The moment we appeared in the door, Father would descend upon Jon like a spider and drag him up to his lair. Jon was hardly permitted to be civil to Mother, so intent was Daddy on some new idea he wanted to share with him. "Jon, what do you think of this—" and "Did you

Garland and Zulime in Hollywood.
(*Courtesy of Victoria Doyle-Jones*)

read the editorial in the *Times* this morning? Don't you agree with me that—" Sitting with my mother in her front bedroom, we could hear the two men laughing together, and Mother's mouth would curve into a tremulous smile.

"It's good to hear Hamlin laugh again. All the time you were away, he hardly laughed at all. He won't admit it yet, but your husband is beginning to mean a great deal to him. I am very grateful to you both."

My own gratitude to my husband was unbounded. Never with my parents did he show the slightest sign of impatience or lack of attention. Smiling, considerate, full of original ideas and topics of conversation, our dinner parties were something to look forward to. It was only when we were at home, alone, that I saw the growing restlessness of his spirit.

"I've got to get going on something soon or I'll go nuts!" he exploded one evening as we were listening to music in what I had fondly imagined was relaxed content.

"But aren't you?" I was surprised, unhappy. "I thought you were working on a new story."

"I am. I was. It's no bloody good, so I threw it out."

Glass in hand, he started to pace our tiny, drawing room. "I'm tired of bits and pieces, of sending things out and having them come back. Sometimes I think I'm just kidding myself. I'm not a real writer at all."

"But you *are*."

He bent over to kiss me. "I have *you* fooled, anyway. But I've been thinking that what I need is a real job, something that will keep me at work, whether I feel like it or not. Would you object if I tried to get a job in radio? I know a couple of important advertising agency guys who might give me a break."

A premonition crept over me. We were no longer an enchanted circle, safe from the world. The wind of change had begun to blow, strong and inexorable. Subconsciously, I had been bracing for it, but something in me cried, "Not yet! Not so soon!"

I sat there silent, and Jon looked at me in concern. "What's the matter? Have I said something I shouldn't?"

I roused myself and tried to smile. "No, of course not. I'd only hoped that we might make a go of it by ourselves. After all, you did sell to the *New Yorker*, twice."

"Two lousy stories in two years," Jon said grimly. "We need a new car, you need some new clothes and I—" He squared his shoulders. "Well, what the hell, why not admit it? I want to be a success, for a change." He sat down beside me and took my hands. "It won't change anything for us. We're a team. Nothing can affect that. Would it interest you to know that I love you more now than I did the night I found out I loved you at all?"

"Yes, it would interest me."

"Well, it's true." He laid his lips on mine for a moment, then he was up, moving around the room again. "But I want to 'do right' by you. All the promises I made, the things I was going to get for you, hang on you. . . ." He shook the dark hair out of eyes that blazed. "Well, I'm going to get them yet. Just wait and see. Let's have another drink on it."

As he charged out to the kitchen in search of more ice, I

leaned back in my chair exhaustedly. Jon was drinking too much—
and the wry thought came to me that though he had asked me a
question, he had not waited for an answer.

Our social life, like Mother's and Daddy's, was practically
nonexistent. Except for the family and Jon's sister, who lived not far
away, we saw almost no one. We had both had a great many friends
in California before we left, but I felt a reluctance to try to get in
touch with them. Many of them, not knowing the circumstances,
felt that I had behaved shabbily to Jimmie and would take the
opportunity of snubbing me, and in any case, most of our friends
had been well-to-do and would not be interested in coming to a little shack in the San Fernando Valley. The Pattens and a few others
opened their arms to me again, but in general, my entire former
social life was swept away. Not that I mourned over it. Jon and I
were too self-sufficient to need anyone else, and the time we had to
spend with our families only made our times alone more precious.

Jon's sister, the only member of his family I ever knew, was
a handsome, bright girl, married to a motion picture producer, and
we dined with them occasionally and they with us. She was a culinary genius, as was her brother, and in outdoing each other we had
some pretty gourmet meals.

Oddly, I don't remember that Christmas. It must have gone
well, for I have no memories to the contrary, but I do remember the
flood not long thereafter. It was one of those California rains that
come down hour after hour, as if the entire heavens had opened.
We were snug at home and the roof was tight, but alarming reports
began coming over the radio. Hundreds of roads and crossings
were impassable, thousands of cars stranded, the Los Angeles
River—ordinarily a comic, little trickle—had reached flood stage
and was cutting away its banks. Power lines were down, no telephone, no electricity. Once again I could visualize my parents imag-
ining the worst for us, and while I knew they must be safe on
DeMille Drive, Jon and I began to worry about Jon's sister, whose
pretty new home was on the riverbank in Studio City. During a
temporary lull in the downpour, Jon decided we must drive down
the boulevard and look into Louise's situation.

The scene was appalling. California had not safeguarded
itself against circumstances such as this, and our first glimpse of the
river at crest was like seeing a mighty, ravening monster. Dark,

churning waters gnawed away at the banks, and now and then, with an ear-splitting roar, huge sections of concrete would tear themselves loose and go swirling and bobbing down toward the sea, in a confusion of engulfed cars, houses, livestock, and according to the news reports, an occasional body.

We crawled carefully down the flooded boulevard to a point opposite Louise's house and stood looking at the ugly flood, unable to reach her, for all the bridges were down, seeing the furious water steadily, remorselessly eating into the banks on both sides. Houses were toppling into the river to the right and left of us, and as we stood there, a roof with a dog huddled on it went twirling, grinding by, only to be shattered to bits at the next bend in the river.

Jon's sister was a fanatic gardener, and Jon gave a shout of relief and amusement. There she was, out on her front lawn with the river slicing ever nearer and nearer, down on her knees, calmly planting spring bulbs! We waved at her across the water and she waved cheerfully back—it was impossible to make one's self heard—and we turned and made our cautious way back to our little snuggery, which fortunately stood on a hillside and was not subject to the flooding that wrecked thousands of homes on the low, flat ground.

I knew Mother and Daddy would be deeply worried—as they had been that momentous New Year's Eve—but Jon and I were touched beyond measure when about five that afternoon there was a knock at our door, and Mrs. Stewart, their housekeeper-chauffeur, stood there. She explained that Mother and Daddy had been so unhappy that they had ordered out the car and at incalculable risk and inconvenience had come the long way round—about a fifty miles drive—and managed to reach us from the west. They were waiting in the car to hear we were safe, and we flung coats over our heads and rushed out to reassure them and speed them on their homeward way, for it was a foolhardy thing to have done, and the forecast was for a still heavier downpour that night. The expression of relief and joy on their faces as they saw us splashing to them through the mud and water was infinitely touching. It is a sobering thing to be so loved.

Speaking of love—my sister's affections were still in a suspended state, and poor Wayne, to Father's frank relief, was the loser.

Whereas they had been in the habit of dining with us once a week or so, Connie now went out with another man and Wayne came alone. Night after night he would wander over to sit by our fire in a gentle melancholy. We were sorry for him, but we did wish sometimes that he would go somewhere else.

My sister had decided to sell her house, and Daddy took it much to heart. "Our lovely little Pomander Walk is gone," he mourned, overlooking the fact that things had been anything but ideal there for some time. My sympathy was with my sister, who had had all the ex-husband and mother-in-law she could stand, but my heart ached for my parents. Though we both promised to remain only a short distance away, it was the difference between looking out your window and seeing your grandchildren romping on the lawn, having Connie drop in for a few minutes in her prettiest frock before going out to dinner with a new conquest, borrowing back and forth between the kitchens, and a general feeling that the houses were almost one. I had been the first to cut into Mother's and Daddy's sense of security. Now, Connie was finishing the job.

Happily, my sister moved into a most amazing and romantic place. It was in fashionable Los Angeles, on Fifth Street, and it was part of a grand old estate. The house had been the "tennis house" beside the private court and was a huge, glass-walled room with a sixteen-foot-high ceiling and a manorial fireplace, adjacent to which was a delightful lean-to kitchen. The forty-foot room took all my sister's handsome, rather heavy furniture and made it one of the most unusual drawing rooms in the city.

In a separate building, down an English garden brick walk, was a long, narrow bedroom with a fireplace, a bath, and a guest room. In a third building, down another brick walk, were two bedrooms, a maid's room, and a bath. It was inconvenient as all get out, particularly when it rained and you had to leave your bedroom, after dressing for dinner, and dart—under an umbrella—across the garden to the main house, where crystal and silverware and high candelabras with high-backed, carved chairs around magnificent refectory table made dramatic contrast to the tall, rain-lashed windows. It was impractical but it was fascinating, and we all loved it—even Daddy. It was not meant to be a permanent home. My sister was looking around for a place to buy, and her thoughts turned more and more toward the San Fernando Valley. John suffered from asthma, and the doctors suggested a move to a dryer climate. The Valley, except during the winter rains, was dry and clear, and there was a vacation atmosphere about it in those days that was attractive. After the rains, the hills came out in a green as emerald as Ireland, and a carpet of almond and walnut and fruit tree blossoms stretched to the foot of the frequently snow-capped mountains. Determined to help find his younger daughter and her two children a suitable rooftree, Father heroically swallowed his disappointment in the breakup of DeMille Drive and set out to systematically explore Los Angeles and its environs.

There was a place in the Valley to which he and my sister returned again and again. Architecturally, it was an anachronism: a sort of white stucco, New York brownstone set high up on a steep hill, with three stories down a tree-shaded swimming pool. It had an impressive sweep of Valley and mountain view, a generous living room and dining room, and four bedrooms and four baths. It was full of sunlight and sweet, untainted air, and it had never been occupied.

The house had been built by a strange little man from New York. He had been a plumbing contractor, so his pipes and fittings were of the finest and the house had been intended to serve his wife and several grown children on the various floor levels, but by the time it was finished, his wife had decided that thirty-five years of marriage was enough and his children elected to stay in the East. When Connie and Daddy first looked at the house, Mr. Shurgan was living a lonely bachelor existence in the little dressing room off the swimming pool.

The trouble was that he would not sell. He had put his place on the market, but each time it came to the point of a genuine offer, he would make excuses and back down. My sister—like our mother—has always had a way with people, and in the course of several visits she and the unhappy little owner became friends.

"Just promise me one thing, Mr. Shurgan," she said, after being disappointed for the third or fourth time, "if you ever *do* get to the point of selling, let me know first."

Mr. Shurgan glumly promised, and that seemed to be that. Daddy, who was deeply enthused over the house, its newness, its view, its convenience, was bitterly disappointed, but my sister was undaunted. "I have a hunch that house is going to be mine someday, and to prove it, I shall keep the last down-payment check I made out. I am in no hurry. I can afford to wait.

Spring came on with a tumultuous rush, as it does in Southern California. No long, slow waiting for buds to unfold. All of a sudden you're knee-deep in summer, and as one perfect day succeeds another, life becomes intoxicating. There was one enchanting afternoon at Connie's Fifth Street house, while we all sat among drifts of flowers and watched her three small Scotty puppies playing with a large deck-tennis rubber ring. Not one of the puppies would relinquish his hold for an instant, and as the tide of strength shifted from one side to another, the ring, with three puppies firmly attached, skittered back and forth across the grass to our delighted amusement.

Spring was beautiful, it was welcome, but all of a sudden our Valley began to get hot. The guest house had not been built to withstand heat, and with no insulation, the sun beating down on the thin shingle roof turned the interior into an oven. There was nowhere to go for relief during the daytime, though the nights were almost always pleasant. Jon had nailed a tin can up under the roof of the front porch as a lure to bird nesters, and one exciting day, a finch moved in and took possession. We loved having her there, and she seemed completely unperturbed by our comings and goings, but as she continued to sit on her eggs and the mercury went higher and higher, she was all but fried alive. We would look up at her in her little tin hell, gasping for breath, and wonder what in the world we could do to help. There was nothing to do but suffer with her, and Jon cursed himself for an idiot in putting the can there in the first place. At the time, it had seemed a safe, protected spot and a wonderful opportunity for us to watch the raising of another bird family. I am happy to report that in spite of the ordeal, the heroine hatched three husky nestlings and launched them all into a summer world, where the temperature was over the hundred mark day after day.

Finally, much as I hated to, I struck. I have always been sensitive to heat, and I became quite desperate. There was nothing for it but to move, so sadly leaving our trees, our birds, our clean, country air, we moved back to Hollywood, into a funny little house not far from Mother and Daddy, on a quiet side street where arching trees gave the illusion of remoteness.

It was there that Jon became very ill. His dentist, in taking out a wisdom tooth, discovered another beneath it, and in getting that out he had to cut into the jawbone, and a dangerous infection set in. That was a hideous time. On the radio constantly were the horrors of the world situation, and on the couch lay my husband in agonies of pain that only alcohol and the strongest of pain pills could alleviate. He who was usually so strong, so competent, was like a suffering child, watching the clock for the moment to take another pill.

It was Connie who, almost literally, saved Jon's life. One look at his tortured face and she called her own doctor for the name of the best dental surgeon in Los Angeles. She and I drove Jon down to Dr. Tholen, who saw he must operate immediately. Connie and I sat in the waiting room for an hour or more—I in unspeakable apprehension—and finally the door opened to reveal my husband, heavily bandaged, his eyes dull, his white shirt covered with blood. It had been an appalling operation in which a large section of the jaw had had to be removed. Dr. Tholen himself, may his name be blessed, looked as if he, too, had been through the mill.

"Take that man of yours home and keep him quiet," he said to me, and I could tell by his voice that it had been a near thing. "And whatever you do," he called after us, "keep him out of fist fights. A week-old baby could knock him out now."

Slowly, Jon fought his way back to health and activity again. I was at home a great deal, taking care of him, and one day, out of the blue, the idea for a mystery novel came to me.[5] It was in the form of a letter written by a granite-souled New England mother to her youngest son in answer to his request for a financial loan, and it was a flat refusal. In a sort of creative trance, I sat down at the typewriter and wrote a cold document offering not the monetary help, which she could very well afford, but to take her son and his young wife under her roof—and domination. I could see Mrs. Comstock down to the last hairpin, and when I had finished the letter, I took it to Jon to get his advice.

"What do you think of this as a springboard for a mystery?"

"Great!" Pale and weak as he was, he kindled at once. "Do you know where you are going from there?"

"I think so. For a little way, anyhow."

"Then get on with it. If you run into trouble, come to me. I may not be much use as a husband these days, but I surely know something about murder mysteries. Remember that first one you asked me about? What happened to it?"

"Love. And marriage. And cooking—and housekeeping—and washing—and dashing back and forth across the country in cars—"

"Poor darling." He drew me down beside him on the couch. "Are you ever sorry?"

"About what?"

"About what you took on when you took me."

"Never."

He was playing with my left hand, turning it so that the light flashed in the topaz of my engagement ring. "I thought by now I'd have a great, fat diamond there—"

"I like this better."

He gripped my hand hard. "Look—" he said earnestly. "It's not always going to be this way. I got in touch with a guy yesterday. He knows the sort of stuff I can do, and he said as soon as I am out of the woods with this jaw thing, to come into the agency and talk to him. He thinks he'll be able to fix me up with something right away—and for good money, too."

"That's splendid."

He took hold of my chin and turned my head so that he could look into my eyes. "You don't sound very enthusiastic."

"Of course, I am. I know how eager you are to—get ahead. It's just that—"

"That what?"

"That I'm afraid of—things coming between us. It has been so wonderful, working together."

"We'll go on working together," he said confidently. "I'll help you with your novel, you'll help me with my radio scripts. We'll be twice as good as anyone else, because we love each other. Something tells me that before long things are going to start to happen. . . . By the way, have you thought of a title for your mystery?"

"What do you think of 'Abandon Hope'?"

"'All ye who enter here,'" he finished the quotation. "Good—for a title, but not for us. Hope is what we've been living on for a long time, but right now I feel it stronger than ever. Darling, our break has come."

Now I was writing again, Daddy was so overjoyed that he was one big beam. Each night I came to dinner, I would bring a chapter and read it aloud. As my characters began to evolve, they became as real to me as the members of my own family, and writing about them seemed merely a matter of putting it down. Surprisingly, I found that I hardly needed to plot, for the characters very often ran away with it, and the reason, I was discovering, was that this time I was writing about people I knew. In my first mystery, the Beach Club one, I was writing about people I neither liked nor understood. How could I conceive, for instance, what a spoiled motion picture beauty like Jean Harlow would do in a given situation? Or Ronald Coleman, or Sam Goldwyn, or C. B. DeMille, for that matter, though I had been in his home many times, had heard him pontificating at the head of his table, and watched him, lord of all he surveyed, on the set. Part of what I wrote about my Hollywood characters was authentic, for I had observed a great many of them, but the rest was frankly borrowed from what I had read or heard. In *Abandon Hope*, which became my first published book, the setting, the people, the motivation were true. "Old S.C." began to take hold, and the book grew encouragingly.

Jon, meanwhile, had made a complete physical recovery and to my carefully concealed regret had become part of the advertising agency-sponsor-radio network "rat race." With his genius for plot and his terse, dramatic dialogue he was a godsend for the industry at that time, and he soon had all the work he could handle.

We were leading a vastly different life these days, and there is no use saying I was happy, for I was not. No walks, no bird-watching, no musical and reading evenings by the fire, no culinary sessions in the kitchen. In the mornings, except when I was working for Daddy, we both wrote, but in the afternoon Jon had to go to the agency or CBS for conferences, coming home later and later, having had far too many drinks. Often, he would have to work in the evenings, too, and I would go alone to dinner at the family's and come home forlornly by myself, to find my husband deep in exhausted, alcoholic slumber on the couch.

Money was coming in, however. We bought another car, and if I felt like buying a porterhouse steak, I bought it. We were still in our funny little house, which we rather liked. It had a cupola bedroom with windows on all four sides opening on a wide view of the sky, but it was small and shabby, and as Jon moved up in the radio-writing business, the question of entertaining his associates arose, and we moved again.

This one was a small house in the Hollywood hills. It was not distinguished but it had a breathtaking view of the city lights, and the night after we moved in we invited Mother and Daddy for dinner. We all stood for a long time looking out at the glitter and shimmer, then Daddy waved his arm.

"Worlds to conquer, young people," he said, smiling.

It had set him thinking, it appeared, for the next time Jon and I dined at DeMille Drive, Father had a surprise for us. It was after dinner, and coffee cup in hand, he was sitting in his big wing chair by the fire, looking handsome and pleased with himself.

"Children—" he began, after an obvious exchange of glances with Mother, in the chair across from him, "I would like to build you a house."

Notes

[1] "The Fortunate Exiles" was to have been the fifth volume of Garland's literary memoirs, not the Middle Border books. The volumes include *Roadside Meetings* (1930), *Companions on the Trail* (1931), *My Friendly Contemporaries* (1932), and *Afternoon Neighbors* (1934). Garland began work on the volume in April 1935, not 1937, as Isabel here suggests.

[2] Stewart Edward White (1873-1946) was a writer of western adventure books who later turned to psychic exploration after he and his wife, Elizabeth (Betty), took part in a séance. *The Betty Book* (1937) is a chronicle of his encounter with spirits, channeled through his wife.

[3] As an itinerant actor, Franklin Garland (1863-1945) had spent relatively little time with the Garland children. He and his wife, the former Alice Field, had relocated to Santa Monica Boulevard in West Hollywood, only two miles away.

[4] Lorado Taft died on October 30, 1936. For the photograph of Taft (with Garland) at the groundbreaking ceremony, see "Art Dream Brought Nearer Reality," *Los Angeles Times*, February 10, 1934, A1. The project died from lack of funding.

[5] The novel is *Abandon Hope* (New York: Mystery House, 1941).

24. The End of the Trail

❧ ❧ ❧

"Daddy!"

"Mr. Garland—"

Daddy lifted a hand. "Wait a minute. Let *me* talk."

I turned to her. "Mother—"

"Your mother and I are in complete agreement on this," Father said calmly. "There is no use appealing to her."

"But—but—"

"Stop sputtering, Mary Isabel, and listen to what I have to say. It has gone on long enough, this fly-by-night renting of cheap, little furnished houses. It is time that you and Jon had a home that is worthy of you, and that is just what I am about to provide."

"But Daddy, you built me one house!"

He smiled. "And took it over. That's the sort of so-called Indian-giving that I do not wish to repeat. The house we build for you will be yours and yours alone. Not large but attractive, tasteful, a place in which you will be glad to entertain your friends. All you have to do is decide on a location."

Jon and I had been tongue-tied long enough; now we both began to speak at once, but Father interrupted again.

"For the moment, I have the floor. You'll have a chance to object later, if you wish. As a matter of fact, I know just about what you're going to say. That Jon is doing well, that before long you will be able to swing this for yourself, but here is the point: I have the money for such a project *now*. In fact, it's burning my pockets, and remember this: no matter what happens it will be a good investment. Southern California is going to go right on booming. If you don't like the house when it's finished, we can sell it and build another. And more important than that, your mother and I would rejoice to see you suitably housed. It might take away some of the guilty feeling we have about occupying a place that was meant for you."

"Daddy, that's ridiculous. You belong in this house and you know it."

"But you do not." If there was a hint of bitterness there it was quickly erased. "Let me say again that I think you are entirely right in wishing to live alone. So long as you are somewhere in the neighborhood, your mother and I will not complain. When I reflect on the parents whose children live thousands of miles away. . . ."

Mother spoke. "Say yes, darling. It would make your father and me so happy."

"But why, *why* should we accept such a tremendous gift from you?"

"Because we wish to make it," Father said quietly. "I haven't much more time in this Vale of Tears, and frankly," a boyish grin transfigured his face, "frankly, I'd like to build one more house before I die."

I didn't cry then, but once we had reached our own home, I dissolved. Jon, though less demonstrative, was as shaken as I. We both needed a drink and a chance to sit down and think things over calmly. We had promised Mother and Daddy to do just that, but for the moment my thoughts were in such a whirl that it was impossible to pin them down. Jon turned on the radio and lit the fire and we sat for a few moments staring into the flames and saying nothing.

Jon spoke first, wonderingly. "I just can't take it in. Your father wants to build a house for us, for *me* who was the villain of the piece!"

"Daddy's very fond of you now, you know that."

"And I'm fond of him, dammit. How could you not be? He's a wonderful guy, your father. I've learned a lot from him."

"Such as?"

"Well, such as how to grow old sportingly, for instance. He's got his troubles, his disabilities, but he's not asking for sympathy. He's still standing on his own feet, looking life and death in the face. Oh, he does plenty of grousing at this insane world, at crooked politicians, yellow journalism, pornography, and God knows what else, but he never whines. And now and then he says something so staunch and revealing that it rocks you back on your heels. Like that 'I'd like to build one more house before I die.'"

"Shall we let him?" I asked slowly.

"Shall we let him!" my husband echoed incredulously, and for a moment I saw him angry. "Look," he said curtly. "I'm not taking charity from anybody. I'm on the road up, now. If you'll just hang on a little longer, I'll build you a house that—"

"That wouldn't be the same." Now I saw my way clear, my way to repay a lot of things. I took Jon's hand and held it tightly. "Listen. Just listen for a minute. All his life Father has been doing things for his family. Giving us things has been his chief joy; dolls first, then books, clothing, jewelry, trips, and when the time came, opportunities. Now he wants the fun of doing it again. When he said he would like to build one more house, he meant exactly that. . . . Oh, Jon, I know you are going to succeed. You're going to give me all those diamonds and things that will please you, but now it is *Father* we must think of. His life is pretty empty, there's not too much to look forward to, but—he's a carpenter, remember— if he can see another roof-tree rising, if he can feel he is providing another set of stout walls to shelter those he loves. . . ."

I trailed off helplessly, but I had not mistaken my husband. He put his arm around me.

"Maybe you're right," he said huskily. "If you think it will mean all that to him—"

"It will." I was as sure of it as I had been of anything in my life before, as sure as I had been of the rightness of our love. "And when you get all that filthy rich, you can insist on paying him back, with interest." I was teasing, but my heart was full of gratitude to my husband for his perception, his fairness, his warmth.

Jon, his face alight, was on his feet. "Do you think it's too late to call them now?"

From that night, Father had a mission. He seemed ten years younger and began issuing orders like a benevolent martinet. "The first thing," he said briskly, "is to find the best possible location. I know you young people are pretty busy, so your mother and I will survey the terrain first. When we have pinpointed half a dozen likely lots, we will all go out in a body and consider them. Just let me know your requirements so I'll have an idea of what size lot to look for."

Our requirements. It was like being given carte blanche in a candy store. We who had been wildly happy in a nine foot "bed-sit" in New York, a raw, little cabin on a remote lake, a minute shack on a Valley back lot, were being asked to consider a thirty-foot living room, air conditioning, an all-electric kitchen, and walls of sliding glass that would make the outside world a mural for our pleasure.

Day after day, doggedly, happily, Mother and Father went forth in their shining new car, their amiable, young housekeeper at the wheel, and gradually narrowed the field down to three or four sites that seemed to have possibilities. We were all agreed on a hill-side and a view, and Jon and I would have liked to have it as remote and countryish as possible, but Daddy was doubtful. There was one romantically hidden location up Nichols Canyon that would have suited us exactly, but Daddy shook his head.

"No, no, it's too lonely, too far away. Another of those big rains and you might be marooned for days. We'll keep looking till we find something that's suitable and not more than a ten-minute drive from us."

In the end they found it, south of Franklin Avenue in Hollywood, high on a picturesque slope of hill, with a wide view of the whole city. Handsome as it was and eminently suitable for the structure that was growing in Daddy's mind, Jon and I exchanged rueful glances. This was going to be a city house, the other end of the scale from our log cabin on the lake. There would be no bird-watching here, that was certain. There were no trees on the proper-ty, and while Daddy talked knowingly of retaining walls and land-scaping, my husband and I were wistfully remembering three thou-sand acres of unspoiled woodland and all the wonders it contained.

Father had engaged an architect and the plans began to grow. Night after night we would go over them, Father glowing, bright-eyed, happily making extravagant changes, insisting on "nothing but the best," till I grew worried and protested.

"Daddy, you mustn't!" I told him one morning. "You'll go broke or something. We don't need all that house, really we don't. We'd be far happier with—"

"Now, now, I know what I am doing." He had the house

plans spread all over his desk and was busily making notes of still further improvements. "But speaking of money. . . ." He leaned back in his chair, put down his pen, and looked at me soberly. "I had a strange experience yesterday morning. You remember my telling you about Stephen Crane, the author of *The Red Badge of Courage*?"

"Yes, certainly."

"I admired Crane as a writer, did what I could to help him along. Many's the five dollar bill he had from me, poor fellow, but yesterday he paid me back a thousandfold."

"What do you mean?"

"A bookseller I know came in yesterday. He knew I had been a friend of Crane's and thought I might have some of his books lying around. It seems the bookseller has an important client who is collecting Crane, and to make a long story short, I dug out a copy of *Maggie, A Girl of the Streets* that Crane had autographed and given me a long time ago, and this man paid me three thousand dollars for it."[1]

"Daddy! How amazing."

Father's face shadowed. "The irony of life, daughtie. What a *hundred* dollars would have meant to Crane in those days. And now some rich collector gives three thousand for a cheap, shabby little book that no one else would look at twice. It makes me feel guilty, somehow, as if I had robbed poor Stephen's grave."

A day or two later, when I arrived for my secretarial stint, I found Father in the depths of gloom. He had sent off the first part of his "Fortunate Exiles" to his fine, loyal friend and publisher, Harold Strong Latham of Macmillan's, and back had come a regretful no. Mr. Latham had felt as I had when I was typing it: it was too low-keyed, too repetitious, too full of the melancholies of old age.[2]

"But what can I do, Mary Isabel?" Father asked me. "I am almost eighty. How can I pretend to a lightheartedness I don't feel? All I can do is plug along at it, try to condense, to heighten the interest here and there, to what end, who knows? After all, during my life I have written and published some forty books. That should satisfy me, don't you think?"

Within the last few years he had published another volume of literary reminiscences, *Forty Years of Psychic Research*, as well as

The Mystery of the Buried Crosses, yet the desire to create was as strong as ever.

"You'll get it in shape, Daddy," I told him confidently, adding his own motto, "The thing is to revise—revise."

He chuckled. "You know, I was sorting out manuscripts this morning about five o'clock and I heard myself saying out loud, "What a toiler this man Hamlin Garland is."

The Sunday afternoon polo games brought Father more actual pleasure than anything. As a horseman, he gloried in the skill and daring, and he always came home rejuvenated, but Saturday afternoons came to be almost equally stimulating. Along with the rest of us, Daddy developed a deep interest in and enthusiasm for football, and during the season we made a point of listening to the big games with him. He had set up a little lined football field on a card table beside the radio, and with a red checker for the ball, he carefully moved it from position to position up and down the field, so that at every time-out we knew where the play was. Daddy used to get as excited as a boy, pounding his knee and shouting with the rest of us at some exciting play. Even Mother sat in on these sessions, and though I don't think she understood very much of it, she liked the sense of action and the feeling of us all being there together. She had definitely improved since we came, was able to make her usual morning walk with Daddy down hill from the Planetarium and go to her afternoon movies again. In his diary Daddy records that he and Mother had just seen Greta Garbo in *Victory* for the fifth time.

It was at this period that we all had an amusing evening. We were deeply fond of the actor George Arliss and his wife, who used to come to Hollywood for the winter months and take a handsome house somewhere.[3] We were entertained often by them. They both loved bridge and Jon and I were asked to play, and the time arrived to return their hospitality.

Mother and I made elaborate arrangements about menu-flowers, an extra waitress. Daddy invested in the finest wines available, and we all put on full evening dress. Mother wore her white brocade, had her hair beautifully coiffed, and came down to the drawing room a vision of regal loveliness. Excitement was high. We loved and admired the Arlisses—he with his expressive face, his dry British wit, his exquisite manner, and Lady Arliss, bright, lively, warm-hearted. Father expanded with pride in his home, his family, the prospect of a magnificent dinner.

We all assembled in the drawing room at the proper hour and waited . . . and waited . . . and waited. They had been asked for seven-thirty, and by eight we were all wondering. At a quarter-past eight we had cocktails. At half-past eight we were getting quite nervous, and at nine I phoned the Arliss home and reached Lady Arliss.

"My dear!" she shrieked incredulously. "It isn't *this* night!"

I assured her it was, and she moaned softly. "How perfectly, perfectly appalling! George and I were so sure it was Thursday night. We've already had our dinner, and to tell the truth we're both tucked up in bed, reading. Oh, my dear, I am *so* sorry!"

There was nothing to do but reassure her and say we would expect them on Thursday, then. I went back to report to my family.

"Very well," said my father cheerily, rising and leading the way to the dining room. "In that case, let us go in and partake of a bang-up dinner. After all, who is more deserving?"

It was really great fun. There we were, as handsomely turned out a family group as you could wish, sitting in state under six tall candles, waited upon by a perfect waitress, eating an exquisite four-course dinner, and drinking wines of rare vintage. All with no social responsibility whatever. Repeated two days later with the Arlisses, it was an anticlimax. *Our* dinner had been perfect.

Father made one more trip to New York. He had been asked to deliver the address at the annual meeting of the American Academy of Arts and Letters, and looking sober and disturbingly small, he went off alone by plane to reap a richly-deserved harvest of affection and admiration.[4]

The hall, he wrote us, was packed to the last seat, and at the end of his address he was forced to rise again and again to acknowledge the applause, the cheers. "It was a most brilliant ending to my life in the East, the climax of my career."

Riding back downtown on the bus, he watched the sun set over the Hudson Palisades and told himself sadly that he would never come this way again. For the first time, he had no wish to linger in "The Imperial City," as he called it. Now his thoughts were directed to California and the building of the new house.

&a &a &a

Reading the last years of Daddy's diaries is almost unbearably poignant. He was so brave, so gallant. The things he would
not worry us with he set down honestly for himself: the acceptance
of age and decay, the ever-nearer approach of "the dark river." The
philosopher in him recognized it all as reasonable and inevitable,
but his still youthful spirit struggled and rebelled. He who had bat-
tled so valiantly for so long in the thick of things found it hard to
become "a tired, little old man puttering in a garden."

Always there was his concern for my mother. It must have
been a shattering and terrible thing to sit by and see the woman
who had shared all those years turn into a listless, almost helpless
invalid, but Father did not shirk his responsibility. In front of
Mother, as indeed before Connie and me, he dwelt cheerfully on the
doings of the day and the plans for tomorrow. Maintaining it was
to please Mother, he bought his yearly new car and this year gloried
in the sleek blackness of a 1940 Pontiac. Often, when I arrived in the
morning, I would find him out in the road with a chamois cloth,
removing the last trace of dust from the glittering splendor. Both he
and Mother still found their greatest relaxation in motoring, and
Connie, Jon, and I drove them far and wide.

A group of Midwestern universities had written Father asking for a "Hamlin Garland Exhibit" to be circulated among them,
and Father asked my help in assembling it.[5] It was an absorbing job.
There were to be manuscripts, letters, longhand poems, family and
personal photographs, with pictures of the various places that had
had a part in his life: the Wisconsin birthplace, the Iowa homestead,
the Seminary, the cabin on the Dakota plains, West Salem, Chicago,
New York, Onteora, all the spots that had roots for this born and
bred American.

I sorted hundreds of old photographs. Here were the
McClintocks, the glorious aunts and uncles of my father's boyhood,
appearing, even in the dim stiffness of old daguerreotypes, a handsome, swashbuckling crew. There was Isabelle McClintock Garland
as a girl, plump, wide-eyed, romantic; and Richard Garland, a slim,
eye-filling young adventurer; the majestic old patriarch, Hugh
McClintock, with his blazing eyes; and Father's two pretty sisters

who had died at fifteen and twenty-one from cold and exposure on the sleet-sheathed Western prairies.[6]

There were countless pictures of Hamlin Garland himself, the first of a solemn, round-eyed, sturdy little boy of six or seven, to whom Christmas was only a candy stick or an orange tossed from a passing sleigh. He was strikingly good-looking as he moved into manhood, with a wide, intellectual forehead, luxuriant dark hair, and a mouth of great sweetness. Then came the young bearded professor, the highly successful author in the late nineteen hundreds who married Zulime Taft, my own beloved father, with a smooth chin again and the warm, round eyes that observed and recorded so much, and lastly the white-haired, distinguished personage, the Academician, still with the flashing, youthful smile that illuminated his whole face.

For days I pored over these links to my past, knowing the story so well through the "Middle Border" books, remembering, matching. In the end, we put together a fascinating exhibit, and though Father insisted no young person would take an interest in it, the universities wrote that its appeal was instant and that they intended to keep it circulating.

It is sad that in his later years Father was obsessed by the idea that he was forgotten, laid away on the shelf. It is true that the book sales grew smaller and smaller, but he had an assured place in American literature and is required reading in most of the high schools and colleges. Requests for reprint rights were constantly on his desk and lecture offers continued to come in. Depressed as he was by growing old and the failure of his physical powers, Father recognized that he had much to be grateful for and expressed it one day to me.

"Your mother and I are together, we have money enough, we have our daughters, who prove their love and loyalty every day, we have two beautiful, intelligent grandchildren with a good inheritance. I tell myself this time after time but. . . ." He smiled wryly. "Where is the reputed 'serenity of old age'?"

There was a poem I used to read on the platform, one that had always had an enormous appeal for me. It was John Burroughs's "Waiting" and it began, "Serene I fold my hands and wait. . . ."

I quoted this to Father, and he laughed. "Do you know how

old John Burroughs was when he wrote that? Thirty! It is easy to be serene and philosophical in a literary way at thirty. It is not quite so easy when you are nearing eighty."

There was no constraint between my father and me in those last years. The disappointment I had been to him was never mentioned. He seemed to take an almost equal satisfaction in his daughters and his son-in-law, of whom he wrote in his journal that he was "intelligent, gifted and most congenial." From my present viewpoint, I wish that I had been of more comfort to my father, but on the other hand, what he really wanted from us was our youth, our enthusiasm, our victories. Feeling out of the race himself, it revitalized him to hear that Jon had sold a radio script, that I was to collaborate on the next one with him, that left out and neglected, as he thought himself, the torch was still being handed on.

It is another of life's ironies that Father never saw a published book of mine. When Uncle Tom Patten read some chapters of my first mystery and pronounced them good, Father wrote in his diary, "I shall now treat Mary Isabel as an author," but though I wrote and published six novels, the first one was accepted about six months after his death. Still, he knew it was coming and believed in me. He often said that it was only a matter of time. He was always keenly interested in the radio, and when Jon and I began writing scripts together, Father was frankly delighted. It was good to feel that we were beginning to justify his faith in us.

Despite the looming menace of war—we had all heard Hitler screaming and ranting on the air one night and it was a moment to chill the soul—Father was a comparatively happy man that night he came up to our house on the hill for dinner. The architect's plans were tucked under his arm, and after dinner we had to go all over them again and approve everything.

Again we protested. "Father, it's too much!"

"Nonsense." The creative light was shining in his eyes, and it was evident that he was going to supervise every nail that went into the structure. We were all standing at the door, and Father flung one arm around my shoulders and the other around Jon's.

"Well, children," he said exultantly, "it's 'full steam ahead!'"

Those were the last words I ever heard my father say.

Notes

[1] Isabel confuses the financing of the DeMille Drive house with this one, for in 1930 Garland arranged for the sale of his brother's copy of Crane's *Maggie, A Girl of the Streets,* as well as other books, to a rare book collector. See Garland to George Ulizio, March 10, 1930, *Selected Letters of Hamlin Garland,* 350-351.

[2] Isabel here disrupts chronology, for Garland submitted the manuscript two years' earlier, in 1936. In his letter declining the manuscript, Latham wrote, "it seems to me that there is too little that is really significant, really important for the present length. It is all very pleasantly written, all very agreeable reading, but it has not the social significance or the power of anything else of yours" (Latham to Garland, May 25, 1936 [USC]). John Ahouse has prepared a reading text of "The Fortunate Exiles" (item 5, USC), together with an introduction and expanded table of contents, all of which are now part of the Hamlin Garland papers at USC.

[3] The British actor George Arliss (1868-1946) was married to Florence Arliss (1871-1950), who appeared with him in a number of films. Arliss won the Academy Award for Best Actor for *Disraeli* (1929) and retired after his last film, *Dr. Syn* (1937). According to Garland's diary, the aborted dinner with the Arlisses took place on January 18, 1938.

[4] Garland delivered the Edwin Blashfield Foundation paper at the Academy's annual meeting on November 10, 1938. The address was published as "Literary Fashions Old and New," *Think* 4 (March 1939): 14, 24, 27.

[5] Here, as elsewhere, Isabel conflates chronology. The exhibit, "Hamlin Garland and His Literary Friends," opened at the Doheny Library of the University of Southern California on April 2, 1936, and lasted through the summer. After that, it went on tour as "The Makers of American Literature" to at least eleven libraries, among them the state libraries of California, Iowa, Ohio, and Wisconsin, as well as to university libraries in Indiana, Chicago, and Ohio.

[6] Harriet Edith Garland (1858-1875) is buried in the City Cemetery in Osage, Iowa; Jessie Viola Garland Knapp (1869-1890) died shortly after her marriage and is buried in the Parkview Cemetery, Columbia, South Dakota.

Index